Ruling Russia

Ruling Russia

AUTHORITARIANISM FROM THE REVOLUTION TO PUTIN

William Zimmerman

PRINCETON UNIVERSITY PRESS

PRINCETON AND OXFORD

Jacket art: *clockwise from top left*:
Vladimir Ilyich Lenin, ca. 1920, (Library of Congress, Prints and Photographs Division);
Mikhail Gorbachev in Aberdeen, on the occasion of receiving the Freedom of the City
award, © Jeremy Sutton-Hibbert/Alamy; Joseph Stalin, (Library of Congress, Prints
and Photographs Division); Vladimir Putin, Bratislava, Slovakia, 2005, © Northfoto,
courtesy of Shutterstock; Russian flag background © Cattallina/Shutterstock.

Library of Congress Cataloging-in-Publication Data

Zimmerman, William, 1936–
    Ruling Russia : authoritarianism from the revolution to Putin / William Zimmerman.
        pages cm
    Includes bibliographical references and index.
    ISBN 978-0-691-16148-8 (hardback)
    1. Authoritarianism—Soviet Union. 2. Authoritarianism—Russia (Federation)
3. Democratization—Russia (Federation) 4. Soviet Union—Politics and government.
5. Russia (Federation)—Politics and government—1991– I. Title.
    JN6531.Z56 2014
    320.947—dc23   2013048288

British Library Cataloging-in-Publication Data is available

This book has been composed in Palatino Linotype

Printed on acid-free paper. ∞

Printed in the United States of America

10 9 8 7 6 5 4 3 2 1

Contents

Acknowledgments

IT TOOK ME SOME WHILE to write this book. In the process I incurred a number of debts. I and three former graduate students—Valerie Bunce, Olesya Tkacheva, and David Rivera—conducted a workshop during which we discussed a draft of the first two-thirds of my book. I repeated the experience via videoconferencing with Russian colleagues— Vladimir Gelman, Eduard Ponarin, Yegor Lazarev, and Kirill Kalinin. All provided valuable oral and written comments on my work at the stage I was in and provided me with useful suggestions about the directions I should take in completing the manuscript. It would not have been possible for me to conduct the two book conferences were it not for the financial support and vote of confidence I received from Teresa Sullivan, who was provost of the university when this project was launched, and the willingness of Vice Provost Lori Pierce to bear with my turgid pace after Professor Sullivan had departed Ann Arbor to become president of the University of Virginia at Charlottesville.

Rivera, Kalinin (currently an advanced graduate student at Michigan), and Tkacheva rendered further assistance in this project—Rivera by providing me with detailed criticisms of every chapter, Kalinin by preparing the figures in Chapters 8 and 9, and Tkacheva by helping me with some transliteration issues. Kelly Grossmann provided valuable assistance in preparing the Selected Bibliography. In addition Kira Youdina exemplified the utility for students and faculty of the university's Undergraduate Research Opportunities Program by chasing down fugitive sources and comparing Russian and English versions of key utterances by various early Bolsheviks.

Special words of thanks go to George Breslauer and Patrick Shields, both of whom made valuable comments on versions of the manuscript. As George has done on multiple occasions and in multiple roles in the course of half a century of friendship, he challenged me to sharpen my thinking about the book. Patrick had good ideas about the ways the manuscript could be improved and kept after me to finish the manuscript. An anonymous reviewer made useful substantive suggestions and also called my attention to ways the manuscript might be made more accessible to upper-division undergraduates.

Earlier versions of parts of some chapters have appeared previously. My comments about Marshal Sokolovsky first appeared as a review essay in the *Journal of Conflict Resolution*. My analysis of Russian citizen assessments of the strengths and attitudes of Russian leaders draws from an earlier Princeton University Press book (*The Russian People and Foreign Policy*, 2002). Undertaking empirically those questions would not have been possible had I not participated in a 1995–96 wave of mass surveys of which Timothy Colton was the principal investigator and if he had not shared data from subsequent surveys. My first effort to show systematically the trend away from mobilized participation and its consequences for the nature of the Soviet system came as a result of my participation in the Soviet Interview Project and appeared in James Millar, ed., *Politics, Work, and Daily Life in the USSR* (© Cambridge University Press, 1987). The section in which I report our ability to estimate changes in Soviet military spending first appeared as an article (coauthored with Glenn Palmer) in the *American Political Science Review* (© Cambridge University Press).

My wife, Susan McClanahan, supported me in multiple ways, most notably by graciously and in good humor accepting the fact that I have done in retirement what I did when I was drawing a salary from the University of Michigan.

This book would not have been possible without the advice, research, and friendship of my former students over the years. For that reason, I take particular pleasure in dedicating this book to them.

Bill Zimmerman
CENTER FOR POLITICAL STUDIES AND
DEPARTMENT OF POLITICAL SCIENCE
UNIVERSITY OF MICHIGAN ANN ARBOR

Ruling Russia

Introduction

THIS BOOK HAS its origins in a paper I wrote half a decade ago.[1] In it I suggested ways that would provide more rigorous answers than were then extant to a question that has animated policy makers, scholars, and plain folk for more than a century and a half, to wit, "Is Russia, was it, or will it ever be a normal country?"—by which people usually have had Western democracy in mind.[2] The first president of the Russian Federation, Boris Yeltsin, declared in 1994 that "we [Russians] live in a normal country." Indeed, so determined was he to make this claim that the first chapter of his book *The Struggle for Russia* was titled "A Normal Country."[3] A decade later the Harvard economist Andrei Shleifer, writing either alone or with Daniel Treisman, a political scientist at UCLA, published a book and a series of papers, including a lead article in *Foreign Affairs* titled "A Normal Country."[4] In these publications, they advanced the argument that Russia's political and economic system was about what one would expect for a country at its level of development—which at their time of writing was what the Organisation for Economic Co-operation and Development (OECD) coded as a midlevel developing country. Their work in turn resulted in critical assessments in *Post-Soviet Affairs* by Peter T. Leeson and William N. Trumbull in 2006 and by me in 2007.[5]

The project turned out differently than I expected. Thinking about whether Russia was a normal country helped me organize my thoughts about the evolution of Russian politics. I have used simple statistical measures in comparing the Russian Federation with other states. I

[1] William Zimmerman, "'Normal Democracies' and Improving How They Are Measured: The Case of Russia," *Post-Soviet Affairs*, Vol. 23, No. 1 (January–March 2007), pp. 1–17. See also Peter T. Leeson and William N. Trumbull, "Comparing Apples: Normalcy, Russia and the Remaining Post-Socialist World," *Post-Soviet Affairs*, Vol. 22, No. 2 (April–June 2006), pp. 225–49.

[2] There are exceptions. See, for instance, Richard Pipes, *Russia under the Old Regime* (New York: Scribner, 1974), p. xxii, who asserts, "Russia belongs *par excellence* [italics in original] to that category of states which in the political and sociological literature it has become customary to refer to as 'patrimonial.'"

[3] Boris Yeltsin, *The Struggle for Russia* (New York: Belka, 1994), pp. 7–8.

[4] Andrei Shleifer and Daniel Treisman, "A Normal Country," *Foreign Affairs*, Vol. 83, No. 2 (March–April 2004), pp. 20–38; Shleifer, *A Normal Country: Russia after Communism* (Cambridge, MA: Harvard University Press, 2005).

[5] Leeson and Trumbull, "Comparing Apples"; Zimmerman, "'Normal Democracies.'"

certainly benefited from bearing in mind the overarching theme of my 2007 paper, which was to avoid making simple mistakes. But as the book progressed, I realized how easy it was to become bogged down in the plethora of uses of the term "normal."[6] I have consequently focused on a use of normality where it was most relevant to the purposes of a volume focusing on the historical evolution of Russian political systems, 1917–2013. I have in mind what leading Soviet and post-Soviet Russian figures advert to when they make reference to normal political systems or situations. It turns out there was a fundamental divide, but that divide was not between Soviet and post-Soviet Russian public figures. Rather, it was between those Soviet and Russian figures for whom "normal" signified stability, security, absence of change and, often, Russian uniqueness, and those for whom it connoted becoming a political system similar to those in the West or some part thereof.

Stability, security, and the status quo were what Gennady Yanayev, vice president of the USSR during the abortive August 1991 coup against Mikhail Gorbachev, had in mind when he referred to returning to normal conditions. It is what Vladimir Putin has generally had in mind as well when he has spoken of normal, though this was not universally the case especially in his first years as president. Examples of those who have had Western political systems in mind in referencing normal (read: Western) political systems would include such diverse public figures as Mikhail Gorbachev, Boris Yeltsin, and the highly visible blogger Aleksei Navalny. (See below, pp. 196, 197, and 301 respectively.)

It turns out though equating normal with Western systems has generally not constrained Russian leaders from seeking to minimize the electoral uncertainty that is central to well-institutionalized Western electoral systems. Rather, Gorbachev, Yeltsin, and Putin all have used various artifices to create conditions characteristic of authoritarian systems where the incumbent is able to "rest easy on the eve of elections."[7] This is part of the reason why the optimistic talk about democratization with its teleological connotation, widespread at the beginning of the twenty-first century, rang increasingly hollow at the end of its first decade. As exemplified by the retrograde pattern of the 2000, 2004, and 2008 presidential elections, Russia was less appropriately termed

[6]Sheila Fitzpatrick, *Everyday Stalinism: Ordinary Life in Extraordinary Times: Soviet Russia in the 1930s* (Oxford: Oxford University Press, 1999), Richard Sakwa, *Putin: Russia's Choice* (New York: Routledge, 1st ed., 2004; 2nd ed., 2008), Martin Malia, *The Soviet Tragedy: A History of Socialism in Russia, 1917–1991* (New York: Free Press, 1994), and Vladimir Shlapentokh, *A Normal Totalitarian Society* (Armonk, NY: M.E. Sharpe, 2001) are examples of the application of normalcy to Soviet or Russian politics or society.

[7]Steven Levitsky and Lucan Way, *Competitive Authoritarianism: Hybrid Regimes after the Cold War* (New York: Cambridge University Press, 2010), p. 12.

a democratic country at the end of the first decade of the twenty-first century than it had been at the onset of that decade.

As we shall see, Gorbachev found it easy to treat being defeated in a general election a normal occurrence for other party officials but not for himself. He was not himself elected by the Soviet citizenry as a whole. Rather, he was selected president by a vote of the Congress of People's Deputies. To be chosen president necessitated that he obtain an absolute majority of the members of the Congress. Without an opponent, he received less than 60 percent of the votes cast. Had the Soviet Union not collapsed in 1991, to continue in office he would have had to stand for election in 1995.

Yeltsin reneged on his promise to hold early presidential elections. He was on the brink of canceling the 1996 elections when he was persuaded not to by a host of public figures and others, most notably his daughter and the economist, Anatoly Chubais. (See below, p. 209, where Yeltsin's sense of guilt and shame for what he almost did is made clear.)

By contrast, Putin managed to finesse the constitutional limit of two successive terms by designating Dmitry Medvedev to be his successor as president in 2008 while he became prime minister. In this respect the 2008 presidential election became one characterized by a "selectorate" consisting of one or at the most two persons—Putin and, arguably, Medvedev. (Following Philip Roeder, I use "selectorate" throughout the book to refer to those who select and remove the leader by established procedures.[8] I term those who have the power to remove through extralegal means such as rallies and coups the "ejectorate."[9]) Putin's decision to select himself again as president in 2012 with Medvedev becoming prime minister was met with strong opposition by some part of the Russian citizenry, especially Muscovites. That opposition at the mass level was so extensive that roughly a month before the March 2012 election Putin acknowledged he might have to face a runoff despite the weakness of the opposing candidates.

The possibility of a runoff in March 2012 brought out two points to which I refer throughout the text. It exemplifies the nonlinear process of the evolution of Russian politics over nearly a century, 1917–2013:

[8] Philip Roeder in *Red Sunset: The Failure of Soviet Politics* (Princeton, NJ: Princeton University Press, 1993), p. 24, refers to the selectorate as those who have the power "to select and remove." See also Susan Shirk, *The Political Logic of Economic Reform* (Berkeley: University of California Press, 1993) and Bruce Bueno de Mesquita et al., *The Logic of Political Survival* (Cambridge, MA: MIT Press, 2003).

[9] Joseph Schumpeter, *Capitalism, Socialism and Democracy*, 2nd ed. (New York: Harper, 1947), p. 272 refers to the electorate's role in selecting a government as including the function of "evicting it."

the collapse of the Soviet Union tempted writers to attach teleological connotations to the term "democratization" and then yield to the opposite temptation, inferring that the retrograde pattern of the 2000, 2004, and 2008 presidential elections bespoke a linear process in which the 2012 election would be even less open and competitive than had been the fraudulent 2008 election—which had been less open and competitive than the 2004 election, which had been less competitive than the 2000 election.

To reduce the likelihood of yielding to these temptations in the future, in this volume I emphasize the importance of bearing in mind "the" Soviet system's *within-system* differences and the analogous *within-system* differences in "the" post-Soviet Russian system.[10]

The accompanying typology (Table I.1) represents my effort to place Russian political systems in an overall context. What I have done is build on the trichotomy used by the broad-gauge comparativists Steven Levitsky and Lucan Way.[11] In their analysis of various regimes since the Cold War they have distinguished among democratic, competitive authoritarian, and what they term "full" authoritarian systems, differentiating among the three on the basis of the status of core democratic institutions, the status of the opposition, and the level of uncertainty.

I have added a fourth column labeled totalitarian or mobilizational. By mobilization I have in mind the use of pressure and/or exhortation to induce people to serve regime goals that they would not otherwise have chosen to engage in.[12] Adding the fourth column allows me to take into account those authoritarian systems with transformative goals that were far more fully authoritarian than Levitsky and Way's "full" authoritarian systems. (I sometimes refer to the latter simply as normal authoritarian systems.) Also added were an additional two rows. One row accounts for the size of the selectorate—and the possibility of an ejectorate. The other considers the regime's overall goals.

---

[10] In this book, the comparisons are largely intertemporal, and to a much lesser extent, cross-national at the level of the state. Much good work is being done by Westerners (e.g., Katherine Stoner-Weiss, Andrew Konitzer, Olesya Tkacheva) and Russians (e.g., Vladimir Gelman, Grigory Golosov) on intra-Russian spatial comparisons, holding the central government constant. Other good recent examples include William M. Reisinger, ed., *Russia's Regions and Comparative Subnational Politics* (New York: Routledge, 2013) and the special issue of *Europe-Asia Studies*, Vol. 68, No. 3 (May 2011), "Russian Regional Politics under Putin and Medvedev."

[11] Levitsky and Way, *Competitive Authoritarianism*, especially pp. 12–16 and 369–71.

[12] This differs only slightly from a definition of mobilization suggested to me by George Breslauer (personal communication).

Table I.1: Regime comparisons: democratic, competitive authoritarian, "full" authoritarian, and totalitarian (mobilizational)

	I. Democratic	II. Competitive Authoritarian	III. Full Authoritarian	IV. Totalitarian (Mobilizational)
Status of core democratic institutions (direct restraints—rule of law) elections	Systematically respected	Exist but systematically violated in favor of incumbent	Nonexistent or reduced to façade status	Façade status or nonexistent
Status of opposition	Competes on more or less equal status with incumbent	Major opposition exists legally but is significantly disadvantaged by incumbent abuse	Major opposition banned or largely in exile or underground	Major opposition banned, parties pro forma or in exile or underground
Level of electoral Uncertainty	High	Lower than democracy, higher than full authoritarianism	Low	Nonexistent
Size of selectorate, possibility of successful ejectorate	Largely universal adult suffrage; ejectorate rare	Largely universal adult suffrage; ejectorate possible	Handful actually select; ejectorate unlikely	Handful (max) actually select; ejectorate quite unlikely
Regime goals	Security international and domestic; largely open to external influence; adjusts policies to complexities of large scale societies	Security international and domestic; largely open to external influence; adjusts policies to complexities of large-scale societies	Security international and domestic; resists external influence; adjusts policies to complexities of large-scale societies	Transformative internationally and domestically; strongly resists external influence; aims to overcome major socializing agents (e.g., family), pluralism of large-scale societies

Sources: This table draws heavily on Zimmerman, "Mobilized Participation and the Nature of the Soviet Dictatorship," in James Millar, ed., *Politics, Work, and Daily Life in the USSR: A Survey of Former Soviet Citizens* (Cambridge: Cambridge University Press, 1987), pp. 332–53; Steven Levitsky and Lucan Way, *Competitive Authoritarianism: Hybrid Regimes after the Cold War* (New York: Cambridge University Press, 2010), and Zbigniew Brzezinski, *Ideology and Power in Soviet Politics* (New York: Praeger, 1962), especially pp. 14–20. Columns I–III stem from Levitsky and Way, *Competitive Authoritarianism*, especially Table 1.1, p. 13 and the accompanying textual elaboration and is reprinted with permission. Column IV relies heavily on Brzezinski, *Ideology and Power*. Rows 4 and 5 draw from Zimmerman, "Mobilized Participation."

In constructing the fourth column I borrowed heavily from Zbig-niew K. Brzezinski's *Ideology and Power in Soviet Politics*[13] as well as from my previous work on mobilization systems.[14] Totalitarian/mobilization systems are ones where the regime has overcome what Brzezinski termed "the natural restraints . . . [including] kinship structure, and particularly the primary social unit, the family,"[15] and the pluralism inherent in large-scale societies,[16] in addition to core democratic institutions, the latter either being nonexistent or having façade status. The citizenry of full authoritarian systems, while subject to repression, sometimes severe, are attentive to extranational sources of information. The regimes adjust their goals and policies to the realities of large-scale societies, the traditional practices and core values of their citizenry, and the dangers they perceive in extranational influences. Totalitarian systems strongly resist external influence by employing autarkic economic policies and by repressing those with ties abroad and are bent on transforming the attitudes and behavior of their citizenry rather than appealing to the citizens' core values.

The reality of Russian politics at various times will not always match up with all the rows in a single column. As a result, the four stylized columnar systems identified in Table I.1 inevitably require some intellectual shoehorning. In some instances the coding is straightforward. The Soviet Union in 1937–38 was clearly totalitarian and 2008 Russia was an easy illustration of what Levitsky and Way term full authoritarianism. Both the Soviet Union and Russia are harder to code for other points in time partly because we attribute to them in those years characteristics of what with hindsight we know they became, partly because they fit most but not every item in a columnar category, and partly because they were on the cusp between, for instance, competitive authoritarianism and normal authoritarianism or competitive authoritarianism and democracy. The schema employed here does, however, provide a method for organizing a complicated and evolving story.

With these criteria in mind the evidence does not sustain the proposition that the Soviet system was totalitarian "from beginning to end."[17] My approach also diverges from that of many who in the 1960s

---

[13] Zbigniew K. Brzezinski, *Ideology and Power in Soviet Politics* (New York: Praeger, 1962), especially pp. 14–19.

[14] William Zimmerman, "Mobilized Participation and the Nature of the Soviet Dictatorship," in James R. Millar, ed., *Politics, Work, and Daily Life in the USSR: A Survey of Former Soviet Citizens* (Cambridge: Cambridge University Press, 1987), pp. 332–53.

[15] Brzezinski, *Ideology and Power*, p. 16.

[16] Ibid.

[17] Shlapentokh, *A Normal Totalitarian Society*, p. 3. In fairness, Shlapentokh "acknowledges significant differences among the various periods in Soviet history," but he also

and 1970s challenged totalitarianism as a concept.[18] What they should have been saying was that the Soviet Union at the time about which they were writing was not totalitarian but, rather, authoritarian. This would have involved differentiating between the Soviet Union circa 1970 and the dreadful years 1937 and 1938 where the case for terming the Soviet system totalitarian is the strongest. It would also have involved taking into account the sparkling research of a handful of Western and Russian scholars (e.g., Terry Martin, Sheila Fitzpatrick, Peter Solomon, and Oleg Khlevniuk)[19] on the years 1937 and 1938 whose work in the Soviet archives documented the features of Stalinist totalitarianism — the atomization and hypermobilization of society, the depths of the terror, and the absence of intraelite norms.

Over time these attributes of Stalinist totalitarianism gradually diminished. Areas of privacy were created, the actual terror attenuated (the threat remained), the society became less mobilized, and modest but significant intraelite norms emerged. Gradually, the mobilization system evolved into a more conventional (read "full" or "normal") authoritarianism, hence the need to distinguish two Soviet systems.

By the same token, Western and Russian scholars have struggled with how to characterize the postcommunist Russian political systems. There have, for instance, been a plethora of labels for the hybrids between democracy and dictatorship used to depict the Russian Federation circa 1996 — competitive authoritarianism (Levitsky and Way),[20] electoral democracy (Michael McFaul,[21] drawing on Adam Przeworski), or a country that was "partly free" (Freedom House). There was no unanimity in the literature as to how to characterize Russia's hybrid political system in the mid-1990s — democracy (Myagkov), electoral democracy (McFaul), competitive authoritarianism (Levitsky and Way).

---

maintains that nevertheless "Soviet society was *totalitarian* [italics in original], as it has been described by various authors in the United States and abroad" and references the usual suspects.

[18] A balanced account of the evolution of thinking about totalitarianism may be found in Abbot Gleason, *Totalitarianism: The Inner History of the Cold War* (New York: Oxford University Press, 1995).

[19] Fitzpatrick, *Everyday Stalinism*; Terry Martin, *The Affirmative Action Empire: Nations and Nationalism in the Soviet Union, 1923–1939* (Ithaca, NY: Cornell University Press, 2001); Oleg Khlevniuk, *1937: Stalin, NKVD, i Sovetskoe obshchestvo* (Moscow: Respublika, 1992); Khlevniuk, *Politbiuro: Mekhanizmi politicheskoi vlasti* (Moscow: Rosplan, 1996); Khlevniuk et al., *Stalinskoe Politbiuro v 30-e gody: Sbornik dokumentov* (Moscow: AIRO-XX, 1995).

[20] Levitsky and Way, *Competitive Authoritarianism*.

[21] "This process of electing leaders must occur under certain or fixed rules, but with uncertain outcomes that cannot be reversed." McFaul et al., "Introduction," in McFaul et al., *Between Dictatorship and Democracy: Russian Post-communist Political Reform* (Washington, DC: Carnegie Endowment for International Peace, 2004), p. 2.

Most Western specialists, however they classified Russia circa 1996, agreed with Levitsky and Way's statement a propos Russia at that juncture, that "[t]he regime was quite open in the early and mid-1990s" with "highly competitive elections," a "legislature [that] wielded considerable power, and private mass media . . . [that] regularly criticized Yeltsin and provided a platform for opposition."[22]

At the same time, whether using McFaul, Levitsky and Way, or Freedom House as their basis for judgment about how to categorize post-Soviet Russian politics, few scholars would dispute the within-system changes in the Russian political system in the dozen years subsequent to the 1996 election. Over that time period, the trend was away from what had been—warts and all—a highly competitive system. Instead, in the period between the 1996 Yeltsin electoral victory and 2008 when Vladimir Putin selected Dmitry Medvedev as his replacement as president, presidential elections became decreasingly open, decreasingly competitive, and increasingly meaningless. (These differences took on added significance at the cusp of the first and second decades of the twenty-first century, when substantial Western and Russian scholars published articles such as one titled "The Sovietization of Russian Politics"[23] and in light of the developments September 2011–May 2012.[24]) There was hyperbole in Gerald Easter's characterization of Russia by 2008 as having become "a normal police state."[25] Grigory Golosov was not, however, out of line to term the 2008 selection of Dmitry Medvedev to serve as Vladimir Putin's replacement an "election-type event." This was much of the basis why, of the thirty-five states Levitsky and Way coded as competitive authoritarian in 1990–95, Russia and Belarus were the two that were coded as "full authoritarian" in 2008.[26]

---

[22] Levitsky and Way, *Competitive Authoritarianism*, p. 191.

[23] Olga Kryshtanovskaya and Stephen White, "The Sovietization of Russian Politics," *Post Soviet Affairs*, Vol. 25, No. 4 (October–December 2009), pp. 283–309.

[24] Cf. especially chapter 9 infra, Vladimir Gelman, "Treshchiny v stene," *Pro et Contra* (January–April 2012), pp. 94–115, his recently published *Iz ognya da v polyma i rossiiskaya politika posle SSSR* (St. Petersburg: BHV-Petersburg, 2013), and three articles, all published in *Post-Soviet Affairs*, Vol. 28, No. 4 (October–December 2012) by Graeme Gill ("The Decline of a Dominant Party and the Destabilization of Electoral Authoritarianism"), pp. 449–71, Gordon Hahn ("*Perestroyka* 2.0: Toward Non-Revolutionary Regime Transformation in Russia"), pp. 472–515, and Karrie J. Koesel and Valerie Bunce ("Putin, Popular Protests, and Political Trajectories in Russia: A Comparative Perspective"), pp. 403–23.

[25] Gerald Easter, "The Russian State in the Time of Putin," *Post-Soviet Affairs*, Vol. 24, No. 3 (July–September, 2008), p. 206.

[26] Levitsky and Way, *Competitive Authoritarianism*, pp. 370–71.

THE OUTLINE OF THE BOOK

In the first substantive chapter, I describe the pattern of elite decision making in the three to four years immediately after the October Revolution involving regularized voting within a narrow selectorate that bore little resemblance to Soviet high politics in the Stalin period. These observances of procedural norms steadily dissipate (Chapter 3) and take place against a backdrop of the repression of the non-Bolshevik parties. What remains are the institutions established in the early postrevolutionary years that facilitated the steady shrinkage of the selectorate to such an extent that from the mid-1930s until Stalin's death in 1953 one might properly argue Stalin himself constituted the selectorate.

Chapter 2 depicts the successes and failures of early efforts to mobilize the Soviet citizenry in the years between the October Revolution and World War II. In terms of relations between regime and society, the initial efforts during War Communism and the Civil War prefigured the worst years of Stalin's rule and illustrated a fundamental way in which for much of the Soviet period Russia differed from what we usually think of as traditional authoritarian states, namely, dictatorships intent on maintaining what they have but not committed to transformative goals. For some fraction of that era the Russian leadership pursued transformative goals, what Kenneth Jowitt termed a "combat task."[27] These in turn had profound consequences for regime-society relations. As we shall see, however, such was not always the case during the Soviet period: a major part of the story of the collapse of the Soviet Union is the steady decline over time in the regime's capacity to mobilize its citizenry to its purposes (Chapter 5).[28]

Chapter 3 traces the gradual decline of the key Party organs, the Central Committee, and the Congress in the decade or so following the 1921 Tenth Party Congress. A decade or so later—the early 1930s—both the Congress and the Central Committee had been relegated at most to selectorate status, with the Politburo constituting the central decision-making body. As Chapter 4 relates, by the latter half of the 1930s, the boundaries between Party members, even Politburo members, and others in the Soviet population had lost all meaning. There were virtually no citizens in the sense that Bueno de Mesquita et al. use the term.

---

[27] Kenneth Jowitt, "Soviet Neotraditionalism: The Political Corruption of a Leninist Regime," *Soviet Studies*, Vol. 35, No. 3 (1983), pp. 275–97.

[28] For greater detail, see Zimmerman, "Mobilized Participation," pp. 332–53; William E. Odom, *The Collapse of the Soviet Military* (New Haven, CT: Yale University Press, 1998); Steven L. Solnick, *Stealing the State: Control and Collapse in Soviet Institutions* (Cambridge, MA: Harvard University Press, 1998).

Everyone, with the exception of Stalin and a handful of his closest aides such as Aleksandr Poskrebyshev ("Stalin's loyal shield bearer"), had become disenfranchised residents.[29]

Chapter 4 focuses on the profound transformations of the 1930s that involved mass mobilization of the citizenry and the systematic application of terror to Old Bolsheviks; to peasants; to priests; to members of nationalities with populations some of whom were in the Soviet Union, and others elsewhere; and, by extension, to people with foreign experience or who had comparatively extensive contact with foreigners.

Chapter 5 shows how at the time, circa 1937, when the Soviet Union was most appropriately labeled totalitarian, when elite politics had basically disappeared—when there was essentially no selectorate save for Stalin himself—and the peacetime mobilization of the citizenry was most extensive, the societal transformations that had taken place and the goals Stalin had set proved counterproductive. In order to strengthen the Soviet state and the citizens' attachment to that state, steps were taken by Stalin to reduce the actual implementation of terror and to render the political system more predictable. A process was set in motion that ultimately led to the stagnation of the Brezhnev era, a phenomenon evidenced by declines in the ability of the regime to mobilize its citizenry effectively and in growing manifestations of documentable group articulations and subtle but substantively important intraelite divergences in views. Chapter 5 also covers the post-Stalin period during which, under Nikita Khrushchev and Leonid Brezhnev, politics within a narrow selectorate reemerged, modest intraelite norms developed, and the ability of the regime to mobilize the Soviet citizenry attenuated noticeably. Absent the systematic application of terror and the kind of grandiose design characteristic primarily of the Stalinist period (but also, partially, the Khrushchev era), as the twentieth century wore on, regime-society relations and intraelite interactions came increasingly to conform to norms more characteristic of normal authoritarian regimes.

Chapter 6 describes Gorbachev's emergence as a system-changing political leader.[30] It depicts his effort to create the preconditions for a system that involved a national selectorate and involved the uncertainty that attends democratization for others while retaining for himself the certainty appropriately associated with authoritarianism until several years down the road—after he had succeeded in transforming Soviet politics, the unsuccessful efforts by an ejectorate to remove him, and the emergence of Yeltsin as the dominant political force in Russian politics.

[29] Bueno de Mesquita et al., *The Logic of Political Survival,* p. 39.
[30] George W. Breslauer, *Gorbachev and Yeltsin as Leaders* (Cambridge: Cambridge University Press, 2002).

Chapter 7 accepts the argument by Levitsky and Way that, while the 1996 election was highly competitive, it still fell short of democracy, whether one used their or Schumpeterian criteria. However competitive it was, the 1996 election was not, however, a data point presaging further democratization. Rather, the progression through 2011 described in Chapter 8 was one in the other direction, culminating in the mockery of an election that ratified Dmitry Medvedev's anointment as president in 2008.

Chapter 9 describes the extraordinary developments attending the 2011–12 electoral cycle. Once again Putin and Medvedev announced in September 2011 that one of them would be the candidate for president and the other would become prime minister. This time, however, they would reverse their roles. Putin would become president. On Putin's election as president, Medvedev would become prime minister. The December Duma election turned out, however, not to be as anticipated. The official count for United Russia was less than 50 percent, well short of the number required to amend the Constitution. Large rallies protesting vote falsification and agitating against Putin's presidential candidacy followed, which were in turn followed by electoral reforms. Roughly a month before the March presidential election the uncertainty that attends democratic and competitive authoritarian systems prevailed and it was problematic whether Putin would obtain a majority in the first round. The Kremlin, however, successfully marshaled enormous resources to avoid a repeat of United Russia's experience in December 2011, with the result that in March 2012 Putin was elected in the first round. In the months that followed, Putin and the majority in the Duma launched systematic efforts to ensure that anti-Putin rallies of the sort and magnitude of those occurring in the winter 2011–12 would not be repeated.

In the conclusion I build on the clear understanding on the part of many ordinary Russians (especially Muscovites), and Mikhail Gorbachev and Boris Yeltsin as well, that the Soviet system was abnormal. As the regime's ability to mobilize society diminished in effectiveness, all the above indicated a desire to live normally (*zhit' normalno*). Generally, this phrase translated to mean "live like a European" and ultimately adopt European institutions. These aspirations notwithstanding, in the second decade of the twenty-first century, it was unclear whether in the short run the bulk of the Russian adult population, after brief flirtations with authentic participation, would prove to be citizens or residents.

This showed up starkly in the retrograde movement exemplified by the 2000, 2004, and 2008 presidential elections, a trend somewhat reversed in the 2011–12 electoral cycle. That cycle lacked the attributes of a fully authoritarian regime that had been evidenced in the 2008 election cycle, though it bore some resemblance to a modernized analogue to the Soviet system with its "circular flow of power,"[31] to wit, a one-person selectorate accompanied by some cheering from the sidelines by a small but growing group who felt entitled to express their views regardless of their actual impact on the outcome.

It was also not democratic, falling short by Schumpeterian criteria—largely free press, freedom of discussion, and all serious candidates competing—and by the criteria employed by Levitsky and Way—an opposition competing on more or less equal status with an incumbent, the latter operating at a high level of uncertainty.[32] Instead, the 2011–12 electoral cycle fit well with the behaviors Levitsky and Way associate with competitive authoritarianism.

What about the longer run? It is manifestly clear that in the political realm Russian openness declined in the first decade of the twenty-first century. The outburst in response to the Putin "castling" in 2011 altered for a moment the relationship between the authorities and the public. The factors that would point to a more democratic outcome are fairly straightforward and are discussed at greater length in the conclusion. It is conceivable that the regime could convince the middle class in cities other than Moscow that the putatively draconic laws adopted after Putin's May 2012 inauguration were for show and may be safely ignored. A year after Putin's inauguration that does not seem to have been the case. By the same token, the regime has the capacity to bring about its own demise by inculcating mass protest and dividing the elite over some matter that large numbers discern as a moral issue.

The opposition could also bring about its own demise. The December 2011 Duma election was remarkable in that many people could oppose United Russia by voting for any approved party rather than by abstaining or destroying their ballot. Putin is unlikely to make voting strategically that easy often. On the basis of prior experience, the likelihood of a united opposition seems remote unless they pick their battles carefully. They have demonstrated a capacity to be clever and insistent. In the aftermath of the 2012 election, Boris Akunin, the distinguished writer, exercised his constitutional right to a morning constitutional. The well-known blogger Aleksei Navalny joined the board of

---

[31] Robert V. Daniels, "Soviet Politics since Khrushchev," in John W. Strong, ed., *The Soviet Union under Brezhnev and Kosygin: The Transition Years* (New York: van Nostrand Reinhold, 1971), p. 20.

[32] These are, intentionally, minimalist criteria. For an example of essays focusing on a broader conception of democracy and dealing with postcommunist systems, see Richard D. Anderson, Jr. et al., *Postcommunism and the Theory of Democracy* (Princeton, NJ: Princeton University Press, 2001).

Aeroflot (evidently only briefly);[33] his sponsor, the banker Aleksandr Lebedev, announced his intention to create a credit card (subsequently scrapped)[34] that would fund Navalny's anti-corruption efforts and declared he would give the first card to Putin. The editor of *Novaya Gazeta*, Dmitry Muratov, demanded an apology from the head of the Investigative Service, Aleksandr Bastrykin, for threatening to kill Sergei Sokolov, a *Novaya Gazeta* staff person—and got it.

But—and it's a big but—the Kremlin will probably retain control over three major resources: the various armed units, the media near monopoly, and persons subject to mobilization under threat to their jobs or their social welfare payments. If a leader who is a real focal point emerges and is able to put together some combination of the street, a fraction of a divided elite, and some key societal grouping in addition to the Moscow urban middle class—the elderly, say, the working class, even the urban middle class in the eleven[35] cities other than Moscow with a population of a million or more—in short, an opposition party, he or she might succeed in ousting Putin—assuming the latter remains in good health—at some point up to and including the 2018 presidential election. The more likely outcome, though, is that those with the most resources will carry the day and that it will again be Putin as it was in 2000, 2004, and 2008 (through his surrogate Medvedev) and 2012.

[33] Reuters, February 26, 2013, reported he was not on the list of board candidates for 2013.
[34] "Bank Buries Navalny Debit Cards," *RIA Novosti*, December 13, 2012.
[35] Perm did have more than a million residents, but in the most recent census its population dropped below a million.

CHAPTER 1

From Democratic Centralism
to Democratic *Centralism*

THE BOLSHEVIKS SUCCESSFULLY seized power in the fall 1917. Historians dispute the support the Bolsheviks received in accomplishing that goal.[1] This is an argument among people with strong views, some of whom are more reasonable than others. What is beyond dispute is that the phrase "Bolshevik coup d'état" presupposes the existence of an état. The wags' retort that there was no état to coup, its flipness notwithstanding, is to the point. The key institutions of the entire Soviet period emerged out of that institutional vacuum during the four-year period from October 1917 to the March 1921 Tenth Party Congress, when the ban on factions within the Party and the New Economic Policy (NEP) were adopted.

What bears in mind in reading the present chapter are two points. First, the period was initially characterized by more open politics and greater attention to regularized voting within a small selectorate than at any time from March 1921 until the late 1980s during Mikhail Gorbachev's tenure as CPSU general secretary. Second, the story of the four years after the seizure of power is one of a steadily narrowing selectorate as the country became increasingly authoritarian. Among the party leaders disregard for procedural niceties grew but regularized voting remained an important aspect of decision making. It got far worse subsequently. (The colossal violence that attended regime-society relations during War Communism is described at the beginning of the next chapter, where the central argument is that aside from the interventions of multiple foreign states there not only was a civil war between the White and the Reds but an at least equally violent civil war between the Reds and the Greens.[2])

[1] In a vast literature see especially Richard Pipes, *The Russian Revolution* (New York: Vintage Books, 1991) and Alexander Rabinowitch, *The Bolsheviks Come to Power: The Revolution of 1917 in Petrograd* (New York: Norton, 1976).

[2] On the Greens see Vladimir Brovkin, *Behind the Front Lines of the Civil War* (Princeton, NJ: Princeton University Press, 1994), especially pp. 145–50. On pp. 145–46, Brovkin describes the Greens as "peasant rebels," largely army deserters, who were found "in every

By far the most open election in Russian politics prior to the Gorbachev era occurred almost immediately after the Bolshevik seizure of power. I have in mind the election of the Constituent Assembly. It was, Oliver H. Radkey tells us, a "fundamentally free election, contested by definitely organized and sharply divergent parties, on the basis of universal, equal, direct, and secret suffrage."[3] In an overwhelmingly peasant country, it is not a surprise to learn that the Socialist Revolutionaries (SRs), a strongly pro-peasant party, got the most votes by a large plurality. The Bolsheviks finished second overall and way ahead of the other parties, but well behind the SRs.

In the strategically significant cities, as Radkey again makes clear, two trends stand out from examining the voting results. First, the cities became increasingly polarized between June and December 1917. Voters were increasingly taking sides with either the Bolsheviks or the strongest "bourgeois liberal" party, one that favored constitutional democracy, the Constitutional Democrats (hence the abbreviation, Kadety). In Moscow (the pattern is rather similar for Petrograd [now again St. Petersburg]), elections for various levels of government took place in June, September, and November. From June to November, the vote for the SRs shrank from approximately 375,000 to about 62,000, with roughly the same number of votes cast in November as in June. The vote for the Kadets increased from slightly less than a 110,000 to almost 264,000, while the Bolshevik vote increased from 75,000 to 366,000.[4]

Second, as these figures bear out, the shift in the Bolsheviks' favor gave them some claim that they were on the side of history. Persuading themselves that this was the case, Lenin's "Theses on the Constituent Assembly" made clear that he and the majority of the Bolshevik leadership were reluctantly allowing the vote to take place but that they would brook no notions that the Constituent Assembly should in any way interfere with "Soviet power." Should it attempt to do so, matters would be "settled in a revolutionary way."[5] This is what happened: the Bolsheviks disbanded the Assembly a day after it first met.

---

province of European Russia under Bolshevik control" who used the forests (where they existed) for cover.

[3] Oliver H. Radkey, *Russia Goes to the Polls: The Election to the all-Russian Constituent Assembly, 1917* (Ithaca, NY: Cornell University Press, 1989), p. 3. The overall results appear at pp. 18–19.

[4] Ibid., p. 55.

[5] I have used an English-language version that appears in Robert C. Tucker, ed., *The Lenin Anthology* (New York: Norton, 1975), pp. 418–22 at p. 422. Apparently, some Bolshevik leaders were willing to have the Constituent Assembly take steps that might have jeopardized the Bolsheviks' seizure of power. Lenin chastises "a few Bolshevik leaders," for not having understood that supporting the Constituent Assembly "would be a

The timing of the voting for the Constituent Assembly has engendered some confusion. Despite the occurrence of the actual voting in the weeks immediately after the Bolsheviks seized power, it was the Provisional Government and not the Bolsheviks that authorized the election of the Constituent Assembly delegates. The resulting election has been properly termed "one of history's first universal adult suffrage voting systems."[6] It is a mistake,[7] however, to characterize it as part of a Bolshevik grand strategy of combining closely held power with symbolic universalism. That came later.

Rather, the elections the Bolsheviks themselves conducted prior to the adoption of the 1936 "Stalin" Constitution were ones in which categories of people were systematically underrepresented or disenfranchised. The 1918 Constitution explicitly disenfranchised "those who employ others for the sake of profit," capitalists, private business men, "monks and priests of all religious denominations," the tsarist police and its agents, members of the former ruling family, and those who are "mentally deranged or imbecile."[8]

Similarly, in a manner akin to the elections to the Duma after the Russian Revolution of 1905 and prior to World War I, the peasantry were systematically underrepresented.[9] Both the Russian Constitution of 1918 and the first Soviet Constitution (1924) established that the Congress of Soviets would consist of "representatives of city and town soviets on the basis of one deputy for each 25,000 voters and of representatives of provincial and district congresses of soviets on the basis of one deputy for every 125,000 inhabitants."[10] Clearly, given that the villagers were explicitly discriminated against, it makes little sense to consider them as a group as part of a selectorate or to regard elections in which they were treated as second-class citizens as "universal adult suffrage voting systems."[11] Prior to 1936 (by which time the kulaks had been liquidated as a class and the putative capitalist exploiters had

---

betrayal of the proletariat's cause." Ibid., p. 421. For details, see William Henry Chamberlin, *The Russian Revolution, 1917–1921* (New York: Macmillan, 1935), vol. 1, pp. 365–71.

[6] Bueno de Mesquita et al., *The Logic of Political Survival*, p. 6.

[7] Ibid.

[8] James H. Meisel and Edward S. Kozera, eds., *Materials for the Study of the Soviet System: State and Party Constitutions, Laws, Decrees, Decisions, and Official Statements of the Leaders*, 2nd ed. (Ann Arbor, MI: Wahr, 1953), p. 88.

[9] Elections after the 1905 revolution and before World War I heavily discriminated against peasants and workers. Terence Emmons, *The Formation of Political Parties and the First National Elections in Russia* (Cambridge, MA: Harvard University Press, 1983), p. 238.

[10] Merle Fainsod, *How Russia Is Ruled* (Cambridge, MA: Harvard University Press, 1953), p. 309.

[11] Bueno de Mesquita et al., *The Logic of Political Survival*, p. 6.

largely been killed or imprisoned) only the urban working class was fully enfranchised.

In the earliest months of the Bolsheviks' tenure in power, when Lenin himself chaired the meetings of the Council of People's Commissars (Sovnarkom), a case could be made that the workers in general should be considered part of the selectorate. They were certainly beneficiaries of the new regime. During periods of extreme hardship they stood at the head of the line for bread and other food provisions.[12] They were explicitly favored in selecting the All-Russian Congress of Soviets, which selected the Central Executive Committee, which in turn chose membership of Sovnarkom. Quickly, though, Russian workers lost the weapons workers everywhere have traditionally relied on as sources of power—independent trade unions and the right to strike. This had the effect of subordinating them to regime discipline and mobilization in much the way as soldiers in the Red Army. Still, for a brief period it could be argued that their vote counted in that the Congress of Soviets selected the Central Executive Committee and it selected the Sovnarkom. It was a brief period, however; slightly fewer than two-thirds of the members of the Congress of Soviets in March 1918 were Bolsheviks. By the end of 1919, Party membership in the Congress had reached 97 percent. Party discipline had predictable consequences.[13] As a result, voting for the All-Russian Congress of Soviets became routinized and merely an opportunity for the Party to mobilize the citizenry, while Sovnarkom soon became a locus where Party decisions were ratified.

But in 1918–20, Sovnarkom mattered. All major decisions were made by the Party Central Committee, but the Council of People's Commissars initially played an important role. Rapidly, though, the various governmental institutions became either symbolic, as in the case of the Congress of Soviets, or administrative organs, as in the case of Sovnarkom. The outlines of the party-state emerged over a brief time span. "Except for the brief period between December 22, 1917, and March 15, 1918, when three Left SR's held portfolios in the Sovnarkom,"[14] it was populated only by Bolsheviks. During that period, Lenin himself chaired the sessions. Philip Roeder notes that initially, moreover, Sovnarkom "enjoyed considerable autonomy in its daily operation, including independence in the appointment of its own members."[15] Vigorous debates took place over important matters, such as the debate

---

[12] Lars T. Lih, *Bread and Authority in Russia, 1914–1921* (Berkeley: University of California Press, 1990).

[13] This paragraph draws heavily on Roeder, *Red Sunset*, p. 48.

[14] Fainsod, *How Russia*, p. 124.

[15] Roeder, *Red Sunset*, p. 45.

whether to ratify the Treaty of Brest-Litovsk and decisions relating to the links between the Party and the trade unions.

As the Party apparatus developed, Sovnarkom evolved into an administrative organ the function of which was to implement the Party Politburo's decisions. Several things led to its downgrading. Lenin was strategic in using both government and Party organs in his efforts, not uniformly successful, to achieve his goals. His first stroke in 1922 effectively removed him from a key role in decisions. From October/ November 1917 until Yakov (Jakob) Sverdlov's untimely death in early 1919, Sverdlov was, for all intents and purposes, the Party Secretariat. Fainsod notes that "he [Sverdlov] functioned largely without staff, and the only complete record of his transactions was in his head."[16]

Following his death, the Party apparatus grew rapidly. With the creation of the Organization Bureau (Orgburo) and the rapid growth in the size of the Secretariat, it quickly developed that a sizeable fraction of key governmental commissariat (later, ministry) appointments were made either by the Secretariat, the Orgburo, or, in the most important cases, the Politburo. "Between April 1920 and February 1921 these central party organs [the Politburo, the Secretariat and the Orgburo] reportedly made 1715 appointments to Sovnarkom positions in Moscow."[17] (At this juncture [early 1920], Stalin was the only member of the Orgburo who was also a member of the Politburo. In April 1922, the post of general secretary was established. Stalin became the first general secretary. From that time on, he was the only person on all three key bodies: the Politburo, the Secretariat, and the Organization Bureau.) By 1923, Orgburo was creating the famous lists of appointments for administrative positions known to all as the *nomenklatura*.

Thus, in a brief time span, legislative and governmental institutions that at that juncture might have resulted in the workers constituting the selectorate became harnessed to the dominant Party institutions. War Communism, as implemented, had transformed trade unions largely into administrative organs of the enterprise. Party discipline in Congresses of Soviets that were almost unanimously composed of Party members anticipated the subsequent Congresses where voting unanimity was pervasive. Lacking a central dominating figure like Lenin, Sovnarkom became the administrative arm of the Party, not a place where key substantive decisions were rendered. The Party apparatus, composed of the Politburo, Orgburo, and the Secretariat, held control over appointments both to the regional Party positions and also to key administrative positions in the economy. It remained the case in 1921

---

[16] Fainsod, *How Russia*, p. 154.
[17] Roeder, *Red Sunset*, p. 47.

that one could talk of a sizeable electorate. But it was membership in the Party, no longer status as a worker or a toiler, which best delimited the selectorate. It would narrow still further as the 1920s progressed. Along with those disenfranchised by the 1918 Constitution and hunted by the Cheka, the majority of peasants and workers had by the Tenth Party Congress in March 1921 or certainly by the defeat of the Workers' Opposition in March 1922 at the Eleventh Party Congress (see below, pp. 30–35) become, in Bueno de Mesquita, Smith, Siverson, and Morrow's term, "residents."[18]

Within the Party, however, vigorous debate was initially the norm. In the first months after the seizure of power, debates in various fora among the Bolsheviks over what became the Treaty of Brest-Litovsk exemplified the initial style of politics within the Party. (Brest-Litovsk was the 1918 treaty between Germany and its allies [other signatories on the German side were Austria-Hungary, Bulgaria, and Turkey] and Russia that allowed the latter to extricate itself from the First World War.) It came at what was, on its face, enormous cost. "By this agreement Russia lost 34 percent of her population, 32 per cent of her agricultural land, 85 per cent of her beet-sugar land, 54 percent of her industrial undertakings, and 89 per cent of her coal mines."[19] These losses proved of short duration. When Germany lost World War I, the Bolsheviks succeeded in quickly reclaiming most of the tsarist patrimony it had ceded to Germany and its allies. What proved to be far more important was that the Treaty of Brest-Litovsk made it possible for the Bolsheviks to stay in power.

That said, the title of John Wheeler-Bennett's book, first published in 1938, *Brest-Litovsk: The Forgotten Peace, March 1918*, was apt for Western readers then. It is probably even more a propos for Westerners ninety years after the event and seventy years after the publication of the Wheeler-Bennett book. I draw blank stares from both my students and some of my colleagues when mention of the Treaty of Brest-Litovsk is made. That is unfortunate given its role in perpetuating the Bolsheviks' tenure in power and how open was the decision process that led to its ratification in comparison with what came soon after its ratification in 1918. In this chapter I am largely unconcerned with the particularities of the treaty, the quite intriguing dimensions of the negotiations, or the profound significance for our understanding of the ways Russian foreign policy was and was not that of a conventional great power at the very dawn of the Soviet period.

[18] Bueno de Mesquita et al., *The Logic of Political Survival*, p. 39.

[19] John Wheeler-Bennett, *Brest-Litovsk: The Forgotten Peace, March 1918* (1938; repr., New York: Norton, 1971), p. 269, based on the State Department's *U.S. Foreign Relations, 1918*.

Rather, in this section I describe the political processes by which the Bolsheviks reached agreement to get out of the war. I am not the first to do so. These have been described well in standard accounts.[20] Historians of the period have also provided clear accounts of the active debates that took place, primarily among the Bolsheviks themselves, concerning the negotiations with the Germans at Brest-Litovsk. But the story pays retelling in some detail both because these debates were over what was literally a life-or-death matter with respect to the survival of Soviet power and because relatively recent research has highlighted the stark contrast between these debates and what follows in the ensuing seventy years. Historians and political scientists have similarly depicted the process of narrowing the selectorate that takes place in the years 1917 to 1921 that culminates in the Tenth Party Congress in March 1921. It is then that the famous Article 7 was adopted prohibiting factions that results in the Bolsheviks in power resembling the narrow conspiratorial party for power *seizure* that Lenin advocated in *What's to Be Done*, published in 1902.[21] That evolution is covered subsequently (pp. 35–37).

In the pages that follow immediately the story is one of shifting coalitions, threats to resign and actual resignations, strategic voting, and sharply polarized views and rhetoric—the stuff of which in countries even with very large selectorates are considered conventional politics. In these respects, the decisions culminating in the Treaty of Brest-Litovsk are comparable to the procedures observed by standard-issue oligarchies with quite small selectorates. The Bolsheviks operated with clear majoritarian procedural norms but severely limited the number of those who counted politically. Lenin was routinely outvoted. He had to threaten to quit to have his way on the most crucial votes. On the single most important vote relevant to the Russian decision to ratify the

---

[20] The best accounts remain Wheeler-Bennett, *Brest-Litovsk* and Louis Fischer, *The Soviets in World Affairs: A History of the Relations between the Soviet Union and the Rest of the World* (London: Jonathan Cape, 1930), vol. 1, pp. 15–78. Ronald I. Kowalski, *The Bolshevik Party in Conflict: The Left Communist Opposition of 1918* (Pittsburgh: University of Pittsburgh Press, 1991) augments the debates among the leadership with a thorough accounting of regional Party and state organs' views on negotiating with the Germans. Standard accounts of the seizure of power and the early years of Soviet power that treat Brest-Litovsk include Pipes, *The Russian Revolution*, pp. 567–605; Leonard Bertram Schapiro, *The Origin of the Communist Autocracy: Political Opposition in the Soviet State, First Phase, 1917–1922* (London: London School of Economics and Political Science, 1955), pp. 89–110; Fainsod, *How Russia*, pp. 126–32; Rabinowitch, *The Bolsheviks Come to Power*; Rabinowitch, *The Bolsheviks in Power: The First Year of Soviet Rule in Petrograd* (Bloomington: Indiana University Press, 2007).

[21] Roeder, *Red Sunset*; Schapiro, *The Origin*; Fainsod, *How Russia*; Malia, *The Soviet Tragedy*; Pipes, *The Russian Revolution*; and many more.

treaty, he failed to obtain a majority of the members of the Party Central Committee. Rather, he carried the day only because Trotsky and his coalition partners abstained. Other leading Party members also threatened to resign if their view was not accepted and did so when they lost.

From the moment they seized power in Petrograd, the Bolsheviks wanted to get out of the war. While a certain amount of posturing was involved, it is suggestive that the Declaration of Peace was the first act of the new government. Within a matter of weeks, the Germans and their allies had agreed to negotiate with the Bolsheviks at Brest-Litovsk about an armistice. Both sides agreed to send their representatives there to negotiate.[22] (From the beginning, though, some Petrograd communists opposed "treaties with any of the imperialist states."[23]) After some delays an armistice was agreed to in mid-December 1917 and negotiations over a peace treaty commenced on December 20.

The Soviets opted to stall in hopes that fraternizing would result in upheavals on the German side. The negotiations ground on. The Bolsheviks faced a choice among three alternatives. The first airing of views at the national decision making level took place in an informal session of party leaders[24] on January 21, 1918, in which, as Lenin noted, "three points of view were advanced: (1) sign a separate, annexationist peace, (2) wage a revolutionary war, (3) declare the war ended, demobilize the army, but do not sign the peace."[25] Lenin strongly favored the first view, Nikolai Bukharin (at this juncture very much on the left among the Bolsheviks) the second, and Trotsky the third—neither war nor peace. Both Lenin's and Trotsky's views were rejected by those present, with fifteen endorsing Lenin's position, sixteen for Trotsky's, and thirty-two for Bukharin's call for revolutionary war.

The result was that on the day after, January 22, at a meeting of the Party Central Committee in a series of decisions binding on the

---

[22] As all accounts agree, the Russian negotiators were a motley blend. They naturally included Bolshevik leaders, including the head of the delegation, Adolf Ioffe (Joffe), and military officers. But they also co-opted a Social Revolutionary woman assassin, a soldier, a sailor, a worker, and a peasant. How the peasant was included is instructive about the atmosphere in those days immediately after the revolution. As Wheeler-Bennett relates, on the way to the Warsaw station the leaders of the delegation realized that the "peasant class was unrepresented" in the delegation and happened upon "an old man in a peasant's coat" who was obviously on his way to some railroad station. "Come with us to Brest-Litovsk and make peace with the Germans." Wheeler-Bennett reports the peasant being told. And after "a little more persuasion, a little money promised" so he did, to round out the negotiating team. As far as I am aware, this was the first instance of what came subsequently to be called "political correctness" (*Brest-Litovsk*, pp. 86–87).

[23] Kowalski, *The Bolshevik Party*, p. 11.

[24] Wheeler-Bennett, *Brest-Litovsk*, p. 187.

[25] Fischer, *The Soviets*, vol. 1, pp. 48–49.

Sovnarkom, the Central Committee decided by a vote of eleven to two with one abstention not to endorse Bukharin's position but, by a twelve to one vote, to follow Lenin's recommendation to continue to drag out the negotiations. The key vote was whether to adopt Trotsky's "no war–no peace" tactic. It carried by a nine to seven vote.[26] The negotiations resumed with Trotsky handling the negotiations for the Soviet side. They stalled yet again. Trotsky left the negotiations declaring that "[w]e are out of the war but we refuse to sign the peace treaty" the Germans were proposing. On February 15, 1918, the Germans announced that armistice would terminate as of February 17 and quickly advanced deep into Russian territory. They met no resistance. Their rate of advance was astonishing. In the middle of a Russian winter "in 124 hours . . . [the Germans] covered 150 miles."[27]

The Russian leadership's reaction was swift. The Party Central Committee met in the evening of February 18. As Louis Fischer describes the meeting, "This was no time for talk. Even the Russians realized that."[28] In a meeting in which the proponents and opponents of each position were limited to two 5-minute speeches apiece devoted to addressing the question, "'Shall we wire the German and sue for peace?'"[29] Lenin and Zinoviev argued in favor. Trotsky and Bukharin argued against. Lenin, always the realist, advocated capitulation. He lost six to seven.

Later the same evening, however, the Central Committee reconvened. This time, after a much longer discussion—and to a good measure in response to the events of the day on the battle field, Trotsky voted with Lenin. The vote this time was seven to six in favor of suing for peace. The Council of People's Commissars was convened that same evening. At that juncture it contained seven Left Social Revolutionaries along with the Bolsheviks. What the Left SRs did not know was the result of the Bolsheviks' discussions in their Central Committee. Four of the seven Left SRs supported the seven Bolsheviks who voted in favor, with the result that Lenin carried the day eleven to nine.

But the Germans did not stop. In desperation, the Soviets turned to the Western Allies for assistance. The French, apparently, provided some specific assurances as to what they would do. Yet another Central Committee meeting was called on the evening of February 22, where by a six to five vote those favoring receiving assistance achieved a majority over Bukharin and the others on the left who favored "revolutionary war." Lenin was absent from the meeting and cast his vote in absentia.

[26] Wheeler-Bennett, *Brest-Litovsk*, p. 193.
[27] Ibid., p. 245.
[28] Fischer, *The Soviets*, vol. 1, p. 60.
[29] Ibid.

"Please add my vote *in favor* of taking potatoes and weapons from the Anglo-French imperialist bandits."[30] Tangible aid was not forthcoming. The Russians faced the German army alone.

Once again, this time on February 23, the Party Central Committee met. Lenin made quite explicit his threat to resign, a threat that also appeared in *Pravda*.[31] He lambasted both revolutionary war (Trotsky's preferred position) and revolutionary phrases (Lenin's characterization of Bukharin's position). On the crucial question, "Shall we immediately accept the Germans terms?" Lenin received a plurality, seven to four to four. To allow Lenin to carry the day and despite his preferences, Trotsky and three of his followers abstained. Those who voted against "offered their resignation from all responsible posts held by them, and reserved their right of 'freely agitating both within the party and outside it,'" though in an action akin to Bueno de Mesquita et al.'s loyalty norm,[32] they subsequently "no longer reserved the right to agitate outside the party."[33] Dzerzhinsky, Ioffe, Krestinsky, and Trotsky took the view that it was more important to avoid a split in the Party targeted at Lenin than not to sign the Treaty of Brest-Litovsk. Schapiro maintains Lenin, too, "was anxious at all costs to prevent a split inside the party" and "silenced" Stalin, who had suggested that resigning from "responsible positions should be considered resigning from the party."[34]

There then followed additional votes that evening by the Central Executive Committee and the Petrograd Soviet, both of which were in session. In both, the rhetoric targeted at Lenin's position and at Lenin himself by the Left Communists and the Left Social Revolutionaries was vicious. Karl Radek, a leading Left Communist, is reported by Wheeler-Bennett as having said, "We want peace but not a shameful peace, not a peace of traitors and blacklegs."[35] Aleksandra Kollontai accused Lenin of "opportunism" and "compromising with imperialism."[36] The invective from the Left SRs was even more astringent, accusing Lenin of treason. Ultimately, Lenin carried the day, or rather the night, despite the strenuous opposition. Once again, as in the crucial seven to four to four vote of the Central Committee, Lenin required strategic behavior by other Bolsheviks. This time, rather than Trotsky, it was the Left Communists headed by Bukharin whose strategic behavior allowed Lenin

[30] V. I. Lenin, *Polnoe Sobranie Sochinenii*, 5th ed. (Moscow: Gosizdat, 1970–85), p. 489, italics in original.

[31] Wheeler-Bennett, *Brest-Litovsk*, p. 257 and p. 257n2.

[32] Bueno de Mesquita et al., *The Logic of Political Survival*, pp. 65–68.

[33] Schapiro, *The Origin*, p. 106.

[34] Ibid., p. 107.

[35] Wheeler-Bennett, *Brest-Litovsk*, p. 259.

[36] Ibid.

to have his way. They elected to walk out, rather than vote against. This made it possible for Lenin to win. Of those who remained to vote, Lenin's position was victorious, 116 to 85, with 26 abstentions.

While the Russians realized this was the time for deeds not words, they remained divided as to what those deeds should be. The governmental Central Executive Committee decided on February 26 to survey local Soviets on the issue of war or peace. Regional opposition, both in Soviets and in Party committees, had been quite strong in December and January. While that opposition attenuated when the Germans resumed their advance in mid-February, there were still places where opposition was strong even after the treaty was signed on March 3. Those on the left who favored revolutionary war were able to claim that a slim majority (105) of the 200 Soviets polled associated themselves with Bukharin's position, and could argue that those who favored revolutionary war were predominantly in the cities while those Soviets whose views coincided with Lenin's were heavily peasant in composition, thus providing the left the opportunity to charge Lenin with appeasing the peasants.[37]

The decision continued to be a topic of fierce discussion well into March at both the regional and national leadership levels despite the signing of the Treaty of Brest-Litovsk on March 3. Kowalski reports that even as the Germans were advancing, local opposition to signing a separate peace was strong in both Petrograd and Moscow, views that were shared by the major northern cities such Archangelsk and Murmansk, a pattern that was repeated in the Volga region, especially in Saratov. There the Soviet "mandated its delegates to the forthcoming Fourth All-Russian Congress of Soviets [scheduled for March 14–16] to resist ratification of the Brest peace."[38] In Siberia, too, opposition persisted even after the Seventh (extraordinary) Congress of the Party (March 4–6) and the mid-March Congress of Soviets. On March 22, "the executive committee of the Siberian Soviet continued to refuse to countenance . . . [ratification of the Treaty], while 'the Siberian Council of People's Commissars even declared itself still at war with the Central Powers.'"[39]

At the national leadership level, the debate over ratification played out first at the Seventh Congress of the Party and then in Moscow at the Congress of Soviets. The sharpest divide at the Seventh Party Congress was between Lenin and Bukharin, but their views were to a considerable extent a rehash of the debates in late February. What was new was that

---

[37] Kowalski, *The Bolshevik Party*, p. 15. This view contrasts with that of Wheeler-Bennett, *Brest-Litovsk* (p. 191), who says only a couple of localities opposed. Kowalski's account on regional actions seems more well based factually.

[38] Kowalski, *The Bolshevik Party*, pp. 13–14.

[39] Ibid., p. 14 citing O. [Oskar] Anweiler, *The Soviets: The Russian Workers, Peasants, and Soldiers Councils, 1905–1921*, 1st American ed. (New York: Pantheon Books, 1975), p. 222.

while the Seventh Congress was meeting, the Petrograd city Party committee and the Petrograd regional committee began to publish a daily, *Kommunist*, the editors of which were Bukharin, Radek, and Uritsky, all Left Communists, and "devoted to popular agitation for revolutionary war."[40] It began publication on March 5. Two days later, the Left Communists were criticized at a Petrograd Party Conference for having an "independent organizational existence"[41] and *Kommunist* was accused of "splitting tactics"[42] and closed down, only to reappear in Moscow in April as a weekly, this time with Bukharin, Radek, V. V. Obolensky, and V. M. Smirnov as the editorial board. As Schapiro relates, in this version "revolutionary war was now completely discarded." In its place were theoretical discussions of what they conceived to be the proper domestic policies to be pursued in light of what they considered a capitulation both to the Germans and to "the less advanced and least revolutionary sections of the proletariat and peasantry."[43]

Significantly, all the members of the Central Committee were severely constrained. Lenin sought to combine winning with avoiding a split. Bukharin resigned and organized a call for revolutionary war but acted in such a way that Lenin could have his way once the decision reached the Congress of Soviets. Trotsky, as we have seen, was highly strategic in his voting on the crucial issue within the Central Committee. His explanation why he could not support Bukharin's call for revolutionary war is telling: "A revolutionary war would have meant a split in the Party," Fischer concludes. He cites Trotsky as having asserted that "'[i]t is impossible to conduct a war against the Germans and against our *bourgeoisie* . . . when you have opposed to you half or more than half of the party led by Lenin.'"[44] Pipes argues that Lenin made clear that for the latter, peace was "'a breathing space for war.'"[45] The facts on the ground had shifted the distribution of views sharply in favor of peace with Germany: as the German army continued its advance, the option of revolutionary war became steadily less appealing and the case for capitulation more apparent.

As a result, at the national level, the Left Communists were in a decided minority by the Seventh Party Congress. The Congress vote was twenty-eight to nine with one abstention. To anticipate charges he had lost his revolutionary fervor, "Lenin then asked the Party Congress to pass a secret resolution, not subject to publication for an indefinite

[40] Schapiro, *The Origin*, p. 134 and Kowalski, *The Bolshevik Party*, p. 17.
[41] Schapiro, *The Origin*, p. 134.
[42] Kowalski, *The Bolshevik Party*, p. 17.
[43] Schapiro, *The Origin*, p. 135.
[44] Fischer, *The Soviets*, vol. 1, p. 68.
[45] Pipes, *The Russian Revolution*, p. 600.

Table 1.1 Key votes (all votes 1918) by Bolshevik leaders regarding the Treaty of Brest-Litovsk: Votes for or against (for revolutionary war) Lenin's position or abstaining (no war, no peace)

Date (all 1918)	For	Against	Abstaining
January 21	15	32	16
January 22	7	9	—
February 18 day	6	7	—
February 18 night	7	6	—
February 23	7	4	4
March 7	30	12	4
March 16	784	261	Left communists abstained

Sources: For the January 21 and 22 votes, see Richard Pipes, *The Russian Revolution* (New York: Vintage Books, 1991), p. 583. The February 18 votes are reported in Leonard Bertram Schapiro, *The Origin of the Communist Autocracy: Political Opposition in the Soviet State, First Phase, 1917–1922* (London: London School of Economics and Political Science, 1955), pp. 103–4. For the February 23 vote, see Louis Fischer, *The Soviets in World Affairs: A History of the Relations between the Soviet Union and the Rest of the World* (London: Jonathan Cape, 1930), vol. 2, p. 65. Alexander Rabinowitch, *The Bolsheviks Come to Power: The Revolution of 1917 in Petrograd* (New York: Norton, 1976), p. 198, quotes the Seventh Party Congress meeting on March 7, whereas Pipes and Fischer both have the vote as 28-9-1. The March 16 meeting of the Congress of Soviets as reported by John Wheeler-Bennett, *Brest-Litovsk: The Forgotten Peace, March 1918* (New York: Norton, 1971), p. 304.

period, giving the Central Committee 'the authority at any time to annul all peace treaties with imperialist and bourgeois governments, and in like manner, to declare war on them.'"[46]

Finally, the Congress of Soviets met and acted on the night of March 16/17. In the caucus before the Congress, the vote was 453 to 36, with 8 abstentions, against the Left Communist position.[47] The treaty was approved overwhelmingly by the Congress as a whole by a vote of 784 in favor, 261 opposed, with the Left Communists abstaining.[48] Its decision gave the previous actions by Party and state organs a veneer of legitimacy in that it was an all-Russian body that had voted overwhelmingly in favor of ratification (see Table 1.1).

[46] Ibid.

[47] Robert V. Daniels, *The Conscience of the Revolution* (Cambridge, MA: Harvard University Press, 1960)., p. 88.

[48] Fischer, *The Soviets*, vol. 1, p. 74 and Wheeler-Bennett, *Brest-Litovsk*, p. 304; Pipes (*The Russian Revolution*, p. 603) says 724–276–118 but these may be different key votes. Regardless, the 75–25 pattern is clear.

We benefit from the hindsight that comes with knowing what would soon be in the cards. The political system became ever more restrictive within a matter of years and in major respects even months. Against the framework of subsequent Soviet politics, several points warrant emphasizing. First, it was felt desirable to consult regional Soviets on a matter of such importance as the ratification of the treaty, both because it reflected the importance of governmental rather than Party entities at this juncture and because the views of regional governmental and Party bodies on key *foreign* policy decisions mattered in 1918. Second, it pays emphasizing how Lenin, universally regarded as *the* Bolshevik leader, behaved with respect to Trotsky and the Central Committee members who had opposed the decision to accept the German terms. He did not feel in a position to have his way without risking an irretrievable split in the coalition that had assumed power. Wheeler-Bennett again: Lenin was convinced that Trotsky's "no war-no peace" policy would fail but "short of a second *coup d'état* and a split within the party from which it might never recover, he could not succeed in imposing his own views upon his colleagues. He consented to give Trotsky's policy a trial. 'We, [Lenin is reported as having said] will only risk losing Estonia or Livonia [split between Latvia and Estonia after the collapse of the tsarist empire], and for the sake of a good peace with Trotsky,' Lenin added with a deep chuckle, 'Livonia and Estonia are worth losing.'"[49]

Pipes, who is often scathing about Lenin,[50] describes him as "having gotten what he wanted," but that to do so, he "pleaded with Trotsky and the Left Communists not to act on their resignation until after the Russian delegation had returned from Brest" and that "he displayed brilliant leadership, alternately cajoling and persuading his followers, never losing either patience or determination."[51]

Third, the Left Communists had an "independent organizational existence" to back up their positions and used it (briefly) to advance their views—initially to defend their preferred policy, "revolutionary war." Then, after the Party Congress and the Congress of Soviets had endorsed the Party Central Committee's decision to ratify the treaty, the Left Communists were still able, briefly, to publish a weekly magazine that articulated their rationale for a series of steps designed to implement their domestic policies in light of the changed external environment. Especially with the knowledge in mind of what transpires in subsequent months—and how non-Bolshevik socialist parties were

---

[49] Wheeler-Bennett, *Brest-Litovsk*, p. 193.

[50] See, especially, Pipes, ed., *The Unknown Lenin* (New Haven, CT: Yale University Press, 1996), passim.

[51] Pipes, *The Russian Revolution*, p. 593.

already being treated, Fainsod's summary observation concerning the process leading to the ratification of the Treaty of Brest-Litovsk is pithy and to the point: "No sanctions were invoked against members of the opposition."[52]

Narrowing the Selectorate

Lenin's victory over Brest-Litovsk came at a cost. Socialist opposition— Left Communists, Mensheviks, and SRs—to Lenin's policies persisted for months after the ratification of the Treaty of Brest-Litovsk. In 1918, despite the Red Terror (targeted primarily against class enemies— defined increasingly broadly), working-class discontent was vividly manifest in local elections in major cities in European Russia. Mensheviks and Right SRs played major roles in these elections. Vladimir Brovkin reports that they "won city soviet elections in Tula, Iaroslavl', Kostroma, Sormovo, Briansk, Izhevsk, and other industrial centers—in the majority of provincial capitals of European Russia where soviet power actually existed." He also adds, pointedly, "The Bolsheviks disbanded all of these newly elected soviets by force."[53]

At the national level, while the Moscow version of *Kommunist* was quickly closed, the Left Communists had their way with respect to domestic economic policy in the spring and early summer 1918. What came to be called War Communism—effectively eliminating money as a means of exchange, full-scale nationalization, and a limited role for "bourgeois specialists"—was implemented with a vengeance over Lenin's opposition.

The disarray that resulted produced efforts by Lenin and Trotsky to impose more traditionally hierarchical relations at the enterprise level such as the appointment of a single enterprise leader and the harnessing of the trade unions to the purposes of the Party. Trotsky, Lenin, and many of the communist trade union leaders agreed that the trade unions should implement Party policy. Trotsky and Lenin were at odds with many in the trade unions as to the role of trade unions but differed themselves how the trade unions would be induced to implement Party policy. Disputes over the nature of workplace decision making persisted until the Tenth and Eleventh Party Congresses in 1921 and 1922,

---

[52] Fainsod, *How Russia*, p. 132.

[53] Brovkin, "Workers' Unrest and the Bolsheviks' Response in 1919," *Slavic Review*, Vol. 49, No. 3 (Autumn 1990), pp. 350–73 at p. 351. See also Brovkin, "The Mensheviks' Political Comeback: The Elections to the Provincial City Soviets in Spring 1918," *Russian Review*, Vol. 42, No. 1 (January 1983), pp. 1–50.

respectively. Central to this opposition were disputes about the role of workers, trade unions, "bourgeois specialists," and management in industry under what was putatively proletarian dictatorship. Initially, the dispute was between a largely unified Central Committee on the one hand and various regional and trade union figures on the other. Lenin's advocacy of one-man management met particular resistance.

As had also been the case with regard to the appointment of former tsarist officers to Red Army posts, there was great resistance to the hiring of civilian "bourgeois specialists." In industry, the suspicion of such specialists was dealt with by the creation of elected boards, which, as the name suggests, entailed joint management of both enterprises and branches of industry. Lenin was determined to introduce one-man management to overcome the inefficiencies that joint management entailed. The list of resistors, as summarized by Schapiro,[54] is impressive. Lenin "was outvoted," he reports, in the Party fraction of the All-Russian Central Council of Trade Unions meeting in early 1920. The subsequent Congress of Councils of National Economy endorsed "a resolution in favour of board management." Party conferences in Moscow and Kharkov rejected one-man management. Tomsky, a Central Committee member and the leading trade unionist, opposed Lenin's policies at the Ninth Party Congress in 1920. The so-called Democratic Centralists and Lutovinov (on behalf of a minority of trade union leaders) all opposed Lenin's views at the Ninth Party Conference. At the Congress, however, Lenin had his way. In part this was because the economy was in shambles and the civil war was still in process. In part, too, ongoing institutional developments, specifically the introduction of the Orgburo in 1919, affected how vigorously folks pursued policies at variance with the Central Committee consensus. Beyond these contextual changes, the trade union leaders (not the workers) often had a stake in the policies Lenin proposed. Trotsky consistently advocated the militarization of the workplace. As Schapiro notes, "Trotsky quite openly urged militarization and compulsion as the normal methods of the proletarian state."[55] Lenin's utterances combined defense of centralization with sops at the Ninth Party Congress, which helped make it possible for a trade union leader like Tomsky to continue as a member of the Central Committee while at the time arguing that he had represented the interests of the workers. (Tomsky's fence straddling, obvious in 1920, became particularly manifest in his behavior at the Tenth Party Congress in 1921.) Thus, Lenin's insistence on *individual authority* was quite explicit: "'The elective principle must be replaced by the principle

[54] Schapiro, *The Origin*, p. 230.
[55] Ibid., p. 277.

of *selection*'" and "'The *collegial principle* . . . must unconditionally yield its place to *individual authority* in the process of execution.'"[56]

The resolutions adopted at the Ninth Party Congress also provided that trade union leaders could participate in the management of an enterprise either as assistants to the manager or commissars (much like the military advisers), or in some instances, the trade union leaders could even become the managers of the enterprise. Moreover, successful boards were allowed to continue and the trade union leadership was assured of consultation rights on appointments.[57] The central thrust of Lenin's position was clear-cut: he skillfully papered over the disputes in a way that held the Central Committee together—the civil war was not yet over—but co-opted those senior Communists, some of whom, such as Tomsky, were members of the Central Committee, by combining one-man management with a continued role for trade union leaders.

Splitting the trade union leaders and the workers over the issue of one-man management went a long way in the direction of eliminating ordinary workers as part of the selectorate even with respect to enterprise leadership. The compromises that were adopted at the Ninth Party Congress constituted a huge step in the direction of a role for trade unions that was premised on the assumption that the Party, not the workers, knew best the workers' interests. The trade unions constituted a considerable force to be reckoned with and channeled. The controversy over the management of enterprises provided renewed evidence that regional or functional organizations sometimes did oppose Lenin and the Central Committee, though with less by way of political weaponry and organization than the Left Communists had had in the dispute over the Treaty of Brest-Litovsk.

The decision to opt for one-man management did not end the debate about the role of trade unions in a proletarian state. Instead, in late 1920 the Central Committee found itself divided about the governance of the trade unions. It began when the Central Committee established a Joint Central Transport Committee (Tsektran), headed by Trotsky, to oversee transportation, notably the railroads, which amounted to a direct challenge to the national trade union organization. Tsektran did not sit well with the rank-and-file workers and with some trade union leaders, including Tomsky.

What to do about Tsektran became transformed into a larger debate about the role of trade unions. The verbiage Lenin and Trotsky used to

---

[56] As cited in Daniels, *The Conscience*, p. 109. Italics in original.

[57] The above draws on Schapiro, *The Origin*, p. 232. See also Daniels, *The Conscience*, p. 109.

depict their preferred outcomes in this matter differed substantially.[58] Trotsky explicitly advocated fusion of the trade unions and the government. Lenin's public posture was more politically astute. For Trotsky, "in the workers' state . . . [t]he thoughts and energies of the communist party, of the unions, and of the government organs must be directed towards fusing in the more or less near future economic organs and trade unions."[59] Lenin's overt posture was that "'[t]he rapid fusion of the trade unions in the state would be a great political mistake. . . . The trade unions are already at present carrying out certain state functions' and 'these will gradually increase.'" What he opposed was "'any artificial speeding up of the tempo of fusion of state and unions.'"[60] Trotsky once again articulated the view that for socialist states militarization should be standard practice, going so far as to term differentiating between "military" and "trade union" methods as "'a Kautskyite-Menshevik-S-R prejudice.'" Lenin evidently shared that "Kautskyite-Menshevik-S-R prejudice" and was by comparison with Trotsky more politic: "'The principal method of the trade unions is not compulsion, but persuasion—though this in no way prevents the unions, where necessary, from successfully applying the method of proletarian compulsion.'"[61]

One of the oldest axioms in politics is that small groups, if in agreement, that meet frequently have agenda control and dominate larger and more diffuse groups that meet less frequently. This proposition applies to Central Committees (and subsequently to an even smaller group, the Politburo) and Congresses as well as in American universities, departmental executive committees, and meetings of the faculty as a whole.

In this instance, the Central Committee was divided, with Lenin and Zinoviev the primary defenders of one position, and Trotsky and Bukharin the defenders of a second perspective. Both sides agreed that the Party, not the trade unions, should play the primary role in industrial management but diverged on how this was to be accomplished. The division—exacerbated by Zinoviev's ad hominem attacks on Trotsky—raised the specter that the Central Committee would lose its ability to dominate the larger body of communists, the upcoming Tenth Party Congress in March 1921. Persons outside the Central Committee sought a far greater role for trade unions in the control of industry and used the existence of the Central Committee divide to raise a far wider

[58] Trotsky's and Lenin's differences were exacerbated by Zinoviev's active cultivation of opposition to Trotsky on the part of trade union officials and others outside the Central Committee.

[59] Trotsky, as cited by Schapiro, *The Origin*, p. 277.

[60] Ibid.

[61] As cited in Schapiro, *The Origin*, p. 278.

range of questions pertaining what they saw, correctly, as the increasingly dictatorial relation of the Central Committee to lower level units of the Party and to governmental and social-political institutions such as trade unions. Within the Party, these were the groups who came to be known as the Workers' Opposition and the Democratic Centralists.

What makes the divided Central Committee's behavior particularly interesting is two things. First, its members decided to allow a kind of great debate to occur to assess the merits of the various positions being advocated. An ongoing public debate ensued that lasted for about two months. It began with a flourish December 30, 1920, at the Bol'shoi Theater in Moscow. At that meeting a variety of views were presented to the public, most notably those of Lenin and Zinoviev, on the one hand, and Trotsky, on the other. In the course of the two-month debate, many platforms were presented, of which only three were discussed when the debate terminated at the Tenth Party Congress in March 1921. These were Trotsky's theses, the theses of the Workers' Opposition, and a compromise formula by Lenin and nine others (known, unsurprisingly, as the Platform of the Ten).

Second, by a vote of eight to seven,[62] with Lenin this time in the majority, the Central Committee decided that delegates to the Party Congress would be elected by separate platforms. This proposal emanated from the Petrograd Party organization, which Zinoviev dominated thoroughly. It was a two-sided weapon. Daniels characterizes it as "the nearest the Communists came to legalizing a multiparty system within their ranks."[63] Schapiro, in contrast, had a better grasp of the implications in practice of adopting such a rule: it "compelled their adversaries to crystallize into open opposition groups, and also, incidentally, in the absence of secret voting at party meetings and conferences, forced all party members to reveal their affiliations."[64]

The proposal initiated from Petrograd infuriated many members of the Moscow Party organization. In early 1921 it was divided almost equally between those who preferred the Program of the Ten or some other proposal. Daniels reports that in a poll Lenin's position received nineteen votes; Trotsky and Bukharin combined, eleven (seven for Trotsky); and others including Democratic Centralists, the Workers' Opposition, and the Ye. N. Ignatov group, seven.[65] Sufficient unity of views among the advocates of various proposals other than that of the

---

[62] Daniels, *The Conscience*, p. 141.

[63] Ibid.

[64] Schapiro, *The Origin*, p. 288.

[65] Daniels, *The Conscience*, p. 140. Subsequent to this vote Ignatov sided with the Workers' Opposition (ibid., pp. 132–40).

Program of the Ten existed that the Moscow city organization, by a vote of fourteen to thirteen, censured the Petrograd organization "for not observing the proper rules of controversy." More to the point, it noted "'the tendency of the Petrograd organization to make itself a special center for the preparation of the party congress.'"[66]

Given the misbehavior of the Party organization in the northern capital, supporters of Trotsky's militarization thesis, given Zinoviev's hostility to Trotsky, could find common ground with those who sought to have the trade unions dominate industry. But that unity extended only so far. Those in the Moscow committee who associated themselves with Trotsky's views or Bukharin's positions (plural intended)[67] adamantly opposed the views of the Workers' Opposition.

Trotsky and Zinoviev were clearly ranged against each other. They, Bukharin, and, of course, Lenin, though, were as one in opposing proposals that would constitute fundamental challenges to the centrality of the Central Committee in making decisions that pertained to the role of the trade unions in industry. The Democratic Centralists overstated the similarity between the Program of the Ten and Trotsky. In their reading, both were "militarizers." In a sense this was right: Lenin clearly believed that the unions should play the role of "the transmission belt from the Communist Party to the masses."[68] But Lenin's statements also implied that education and agitation would be the first steps in controlling the trade unions and in turn the workers. Trotsky saw the workers as the civilian counterpart to the Red Army of Workers and Peasants. Blair Ruble's brief discussion of the Group of Ten and the evolution of the trade unions in the 1920s argues that Lenin shared with Trotsky the view that "unions should help raise productivity" but unlike Trotsky "on condition that they guarantee workers' legitimate rights against infringements by management."[69] Trotsky's trade union militarization for production became fully implemented only in the 1930s under his arch-nemesis, Stalin.

Where all the members of the Central Committee and even the Democratic Centralist leadership found common ground was in defending the dominance of the Central Committee over the trade unions against the proposals of the Workers' Opposition. Schapiro is right to assert that neither those who became known as the Workers' Opposition nor

[66] Ibid., p. 140.

[67] For a comparison of Bukharin's views in January 1921, when his views seemed fairly close to the Workers' Opposition, and at the Tenth Party Congress, when he sided completely with Trotsky against the Workers' Opposition, see Schapiro, *The Origin*, pp. 286–87.

[68] Blair Ruble, *Soviet Trade Unions: Their Development in the 1970s* (Cambridge: Cambridge University Press, 1981), p. 12.

[69] Ibid., p. 11.

the Democratic Centralists were "an opposition in any real sense of the term. They had no separate organization, no fixed membership, no press or publications of their own."[70] He is misleading, though, when he adds, "and [had] no platform or policy as an alternative to the official communist programme."[71] In fact, in the lead-up to the Tenth Party Congress (March 1921) both, as he thoroughly documents, presented and published alternative platforms concerning the role of the trade unions in the Soviet context. (I say "misleading" because a fair retort would be that the publication of these platforms became possible only because of a decision by the Central Committee to allow various groups to present their views in various fora.)

The Workers' Opposition called for the management of industry and of individual factories by the communists in the trade unions. Crucially, leadership positions would be elected. Union officials would be elected. Union officials would not be appointed by the Central Committee or by the rapidly emerging central organs—the Orgburo, the Secretariat, or the Politburo (all of which had been established or, in the case of the Politburo, reconstituted in 1919). "This policy [electing the leadership]," Schapiro notes, "was aimed at breaking the power of the Central Committee of the party and even of the local party organizations over the unions."[72] Writing in 1956, a Soviet historian, S. N. Kanev,[73] in an article that way overdoes the differences between Lenin's and Trotsky's views, nevertheless was correct when he argued that the trade union dispute was part of a much larger issue: Central to the discussion was "the question about the Party, its place in the system of the dictatorship of the proletariat, the methods of approaching the masses," and the means of involving the mass in socialist construction. Disregarding the jargon, he nails the challenge that the trade union controversy represented. The trade unions and the Workers' Opposition sought the dictatorship of the proletariat, not the Party dictatorship over the proletariat. That challenge would not have been tolerated regardless of what decisions were taken at the March 1921 Tenth Party Congress, though Ruble[74] is correct when he asserts that the rationale for responding as Lenin did was strongly influenced by events.

[70] Schapiro, *The Origin*, p. 224.
[71] Ibid.
[72] Schapiro, *The Origin*, p. 285.
[73] S.N. Kanev, "The Party Masses in the Struggle for Unity of the Russian Communist Party in the Period of the Trade Union Discussion, 1920–21," *Voprosy Istorii* No. 2, (February 1956), 17–27 and reproduced in *Current Digest of the Russian Press*, Vol. 8, No. 14 (May 16, 1956), 15–19, dlib.eastview.com/browse/doc/13974718. Thanks to Olesya Tkacheva for calling my attention to this article.
[74] Ruble, *Soviet Trade Unions*, pp. 10–12.

"By events" here of course refers mostly to the Kronstadt Rebellion—with its slogan, ominous to the Bolsheviks, of Soviets without Bolsheviks—which took place while the Tenth Party Congress was in process. This was a Congress that transformed Russian politics in fundamental ways; these persisted until the perestroika era of the late 1980s. With respect to regime-society relations, the adoption of the New Economic Policy amounted to a truce with the peasantry and the restoration of a market economy with the state maintaining control over the commanding heights.[75] It was clearly a retreat.

Lenin knew what to say and do about behavior during retreats. While loosening the restraints on the peasantry, the modest tolerance for noncommunist socialist participation in regional-level and trade union politics ended. The Mensheviks had made the mistake of being right. They would not be allowed to remind folks of that. They, along with the Workers' Opposition, had taken seriously the 1920 statements about freedom of discussion and paid the price. Lenin made clear that what little there was left of SR and Menshevik participation in politics in 1921 would be eliminated. "We shall keep the Mensheviks and SRs (whether they are now open or disguised as 'nonpartisans') in prison."[76]

But Lenin was not intent merely on eliminating noncommunist, albeit socialist, opposition. Rather, he sought to restrict severely *communist* opposition to Central Committee decisions. The era of relatively free discussion came to an abrupt end. Because the Workers' Opposition's views meshed in some ways with those held by Mensheviks, they were accused of sympathizing with the latter. In one of his most frequently cited quotes, Lenin declared, "Now it is a great deal better to 'discuss with rifles' than with the theses offered by the opposition. We need no opposition now, comrades, it is not the time! Either on this side, or on that, with a rifle, but not with the opposition. . . . And I think that the Party Congress will have to draw that conclusion too . . . that the time has come to put an end to the opposition, to put a lid on it; we have had enough of opposition now."[77]

The decisions taken at the Tenth Party Congress culminated a process that had been ongoing since the Bolsheviks seized power. During a brief time span (three and a half years), the Party had become *the* Party. The Party had asserted its claim to appoint trade union employees, thus virtually disenfranchising workers without regard whether they were

[75] In a vast literature, Paul Gregory, *Before Command: An Economic History of Russia from Emancipation to the First Five-Year Plan* (Princeton, NJ: Princeton University Press, 1994) stands out.

[76] Cited in Roeder, *Red Sunset*, p. 43.

[77] In virtually all standard sources for the period. E.g., Fainsod, *How Russia*, p. 134.

communist or not. At the Tenth Congress, what Lenin had written in 1902 in *What's to Be Done* had morphed into Marxism. The resolution attacking the Workers' Opposition declared that *"Marxism* [mine] teaches us that only the political party of the working class, i.e. the communist party, is capable of uniting, educating, and organizing such a vanguard of the proletariat and of the working masses as is capable of resisting the inevitable petty bourgeois waverings of these masses . . . [and] their trade union prejudices."[78] Then to top matters off, the Congress adopted the Resolution on Party Unity with its well known Article 7 prohibiting factions:

> In order to ensure strict discipline within the Party and in all Soviet work and to secure the maximum unanimity in removing all fractionalism, the Congress authorizes the Central Committee, in cases of breach of discipline or a revival or toleration of fractionalism, to apply all Party penalties, including expulsion, and in regard to members of the Central Committee to reduce them to the status of alternate members and even, as an extreme measure, to expel them from the Party.[79]

Moreover, the Communist Party was rapidly becoming transformed into a large administrative apparatus, the leadership of which was capable of enforcing its policy preferences. It was a radically different organization in March 1921 than it had been as recently as two years before. Developments in the next two years further transformed the Party as an organization into what was basically the entity that persisted until glasnost and Mikhail Gorbachev in the mid-1980s. Until Sverdlov's death in March 1919, he had been the secretariat. At the Eighth Party Congress in 1919, an Orgburo, and the Secretariat had been established. In addition, the Politburo (which had existed in 1917 but fell out of use after the October Revolution) was reconstituted and authorized to make important decisions between Central Committee meetings. These institutional developments were followed in 1920 by the establishment of a Central Control Commission, which took on an increasing role in the early 1920s.

The importance of these institutions grew rapidly. Strictly speaking, the Politburo was initially a subcommittee of the Central Committee. Initially, the relative weight of the two bodies was governed primarily by the progress of the civil war. While it was going on in the first several months of 1920, the Politburo met far more frequently than did the full Central Committee. Once the danger had passed and the Central

---

[78] Schapiro, *The Origin*, p. 318.
[79] Again in every standard source, e.g., Fainsod, *How Russia*, p. 135.

Committee members had returned to Moscow, the ratio of meetings was reversed for the latter half of 1920.[80]

Central Committee plenum meetings decreased rapidly after the Tenth Party Congress. From 1922 on, the Politburo (see pp. 94–99 below for the diminished role of even the Politburo in the 1930s) was the dominant organ of the two. The Central Committee's growth in size (below, p. 83, table 3.1) was paralleled by a decrease in power, playing a major role only in those circumstances when the Politburo was divided, as in the famous dispute in 1957 between Nikita Khrushchev and the Anti-Party Group who sought to oust Khrushchev from his sinecure as Party leader.

The Secretariat staff in Moscow "grew between 1919 and 1921 from 30 to 602; by August 1922 'responsible workers' numbered 325 in the central and regional bureaus and an estimated 15,000 in provincial and local organizations."[81] The increased numbers increased the influence of the Secretariat both in making appointments in regional Party organizations and in non-Party institutions in Moscow (most notably in the government, the trade unions, and in the armed forces). Since this is a story of the consequences of institutional development for the size of the selectorate, it warrants emphasizing that both Ye. A. Preobrazhensky and N. M. Krestinsky, the first active secretaries of the Party, were relatively tolerant of dissent. ("Active" is inserted here to indicate the Central Committee initially appointed three secretaries. The third, L. P. Serebryakov, became ill and as a consequence played almost no role.) Preobrazhensky in particular was committed to free discussion within the Party and was not a zealot when it came to using the organizational weapon to harness discrepant views in regional Party organs.[82] Both were Trotsky supporters. Nevertheless, appointments by the Party to the government bureaucracy quickly reduced the government's role in decision making despite Lenin's leadership of Sovnarkom and Preobrazhensky's and Krestinsky's support of Trotsky. The first nomenklatura list of roughly five thousand *state* officials requiring approval by the central Party organs appeared in October 1923.[83]

Another indication of the increased concentration of power pertains to meetings of many governmental institutions. The state certainly did not begin to wither away. The transformation to a party-state was well launched as early as December 1919. By then, "the All-Russian Soviet

[80] Graeme Gill, *The Origins of the Stalinist Political System* (New York: Cambridge University Press, 1990), pp. 25–122.

[81] Roeder, *Red Sunset*, p. 46.

[82] See, for instance, Daniels, *The Conscience*, p. 151.

[83] Roeder, *Red Sunset*, p. 47.

congress had not met for a year . . . the Central Executive Committee had scarcely met at all and had barely debated or voted a single decree; all legislation was conducted either by the Presidium of the Central Executive Committee or by the Council of People's Commissars (the two bodies were largely identical in composition)."[84]

By successfully dominating major appointments in the trade union, the communists had effectively eliminated ordinary workers from the selectorate while continuing to regard the trade unions as a force to be reckoned with. In the terminology being employed here, the workers were excluded from the selectorate, but, had the Kronstadt rising spread to the workers in the two capital cities rather than being repressed, one can tell a story in which the workers would have effectuated the Kronstadt slogan of "Soviets without Bolsheviks" by constituting themselves as an ejectorate and removing the Bolsheviks from power.

Likewise, the regional Party organizations were increasingly brought to heal. At the Ninth Party Congress in 1919,[85] the Orgburo had received the power to transfer and appoint Party officials without recourse to the Politburo or the Central Committee "except for appointments within the central apparatus." By 1920, it was in a position (prior to then it really did not have adequate records to know what was going on in the regions) to use the transfer and appointment power as an effective weapon to control local Party organs, at least in the major industrial centers. Initially, only limited use was made of that power with regard to regional Party organs. Roeder mentions the example of the Ukrainian Central Committee, which was removed by the center in 1920 and the Samara Regional Committee, which Moscow removed in 1921. In both cases, Moscow picked the replacements.[86] Prior to March 1921 such examples as these were infrequent.

The difference between the situation a year before the Tenth Party Congress meeting in 1921 and 1922, a year after, was stunning. After March 1921, what Roeder terms reciprocal accountability became the emerging pattern: It "is found where selectors . . . can be appointed and removed by the very leaders whom they appoint and remove."[87] The Central Committee, through the Secretariat and the Orgburo, appointed those whose jobs warranted their participation at Party Congresses. The pace accelerated. "In 1922 [the Secretariat] reported removing or transferring thirty-seven *guberniia* (province) [forerunners to the oblast] secretaries and making recommendations in forty-two elections. . . . It

[84] Schapiro, *The Origin*, p. 261.
[85] Ibid., p. 264.
[86] Roeder, *Red Sunset*, p. 51.
[87] Ibid., p. 27.

made approximately 5,000 assignments of 'responsible officials' and at least as many assignments of other personnel"[88] to lower levels of the Party in the same year.

Those whose positions warranted participation at Party Congresses in turn would elect the members of the Central Committee through what Robert Daniels famously termed the circular flow of power—in which, for instance, the general secretary used the central Party Secretariat to appoint regional secretaries. The latter would then appoint delegates (themselves very much included) to the All-Union Congress. The Congress would then designate the Central Committee, which would elect the Politburo and the gensek.[89] The same practice obtained subsequently as the Congresses became increasingly substantively irrelevant—a "rally,"[90] as Fainsod termed it—for the faithful. Instead, it became no longer appropriate to consider the Central Committee, sometimes augmented by the Central Control Committee, the winning coalition, but the selectorate of the Politburo. In turn, in the post-Leninist Soviet period (Lenin died in 1924), the Politburo or increasingly often a majority of its membership became the real selectorate. In the 1930s, meetings of Politburo in turn decreased sharply to the point that, as we describe below (p. 85, table 3.2), there really was a selectorate of one, Stalin.

IMPLICATIONS FOR THE SELECTORATE

Through no fault of their own, the Bolsheviks' tenure in power began with an almost universal electorate. This ended quickly with the disbanding of the Constituent Assembly. Through repression and institutional design, they systematically disenfranchised, coerced, and in many instances slaughtered those whom they considered their class enemies, both in the town and in the countryside. They mimicked their tsarist predecessors in creating an electoral system that vastly underrepresented the small peasants in the countryside whom theoretically they did not regard as their enemy. By extending the appointment and transfer power of the central Party organs to the trade unions, they effectively rendered their core class constituency, the bulk of the working class, impotent even with respect to the choice of the factory leadership and irrelevant to the selection of political leaders.

[88] Ibid., p. 47.

[89] John W. Strong, ed., *The Soviet Union under Brezhnev and Kosygin: The Transition Years* (New York: Van Nostrand, 1971), p. 20.

[90] Fainsod, *How Russia*, p. 187.

Over the course of the first three or four years of Soviet power, the communists took decisions that disenfranchised and often imprisoned noncommunist socialists. By the Tenth and Eleventh Party Congresses (1921 and 1922, respectively), they were also constraining the kind of intra-Party parliamentary majoritarianism that had characterized the decision to capitulate to the German demands at Brest-Litovsk. Of these growing constraints, two were especially noteworthy as institutional developments facilitating manipulation. One was the decision to require the election of blocs defined by their support of resolutions before an upcoming Congress. The other was to require attendees to vote publicly. Both tended to produce fewer votes than otherwise at Congresses at variance with the Central Committee view or with the majority view of the Central Committee.

In addition, while voting continued to be the mechanism of resolving disputes within the Central Committee, a variety of techniques became increasingly employed to bring regional bodies in line. Representatives were sent to regional Party meetings to articulate the Central Committee's position. Three months after the March 1921 Tenth Party Congress, the Central Committee reacted sharply to a resolution adopted by a fifteen hundred to thirty vote at the Fourth All-Russian Trade Union Congress, which, while it affirmed the "over-all control of the party" in the "selection of directing personnel for the trade union movement," also maintained that "in the trade unions . . . above all, the selection of leaders should be made by the organized party masses themselves."[91]

An uproar ensued. Tomsky was replaced as the Central Committee representative to the Congress and the Communist "fraction" at the Congress was obliged to reverse itself on the same resolution it had overwhelmingly passed by fifteen hundred to thirty the previous day.[92] Finally, it cannot be overemphasized how powerful was the loyalty norm among the communists even in the early days post-October. In part this took the form of deference to Lenin per se. (Note though that the feeling was mutual, as Lenin's concessions to Trotsky [above, p. 27] over the debate over the negotiations with Germany at Brest-Litovsk illustrated.) Trotsky's behavior in the debate over the trade unions in early 1921 was certainly shaped by such feelings. A host of lesser lights also deferred to Lenin. In addition many communists had internalized the notion that the Party was always right. This notion came back to haunt communists in the 1930s—especially those who were Party members before the Revolution (the Old Bolsheviks). Karl

[91] Schapiro, *The Origin*, p. 324.
[92] Ibid., p. 325.

Radek epitomized the dilemma many experienced in 1921 in his oft-cited explanation why he was voting for the Program of the Ten. "In voting for this resolution, I feel that it can well be turned against us, and nevertheless I support it. . . . Let the Central Committee in a moment of danger take the severest measures against the best party comrades, if it finds this necessary. . . . Let the Central Committee even be mistaken! That is less dangerous than the wavering which is now observable."[93]

In addition, there was another kind of loyalty norm in play as well. As we have seen, the communist leadership was not about to yield power vis-à-vis the trade unions regardless of the division within the Central Committee. The Central Committee plus the leadership of a few key regional Party organs and a handful of those who controlled the regional Party organizations who were not full members of the Central Committee were unified in the belief that it must retain power and that defecting was dangerous. Trotsky and Zinoviev might quarrel to the point of despising each other. Bukharin said nice things about the Workers' Opposition. But when push came to shove, not even he was willing to risk the controlling position the Central Committee occupied by supporting the measures the Workers' Opposition proposed, which had the effect of eliminating the decisional centrality of the Central Committee. Indeed, he strongly supported the use of the appointments and transfer weapon as a way of bringing to heel the Moscow city organization, a hotbed of support for the Workers' Opposition: "The Moscow organization must be *made healthy*. . . . It is necessary to remove . . . the most factious element, to send in *new*, fresh faces.[94]

In short, the communist leadership had narrowed severely the selectorate and created a situation in which the distribution of power between, on the one hand, the Central Committee and the growing apparatus and, on the other, potential challengers vastly favored the former. The Congress continued to play some role. When members of the Workers' Oppositions persisted in stating their view, even to the extent of expressing their dismay to the Communist International at developments,[95] the Central Committee sought unsuccessfully to have the Congress exclude five of the leading members of the opposition from the Party. The Congress went along with the exclusion of two of the five but successfully resisted the efforts to exclude three long-term

---

[93] Schapiro, *The Origin*, p. 320.

[94] Quoted in Daniels, *The Conscience*, p. 138. (Italics in original.)

[95] The Communist or Third International was an international labor organization explicitly opposed to the Second or Socialist International. It was formed in the aftermath of World War I and dominated by the Russians from its inception. As a gesture to the USSR's wartime allies, the United States and the United Kingdom, it was dissolved in 1943.

communists. To that extent, despite the growing significance of the appointment and transfer power of the Secretariat in the selection of Congress members—Roeder's reciprocal accountability, Daniels's circular flow of power—those nominally empowered to serve as a selectorate continued to act to some modest degree as though such were actually the case.

But that observation does not diminish the central conclusion of this chapter. Over the first few years after October 1917 the selectorate narrowed substantially and became increasingly constrained by the rapidly developing system of reciprocal accountability, which was in turn primarily a product of the growing Party apparatus. The ruling coalition in turn also narrowed. The Central Committee fought vigorously and successfully to thwart efforts to have some other groups make authoritative decisions and were as one in projecting a united front to all outside groups. It was, however, not unified internally. As the burgeoning apparatus (especially as Lenin's health deteriorated) became a political resource—the 1919 Party rules had specified that the center "'distributes the forces and funds of the party'"[96]—it became clear a majority, first in the Central Committee and soon in the Politburo, could utilize that weapon to mobilize regional Party units and the Central Committee itself against opponents, including members of the Central Committee.

[96] As cited in Roeder, *Red Sunset*, p. 51.

CHAPTER 2

Alternative Mobilization Strategies, 1917–1934

STATES VARY IN THEIR ability to extract resources from their citizens. In this chapter I discuss the Soviet effort to mobilize its own citizenry in the years prior to the Great Purge. This entailed initially the effort to mobilize the peasantry in the aftermath of the Bolshevik Revolution; the formation of the Red Army of Workers and Peasants (RKKA)— overwhelmingly the peasantry in arms; and the harnessing of the urban population in a manner akin to the military. In the historical chronology, there then follows the New Economic Policy of the 1920s. NEP was a period during which the regime consolidated its power in a manner analogous to those of other normally or "full"[1] authoritarian states rather than one bent on mobilizing and transforming the society in pursuit of Jowitt's "combat task."[2] There then follows a period which in turn was followed, in the country, by the horrors of collectivization and, in urban areas, the penetration of virtually all manner of arts and sciences by Party doctrine among professional, scientific, and artistic groups. We discuss these in turn.

The story of peasant resistance to Bolshevik efforts—efforts rendered far more difficult by several Bolshevik policies—has been amply documented elsewhere. (Thus, for instance, the rampant inflation, exacerbated by Bolshevik notions that money could be eliminated as a means of payment, along with the absence of consumer goods, greatly increased the peasants' propensity to hoard the grain.)

Having come to power in the cities—unlike Mao and Tito, who seized power in the country and then advanced on the cities—the Bolsheviks sought to extend their power in the countryside. A half year after the seizure of power, Yakov Sverdlov was exaggerating when he observed that "revolutionary Soviet authority is sufficiently strong in the cities" but on the money in asserting that "the same cannot be said in regard to the village." To remedy the situation, the Bolsheviks set out, again in Sverdlov's words, to split "'the village into two irreconcilably hostile

---

[1] Above, pp. 4–6 and Levitsky and Way, *Competitive Authoritarianism*, p. 13.
[2] Jowitt, "Soviet Neotraditionalism," pp. 275–97.

camps, . . . to inflame there . . . civil war.'"[3] This they did in three ways: by creating the Committees of the Poor within the villages, by turning loose on the countryside the "food detachments" of armed workers to march on the villages to enforce the state monopoly on the trade of grain, and by loosing the newly established Red Army on the country-side. They got their civil war.

Indeed, there were multiple civil wars. There was the well-known war between the Whites and the Reds which, it is usually argued, the Reds won because the peasants disliked the Whites more and feared the return of the landowner. There was also war with the Greens. Both, along with the various foreign interventions, left an indelible mark on Russian society. The clashes between the Greens and the Reds often took the form of guerilla warfare in which the Greens would use the forests as a shield and then ambush detachments of Committees of the Poor, the armed workers sent to the countryside, and the Red Army. The Reds sought two specific goals and a broader one as well. The two specific goals were to requisition the grain and to establish Soviet power in the countryside, while the broader one was to intimidate the citizenry. As marginal as the Bolsheviks' presence outside the big cities was for years, they succeeded better in inserting regional governments than in their efforts to acquire grain by coercion. Both Vladimir Brovkin and Robert Conquest argue that "the magnitude of the Bolshevik war against peasants ["the Greens"] on the internal front eclipsed by far the frontline civil war against the Whites."[4]

This is an underresearched area,[5] but Brovkin's research certainly makes this a plausible claim. We know some things. A few of the largest risings, Tambov being the obvious example,[6] and most organized opposition to Bolshevik incursions into the countryside have been analyzed in detail. It is clear that typically peasant passive resistance—hiding grain, reducing plantings, and the like—was extensive. Likewise, many what Russians term *bunty* (small local peasant risings) occurred that often resulted in the dispatch of a "punitive detachment."[7] Brovkin cites American intelligence sources as having reported that "'the rural population of the districts of Novgorod, Petrograd and Tver have recently organized a vast movement. In most of the districts the peasants are well armed and even possess a canon [*sic*],

---

[3] As cited in Pipes, *The Russian Revolution*, p. 728.

[4] Brovkin, *Behind the Front Lines*, p. 127.

[5] Ibid., p. 6.

[6] Ibid., pp. 312–18; Oliver H. Radkey, *The Unknown Civil War in Soviet Russia: A Study of the Green Movement in the Tambov Region, 1920–1921* (Stanford, CA: Hoover Institution Press, Stanford University, 1976).

[7] Brovkin, *Behind the Front Lines*, p. 156.

machine guns and hand grenades.'"[8] Likewise, he reports communist sources to the effect that fifty thousand Green rebels in Tver' in central Russia and almost fifty-five thousand in Ryazan were arrested.[9] The problem, as Brovkin recognizes, is we don't know how typical such occurrences were. It is safe to say, though, that however much Lenin encouraged efforts to mobilize villagers against each other and armed workers and the newly formed Red Army against the villages, these efforts had limited success.

It is also clear that the violence on both sides was horrific, as is commonly the case in civil wars. Lenin insisted on hostage taking, a policy that segued into the Red Terror in which the Cheka operated almost without control. In response to an uprising in Penza, Lenin demanded that it "be **mercilessly** suppressed":

1. (hang without fail so **the people see) no fewer than one** hundred **known** kulaks, rich men, bloodsuckers.
2. Publish their names.
3. Take from them **all** the grain.
4. Designate hostages—as per yesterday's telegram.[10]

Anatoly Lunacharsky informed Lenin of the Urenskoe affair in Kostroma which, he wrote, was "'nothing but a nightmare. Its conclusion was horrible. The peasants killed, froze to death, and burned alive twenty-four of our comrades, having subjected them to horrible tortures.'" "But, at the same time," he added, probably in unintentional understatement, "I am not completely sure that the blame falls on peasants exclusively . . . it started with machine gun fire upon them.'"[11]

Perhaps, however, the most telling data on the regime's limited political capacity pertain to those Russians who occupied the dual role of peasant and army conscripts. In the section that follows I depict the growth of the RKKA, which was in several respects a great achievement, primarily through Trotsky's efforts. But if mobilizing the peasant to yield grain to the cities produced few results, then it pays examining the success that the Bolsheviks had in recruiting the tax collectors, who were also overwhelmingly peasant.

It is not altogether a success story. A sizeable fraction of those inducted, coerced, or railroaded into the military deserted. Estimates by such leading Western historians as John Erickson and Mark von Hagen

---

[8] Ibid.

[9] Ibid., p. 146.

[10] Richard Pipes, *The Unknown Lenin: From the Secret Archives* (New Haven, CT: Yale University Press, 1996), p. 50, bold in original.

[11] Brovkin, *Behind the Front Lines*, p. 157.

put the number not caught at a million or more. These numbers constitute a huge qualification to what follows, which depicts the transformation of what military forces there were immediately after the Revolution into what quickly became the RKKA.

But the transformation must also be recognized. It would be difficult to imagine an army subordinate to Soviet power performing the tasks it did in 1919–20 accomplishing anything like those same tasks in the immediate aftermath of the Bolshevik seizure of power in Petrograd. Armies are usually disciplined and hierarchical organizations. The Bolsheviks initially adopted resolutions that had the effect of continuing the policies they had pursued prior to their seizure of power. These had been designed to exacerbate the fissiparous tendencies of an army in disarray. Merle Fainsod[12] is succinct on this score: "The dream of an egalitarian people's army . . . possessed the minds of the Bolshevik leadership and guided the early army decrees. The order of December 29, 1917 abolishing military ranks and titles was followed by another decree of the Council of People's Commissars[13] on January 12, 1918, proclaiming the formation of a socialist army which was to be 'built up from below on the principles of election of officers and mutual comradely discipline and respect.'"

This was not a step that would result in anything like the usual European army, as the majority of the Bolsheviks, Lenin and Trotsky in particular, quickly came to realize. The initial steps did address one problem in part, that of increasing the prospects of loyalty within the ranks to a government claiming to represent the workers in a country, three-quarters of whom were peasants. They accomplished this initially by recruiting only among the urban working class and requiring a kind of loyalty check in the form of an endorsement by a Party organization, a trade union or "'democratic organizations standing on the platform of the Soviet Government.'"[14] But for an initially volunteer army, this was of little avail. To be sure, some joined for reasons compatible with the regime's goals. But, as Trotsky observed, "'the majority of those who enlisted were vagabonds of the worst kind.'"[15]

The beginnings of a sharp move in the direction of creating a more conventional army date with the appointment of Trotsky as people's commissar for war in March 1918, though officially February 23, 1918, was designated as the date for the formation of the Workers-Peasants

---

[12] Fainsod, *How Russia*, p. 391.

[13] In 1946 the Council of People's Commissars became the Council of Ministers when labels such as People's Commissars became unfashionable.

[14] Fainsod, *How Russia*, p. 391.

[15] As cited in ibid.

Red Army. In April, compulsory military training was inaugurated and its ramifications were extended across age and class cohorts in the ensuing months. An army that had dwindled to about 300,000 men by May 1918 grew to 3 million by January 1, 1920, and in excess of 5 million during that year, though, as Erickson[16] makes clear, the numbers are to some extent notional and the units consisted of an incredible mélange: "Latvian riflemen, Bolshevik sailors, the workers of Moscow, Petrograd and the Urals, volunteers from the old Imperial Army, ex-prisoners of war and peasants shuffling about in local militia units, all these milling about at the center or scattered about the provinces, or yet again organized into miniature, swaggering 'armies.' . . ." In addition, Trotsky took steps to centralize decision making, to bring former tsarist officers and NCO's into command structures, to establish discipline, and to train the ordinary soldiers to perform simple but essential tasks that ordinary soldiers in a large mass army have to do in order to perform effectively.

The election of officers was ended as a result of decrees dated March 21 and April 22, 1918, and the death penalty was restored.[17] Euphemistically termed "military specialists," almost 50,000 former officers enlisted in the Red Army in the course of the civil war. Two means were adopted to ensure their loyalty. The first was the establishment of a system of political commissars who, as Trotsky put it, would stand alongside the specialists "one on the right and another on the left, revolver in hand."[18] The second was to make hostages out of the military specialists' families, who were threatened with "immediate arrest." Betrayal of the Bolsheviks, Trotsky declared, also constituted "'betraying members of their own families. . . .'"[19]

Their role in the new army produced sharp criticism from many Bolsheviks, especially in the army itself. The criticism was to some extent well founded since, as Trotsky recognized, many of the former tsarist officers defected to the Whites.[20] However, in general the officers complied with the new reality. Aborting the policy of a decisive role for the military specialists, Trotsky again declared, would be as counterproductive as "'to drive out all the railway engineers . . . because there are a few saboteurs among them.'"[21]

[16] John Erickson, "The Origins of the Red Army," in Richard Pipes, ed., *Revolutionary Russia* (Cambridge, MA: Harvard University Press, 1968), pp. 224–58 at p. 229.

[17] R. Craig Nation, *Black Earth, Red Star: A History of Soviet Security Policy, 1917–1991* (Ithaca, NY: Cornell University Press, 1992), p. 18.

[18] As cited in Pipes, *The Russian Revolution*, p. 629.

[19] Fainsod, *How Russia*, p. 395.

[20] As cited in ibid.

[21] As cited in ibid., p. 395.

Perhaps most important in the movement toward a conventional army, however, was Trotsky's determined effort to achieve the basics: "Every army unit must receive its rations regularly, foodstuffs must not be allowed to rot, and meals must be cooked properly. We must teach our soldiers personal cleanliness and see that they exterminate vermin. They must learn their drill properly and perform it in the open air as much as possible. They must be taught to make their political speeches short and sensible, to clean their rifles and grease their boots. . . . That is our programme [for the near future]."[22] Craig Nation is correct in pointing out that the RKKA's "aspirations . . . remained distinct" and distinctive inasmuch as they were "'defined by the presence of a moral idea— therefore it triumphs.'"[23] Michael Morozow was nevertheless also on target in asserting this represented a "'return to normal conditions'"[24] because, as Nation acknowledges, "the common environment imposed by the battlefield" required that the Red Army adopt "methods resembling those of its enemies."[25]

Moreover, there were some important successes. Nation writes that "[i]n the space of a single year a defeated nation presumed to be at the end of its tether had mobilized a mass army, assured it a qualified leadership, and successfully projected an inspirational vision of its goals. It was an army that, as events were to demonstrate, could fight and win."[26]

This, however, needs to be placed in a larger context. The newly formed Red Army faced a wide range of tasks, some of which it performed better than others. The results of the Red Army's efforts to gather food in the countryside to feed itself and the cities, as we have seen, were desultory and provided the opportunity for vast numbers to desert rather than risk their lives. When one asks what armies do, the obvious answer is one of the key tasks armies perform is provide security from external and internal threats.

In the setting of a collapsed empire, however, conventional notions of external and internal threat were essentially meaningless in 1919. An enumeration of the countries the troops of which were located on Russian territory suggests the magnitude of the task confronting the Red Army. At some time or other during the time span November 1917 to March 1921, they faced threats from the Allies (Great Britain, France,

[22] As cited in ibid., p. 394.

[23] Nation, *Black Earth*, p. 19, citing Trotsky. This is an early example of the view among Soviet leaders that socialists were uniquely advantaged in war. Stalin was the most prominent articulator of that position as captured in his concept of "permanently operating factors."

[24] As cited in Nation, *Black Earth*, p. 19.

[25] Ibid., p. 19.

[26] Ibid., p. 21.

and the United States), the Germans (with and without weaker allies), the Japanese, the Czechoslovaks, the Poles, and the Whites.

The waffling "some time or other" is important to keep in mind. Initially, the Bolsheviks looked for assistance from the Allies against the Germans. Raymond Robins's telegram to the American Ambassador (dated March 21, 1918)[27] declared, "Wire from Murmansk states that English and French are co-operating with the Soviet Government in the protection of the port and railroad, under express orders from Moscow." Likewise, the Czechoslovak control of the Trans-Siberian constituted a real threat and was a major impetus to the decisions to convert the army into something far more akin to other conventional armies. But Pipes[28] asserts that "several hundred Czechs" landed with the British at Murmansk who were initially going to aid the Bolsheviks. Similarly, while the German advance after the collapse of the negotiations at Brest-Litovsk threatened to terminate the Bolshevik Revolution at its inception, the Germans subsequently played a role in sustaining the Bolsheviks in power.

In addition to fighting armed forces from foreign states, the Whites, and the Greens, the Red Army also was tasked with many other responsibilities. Trotsky came up with the idea of requiring units that had been withdrawn from combat zones to continue in uniform but be assigned "to such tasks as repairing railroad beds, transporting fuel, and fixing agricultural machinery."[29] In assuming these tasks, it was scarcely the only army to take on such typically civilian roles, especially in the aftermath of catastrophes, whether they be the result of war or insurrection or severe weather.

The Bolshevik leadership envisaged the RKKA playing an even larger role. They saw the army as the means by which the revolution in Russia would be linked to revolutions in Eastern and Central Europe, which they initially regarded as the sine qua non for staying in power in Russia. Nation makes clear the Bolsheviks intended to use it not only for defense but also to intervene in the revolutions in Europe. The Poles, who waited until it was clear that the Reds were going to win against the Whites, attacked the Ukraine in 1920. Initially, the Red Army had considerable success in rebuffing the Polish incursion. The Soviet leadership was quick to realize and exploit Russian nationalism as a mobilizing sentiment against outside threats. It was no more than three months after the Bolsheviks had seized power in Petrograd that Lenin and others found themselves urging, with considerable success,

---

[27] Cited in Chamberlin, *The Russian Revolution*, vol. 2, p. 398.
[28] Pipes, *The Russian Revolution*, p. 599.
[29] Ibid., p. 707.

the Russian citizenry to rally to the cause: "The socialist fatherland is in danger!"

But, as events in Poland bore out, when the Red Army, energized by slogans of "Give us Warsaw!" counterattacked against the Polish army and crossed into what were ethnically Polish lands, the situation was rapidly transformed. In the first chapter in a recurring story throughout the Soviet period, Soviet leaders failed to appreciate the role of nationalism as a motivating force that would thwart their aspirations (most egregiously Khrushchev's secret speech in 1956 and Gorbachev on the reaction of East Europeans to glasnost). The RKKA quickly found itself in an exceedingly untenable position, to a large extent because the Polish workers and peasants viewed the army as Russian imperialist occupiers and not liberators and potential revolutionary enablers who would link the revolution in Russia with the revolution in Germany and perhaps elsewhere in Eastern-Central Europe. The formation of a sizeable and successful Red Army, grounded firmly in the hierarchical and disciplinary modes of other armies, but augmented by a sizeable dose of revolutionary enthusiasm and political controls, demonstrated that the Red Army could compete on a par with the armies of European states such as Poland, though not yet the armies of the major European powers. Like other armies as well, though, in the early years of Soviet power it was far superior at the task of defending the mother- or fatherland than at force projection; that would come later.

The effort to achieve the hierarchy and discipline characteristic of other armies was part and parcel of the overall effort to harness the society to the regime's purposes. It was obviously primarily the military that had to cope with the Czechoslovak Legion, the Whites, and foreign interventions. Early on, they were tasked with suppressing the peasants and obtaining grain to feed the cities at gun point. They, Committees of the Poor (kombedy), and other Bolshevik supporters were unleashed on the countryside. Their opponents fought back on a national scale with vigor but with limited firepower and little by way of organization. Pipes points out that the introduction of compulsory military service and Lenin's instructions to rename the Commissariat of War the Military-Supply Commissariat occurred on the same day. Indeed, Lenin's very first point in arguing for that change in title was that "'[t]he Commissariat of War is to be transformed into a Military-Supply Commissariat—that is, nine-tenths of the work of the Commissariat of War is to concentrate on adapting the army for the war for bread and the conduct of such a war for three months, June-August.'"[30]

In addition, the Bolsheviks coupled the tasks for the military with the larger effort to militarize the entire society. It is widely asserted that

---

[30] Pipes, *The Russian Revolution*, p. 734.

War Communism was a response to the civil war and foreign interventions. Indeed, the earliest decree (November 29, 1917) about the role of labor had a markedly syndicalist bent, providing for Workers' Control, a provision that affirmed, inter alia, the right of the "organs of Workers' Control" "to supervise production, fix the minimum of output, and determine the cost of production" in the factories. Control, furthermore, was ostensibly to be exercised "through [the workers'] elected organizations."[31] But the belief in complete state ownership, a planned economy, and 'the leading role of the party'[32] preceded the Civil War. Moreover, as Paul Gregory points out, not only did the wholesale nationalizations take place in 1917, prior to the outbreak of the civil war, "the most extreme nationalization decree was passed in November 1920 after the civil war had largely ended."[33] Indeed, by 1920 the Whites had been virtually defeated. It was then that the Bolsheviks, most notably but not just Trotsky, introduced the steps that resulted in establishing what amounted to the dictatorship *over* the proletariat rather than the dictatorship *of* the proletariat.[34]

The transformation of the status of workers in the factories was similar to the transformation of the army and took place almost in parallel to those changes but met greater resistance. The factory committees lost much of what they had received in November 1917 at the First Congress of Trade Unions in January 1918.[35] In the same month, in addition, the regime issued "the Declaration of the Rights of the Toiling and Exploited People," which, "with a view to the destruction of the parasitic classes of society and the organization of the national economy," declared that "universal labor service is established."[36] This was followed by a decree in October that declared that "all citizens of the RSFSR . . . [with some exceptions] are subject to compulsory labor. What amounted to a civilian draft began in November and December 1918. Much like the military specialists, the civilian workers and technicians were "'mobilized for military service' and subject to court martial."[37]

Pipes' extensive list warrants citation: "The first civilians to be 'mobilized' were railroad workers. (November 28, 1918). Other categories

---

[31] For an English translation, see Meisel and Kozera, *Materials for the Study of the Soviet System*, p. 27.

[32] Paul Gregory, *The Political Economy of Stalinism: Evidence from the Soviet Secret Archives* (Cambridge: Cambridge University Press, 2004), p. 29.

[33] Ibid., p. 28.

[34] To be sure, the proletariat had privileges when it came to allocations of food that many others did not have and they were constitutionally privileged in comparison with the peasants.

[35] Pipes, *The Russian Revolution*, p. 709.

[36] Meisel and Kozera, *Materials for the Study of the Soviet System*, p. 58.

[37] Pipes, *The Russian Revolution*, p. 706.

followed: . . . medical personnel (December 20, 1918), employees of the river and ocean fleets (March 15, 1919), coal miners (April 7, 1919), postal, telephone, and telegraph employees (May 5, 1919), workers in the fuel industry (June 27, 1919, and November 8, 1919), wool industry workers (August 13, 1920), metalworkers (August 20, 1920), and electricians (October 8, 1920)."[38] Symbolic of the fusion between the military and civilian sectors, Trotsky, who had become commissar for war in March 1918, took on the additional post of president of a Commission on Labor Organization in December 1919. In such a setting, it followed logically that trade unions were not organizations to defend the worker against management's caprices, as they had been under capitalism. Rather, they increasingly became, as they remained throughout the Soviet period, instruments of the state. They were, as Trotsky in his usual indelicate manner put it, "not to struggle for better working conditions—this is the task of the social and political organization as a whole—but to organize the working class for the purpose of production . . . hand in hand with the government in an authoritative manner to bring workers into the framework of a single economic plan."[39]

Thus, it is Trotsky, usually endorsed by Lenin, who created an army that in its attachment to details, to discipline, order, and hierarchy, bore many of the attributes of a conventional early-twentieth-century army. But that army had a quite wide mandate in comparison with other armies even in wartime. This was because the intention was to use it not only to solidify power domestically and to thwart the actions of foreign armies, but because the regime's goals were to control the entire economy and to use the army to support revolution elsewhere. Similarly, it was Lenin and Trotsky, not Stalin, whose idea it was for the civilian sector to emulate the Red Army pattern—complete with bourgeois specialists, absence from work considered as desertion, and the assignment of tasks by Moscow. Chamberlin nicely describes how in early 1920, the communist leaders "were not yet ready to admit that war communism . . . was not capable of bringing the country back to normal productivity of industry and agriculture and to tolerable living conditions." He quotes the Central Committee at the Ninth Party Congress in early 1920 as having endorsed "the mobilization of the industrial proletariat, liability to labor service, militarization of economic life and the use of military units for economic needs."[40] The repressive moves against both urban dwellers and the countryside provoked nontrivial

---

[38] Ibid., p. 706.

[39] Trotsky, *Kak vooruzhalos'* II, pt. 2, p. 78, as cited in Pipes, *The Russian Revolution*, p. 710.

[40] Chamberlin, *The Russian Revolution*, vol. 2, p. 293. His source is Trotsky, "The Economic Upbuilding of the Soviet Republic," pp. 107–14.

uprisings across the country, especially once the danger that the Whites might win had passed. The economy was in ruin. Desertions in the military proliferated. The most well-known peasant rising of several took place in 1920 and continued in 1921. From the Bolsheviks' perspective, the most alarming workers' work actions were the strikes in Petrograd in March 1921, which prompted the sailors on the island of Kronstadt, just off the coast from Petrograd, to rebel in support of the strikers. The rising, which took place during the Tenth Party Congress, ominously called for "Soviets without Communists." It was severely repressed.

But Lenin got the message. The regime was in serious danger. The result was the New Economic Policy, the central points of which for regime-society relations were an end to the confiscation of grain and the introduction of a "proportional tax on agriculture," the stabilization of the currency, and the legalization of private trade.[41] This amounted to an enormous concession to the peasantry and a substantial retreat from the mobilization system that the Bolsheviks aspired to create. Simultaneously, it adumbrated an acceleration in the trend to a more closed political system.

THE NEW ECONOMIC POLICY

NEP is best thought of as a truce with the petit bourgeoisie (read here: the moderately well-to-do peasantry) at home and an analogous truce with the bourgeoisie abroad (the Anglo-Russian trade agreement, the reciprocal recognition of Ataturk's Turkey, and secret military deals with Germany).[42] Domestically, such relations, as will be seen, were much like those characteristic of other non-totalitarian authoritarian regimes. They are then juxtaposed to the effort during the peak Stalinist years to harness the entire society to achieving the regime's combat task[43] of catching up and over passing the industrialized West.

With respect to the bulk of the society—i.e., the peasantry—this entailed "the liquidation of the kulak as a class," as Stalin put it, and massive and rapid collectivization. For the urban worker, it meant first the initial Five-Year Plan and then the Five-Year Plan in four. For those in the arts and sciences, the phrase "Cultural Revolution," while not

[41] See, among many sources, Gregory, *Before Command*, pp. 86ff. and Gregory, *The Political Economy*, pp. 28–29.

[42] On NEP in foreign policy, see the general treatments by Fischer, *The Soviets*; Adam Ulam, *Expansion and Coexistence* (New York: Holt, Rinehart and Winston, 1974). On *British-American Commercial Relations with Soviet Russia 1918–1924*, see Christine White's book by that title (Chapel Hill: University of North Carolina Press, 1992).

[43] Jowitt, "Soviet Neotraditionalism," pp. 275–97.

quite a fit for all areas of scholarship and specialist training, captured a sizeable fraction of the regime's efforts to impose Party dictates across a vast array of areas of thought ranging from literature to ichthyology. The initial years of these efforts were termed the Great Breakthrough (*Velikii Perelom*) and involved, along with repression, nontrivial support by what might be delicately termed policy entrepreneurs. These were people of various sorts who were strong supporters of revolutionizing particular domains of Soviet urban and rural society and who often had specific careerist reasons for rendering such support.

It's an overgeneralization to maintain that those acting in the name of Soviet power alternated between two approaches to regime-society relations: War Communism and NEP. It does, though, bring home a central fact. For the rural citizenry as well as for scientists, skilled managers, and persons in the arts and social studies, under NEP those who were not against the Soviet regime, or more precisely, not categorized as being against the Soviet regime, were treated as though they supported that regime.

The deal the regime offered the peasantry under the rubric of NEP was straightforward and far removed from the political use of terror in the villages with its concomitant campaign vocabulary—struggle, front, battle—of War Communism. The basic ingredient in the deal was what is usually described as a tax in kind. (Initially, it was that, but beginning in 1924 the peasants paid in cash.) A proportional tax on agriculture"[44] replaced the practice of requisitions at gunpoint. The tax burden fell unevenly on peasants with different land holdings. Those with the larger plots—who were also the peasants most likely to produce amounts of grain over and above that necessary to feed themselves and their family—were taxed at a higher rate. In the first years of NEP the tax, however, was not at such an onerous level as to thwart the incentive of the relatively affluent richer and middle peasants (the kulaks and *serednyaks* ["middle"] peasants) to grow and sell grain, which after taxes they could sell on a more or less open market. (Needless to say, once collectivization was launched, criteria specifying who was a kulak were often ambiguous and subject to political manipulation. The result was that defining someone as a kulak often became a weapon targeted against recalcitrant peasants regardless of their land holdings, grain production, or the number of people they employed.) To the extent the peasants were mobilized during NEP, they were mobilized by price incentives and taxation policy, not coerced at gunpoint.

[44] Gregory, *The Political Economy*, p. 28.

The incentive structure for the peasants was such that it made sense to maximize the growth of grain.[45] At least that was so if they had grown the grain necessary for consumption by their family after the government had taken its share and there was something to buy with what they had left over. This the regime did. It not only permitted but encouraged motivated peasants—this applied primarily to the middle and moderately well-to-do peasants—to produce more by rendering it legal to lease land and to hire farm workers. In addition, NEP affected the urban work setting as well, and the peasants' propensity to consume, by denationalizing all but the "commanding heights" of the industrial sector and stabilizing the currency, thus creating the preconditions for money to serve, as it usually does, as a means of exchange and for there to be a market for consumer goods.

NEP worked. By 1926 agriculture had recovered to prewar levels.[46] As Gregory observes, "by all normal indicators, NEP was a resounding success. The economic recovery that began in 1921 was one of history's most rapid."[47] By 1927, however, "*state procurements*, not . . . overall agricultural marketings,"[48] had declined substantially and declined even further in 1928 and 1929. The result was that it became necessary "to import grain for the first time in Russian history."[49] As the accompanying chart from Gregory makes clear (Table 2.1),[50] it is almost certain that the reason state procurements had decreased was because the ratio between state prices and prices on the private market had shifted. Given that shift, the peasants, reasonably enough, sold more grain on the private market and altered somewhat their plantings to generate more profitable crops. He bolsters this intuition by using econometric models to argue that "if the agricultural year 1925–26 is taken to represent 'normal' behavior, the peasant economy reacted to every percentage point reduction in the relative state/private grain price by reducing its marketing to the state by thirteen percentage points. . . . [But] by 1927–28 administrative measures dominate private economic decision making. The econometric model no longer shows 'normal' responses to relative price incentives. By the 1928–29 agricultural year . . . extraordinary measures were required to extract grain from an unwilling peasantry. Command had replaced markets."[51]

[45] Ibid.
[46] Gregory, *The Political Economy*, p. 26.
[47] Ibid., p. 24.
[48] Ibid., p. 33, italics in original.
[49] Ibid., p. 32.
[50] Gregory, *Before Command*, p. 110 and *The Political Economy*, p. 33.
[51] Gregory, *Before Command*, p. 112.

Table 2.1 Output, price of wheat, and state purchases

Purchases	1926–27	1927–28	1928–29
Grain produced (millions of tons)	74.6	72.8	72.5
Grain state collected (millions of tons)	11.6	11.1	9.4
Private market price in kopecks per centner	861	892	1,120
State price in kopecks	648	622	611

Source: Paul Gregory, The Political Economy of Stalinism: Evidence from the Soviet Secret Archives (Cambridge: Cambridge University Press, 2004), p. 33.

It most certainly had. Arguing that the peasantry had conspired to thwart Soviet power, playing on the fear of war, and asserting that rapid industrialization was imperative and impossible unless collectivization occurred, Stalin demanded the liquidation of the kulaks as a class and massive and rapid collectivization of agriculture. The literature divides on the extent to which the events in the countryside that followed were harnessed by Moscow and the extent to which the mobilization that occurred initially was prompted by local Party officials or motivated by patriotic and careerist considerations of urban dwellers mobilized to carry out Party dictates in the countryside. Among the latter, particular mention should be made of, to use the title of a major book by Lynne Viola, The Best Sons of the Fatherland[52]—the so-called 25,000ers. These "best sons" were a motley group: "skilled or highly skilled cadre workers, civil war veterans, shock workers, factory activists, Communist party members"[53] who were sent to the villages across the Soviet Union to accelerate the pace of collectivization and often stayed to serve as the first chairman at various kolkhozes.

Such instructions as there were from the center were vague and varied across time. (The Politburo approved model kolkhoz guidelines on March 1, 1930, the same day that Stalin gave his famous "dizziness with success" speech that signaled a temporary halt to collectivization.[54]) The availability, first in Russian and more recently in English, of important documents taken from Soviet archives,[55] reinforces the arguments key

[52] Lynne Viola, The Best Sons of the Fatherland: Workers in the Vanguard of Soviet Collectivization (New York: Oxford University Press, 1987).

[53] Ibid., p. 3.

[54] Sheila Fitzpatrick, Stalin's Peasants: Resistance & Survival in the Russian Village after Collectivization (New York: Oxford University Press, 1994), p. 49.

[55] See, for English translations, the exchange of documents and letters in Lynne Viola et al., The War Against the Peasantry, 1927–1930: The Tragedy of the Soviet Countryside (New Haven, CT: Yale University Press, 2005), especially pp. 199–201. For more on Syrtsov, see below, pp. 89–93.

specialists of the period such as Viola and especially Fitzpatrick that the vagueness was intentional and strategic. Thus, Stalin intervened in S. I. Syrtsov's speech at the November 1929 Central Committee plenum to scoff at the idea that "everything can be 'organized in advance.'"[56] Both he and Molotov pressed hard to make the document a Politburo commission was preparing in December 1929/January 1930 on collectivization far shorter and less specific in order, in Stalin's words, to provide "maximum support for the growing collective-farm movement."[57] As Fitzpatrick remarks, "The regime's failure to give adequate instructions on collectivization and dekulakization was not simply an oversight. Rather, it appears to have been a strategy . . . to get local cadres pushing for the absolute maximum. . . . The cadres going out to collectivize . . . knew very well that it was better (for their own careers, as well as for the cause) to go too far in collectivizing than not to go far enough. . . . They knew, too, that observing the letter of the law was not the way to achieve revolutionary social transformations."[58] Fitzpatrick's jaundiced view of the motivations of those such as the 25,000ers who went to the countryside in 1930 is entirely appropriate. It is, though, worth keeping in mind the atmosphere of the times symbolized by the terms "Cultural Revolution" and "Great Breakthrough." In the late 1920s and the early 1930s, as we will see below, the regime, and Stalin in particular, fostered the sense of a new revolutionary period in which traditional approaches were challenged and a strong sense obtained of the desirability of introducing truly socialist practices and thought across a range of spheres of life. Many, especially among urban dwellers, were mobilized by the sense of participating in a Great Breakthrough. The vast mobilization of the citizenry was not achieved merely by repression but by a mix of repression and the successful mobilization of (largely urban) believers and entrepreneurs. That said, repression was the core to the radical transformation of the countryside.

The result was civil war with some active peasant resistance and enormous human suffering, along with widespread passive resistance on the part of the peasantry. (While the estimates diverge somewhat, economists have concluded that what did not happen was that collectivization increased the net saving to industry[59]—the usual rationale for Stalin's decisions in this regard.) We now have plausible reports that

[56] Viola et al., *The War Against the Peasantry*, p. 167.
[57] Ibid., p. 201.
[58] Fitzpatrick, *Stalin's Peasants*, p. 49.
[59] Holland Hunter and Janusz Szyrmer, *Faulty Foundations: Soviet Economic Policies, 1928–1940* (Princeton, NJ: Princeton University Press, 1992); Gregory, *Before Command*, pp. 117–18. Gregory, *The Political Economy*, p. 47, cites James Millar, Michael Ellman, and A. A. Barsov, who argue "there was virtually no surplus."

were produced by the secret police (at this juncture termed OGPU) that convey some sense of the resistance by the peasantry and the human costs that collectivization entailed. The magnitude of the resistance is illustrated by a top-secret OGPU report prepared in 1931. According to it,[60] there were 13,754 mass disturbances in 1930 (ten times as many as in the previous year) involving "more than 2,468,000 people" or an average of roughly 170 people per "disturbance." The secret police categorized 176 such incidents as being "of an insurrectionary nature." The report indicates that in 1930 alone almost 1200 officials and other collectivization supporters had been murdered and that murder attempts had been targeted at half again as many other collectivization supporters.

In some ways even more telling of the intensity of the resistance is the report's depiction of how shaky Soviet power had become in some areas. In March/April 1930, OGPU observed,

> A shift by the kulaks and counterrevolutionaries . . . to an open armed struggle against the soviets [took place]. In the Central Black Earth Oblast, in Ukraine, in the Northern Caucasus Krai, in Transcaucasia, in the Lower Volga Krai, in the Belorussian SSR, in Moscow Oblast, in Siberia, the Far Eastern Krai, Buriato-Mongolia, and Kazakhstan, kulaks and antisoviet elements in a number of instances made attempts, not without success, to coordinate individual local disturbances with the insurrectionary movement of entire raions . . . and to make them counterrevolutionary in nature. . . . Soviet power, in effect, did not exist for several days. . . . In Mozyr Okrug, Belorussian SSR, participants in disturbances put up tenacious resistance even to OGPU operational detachments.[61]

The human consequences were ghastly. Millions, some under duress, others in response to the first Five-Year Plan, moved to the cities.[62] The January 30, 1930, Politburo decree categorized kulaks into three categories: Category 1 kulaks were to be "immediately" liquidated "by incarcerating them in concentration camps, not stopping at the death penalty for organizers of terrorist acts, counterrevolutionary disturbances, and insurrectionist organizations." Category 2 consisted of the remaining "richest kulaks and quasi-landowners . . . to be exiled to remote

---

[60] Viola et al., *The War Against the Peasantry*, pp. 340–69. The figure for the number of disturbances is on p. 341, the total involved at p. 343, and the number of murders and attempted murders, p. 368. See also Viola, "The Other Archipelago: Kulak Deportations to the North in 1930 (Dekulakized Peasant Families in the Soviet Union)," *Slavic Review*, Vol. 60, No. 4 (Winter 2001), pp. 730–55.

[61] Viola et al., *The War Against the Peasantry*, pp. 357–58.

[62] Sheila Fitzpatrick concludes that about 12 million moved from villages to urban areas in the period 1928–32 (*Stalin's Peasants*, p. 80).

localities of the USSR and within the borders of a given region, to remote areas of the region." Category 3 deportees, the residual category,
were to be left in the raion where they lived but "outside collective
farms."[63] Sixty thousand first category kulaks were scheduled to be arrested initially. But in fact by mid-April 1930 the number arrested way
exceeded the original number called for. One OGPU document puts the
number at about 140,000, an overfulfilling of the plan that Viola says
may have been the result of "Bolshevik tempos, social purging, and a
police head more concerned with cases than kulaks."[64] The head of the
secret police, Genrikh Yagoda, informed Stalin that 1.4 million persons
had been deported as of January 1932.[65] Thousands died while in route.
Thousands more died in their first winter in Siberia or Kazakhstan.

Directly related to the struggle between the regime and the peasantry was the famine of 1932–33. Fitzpatrick notes that "some degree
of government responsibility—and popular perception of government
responsibility—are more the norm than the exception" in famines and
that "the 1932–33 famine was an egregious case." It matters not a wit
to the thousands who died, but scholars debate whether it should be
coded as manslaughter or murder. It does matter for our story that the
regime explicitly forbade mention of the famine in the press—the code
term was the "well-known events," that foreign journalists were not allowed to visit areas experiencing the famine, that publicly and privately
Soviet commentators asserted that the peasants "were trying to *stage a
famine*," "*passing themselves off* as ruined kolkhozniks," and even that
"one delinquent peasant 'starved his family and *made propaganda* out of
it.'"[66] Stalin and his supporters were at war with the village. Perhaps the
most explicit recognition of this reality was expressed by M. M. Khatae-
vich, a high Ukrainian Party official, who told Viktor Kravchenko, "A
ruthless struggle is going on between the peasantry and our regime. . . .
This year was test of our strength and their endurance. It took a famine
to show them who is master here. It has cost millions of lives, but the
collective farm system is here to stay. We've won the war."[67]

A majority of the peasants who had not died during the years 1929
to 1933 had been harnessed to the regime's goals. Large numbers were

---

[63] Viola et al., *The War Against the Peasantry*, pp. 228–29.

[64] Lynne Viola, *The Role of the OGPU in Dekulakization, Mass Deportations, and Special
Resettlement in 1930*, The Carl Beck Papers in Russian & East European Studies (Pittsburgh:
Center for Russian & East European Studies, University of Pittsburgh, 2000)., p. 21.

[65] Fitzpatrick, *Stalin's Peasants*, p. 83.

[66] Ibid., p. 75. (Italics in original.)

[67] Viktor Kravchenko, *I Chose Freedom* (New York: Scribner, 1946), p. 130, as cited in
Tucker, *Stalin in Power: The Revolution from Above, 1928–1941* (New York: Norton, 1990),
p. 195.

incarcerated in the camps, enslaved in the construction of such projects as the White Sea Canal or exiled to the far reaches of the Soviet Union where they often perished. Those who became kolkhozniks found that they were in effect almost as constrained in their movements as those in the camps or exile once the implications of the law on internal passports adopted in December 1932 began to take effect. Put bluntly, this, in combination with the system of obligatory work days for the collective,[68] amounted to the restoration of serfdom. Urban dwellers could move from job to job. Although in practice the kolkhozniks were more able to secure permission to leave than the rules implied, still what had begun initially as a war on the kulak had resulted in the virtual captivity of the entire peasantry, whether in a kolkhoz that encompassed the peasant's village, in the camps, or in exile in northern Siberia, the Urals, or Kazakhstan. The peasantry had resisted, a resistance that led to Stalin's "Dizziness with Success" speech and the brief collapse of the collectivization impetus in 1930. Lynne Viola rightly maintains that the collectivization was both a top-down and a bottom-up phenomenon.[69]

What is missing in that formulation is a sense of the asymmetric interdependence of the top-down and bottom-up factors. "Dizziness with Success" was in part Stalin's response to the vigorous peasant opposition to collectivization. But the bottom-up behavior was engendered, in a fashion well captured by Fitzpatrick, by the political environment created by Stalin, an environment in which overachieving and zealousness usually was a path to success. To use a bridge analogy, it is often good practice to concede a trick in order to make the small slam bid. The energetic reaction in late 1929 and much of 1930 produced a trick for the defense. But only one trick. The peasantry had little else with which to defend themselves and their property. Active resistance had some measure of success, as opposed to the usual passive peasant behavior such as the hiding of grain, but was much reduced when the pressure to proceed with collectivization was resumed in the fall 1930.

THE GREAT BREAKTHROUGH IN THE CITIES

The Shakhty trial in May and June 1928 and its successor, the Industrial Party trial, adumbrated the Cultural Revolution of the late 1920s and early 1930s and the purges and show trials of the mid- and late

---

[68] The analogy to the French prerevolutionary *corvée* and the Russian prerevolutionary *barshchina* is convincingly drawn by Tucker, *Stalin in Power*, pp. 195–99. See also Fitzpatrick, *Stalin's Peasants*, pp. 128–42, and Robert V. Daniels, *The Rise and Fall of Communism in Russia* (New Haven, CT: Yale University Press, 2007), especially p. 202.

[69] Lynne Viola, ed. *Contending with Stalinism: Soviet Power and Popular Resistance in the 1930s* (Ithaca, NY: Cornell University Press, 2002); Viola, *The Best Sons*.

1930s. The Shakhty trial in May and June 1928 targeted "bourgeois specialists" who, it was alleged, had been wreckers, working for foreign governments and "international capital." (Given the inexperience of management and workers alike, it was small wonder that the products produced were shoddily built and that there were major industrial accidents. No evidence exists that substantiates the idea of a foreign-funded conspiracy to thwart Soviet industrialization.[70])

The connection between the Shakhty trial and the Cultural Revolution was that the political message of the Shakhty trial was the need for truly Soviet engineers and scientists who had no links with the past or with foreign powers. Likewise, an overarching theme of the Cultural Revolution (launched in 1928) was the appropriateness of a new, truly revolutionary, and truly socialist science, public institutions, and literature. This provided a milieu in which it was open season on leading non-Bolsheviks or non-Stalinist communists in institutes of the Academy of Sciences and universities. It also contributed to suspicion of a wide range of things non-Soviet, a suspicion that persisted throughout the 1930s notwithstanding the brevity of the period (not much more than the duration of the first Five-Year Plan) during which radical thinking in many areas seemed paramount. Soviet scholarship either was or should become radically different from bourgeois scholarship. There developed a pervasive strand of xenophobic thinking that carried forward throughout the 1930s and resulted in thoroughgoing repression among various elites but also the targeting for repression of nationalities with cross-border populations. The Shakhty and the Industrial Party trials are also appropriately viewed as dress rehearsals for the political trials of 1937. But they were notably sloppier than the subsequent show trials: "only ten of the fifty-three defendants made full confessions and implicated the others; another half-dozen made partial confessions; the rest maintained their innocence and fought the charges."[71] It was also more transparently obvious that they were show trials. This is illustrated by Tucker, who in *Stalin in Power* reproduces an English-language translation of the indictment that is indistinguishable from a playbill and is actually labeled "The Plot."[72]

[70] John Scott, *Behind the Urals: An American Worker in Russia's City of Steel* (Boston: Houghton Mifflin, 1942); also Loren Graham, *The Ghost of the Executed Engineer: Technology and the Fall of the Soviet Union* (Cambridge, MA: Harvard University Press, 1993). A plausible account of Politburo debates over the Shakhty trial is contained in Michael Reiman, *The Birth of Stalinism: The USSR on the Eve of the "Second Revolution"* (Bloomington: Indiana University Press, 1987), pp. 57–66.

[71] Tucker, *Stalin in Power*, pp. 77–78.

[72] Ibid., p. 99. The key villain, P. A. Palchinsky, the "playbill" announced, had already been executed prior to the trial. See also Graham, *The Ghost*, especially p. 46, where he reports that a central charge against Palchinsky was that he had published "'detailed

The trials provided a backdrop to the Cultural Revolution by conveying the sense of capitalist encirclement and its dangerous domestic manifestations, most notably wrecking. It fostered the demands for homegrown engineers and scientists to carry out the industrialization plans epitomized by the extraordinary conceit of the Five-Year Plans. In a brilliant essay, Richard Lowenthal[73] argued that the utopian dreams of the revolution ultimately gave way to the more quotidian tasks of development.

But the story in the Soviet Union is more complicated. There is a kind of dialectical process in play. In the years of the Great Breakthrough we witness quite radical approaches across the board which then, as the 1930s progress, often become replaced by very traditional, indeed often Victorian-like, or nationalist, symbols, strategies, and norms. The Great Breakthrough provided the backdrop and much of the rationale for a radical and truly socialist science. This resulted in assertions that in various fields bourgeois science needed to be replaced by socialist, proletarian science. Such charges were made virtually, but not completely, across the board. Tucker has a list that makes the point nicely: "In economics there were the wrecker theories of planners like B. Bazarov and N. Kondratiev (whose views did not envisage anything like the heroic Stalinist tempos of industrialization as feasible). Wrecking was rife in forestry science, melioration theory, mining science, high tension technology, microbiology, and even in ichthyology."[74]

Ichthyology illustrates a core premise in all of this. Normal science (the term is Thomas Kuhn's) implied that the Five-Year Plan was inappropriate for fish whose behavior were not governed by such matters. People who thought that way made the fundamental error of thinking there were no differences between a capitalist country and the Soviet Union.[75] In some areas, the idea of socialist distinctiveness persisted well into the post-Stalin period. It was not, for instance, until after the 1962 Cuban Missile Crisis that the Soviet leadership pointed out to the Chinese that the "atomic bomb does not observe the class principle."[76]

---

statistics' on the mining and petroleum industries." Before the revolution, Palchinsky published data on labor issues in the Don Basin. The *tsarist* government exiled him for that (ibid.).

[73]See Lowenthal's chapter, "Development vs. Utopia in Communist Policy," in Chalmers Johnson, ed., *Change in Communist Systems* (Stanford, CA: Stanford University Press, 1970), pp. 33–116.

[74]Tucker, *Stalin in Power*, pp. 100–101.

[75]Ibid., p. 101.

[76]*Pravda*, July 14, 1963, and cited in William Zimmerman, *Soviet Perspectives on International Relations* (Princeton, NJ: Princeton University Press, 1969), p. 5.

But there is a developmental counterpoint that it also evident from the beginning of the Great Breakthrough. As cultural historians are prone to observe, this was a period of enormous mobility both horizontally and vertically.[77] And along with that developmental reality, Stalin early on began to signal the dangers of taking radical innovations too seriously. The Cultural Revolution was a time when scholars and policy advocates pushed hard on the theme of the withering away of various key "bourgeois" institutions and when egalitarianism was in good odor. Not just the state but also related institutions such as the law and the school were ostensibly to wither away. But Stalin's perspective was consistently on development, the power of the state, and the rationale for state power, capitalist encirclement. (The latter pointed directly to the next large social aggregates to be targeted after the war on the peasants, namely nationalities with cross-border ties.)

As early as 1931, at a congress of industrialists, he attacked "leftist egalitarianism (*uravnilovka*) in the sphere of pay." Even earlier, while the Cultural Revolution was at its peak, he declared that "the Marxian formula" entailed "the highest development of governmental power for the purpose of preparing the conditions for the withering away of governmental power." Of course, he recognized, it "is 'contradictory.' . . . But this contradiction is life, and it reflects completely the Marxian dialectic."[78]

Overall, the theme of the period of the Five-Year Plans is the withering away of withering away. By the end of the 1930s it was no longer the case that the state was being strengthened in order to pave the way for its withering away. Instead, by 1939 Stalin had fully dismissed the idea of the withering away of the state as long as capitalist encirclement persisted. "It is sometimes asked: 'We have abolished the exploiting classes; there are no longer any hostile classes in the country; there is nobody to suppress; hence there is no more need for the state; it must wither [Fainsod: die away] away. . . . Is it not time we relegated the state to the museum of antiquities?" Such questions, Stalin made clear, "not only betray an underestimation of the capitalist encirclement, but also an underestimation of the role and significances of the bourgeois states and their organs, which send spies, assassins and wreckers into our country and are waiting for a favorable time to attack it by armed force. They likewise betray an underestimation of the role and significance

---

[77] Sheila Fitzpatrick in Fitzpatrick, ed., *Cultural Revolution in Russia, 1928–1931* (Bloomington: Indiana University Press, 1984), p. 3.

[78] I have cited Fainsod, *How Russia*, p. 111, who in turn quotes Stalin's Political Report of the Central Committee to the Sixteenth Congress of the All-Union CP [b] from the latter's *Sochineniya*, Vol. 12, pp. 369–70.

of our socialist state and its . . . organs ["organs" here means the secret police and other wielders of the instruments of violence]."[79]

Nor did Stalin believe that capitalist encirclement was a geographical concept. The formation of the Soviet Bloc after World War II did not eliminate capitalist encirclement in Stalin's view. Writing in 1950, after communist takeovers in Eastern Europe and in the Far East, he still declared that "in the face of capitalist encirclement, when the victory of the socialist revolution has taken place in one country alone while capitalism continues to dominate in all other countries, the country where the revolution has triumphed must not weaken but must strengthen in every way its state, state organs, intelligence agencies, and army if it does not want to be destroyed by capitalist encirclement."[80] Not until the late 1950s, when Khrushchev noted that it was "no longer certain who encircles whom,"[81] was the underlying rationalization for the persistence of terror—the existence of capitalist encirclement—authoritatively dismissed. (It is, though, important to recognize that Stalin's heir apparent, Georgy Malenkov, had in effect challenged the capitalist encirclement doctrine in 1949 by observing that "[n]ever before in all its history has our country been surrounded by neighboring countries so friendly to our state."[82])

But this came long after the Cultural Revolution had itself withered away by the mid-1930s. Readers will want to explore other areas of scholarship[83] to obtain a full picture of what transpired. But examples from professional areas—law and education—where withering away was seriously proposed; from literature and history, where radical Marxist scholars seemed to prevail during the Cultural Revolution, only to have their efforts thwarted by the Party's intensified mobilizational intrusion in their realms of inquiry; and a passing reference to physics and biology, where the immediate damage from the Cultural Revolution was modest, but evolved into a catastrophe for biology and biologists, will suffice. These examples provide a sense of the transformative nature of the times and the extent of the mobilizational efforts of the regime that attended the Cultural Revolution. They also enable a deeper understanding of how it came to pass that the Cultural Revolution segued into regime-society relations that combined nearly unique

[79] Fainsod, *How Russia*, p. 357.

[80] Ibid.

[81] Nikita S. Khrushchev, *K pobede v mirnom sorevnovanii s kapitalizmom* (Moscow: Gospolitizdat, 1959), p. 154.

[82] Malenkov, November 6, 1949, as cited in Robert C. Tucker, *The Soviet Political Mind: Stalinism and Post-Stalin Change*, rev. ed. (New York: Norton, 1971), pp. 94–95.

[83] A good place to begin is Fitzpatrick, *Cultural Revolution*.

levels of terror and the greatly intensified use of traditionalist symbols and incentives.

The transformative quality of the Cultural Revolution may be thought of in three different ways. One pertained to arguments that the approaching achievement of socialism implied entirely novel sciences—*Soviet* sciences or arts that were separate from and better than scholarship in the West or that prior to the triumph of Soviet power in Russia. The second was the view that, in light of the gains in the direction of achieving socialism, fundamental institutions of "bourgeois" societies—the state, the legal system, and the school—were far less required and as a result might begin to wither away. The third transformative element amounted to claims that the nature of man was in the process of being transformed, that a New Soviet Man was being created. (A generation later Aleksandr Solzhenitsyn published "Matryona's House,"[84] a wonderful short story, the heroine of which, intentionally, was an old Russian woman.)

Developments in physics and biology provide alternative examples of how the impetus to differentiate Soviet and bourgeois science played out in the natural sciences during the Cultural Revolution. In the case of physics, as Loren Graham has shown, a "possibility arose that an alliance of Marxist ideologues and Stalinist bureaucrats would result in restrictions on physics itself, perhaps even to the proscription of relativity physics and quantum mechanics."[85] Unlike other areas of inquiry (discussed in succeeding pages), the turmoil that occurred largely involved attacks (less by physicists and more by philosophers) on the underlying philosophical assumptions of modern physics rather than on physics itself. Indeed, Graham shows that the late 1920s and early 1930s were a period of great intellectual achievements in Soviet physics. Moreover, in the early 1930s Soviet physicists largely took the position that the analytical power of relativity and quantum mechanics could be decoupled from Western physicists' philosophical predilections. (One particularly well-known articulation of this belief was a famous paper by the physicist Boris Hessen that he presented at a conference in Great Britain in 1931. In it, he made that point concerning Newton's work, but which he meant to apply to contemporary Western physics as well. Unfortunately, he made the mistake of going to the conference as a member of a Soviet party of eight including Bukharin. He died in the purges.[86])

---

[84] In Aleksandr Solzhenitsyn, *Stories and Prose Poems* (London: Bodley Head, 1971).

[85] Loren R. Graham, *Science in Russia and the Soviet Union: A Short History* (Cambridge: Cambridge University Press, 1993), p. 113.

[86] Ibid., pp. 149–51.

The real challenge to physicists came later in the 1930s and after World War II. It was not until 1936 that a serious challenge to quantum mechanics appeared in a physics journal.[87] Physicists were hard hit during the 1937–38 purges and subject to pressure during the post–World War II Zhdanovshchina, but no approaches or areas of inquiry were ever completely prohibited.

The same was not the case concerning genetics. The Soviet Union missed out on a number of the great revolutions of the twentieth century; one of these was the genetic revolution. This occurred as a direct outgrowth initially of the Cultural Revolution and the collectivization of agriculture, and the rise to dominance in biology of Trofim Lysenko. Lysenko gained visibility during the Cultural Revolution because in 1931 the Ministry of Agriculture decided to try out his approach to plant physiology. Just as in the case of physics, however, the really destructive events occur in the mid-1930s and then in 1948 when genetics was explicitly banned after a speech by Lysenko that, we now know, was edited by Stalin who emphasized the "'reactionary character' of 'foreign science.'"[88] Lysenko was a charlatan and a huckster who offered bogus products and ultimately an entire bogus theory of how, by disregarding (Western) science, agriculture could be miraculously transformed in the Soviet Union, which appealed to Stalin and subsequently Khrushchev.

By contrast, far more serious Soviet scholars took the position that the approaching achievement of socialism implied that Soviet power would be truly distinctive from normal bourgeois states inasmuch as it implied the absence of what Marxists had defined as the essential core of the state,[89] namely the instruments of coercion.[90] In several publications,[91] Robert Sharlet has depicted Ye. V. Pashukanis's role during the Cultural Revolution in attempting to further the withering away

---

[87] Graham, "Quantum Mechanics and Dialectical Materialism," *Slavic Review*, Vol. 25, No. 3 (September 1966), p. 383.

[88] As reported by Graham, *Science in Russia*, p. 133. See also Ethan Pollock, *Stalin and the Soviet Science Wars* (Princeton, NJ: Princeton University Press, 2006), pp. 41–71.

[89] Alfred G. Meyer, *Marxism: The Unity of Theory and Practice; a Critical Essay* (Cambridge, MA: Harvard University Press, 1970).

[90] The call for the withering away of the law that achieved high prominence during the Cultural Revolution and the first five-year plan was actually the second instance Russian legal specialists had pressed hard for the withering away of law, the first in the months immediately after the Bolshevik seizure of power in 1917. Quickly, however, a legal system developed that looked much like what someone like John Hazard could code as a European civil law system. Hazard, *Settling Disputes in Soviet Society: The Formative Years of Legal Institutions* (New York: Columbia University Press, 1960).

[91] See especially Sharlet's chapter in Fitzpatrick, *Cultural Revolution*, pp. 169–88, on which this section largely depends. See too his "Stalinism and Soviet Legal Culture," in

of law, an effort that began toward the end of NEP and continued into the Cultural Revolution, terminating when he became one of the thousands executed in 1937. For Pashukanis, law resulted directly from the institution of private property and commodity exchange. For him, the state as an institution of class rule—"the political state"—was, in Scarlet's words, a "meta-juridical phenomenon beyond the scope of legal theory."[92] As socialism and the plan replaced the market and law, "the legal state" would wither away. These views were enormously influential at the end of the 1920s and the beginning of the 1930s, "especially in criminal and civil law and procedure and the administration of criminal justice."[93] As part of the more general trend to remove "bourgeois" specialists, Pashukanis and his supporters were effective in removing senior professors from law schools and from the state apparatus.

The problem Pashukanis and his confreres faced was that as early as mid-1930 Stalin had explicitly ruled out the possibility that the state would wither away in anything like the near future. As was the case in many other domains of scholarship as the Cultural Revolution was brought to an end, Pashukanis was forced to engage in self-criticism and to modify his views, though he continued to play a major institutional role until the mid-1930s. By then, it was manifestly clear that "Stalin needed law both to stabilize his 'revolution from above' and as an instrument for future social engineering."[94] Ironically, Sharlet concludes, Pashukanis's final undoing was the adoption in late 1936 of the new Soviet (Stalin) Constitution, which, inter alia, guaranteed the right of "'personal property' . . . [and] a stable legal system."[95] His arrest and disappearance (presumably to the camps) in early 1937 followed quickly thereafter. From that time forward, Stalin's famous remark that "stability of the laws is necessary now more than ever" served to define the tasks of Soviet lawyers, judges, and law schools. "Essentially, Pashukanis' successors revived the NEP legal culture along with its Stalinist additions,"[96] a legal system that, despite such monstrous abnormalities as Article 58 of the RSFSR code (a deliberately vague article that sanctioned "terrorism, counterrevolutionary agitation and wrecking"[97]), was recognizably Continental.

Robert Tucker, ed., *Stalinism: Essays in Historical Interpretation* (New York: Norton, 1977), pp. 155–79.

[92] Sharlet in Fitzpatrick, *Cultural Revolution*, p. 172.

[93] Ibid., p. 180.

[94] Sharlet in Tucker, *Stalinism*, p. 163.

[95] Sharlet in Fitzpatrick, *Cultural Revolution*, p. 187.

[96] Sharlet in Tucker, *Stalinism*, p. 178.

[97] Peter H. Solomon, *Soviet Criminal Justice under Stalin* (Cambridge: Cambridge University Press, 1996), p. 92.

Education was another professional area[98] where the Cultural Revolution had profound effects, ones that directly connected to the Shakty trials. Cultural Revolution defined as class war intensified demands that student bodies be "proletarianized" and that members of the older intelligentsia be removed from the faculty. The social composition of the universities shifted dramatically in favor of workers and the curriculum emphasis shifted toward training with immediate applications in the factory. It was in this milieu that V. N. Shulgin had a brief moment of fame. To him, the school was to play an ever-decreasing role in the training of students: "the soviets, the Party, professional associations, mass organizations, these were for Shulgin the real 'school of the masses.'"[99] This played well in the years 1928 to 1930 when Bukharin and his allies on the right were the main political targets. Shulgin's transformationist instincts initially resonated well. Stalin, with his eye on economic development, was not likely to view the withering away of the school any more favorably than the withering away of the state. As Lapidus observes pointedly, "By 1931, left deviation was already being singled out as the main danger."[100]

The radical moment in education served a purpose by undermining the position of prerevolutionary specialists whether as teachers or researchers and by politicizing the school environment. But that quickly gave way to the view that the core tasks of education were the preparation of workers to engage in ordinary jobs and, on another track, the training of those who would carry on their academic training beyond the junior secondary level. Uniform practices nationwide became the norm. The curriculum and the school system more generally rapidly took on attributes that were directly evocative of the school system under the tsars cum the far greater role for Party indoctrination than during either NEP or the Cultural Revolution. Lapidus cautions her readers not to view these developments as "a response to the universal functional requisites of modernization."[101] Stalin's revenge of the superstructure (an obvious coinage, I think initially by Richard Lowenthal) on the base of Soviet society coupled with the rigidly hierarchical nature, after the Cultural Revolution, of the regime's relationship to all aspects of society including the schools, Lapidus observes, "gave a very special character to Soviet patterns of modernization."[102] True enough, but the restoration of grades and examinations, the shift away from

[98] Gail Lapidus, "Educational Strategies and Cultural Revolution," in Fitzpatrick, *Cultural Revolution*, pp. 78–104.

[99] Ibid., p. 96.

[100] Ibid., p. 99.

[101] Ibid., p. 103.

[102] Fitzpatrick, *Cultural Revolution*, p. 103.

affirmative action for children of workers, and the restoration of uniforms, coupled with the tracking of students, rendered Soviet schools readily recognizable to persons who were familiar with stereotypically traditionalist Western European or American schools or nineteenth-century tsarist schools.[103]

Education and the law were only two of the many domains hit hard by the Cultural Revolution. During the years 1928 to 1931 efforts to create radically different and truly Soviet cultural and/or scientific areas proliferated. One such area, much covered by Western and Russian scholarship,[104] where efforts were made to create something truly distinctive was that of literature and art. Basically what occurred was a demand by cultural figures, who were not themselves of lower social class origins, that literature and art be "proletarianized" and that they, as spokesmen for the proletariat, be entitled to call the shots.

With respect to literature, this largely meant achieving a hegemonic position in the cultural community for a body they had hitherto dominated, namely, the Russian Association of Proletarian Writers (RAPP). For most areas of culture, including literature, it also entailed the ouster from positions of prominence somewhat older, often noncommunist, fellow travelers and the succession to these positions of radical elements. Those behind RAPP had some redeeming virtues. Western literary scholars praise their commitment to an unvarnished realism and the author's right to assess his or her own work—with the caveat that these attributes be within a class-based framework.[105] Once again, though, as in the case of education and the law, the radical Marxism for which they spoke ran afoul of Stalin's preoccupation with providing an environment in which the dominant mobilizational themes would be state building, industrialization, and the Soviet people's ability to achieve superhuman tasks.

This called for a different organizational structure and an entirely different kind of realism. The result in literature institutionally was the demise of the radical but not all-encompassing RAPP and the establishment in April 1932 of a Union of Writers[106] composed of all writers, communist and noncommunist alike, but in which a communist faction

---

[103] On this, see Nicholas S. Timasheff, *The Great Retreat: The Growth and Decline of Communism in Russia* (New York: E.P. Dutton, 1946), pp. 215–25.

[104] English-language versions of relevant Russian documents may be found in Katerina Clark et al., *Soviet Culture and Power: A History in Documents, 1917–1953* (New Haven, CT: Yale University Press, 2007).

[105] Rufus Mathewson, *The Positive Hero in Russian Literature* (New York: Columbia University Press, 1958), p. 213.

[106] For an English-language text of the Politburo decision, see Clark et al., *Soviet Culture and Power*, pp. 151–53.

played the preeminent role. (It should be stressed that the Central Committee resolution establishing the Union of Writers stipulated that it would implement "analogous *change along this line in the other types of art*" as well.[107]) Socialist realism and the realism of the radical Marxists differed enormously. For the latter, it involved "tearing off the masks" and showing communist heroes in all their complexity. Socialist realism, by contrast, assumed that the "revelation of human complexity [was] politically harmful" and that instead the author's obligation was to depict positive heroes. (Hence the title of Mathewson's book.) He or she, moreover, was obliged to observe the norms of *partiinost'* (awkward in English as "party-ness") in practice, following the Party line, whatever it happened at the moment to be). Realism signified not actual but becoming; the ideal was the real. In this perspective, realism became the depiction of the mythic New Soviet Man, as exemplified by the Stakhanovites, with whose help a new socialist order would be created. (Stakhanovites were, of course, Paul Bunyan–like workers who were alleged to have dramatically overfulfilled plan norms.) As Andrei Zhdanov, Party secretary with responsibility for cultural affairs, made clear, in harnessing society to the regime's purposes, literature, and culture more broadly, like almost everything else, would do its part. The purpose of literature in the Soviet scheme of things was to contribute to the mobilization and transformation of the Soviet citizenry by depicting a new conception of the desirable to which the citizenry would be led. In Zhdanov's words, *"Soviet literature must be able to show our heroes, be able to look into the future. It will not be a Utopia, for our tomorrow is being prepared by planned conscious work today."*[108]

The aspiration to create a New Soviet Man logically extended to psychology. In the 1920s "environmental determinism" represented the prevailing mode in Soviet thinking about human psychology.[109] How much people could change was a matter for discussion, but the trend during the Cultural Revolution was to accept a Marxist perspective on people's behavior. In a repeat of patterns found elsewhere, psychologists in quick order were faulted first for right opportunism, for accepting, it was alleged, the reactionary doctrine that views "the working class as robots."[110] They, especially those working in applied areas such as the factory and the school, were then hammered for leftist tendencies. As Bauer notes, "[M]an [acquired] consciousness and purpose."[111]

---

[107] Ibid., p. 152. (Italics in original.)

[108] As cited in Mathewson, *The Positive Hero*, p. 290, italics in original.

[109] Raymond Bauer, *The New Man in Soviet Psychology* (Cambridge, MA: Harvard University Press, 1952), p. 88.

[110] Ibid., p. 98.

[111] Ibid., p. 94.

Likewise, by 1931 the greatly intensified emphasis on *partiinost'* had the consequence that research that generated the wrong facts—those that challenged existing Party dogmas—were politically harmful and should be repressed. As in other domains of Soviet scholarship, practice, broadly construed, was crucial and thus took precedence over mere scholarly research, something the leftist enthusiasts among psychologists had failed to understand. And so, from 1932 on such basic elements in a psychologist's portfolio as research on attitudes were considered suspect. Open-ended questions might call forth responses that suggested the existence of more than one acceptable answer. By 1936, it was being stated that "'[s]uch questionnaires as concern the subject's political views or probe into the deep and intimate side of life . . . must be *categorically banned* from use.'"[112]

In some ways, the most interesting and instructive example pertains to history. There, Marxists, operating on the assumption that their views were congruent with those of the center, attempted to secure a dominant position in a field members of which had diverse views and diverse institutional loyalties. In this instance, there was not just one but at least two major protagonists in the story, M. N. Pokrovsky and Yemelyan Yaroslavsky, both of whom straddled the academic and Party worlds. In 1930 Pokrovsky was a member of the Presidium of the Party Central Control Commission (CCC) while Yaroslavsky was a secretary to the CCC and a member of the editorial boards of leading Party and state newspapers.

As we have seen in discussing other disciplines, the late twenties were a time when younger generations found it was appropriate to attack non-Party scholars. Such was the case in history. It was an attack that Pokrovsky evidently did not initiate but which he joined in the climate of the aftermath to the Shakhty trial and which he used to foster a Communist Academy, the membership composition of which was as its name implied. He also found himself involved in a serious dispute with an Old Bolshevik historian, I. A. Teodorovich, who had ties with Yaroslavsky.

These disputes were not the genteel academic food fights ubiquitous in the West. Substantive commentary was part of the language of the debates, but so were (literally) dangerous charges of "Trotskyism" and "bourgeois liberalism." The disputes among the historians elevated to the level of the Central Committee and resulted in a Central Committee resolution in March 1931. In October 1931 Stalin wrote his famous letter

---

[112] V. N. Kolbanovsky, a prominent Soviet psychologist, as cited by Bauer, *The New Man*, p. 111, italics in original. On the strictures against empirical social research, see also B. M. Firsov, *Istoriya Sovetskoi sotsiologii* (St. Petersburg: European University, 2001).

to the editors of the journal *Proletarskaya Revolyutsiya*, in which he "attacked 'archival packrats,' and vulgar factologists," by which he clearly meant honest historians, whatever their political views, for whom facts trumped actions and the Party line.

The letter had a devastating impact on historians and had profound consequences for multiple other areas of scholarship as well. John Barber, an English historian whose analysis of the period emphasizes the autonomous actions of the "militant intellectuals [including Pokrovsky] with the party leadership [often] standing aside,"[113] and less Stalin's revolution from above, observes that "historical work virtually came to a standstill."[114] It was a watershed. "Criticism, self-criticism, dismissal from academic posts, expulsion from the party"[115] and in some instances repression[116] followed almost immediately. Yaroslavsky and his associates and Pokrovsky's colleagues were all criticized. Many of them were dismissed. Pokrovsky was not attacked, probably because he was virtually on his deathbed. He died of cancer in 1934. His disgrace came in 1934–36.[117]

In terms of the relation between the regime and scholarly disciplines, there followed two crucial developments. First, the advocates of change had responded to the cues provided by high politics. They often gave vent to revolutionary views in what the cues stemming from the Shakhty trial, the attack on the rightists in the leadership, and the first Five-Year Plan signaled were transformative times. They also used the atmosphere of the times to strengthen their institutional positions, often communicating with central Party leaders to seek the latter's support in such ventures. What happened instead in most of these cases was that they ran afoul of Stalin's commitment to harnessing virtually all the intellectual resources of the academy to state building. In such a milieu, the institutions and quotidian existence of individuals in the academy would be controlled more directly by the pervasive Party organs than they had been during either NEP or the Cultural Revolution. The level of the center's intrusion into the professional institutions and indeed of the day-to-day work of individual scholars took on new and

---

[113] See John Barber, "Stalin's Letter to the Editors of *Proletarskaya Revolyutsiya*," *Europe-Asia Studies*, Vol. 28, No. 1 (1976), pp. 21–41 at p. 25. See also his *Soviet Historians in Crisis, 1928–1932* (London: Macmillan, 1981) and George Enteen, "More about Stalin and the Historians: A Review Article," *Europe-Asia Studies*, Vol. 34, No. 3 (July 1982), pp. 448–54.

[114] Barber, "Stalin's Letter," p. 22.

[115] Ibid.

[116] Enteen, "Marxist Historians during the Cultural Revolution: A Case Study of Professional In-fighting," in Fitzpatrick, *Cultural Revolution*, p. 165, citing the Soviet historian I. I. Mints.

[117] Ibid., pp. 166–68.

more direct forms. In history, Barber emphasizes, "For the first time, the highest political authority told intellectuals precisely what interpretation of a particular subject was to be presented. Henceforth, the party leadership itself would be the arbiter of truth—in history and potentially in every other scientific and cultural field. . . . Since the distinction between obedience to the party and loyalty to the state had been to all practical purposes obliterated, any deviation from the line would not be not only wrong, but disloyal and treasonable."[118]

Thus, members of the Politburo, whom readers might a priori expect would have better things to do, would literally tell authors what to write.[119] Yaroslavsky, for example, received "personal instructions from [Lazar] Kaganovich and Stalin as to just how he should revise his" book on the history of the Communist Party.[120] (Kaganovich at this juncture was the Politburo member charged with the oversight of cultural and scholarly matters.)

Second, the leaders of the Cultural Revolution similarly also often sought to remove senior noncommunist professors to make way for younger, Marxist scholars including themselves. Ironically, the culmination of the Cultural Revolution sometimes left many of the much maligned "bourgeois specialists"[121] in place or restored to their places of influence in the academy—in the case of history largely because their views of prerevolutionary Russian history came closer to the favorable

---

[118] Barber, "Stalin's Letter," p. 25.

[119] But see Gregory, *The Political Economy*, pp. 68–75 on the petty details—the dictator's curse—with which Stalin and other members of the Politburo were preoccupied.

[120] Enteen, "Marxist Historians," in Fitzpatrick, *Cultural Revolution*, p. 166.

[121] The career of Ye. V. Tarle serves as an archetypical example. Tarle was a historian of some stature before the Revolution. During the Cultural Revolution, he was arrested and exiled for five years to the Central Asian city of Alma Ata (now Almaty). His more statist and nationalist views fit more comfortably with where Stalin was heading than did the views of the radical Marxists who had been dominant during the Cultural Revolution. Tarle returned to Leningrad after thirteen months in exile and obtained appointments in major institutes there. He continued to write and publish. His publications included a major volume on Napoleon published in 1936. He had the poor taste to publish it under the editorship of Karl Radek, who by early 1937 had become an enemy of the people. Two scathing reviews were published: one in *Pravda*, the other in *Izvestia*. But, in the words of a twenty-first-century Russian historian of a nationalist bent, "A genuine miracle occurred." (Viktor Vrachev, *Travlya Russkikh istorikov* [Moscow: Algoritm, 2006], pp. 185–88, at 187.) Stalin intervened to defend Tarle, declaring that "in comparison with . . . other bourgeois historians . . . [Tarle] was one of the better" and that consequently "there was no basis for connecting his name with that of his editor, the enemy of the people, the Trotskyite bandit, Radek." Tarle's career flourished subsequently. He won multiple Stalin and Lenin prizes, especially for his work during the Great Patriotic War (World War II) when he published numerous historical monographs and articles the theme of which was how bravely the Russians had fought historically.

view of the Russian state that Stalin increasingly emphasized as the 1930s proceeded. Stalin's letter set off a process that effectively ended the Cultural Revolution generally. In December 1931 Kaganovich dotted the i's by demanding that "Trotskyite contraband" be addressed "in a Bolshevik way."[122] Central figures, such as Pashukanis (law), Shulgin (education; see above, p. 68), and G. E. Deborin (philosophy),[123] in other areas of scholarship were subjected to criticism and self-criticism and forced to recant their views.

The areas of scholarship discussed herein usually shared several things in common. They held views that were recognizably Marxist in that they took into account the impact of the societal base in explaining events. They had an analogous view of the way the social and economic environment shaped the nature of man. By 1932, at the latest, it had become clear that the Stalinist leadership and Stalin himself wanted to have nothing to do with such limiting perspectives. Stalin sought state builders in history, heroes in construction, and conscious and purposeful people in everyday walks of life. What he did not want were scholars and specialists whose analyses emphasized how complicated people or tasks were or who viewed the Russian state in a negative light.

[122] Barber, "Stalin's Letter," p. 23.

[123] On Deborin, see especially David Joravsky, *Soviet Marxism and Natural Science, 1917–1932* (New York: Columbia University Press, 1961), passim.

CHAPTER 3

From Narrow Selectorate to Autocracy

THE STORY OF HOW STALIN managed to outsmart and outmuscle Trotsky and then to move against Zinoviev and Kamenev is well known and widely depicted in the literature.[1] With the decisions taken at the Tenth Party Congress in 1921 and the burgeoning Party apparatus, "The answer to the question 'Who will rule Russia?'" as Robert Conquest observed, became, simply, "Who will win a faction fight confined to a narrow section of the leadership?"[2]

What that generalization misses is that it fails to note that the institutional reference point for the phrase "narrow section of the leadership" changes substantially in the course of the decade or so following the Tenth Party Congress. Congresses and the Central Committee mattered substantially in the early 1920s. A decade or so later—the early 1930s—both the Congress and the Central Committee had been relegated to observer status. Rather, the Politburo constituted the genuine selectorate though even as late as the Seventeenth Party Congress in 1934 members of the Party Congress attempted (unsuccessfully) to play the role of the selectorate. By the latter half of the 1930s, it was a stretch to consider even the Politburo as constituting the selectorate. Indeed, by then, it had become a dubious matter whether any institution—Party or state— might be thought to constitute the selectorate.

We saw telling evidence in the first chapter that the Central Committee, even including the Democratic Centralists, despite being divided over how to handle relations with the trade unions, was united in rejecting the proposals of the Workers' Opposition that would have diminished the Central Committee's governing role.

The successful threat to its position came from Party institutions rather than from such external groups as the Workers' Opposition. During the decade, the Congresses enlarged rapidly in size and, with

---

[1] Schapiro, *The Origin*; Roeder, *Red Sunset*; Fainsod, *How Russia*; Robert Conquest, *The Great Terror: A Reassessment* (New York: Oxford University Press, 1990); Gill, *The Origins of the Stalinist Political System*; Tucker, *Stalin in Power*; Isaac Deutscher, *Stalin: A Political Biography*, 2nd ed. (Oxford: Oxford University Press, 1967).

[2] Conquest, *The Great Terror*, p. 7.

qualifications noted below, took on an increasingly symbolic role. The Central Committee went through the same process. The frequency of meetings decreased, its size increased enormously, and its power diminished. It, in effect, became the selectorate, the institution to which the Politburo appealed when the latter was divided. As the 1920s ground on, the Politburo became the real repository of power, a condition that lasted well into the 1930s when it too became not much more than a ceremonial organization.

In the case of the Congress, the story of its demise as an effective, rather than a symbolic, institution covers both the NEP and the 1930s. The decision to require regional party organizations to participate as blocs strengthened the hand of both members of the Secretariat and members of the Politburo, notably Gregory Zinoviev, with a city-specific power base in Leningrad.[3]

But the overall impact of the changes was twofold. It diminished the Congress's ability to hold accountable the Central Committee or the increasingly powerful central Party organs—the Politburo, the Secretariat, and the Orgburo. The content of Congresses was also transformed. Rather than a locale where serious debates took place over serious matters—case in point the debate over the ratification of the Treaty of Brest-Litovsk at the Seventh Party Congress in March 1918—Congresses became an instrument employed by Stalin and his confreres to harass and intimidate those leaders who had fallen out of favor—even though they usually continued to hold symbolic membership in the Central Committee. Merely the increase in the number of Congress participants and the steady increase in the gap between Congresses would have been sufficient to predict a diminished role for the Congress.

The composition of the Seventh Party Congress in 1918 was approximately the same size as that of the U.S. Senate. The latter of course has 100 members while the Seventh Congress[4] was composed of 106 members, of whom 47 were full (voting) members. More than 2,000 (2,016) persons (of whom 1,227 were voting members) were members of the Seventeenth Party Congress, held in March 1934. Likewise, Congresses occurred much less frequently the longer Stalin was the key figure in Soviet politics. Congresses occurred once every calendar year from 1917 (the Sixth Congress) through December 1925 (the Fourteenth Congress). The Fifteenth Congress took place in December 1927, the Sixteenth in June/July 1930, the Seventeenth (as noted above) in March 1934. The last two Congresses held while Stalin lived took place in

---

[3] Roeder, *Red Sunset*, p. 57.
[4] Gill, *The Origins of the Stalinist Political System*, p. 58.

March 1939 and October 1952, respectively. (World War II may be a part of the story in explaining the length of that gap.)

The enlargement of the Congress and the steady increase in the length of time between Congresses would be sufficient as evidence of the weakening of the Congress. But the dramatic change in the content of the Congresses requires an understanding of how the Orgburo and the Secretariat (with a strong assist from the Central Control Commission[5]) altered the composition of the Congress memberships, an alteration that resulted in the Congresses becoming occasions for the browbeating and bullying of those leaders who, while usually still members of the Central Committee, were no longer part of Stalin's entourage. The Secretariat and the Orgburo appointed local and regional secretaries. They in turn appointed politically reliable persons from their respective regions to be participants in the Congresses.[6] Muscle was applied, inter alia, by sending candidate or full Central Committee members to participate in regional party conferences at which Congress members were selected. It worked. Gill cites both Stalin's depiction of the efforts to stack the Twelfth Party Congress and that of the pro-Trotsky "Group of 46," which, while quite different in tone, are obviously describing the same phenomenon.

STALIN: "For the past six years the Central Committee has never once prepared a congress as it has in the present case."

DECLARATION OF THE 46: "[T]he secretarial hierarchy of the party to an ever greater extent recruits the membership of conferences and congresses, which are becoming to an ever greater extent the executive assemblies of this hierarchy."[7]

The result of these efforts soon became apparent. At the Eleventh Party Congress (1922), the Congress rejected the Central Committee's proposal that A. G. Shlyapnikov, S. P. Medvedev, and Aleksandra Kollontai (who had had the temerity to ask the Communist International to support their position) be expelled from the Party[8] and instead recommended more lenient action. There was also vigorous debate concerning whether the Central Control Commission should be emasculated.

---

[5] On the Central Control Commission, see especially Roeder, *Red Sunset*, p. 59: "Party rules gave . . . enlarged plenary sessions [of the Central Committee and the Central Control Commission] special powers on issues of Party discipline and unity. To manufacture the super majority of two-thirds needed to expel a member of the Central Committee itself, Stalin convened joint meetings with the Central Control Commission, which he dominated."

[6] Especially Gill, *The Origins of the Stalinist Political System*, pp. 140–41.

[7] Ibid., p. 141.

[8] Schapiro, *The Origin*, p. 336. Also Daniels, *The Conscience*, p. 162.

Individual disapproval of the growing role of the Secretariat was registered at the Twelfth Congress but carried little weight. "When the Thirteenth Party Congress convened in May 1924," Daniels observes, "the
activity of the secretarial machinery had been so effective that not a single oppositionist was elected to the congress as a voting delegate."[9] "By
the time of the XIV Congress [December 1925]," Gill adds, "the mass
jeering and shouting down of speakers had become the norm, a pattern
which was to be maintained until the opposition was vanquished."[10]
Moreover, with the exception of Zinoviev's control over the Leningrad
participants at the same Congress, from the Thirteenth Congress on
monolithic unity became the operative descriptive of Congresses, with
the practice of unanimous public votes becoming standard.

But if we dropped the story of the withering away of the Congress as
an effective organ at this juncture, readers would have an excessively
compliant view of the Party Congresses that took place after the Tenth
Congress (1921) and prior to the Eighteenth Party Congress in 1939. For
instance, evidence of a long-festering dispute over the rate of growth
broke out at the Seventeenth Congress between Vyacheslav Molotov, at
that juncture Chairman of Sovnarkom, and Sergo Ordzhonikidze, head
of the Supreme Council of the National Economy (Vesenkha).[11]

But the most striking example that attendees at a Congress were
not completely docile pertains to the issue of Stalin's continuation as
leader, which appears to have come up at the Seventeenth Party Congress in January 1934. We discussed (above, pp. 56–60) the awful years
1930 to 1932 during which the peasants were collectivized at huge costs
in life to both the peasants and their animals. At the level of high politics, Stalin had defeated in sequence Trotsky, Kamenev, and Zinoviev,
and then Bukharin, Tomsky, and Rykov. These events were evidently
very much on the minds of the participants at the Congress. Stalin himself announced that "[w]hereas at the XVth Congress it was still necessary to prove the correctness of the Party line and to fight certain
anti-Leninist groupings, and at the XVIth Congress, to finish off the last
supporters of these groupings, at the present Congress there is nothing
to prove and, it seems, nobody to beat."[12] It was for this reason that the
Seventeenth Party Congress was termed the Congress of Victors.

Apparently, with the crisis prompted by the chaos and devastation
attendant collectivization attenuated, and mindful of the humiliations

---

[9] Daniels, *The Conscience*, p. 239.

[10] Gill, *The Origins of the Stalinist Political System*, p. 142.

[11] Ibid., p. 224; J. Arch Getty, *Origins of the Great Purges: The Soviet Communist Party Reconsidered, 1933–1938* (Cambridge: Cambridge University Press, 1985), p. 17.

[12] Cited in many places including Conquest, *The Great Terror*, p. 31.

experienced by those who had opposed Stalin, conversations took place among a section of the senior delegates to the Congress, notably those who were familiar with the so-called Lenin testament.[13] They were distressed about "'an abnormal situation'" that had arisen within the party.[14] These participants in the Congress evidently concluded "the time had come to remove Stalin from the post of Secretary General and to transfer him to other work."[15]

What would such a situation have meant for these senior communists? Certainly it did not include Stalin's conception of monolithic unity. They probably did consider it normal to adopt such restrictions on Party openness as the Tenth Party Congress prohibition on factions in the context of the temporary retreat vis-à-vis the peasantry that the New Economic Policy entailed. Given what Kirov is reported to have said when he was approached and asked if he would accept appointment as general secretary, certainly he, and very likely the Old Bolsheviks who approached him, did not consider the main policies associated with Stalin to have been abnormal.[16]

Something more than 100 but fewer than 300 of the 1,225 voting members of the Party Congress seem not to have voted for Stalin. Anton Antonov-Ovseenko maintains that there were 292 votes against Stalin in the voting for the slate of persons who would become members of the Central Committee. He reaches this number by reporting the assessment of the vote conducted by a commission headed by Nikolai Shvernik and subtracting that number from the 1,225 eligible voting members certified by the Credentials Committee. The summary report had stated there were only 936 votes for Stalin. (It should be stressed that at this congress, voters were presented with a single slate composed of the Secretariat's and Politburo's nominees of the persons to

[13]Lenin wrote his "testament" in December 1922. In it, he said that "Stalin is excessively rude . . . a defect which cannot be tolerated in one holding the position of Secretary General. Because of this, I propose that the comrades consider the method by which Stalin would be removed from this position." Delegates at the Thirteenth Party Congress were informed of its existence and decided not to act upon it. It resurfaced in 1956 when the delegates to the Twentieth Party Congress were provided copies as a precursor to Khrushchev's "secret speech." The version of the testament cited here is from that speech which is reproduced in Russian Institute, Columbia University, *The Anti-Stalin Campaign and International Communism: A Selection of Documents* (New York: Columbia University Press, 1956), p. 7.

[14]L. Shaumian, "Na rubezhe pervykh piatiletok," *Pravda*, February 7, 1964, as cited in Conquest, *The Great Terror*, p. 32.

[15]Ibid., p. 32

[16]Antonov Ovseenko, *The Time of Stalin: Portrait of a Tyranny* (New York: Harper & Row, 1981), p. 82. The Shaumian article gives no hint that these issues were on the table for those who wanted Stalin transferred to other work.

be "elected" to the Central Committee.) By this count 289 votes were cast against Stalin. Since Kirov had received three votes against, the Politburo member, Lazar Kaganovich, is reported to have decreed that it be recorded that Stalin had also received three votes against.[17] Robert Tucker cites another source[18] that reports a document in the Party archives written by V. M. Verkhovykh, the vice-chairman of the vote-counting commission, in which he wrote in 1960 that either 123 or 125 votes had been cast against Stalin. The article from which Verkhovykh's recollections were taken was published in 1989. It reproduces a photo-copy of the results in the vote for membership of the Central Commit-tee that indicates that 1,059 of the possible 1,225 had been cast. Kirov is shown to have received 1,055 and Stalin 1,056 votes. If all the 166 missing ballots had not supported Stalin, this would imply he had 169 votes cast against him.

Stalin's subsequent behavior may be overdetermined, but surely his behavior in the five-year interim between the Seventeenth and Eigh-teenth Party Congresses indicates that whatever the exact figure, at least to Stalin's way of thinking, the opposition was not trivial—though it bears emphasizing that even three votes not cast in his favor might have set him off. In any event, Stalin dealt with those who might con-ceivably have opposed him at the Seventeenth Congress in his typical manner. Of those who had been either voting or candidate members at the Seventeenth Congress, only 3 percent participated in the Eighteenth Party Congress.[19] According to Nikita Khrushchev in his famous "se-cret" speech at the Twentieth Party Congress in 1956, "Of 1966 dele-gates . . . [to the Seventeenth Party Congress] 1,108 were arrested on charges of anti-revolutionary crimes."[20] Those the Seventeenth Con-gress had approved as Central Committee members fared even worse. Khrushchev again: "Of the 139 members and candidates of the Party's Central Committee who were elected at the XVIIth Congress, 98 per-sons, i.e., 70 percent, were arrested and shot (mostly in 1937–1938)."[21] The Seventeenth Congress's limited effort to play the role of an ejec-torate in 1934 had proved fatal both for its members and especially for those whose selection the voting members of the Congress had ratified.

The Congress had become at most what Fainsod a half century ago termed "a rally of Party and state functionaries,"[22] something to be

[17] Ibid., p. 83.

[18] Tucker, *Stalin in Power*, pp. 260–61, citing "Skol'ko delegatov XVII s'yezda partii golosovalo protiv Stalina?," *Izvestia Ts. K. KPSS*, No. 7 (1989), p. 114.

[19] Gill, *The Origins of the Stalinist Political System*, p. 278.

[20] *Anti-Stalin Campaign*, p. 23.

[21] Ibid., pp. 22–23.

[22] Fainsod, *How Russia*, p. 186.

called at the whim of the leadership rather than the kind of narrow selectorate encountered in typically authoritarian systems. Whereas the gap between the Seventeenth and Eighteenth Party Congresses had been five years, the Nineteenth Congress met in 1952, thirteen years after the Eighteenth Congress, causing Khrushchev, after the fact—and after Stalin's death—to query whether that gap "[w]as . . . a normal situation when . . . our Party and our country had experienced so many important events" in the interim, events that "demanded categorically that the Party should have passed resolutions pertaining to the country's defense during the Patriotic War and to peacetime construction after the war."[23] The question was rhetorical.

The Transformation of the Central Committee

The story is broadly similar in the case of the Central Committee. However much its members might disagree in the first years after the revolution, they were united (above, p. 33) in ensuring that the Central Committee was the key decision making body. (There was considerable membership overlap with other institutions, notably the governmental Sovnarkom, but that does not gainsay the Central Committee's decisive role.) As the 1920s progressed, the body as an institution faced two institutional challenges. One was the Central Control Commission (CCC); the other, the Politburo. The challenge from the CCC was almost thwarted at the 1922 Eleventh Party Congress where "a vote to abolish the control commissions was only narrowly defeated."[24] Instead, the practice, provided for in a part of the resolution on party unity adopted at the Tenth Party Congress that was initially kept secret, became established that on personnel matters the Central Committee and the Control Commission would meet jointly. Since the apparatus (which increasingly meant Stalin) controlled appointments to the latter, this had the effect of diluting the Central Committee's power. This became especially so because "a new forum was established, the joint CC-CCC plenum," the broad mandate of which involved "'the most important general political and general party questions'"[25] but whose focus was overwhelmingly with cadre questions.

In addition, the two factors that had played such an important role in transforming the power of the Congresses also took their toll on the influence of the Central Committee as an institution: increased size and

[23] *Anti-Stalin Campaign*, p. 21.
[24] Gill, *The Origins of the Stalinist Political System*, p. 59.
[25] Ibid., pp. 150 and 151.

an increase in the intervals between meetings. Table 3.1 shows the number of members of the Central Committee 1917–71. The increase in size was a politically shrewd way of weakening the Old Bolsheviks. They continued as members of the Central Committee, but their ability to mediate disputes between factions in the Politburo diminished steadily as the number of members increased. The new members were almost entirely persons nominated by the Secretariat and/or the Orgburo, that is, were Stalinists. They often were Party first secretaries from various regions or key figures from major sectors of the economy and illustrated what Daniels has called job slot representation.[26] Norms developed that occupants of particular posts—first secretary of the Moscow City Committee, first secretary of republics—were entitled to Central Committee membership and, as Table 3.1 reveals, the number of slots implying such an entitlement increased over the years. Daniels notes this had the effect of inflating the "status value of Central Committee membership" for individuals.[27] But it also weakened the Central Committee as an institution. Such an institution could, and did at times, serve as an appellate body to which Stalin could turn to resolve disputes within the Politburo. But as the size of the Central Committee grew its role diminished. As Roeder notes, effective accountability in such a system became "reciprocal" and limited. Although in principle Communist Party secretaries were elected, from the mid-1920s on they were in fact appointed by the Party Secretariat and more specifically by Stalin, who utilized the fact that he was the only person who was a full member of the Politburo, the Orgburo, and the Secretariat to great advantage. The Party secretaries in turn selected representatives from their region, themselves included, to serve as representatives to the Party Congresses. This is what Daniels aptly described as the "circular flow of power."[28] The Congresses approved a list of persons to be members of the Central Committee. "Stalin began . . . to remove oppositionists from that body and from the Politburo." Thus, the "circuit [was] closed": Stalin "controlled the body that nominally elected him."[29] The putative selectee in practice selected the selectorate who completed the circle by selecting him—though as we just saw with regard to the Seventeenth Congress, even this was not always a completely foolproof way for a leader to avoid some measure of accountability.

[26] Robert V. Daniels, "Office Holding and Elite Status: The Central Committee of the CPSU," in Paul Cocks et al., eds., *The Dynamics of Soviet Politics* (Cambridge, MA: Harvard University Press, 1976), pp. 77–95, especially pp. 78–80. See also Roeder, *Red Sunset*, p. 56.

[27] Daniels, "Office Holding," p. 79.

[28] Daniels, "Soviet Politics since Khrushchev," p. 20.

[29] Ibid.

Table 3.1 Numbers of Central Committee members 1917–71

Year	Voting members	Candidate members
August 1917	21	4
March 1918	15	8
March 1919	19	8
April 1920	19	12
March 1921	25	15
April 1922	27	19
May 1924	53	34
1925	63	43
1930	71	50
1934	71	67
1939	71	68
1952	125	110
1956	133	122
1961	175	156
1966	195	165
1971	241	155

Sources: This table draws most heavily on Graeme Gill, *The Origins of the Stalinist Political System* (New York: Cambridge University Press, 1990), pp. 61, 145, and 227. Also Merle Fainsod, *How Russia Is Ruled* (Cambridge, MA: Harvard University Press, 1953), pp. 163–64. For 1952 through 1971, see Robert V. Daniels, "Office Holding and Elite Status: The Central Committee of the CPSU," in Paul Cocks et al., eds., *The Dynamics of Soviet Politics* (Cambridge, MA: Harvard University Press, 1976), p. 80.

The foolproof ways Stalin employed rendered moot the issue whether either the Congress or the Central Committee was in any sense a selectorate as far as the general secretary was concerned but not with regard to the expulsion of members of the Politburo. Diluting the membership was one tack. Another, as Khrushchev has reported[30] (above, p. 80), was to kill a quite sizeable fraction of the members of both bodies, the Congress and the Central Committee, and appoint comrades whose continued existence, not merely their careers, required that they ratify the Kremlin's personnel decisions. In addition, by the late 1930s, cadre appointments at the regional and lower levels had to be approved by the NKVD. Since it was the regional (oblast and republic) secretaries who largely constituted the pool out of which the Central Committee was drawn, this further reduced the possibility that the Central Committee would exercise any effective independent role in selecting members of the Politburo, much less the general secretary.[31]

[30] *Anti-Stalin Campaign*, pp. 22–23.
[31] Gill, *The Origins of the Stalinist Political System*, p. 296.

A final way was to reduce the number of meetings of the Central Committee in precisely the manner that had occurred in the case of the Congresses. The frequency of Central Committee meetings decreased steadily through Stalin's years as general secretary. Intervals between meetings stretched from weeks to months and became quite irregular, despite Party rules that specified their regular occurrence.[32] Indeed, Roeder cites an authoritative Soviet source to the effect that Central Committee "meetings became infrequent: apparently in the last sixteen years of Stalin's rule only six were called."[33]

THE RISE AND DEMISE OF THE POLITBURO

As Gill emphasizes, "The body which undermined the position of the CC within the party was the Politburo."[34] Initially, the Politburo was a real executive committee of the type familiar to many institutions, including departments in American universities. "'Our Politburo of the CC is the operative leadership organ of all areas of socialist construction,'" Politburo member Lazar Kaganovich declared in 1934.[35]

In its first three years, it met at least once a week and often twice a week. Similarly, as Table 3.2 on the next page indicates, Politburo meeting frequency in the late 1920s and at the beginning of the 1930s averaged approximately once or twice a week. In the years immediately prior to those (1937–38) of the great purges the number dropped precipitously. It met fifteen times in 1935 and only nine times in 1936. At no time during 1936 did the Politburo meet more than once a month. After that, it met spasmodically and even more irregularly.

These figures do not include informal caucusing. The latter weakened the Politburo as an institution in that the informal meetings became the actual locus of decision making. This behavior, had it been done by the losers, would have been castigated as factionalism, dated from the early 1920s with the famous meetings of the "seven" in Trotsky's absence but became even more pronounced as Stalin's power increased. During the twenties, during the factional disputes involving first the left and then the Right Opposition, the Stalin clique similarly met in advance on numerous occasions to decide on measures to be undertaken, thus rendering the Politburo something of a shell institution. As Stalin's

---

[32] Ibid., pp. 145, 225–26, and 281.
[33] Roeder, *Red Sunset*, p. 58.
[34] Gill, *The Origins of the Stalinist Political System*, p. 65.
[35] As cited in Khlevniuk et al., *Stalinskoe Politburo*, p. 7.

Table 3.2 Formal sessions of the Politburo 1928–40

Year	Central Committee plenums	Politburo meetings	Number Stalin attended
1928	3	53	51
1929	2	51	49
1930	1	38	30
1931	2	57	47
1932	1	43	30
1933	1	24	16
1934	2	18	14
1935	3	15	15
1936	2	9	7
1937	3	6	6
1938	1	4	4
1939	1	2	2
1940	2	2	2

Source: E. A. Rees, "Stalin, the Politburo and Rail Transport Policy," in Julian Cooper et al., *Soviet History, 1917–53: Essays in Honour of R.W. Davies* (London: Macmillan, 1995), p. 106. Other scholars generate somewhat different tables, e.g., O.V. Khlevniuk, *Politburo: Mekhanizmi politicheskoi vlasti* (Moscow: Rosplan, 1996), p. 288, but they all point to the same conclusion.

letters to Molotov make clear,[36] advance consultation and mobilization was a characteristic feature of how the Stalin-Bukharin et al. coalition confronted the ostensibly "united" opposition of Trotsky, Kamenev, and Zinoviev.[37] Letters to Molotov were read and initialed by several other members of the Politburo.

The practice of caucusing prior to Politburo meetings persisted throughout the 1920s and 1930s. Nevertheless, until the late 1920s, Stalin was attentive to the niceties of achieving Politburo approval,[38] even if it was to considerable degree a sham because his caucus had colluded in advance. When he encountered stubborn resistance within the Politburo, moreover, he could always go to the Central Committee which, as we saw previously (pp. 38–39), had been stacked with his appointees. During the brief time span of 1928 to 1930 the key figures

[36] Lars Lih et al., *Stalin's Letters to Molotov 1925–1936* (New Haven, CT: Yale University Press, 1995), notably pp. 90–93, p. 115, and passim, pp. 97–132; and Khlevniuk, *Politburo,* p. 48.

[37] Stephen E. Hanson, *Time and Revolution: Marxism and the Design of Soviet Institutions* (Chapel Hill: University of North Carolina Press, 1997) is a rare book that takes Zinoviev seriously.

[38] E.g., Gill, *The Origins of the Stalinist Political System,* p. 193.

in the Right Opposition were removed from the Politburo and from job slots that typically warranted Politburo membership. In 1929 Bukharin was ousted as head of the Communist International (Comintern) and then from the Politburo. Tomsky was removed as trade union head in 1929 and lost his place in the Politburo in 1930. Rykov lost his position as head of Sovnarkom and as a member of the Politburo late in 1930.

During the same period Stalin began acting on his own initiative and at variance with Politburo consensus. Two examples, one of major import, the other minor, are provided by Gill. The first was Stalin's decision to force collectivization. The counsel given the regions reflected the divisions in the leadership as to the extent of force to be used in collectivizing and obtaining grain from the peasants. Some Party and government leaders—Gill gives as examples M. I. Frumkin, the deputy commissar for finance, and the Moscow party secretary and candidate member of the Politburo, N. A. Uglanov—advised local Party leaders "to eschew undue pressure in their dealings with peasant producers."[39] Stalin and his close allies—especially Molotov, Kaganovich, and Mikoyan—employed what came to be known as the Ural-Siberian method for acquiring grain, that is, coercive measures reminiscent of War Communism.[40]

Frumkin was central to a lesser example of the erosion of the façade of collective leadership. Writing in his guise as deputy commissar of finance, Frumkin wrote a letter in mid-1928 (while the right still had substantial representation on the Politburo) critical of the means by which collectivization of agriculture was being achieved. "The Politburo," Gill reports, "decided to handle this matter by circulating . . . [the] letter, along with a formal reply by the Politburo, to the CC. . . . Stalin preempted the decision by writing a personal reply," which aggravated sensibilities in the Politburo not just among the Right Opposition.[41]

Stalin's initiatives came increasingly without reference to the Politburo once Bukharin had been removed from the Politburo. One of Stalin's most portentous acts, the December 27, 1929, declaration calling

---

[39] Ibid., p. 193.

[40] E. A. Osokina, *Our Daily Bread: Socialist Distribution and the Art of Survival in Stalin's Russia, 1927–1941* (Armonk, NY: M.E. Sharpe, 2001; Viola et al., *The War Against the Peasantry*, pp. 118–22; and Yuzuru Taniuchi, "Decision-making on the Ural-Siberian Method," in Julian Cooper et al., *Soviet History, 1917–53: Essays in Honor of R.W. Davies* (New York: St. Martin's, 1995), pp. 78–103.

[41] Gill, *The Origins of the Stalinist Political System*, pp. 193–94, where he describes Frumkin as finance minister. See also Stephen F. Cohen, *Bukharin and the Bolshevik Revolution: A Political Biography, 1888–1938* (New York: Vintage Books, 1973), p. 286 and M. Lewin, *Russian Peasants and Soviet Power: A Study of Collectivization* (New York: Norton, 1975), pp. 299–300, where he is described as in the text.

for "the liquidation of the kulaks as a class" came before the commission charged with dealing with "the kulak problem" announced its proposals.[42]

Even as the Right Opposition was being defeated politically, however, this did not signify that in 1929–30 members of the Politburo, virtually all Stalinists, were acquiescing without struggle in the erosion of the Politburo as an institution. While the integrity of the Politburo as an institution steadily eroded, there were instances into the 1930s when the Politburo attempted to retain some manifestation of collective leadership.

Much has been known about these efforts for a long while.[43] The work of O. V. Khlevniuk and his colleagues has greatly enriched our understanding of the dynamics of elite politics[44] throughout the 1930s. These studies give us not only an excellent sense of the worst of the Stalin period in the late 1930s, when the Politburo had become a shadow of its former self, but an appreciation of the considerable difference in the role of the Politburo qua institution and the interaction of its members with Stalin, the general secretary, circa 1930 and in the latter half of the 1930s.

The efforts of the Politburo members to constrain Stalin's increasing power vis-à-vis the Politburo may be illustrated by considering Stalin's ultimately successful efforts to undermine Aleksei Rykov's position as head of the USSR Sovnarkom. Stalin alleged to Molotov that under Rykov's leadership, the Sovnarkom might become a counterweight to the "party leadership" (by which he meant himself). Stalin urged Molotov, in a letter dated September 22, 1930, to agree to replace Rykov. Moreover, he proposed that a standing commission, which he termed a Commission on Fulfillment, "should be established for the sole purpose of systematically *checking up on the fulfillment* of the center's decisions"[45] and, he argued, this matter should be resolved "by the fall." "Otherwise, there will be a split between the soviet [read: government] and party leadership."[46]

The matter was not resolved as expeditiously as Stalin wished. Discussion on this matter in the Politburo continued through the fall. In October, Kliment Voroshilov, evidently on Politburo instructions and

[42] Lewin, *Russian Peasants and Soviet Power*, p. 487.

[43] Conquest, *The Great Terror*, p. 23; Hugh Seton-Watson, *From Lenin to Khrushchev: The History of World Communism* (New York: Praeger, 1960), pp. 163–64.

[44] E.g., Khlevniuk, *Politburo*; Khlevniuk et al., *Stalinskoe Politburo*; O. V. Khlevniuk, *In Stalin's Shadow: The Career of "Sergo" Ordzhonikidze* (Armonk, NY: M.E. Sharpe, 1995).

[45] For an English-language translation of the letter, see Lih et al., *Stalin's Letters*, pp. 217–18, italics in original.

[46] Ibid., p. 217.

expressing Politburo consensus,[47] wrote to Stalin to the effect that "I, Mikoyan, Molotov, Kaganovich, and in part Kuibishev believe that the best outcome of the situation would be the unification of the [party and government] leadership. It would be good to sit you in [the leadership] of Sovnarkom and, in the way that you know how, really take on the leadership of the whole country."[48] The Voroshilov letter also makes it clear that there was opposition to Stalin's idea of yet another commission. "Kuibishev first, and following him, I and Sergo [Ordzhonikidze] expressed doubts about the rationale of the existence of such a commission."[49]

Khlevniuk makes the plausible argument that Voroshilov may well have been cleverly trying to tempt Stalin to imitate Lenin's leadership style (which had been to head the government), a move that, he argues,[50] in 1930 would have had Stalin being constantly involved in the intricacies of day-to-day governance rather than "episodically," as had been Stalin's practice. (Drawing on Khlevniuk's data pertaining to the number of meetings and the number of decisions rendered, Paul R. Gregory argues that the centralization of power to the Politburo and the General Secretary had already resulted in "the dictator's curse."[51]) In the process, Stalin would have lost "the prior ability to exercise direct control over the party apparatus." "Moreover," Khlevniuk argues, "Stalin's colleagues clearly understood this."[52] At the same time, he is careful to assert that "[i]t is difficult to say to what extent Stalin's colleagues were motivated by a wish to reduce his rapidly growing power . . . nor to what extent Stalin suspected them of such aspirations. In any case, Stalin insisted on his variant [of the proposed changes. It was] only ten years after, when Stalin had achieved the powers of an absolute dictator and had achieved the possibility of resolving on his own the fate of any member of the Politburo, that he took on the post of the chair of the Sovnarkom—which Voroshilov had proposed in his letter in 1930."[53] It is worth noting that Voroshilov's proposal was precisely that which Old Bolsheviks were discussing in the corridors of the Seventeenth Party Congress in 1934. Moreover, from the perspective of the evolving role of the Politburo as an institution, it matters little whether Khlevniuk's argument is or is not correct. The central point here is that in 1930 individual Politburo members took views at

[47] Khlevniuk, *Politburo*, p. 41.
[48] Ibid., p. 42.
[49] Ibid.
[50] Ibid.
[51] Gregory, *The Political Economy*, pp. 68–75.
[52] Khlevniuk, *Politburo*, p. 43.
[53] Ibid.

variance with those advocated by Stalin on important cadre questions. Moreover, at least in Stalin's absence, in 1930 the Politburo occasionally attempted to act as an institution distinct from, and at variance with, the interests of the general secretary.

How extensive such individual or collective acts were is difficult to say, though we can say with certainty they were more extensive in 1930 than they were eight to ten years later. Clearly, there were those with intimate knowledge of the Politburo's functioning who were distressed at its declining importance. This is best illustrated by considering briefly the so-called Lominadze-Syrtsov Affair.

That affair is more significant for what it reveals by way of conversations among communists across what was perceived to be the politically appropriate spectrum of views aimed at a minimum at altering the distribution of power between Stalin and the Politburo and probably replacing Stalin as general secretary. Parts of the agenda were certainly also about key policy items,[54] notably the tempo of collectivization.

Vissarion Lominadze was quite close to Ordzhonikidze (who in 1930 was head of the CCC and a member of the Politburo), having worked with him in the Transcaucasus, where he, Lominadze, had been a Party secretary in Georgia in the early 1920s. He returned to Moscow in the mid-1920s to work in the Comintern. In 1929 he was charged with being a leftist. He certainly had opinions, which was often in these years a fatal affliction. Ordzhonikidze tells us that Lominadze "'had strong opinions on questions pertaining to the Chinese Revolution, [and] struggles with the kulak class.'"[55]

He also had opinions about those who had no opinions prior to being told what opinions they should have. This attitude led him to view with distaste the hagiography of Stalin centered on the observance of the latter's fiftieth birthday in 1929 and to express his scorn for those who were essentially deifying Stalin. Khlevniuk reports that in response to the charges of leftist deviation Lominadze wrote a letter to the Party Institute of Red Professors in which he asserted that

[t]here's been a rather rapid expansion of a *special type of Communist* [emphasis Lominadze's]. . . . This type of Communist voices his opinion on any question after he is convinced that a particular viewpoint has been recognized as correct from above. . . . The fundamental trait of this typical representative of the lower party elements is fear of making a mistake, ideological cowardice, and constant trepidation that he could say something that might differ from the leadership's thinking. Of course, this fear

[54]Davies, "The Syrtsov-Lominadze Affair," *Soviet Studies*, Vol. 33, No. 1 (1981), pp. 29–50.

[55]Khlevniuk, *In Stalin's Shadow*, pp. 30–39 at p. 31.

most often leads to mistakes. . . . [This] inevitably places "those afraid to make a mistake" in a dead end at every turn. . . . Any new thought invariably seems to them to be a deviation of the left or right.[56]

These views—and analogous ones entertained by several important figures in the Communist Youth League (Komsomol) leadership—did not resonate well with Stalin. He wrote angrily to Molotov that Lominadze and the Komsomol leaders were "demanding (essentially) the *freedom* to review the general party line, the *freedom* to weaken party discipline, the *freedom* to turn the party into a discussion club."[57]

For an understanding of how the Politburo operated in 1929–30, two aspects of the 1930 Lominadze story deserve attention. The first is that Lominadze had no hesitation in sharing his views with Ordzhonikidze, who was clearly his protector at that juncture—and it turned out, subsequently as well. The second is that these letters put Ordzhonikidze in an extremely awkward spot. Party norms clearly dictated that he share these letters with the Politburo. So doing would likely have had severe, even fatal, consequences for both Lominadze and Ordzhonikidze. Ordzhonikidze tried to conform to Party norms by reading the letter to Stalin while at the same time living up to his promise to Lominadze by refusing to hand over the letter to Stalin, saying "I gave him my word." Stalin never forgot Ordzhonikidze's failure to subordinate the integrity of his word to Lominadze to Party dictates and included Ordzhonikidze's behavior vis-à-vis Lominadze in his attack on Ordzhonikidze after the latter's suicide in early 1937.

It is Syrtsov's behavior, though, that sheds more light on the functioning of the Politburo circa 1930. Syrtsov was an even faster riser than Lominadze and in the late 1920s had had an even more powerful protector, Stalin himself. Identified as a staunch Stalinist while a secretary of the Siberian Regional Party Committee, he became chair of the Russian Republic Sovnarkom in 1928 at the age of thirty-five, a candidate member of the Politburo in 1929, chair of a Politburo commission in September 1930,[58] and someone who might well be a likely prospect to replace Rykov as chairman of the All-Union Sovnarkom. As a candidate member of the Politburo, Syrtsov had the opportunity to experience firsthand the workings of the Politburo as an institution.

Like Lominadze, Syrtsov suffered from a propensity to have and express opinions. The two became good friends and exchanged views on sensitive political topics. The accusations of the existence of a

---

[56] As cited in Khlevniuk, *In Stalin's Shadow,* p. 32.

[57] An English version of Stalin's letter is contained in Lih et al., *Stalin's Letters,* p. 162, italics in original.

[58] Khlevniuk, *In Stalin's Shadow,* pp. 35–38; Khlevniuk et al., *Stalinskoe Politburo,* p. 310.

"left"-right block emerged because Syrtsov, whose views, once in Moscow, had some flavor of Bukharin's critique of the pell-mell pace of collectivization, was accused of right deviationist tendencies, whereas Lominadze, who had been charged with leftist tendencies, shared with Syrtsov reservations about the pace of collectivization.

Sorting out exactly what the two and their colleagues hoped to achieve is a task for others.[59] It is clear, though, that both Lominadze (as noted above) and Syrtsov had provided evidence of having independent minds and reservations about the Great Breakthrough (*Velikii Perelom*). In Syrtsov's case, he had published a "brochure" in early 1930 titled "Our Successes, Failings, and Tasks." It is worth noting that at this juncture Politburo members had access to media sources, an access that became increasingly limited as the 1930s progressed. Using that access Syrtsov talked in public about successes *and* problems—which set him off from Stalin's public stance. He then published (with a print run of ten thousand) a speech on the agricultural "control figures" that prompted Stalin to propose, and the Politburo to adopt, a resolution chastising the publication of Syrtsov's speech and characterizing its publication as "a mistaken political step on the part of C. [for Comrade] Syrtsov."[60]

For our purposes, though, it is Syrtsov's views about the Politburo—of which he was a candidate member—and the views of other Politburo members that are most relevant. He had been meeting with a small group including B. G. Reznikov. Whether Reznikov was a plant is not certain,[61] but in any event he denounced Syrtsov to Stalin. Reznikov, among other things, reported that Syrtsov (along with Lominadze) declared that Stalin had to be replaced. When interrogated by a group headed by Orzhonikidze, Syrtsov insisted he would talk only to the Central Control Committee, even though at that juncture Ordzhonikidze was in fact the head of that institution.

This insistence on procedural niceties had only a limited effect, but it does shed light on his view of the actual functioning of the Politburo. In Reznikov's denunciation, he alleges that Syrtsov maintained that "'a

[59] See Davies, "The Syrtsov-Lominadze Affair" and the various publications cited herein by Khlevniuk.

[60] The above paragraph draws heavily on Khlevniuk, *Politbiuro*, p. 44. The quote in the text is drawn from it as well.

[61] Khlevniuk, in his chapter "Stalin, Syrtsov, Lominadze: Preparations for the 'Second Great Breakthrough,'" concludes that "most probably, Reznikov's repetitive contacts with Syrtsov and other oppositionists were part of a special mission assigned to him by a high party official, if not by Stalin himself." Paul R. Gregory and Norman Naimark, eds., *The Lost Politburo Transcripts: From Collective Rule to Stalin's Dictatorship* (New Haven, CT: Yale University Press, 2008), pp. 78–96, at 84.

significant part of the Party *aktiv* are, of course, dissatisfied with the regime and the policy of the Party. But they believe that it is the whole Politburo, while not Leninist, is after all the [agent of the] Central Committee, which is conducting the existing hard line.'"[62] He has Syrtsov saying that it is "'necessary to dispel this illusion. The Politburo is a fiction. In fact, everything is decided behind its back by a small clique [*kuchka*] that meets in the Kremlin in Tsetkina's former apartment. Kuibyshev, Voroshilov, Kalinin, and Rudzutak are not in this clique while, by contrast, others, not members of the Politburo, for instance, Iakovlev and Postyshev, are.'"[63] Moreover, Reznikov asserts, when pressed as to whether "'some members of the Politburo can be counted on?'" Syrtsov had replied, "'Yes, when the matter becomes somewhat more serious.'"[64]

Syrtsov's direct testimony seems to bear out much of Reznikov's account. We have a stenogram excerpt of Syrtsov's responses when he appeared before a joint committee of the CCC and the Politburo. There he maintained that "'it seems to me that the ruling group of the CC [by which he meant the Politburo] is not fully free in a number of its actions, that here there's a certain automaticity [*avtomatizm*] of actions. . . . It seems to me a not normal situation when a certain group judges in advance a whole range of Politburo decisions. I fully understand when Rykov, as a person having committed rightist mistakes and pursuing an incorrect political line, is excluded. But as far as I understand, Kuibyshev, Rudzutak, and Kalinin do not participate at all in this group and are members of the Politburo in name only [*mekhanicheskimi chlenami*].'"[65]

Syrtsov seems to have drawn blood by his accusations. Stalin felt obliged to deny the charges of the existence of a faction that was the real ruling group given that (with the exception of Rykov) the Politburo by 1930 was made up entirely of Stalin supporters—Trotsky, the left, and the right having in turn been defeated. At a joint session of the Politburo and the Presidium of the CCC ten days after Syrtsov had been questioned, Stalin, Khlevniuk tells us, said, in a classic nondenial denial, that he had met individually with "'Molotov, Kalinin, Sergo [Ordzhonikidze], Rudzutak, Mikoyan'" ostensibly to prepare his speech for the Sixteenth Party Congress. "'Neither Kaganovich, nor Iakovlev, nor Postyshev . . . were in this apartment. Did we sometimes meet with

---

[62] Khlevniuk et al., *Stalinskoe Politburo*, p. 97 and reproduced from Soviet archives.
[63] Ibid.
[64] Ibid.
[65] Ibid., p. 99, deletions by Khlevniuk et al., and excerpted in Khlevniuk, *Politburo*, p. 46.

several members of the Politburo? Yes, we met. We met mainly in the facilities of the Central Committee. What's bad about this?'"[66]

In the bad old days of the Soviet Union, cynics defined "creative Marxism-Leninism" as revisionism by those in power. "Meet[ing] with several members of the Politburo" turned out to be factionalism in power. That being said, it is important to realize that in the early 1930s Stalin's standard modus operandi was to act as though he felt he could not act on his own without clearing a decision with the members of the Politburo or a sizeable sample thereof. A Politburo member such as Sergo Ordzhonikidze had enough independent stature and resources that Stalin felt he needed to treat "Sergo" with sensitivity.[67] Moreover, Ordzhonikidze could sometimes protect his friends and clients,[68] and that is apparently why Lominadze—and by extension perhaps Syrtsov—was treated relatively mildly in response to what might have been viewed as treasonous conspiring.

Ordzhonikidze played the political game pretty well. During the discussion of what was to be done about Syrtsov and Lominadze, he was the most strident, saying that there was no place in the Party for double dealers. In practice, however, neither Lominadze nor Syrtsov was actually expelled from the Party. According to Khlevniuk,[69] Lominadze was expelled "only" from the Central Committee, relatively mild punishment for his misdeeds. Ordzhonikidze advanced Lominadze's career throughout the first half of the 1930s. "In August 1933, Lominadze was awarded an Order of Lenin and soon . . . left Moscow to become the secretary of the city party committee in Magnitogorsk."[70]

There is a certain irony to the treatment of Syrtsov and Lominadze. They really were double dealers. This phrase, which became a pervasive theme after the Seventeenth Party Congress and the murder of Kirov in December 1934, came to be applied by Stalin to vast numbers of people who had never engaged in any actions against the regime. It

[66] Khlevniuk, *Politburo*, p. 48.

[67] An example from Lih et al., *Stalin's Letters* (p. 123) where Stalin asks Molotov to smooth a matter over with Ordzhonikidze is revealing: "The sooner you take care of this little thing, the better."

[68] This is Khlevniuk's argument. See Khlevniuk, *Politburo*, p. 170.

[69] Khlevniuk, *In Stalin's Shadow*, p. 39. In Lih et al., *Stalin's Letters*, p. 197 it is reported that Lominadze was "expelled from the party." This seems to be in error. Likewise Getty, *Origins of the Great Purges*, p. 19, has "Lominadze expelled from the party for a short time, but soon readmitted and appointed the party secretary . . . [for] the Magnitogorsk construction project." The direct quote, cited in Khlevniuk et al. (*Stalinskoe Politburo*, p. 106), of the resolution adopted by a joint session of the Politburo and the Presidium of the Central Control Commission speaks only of a decision "to remove Syrtsov and Lominadze from membership" of the Central Committee.

[70] Khlevniuk, *In Stalin's Shadow*, pp. 69–70.

is best epitomized by Stalin's "Saboteurs disguise themselves by over fulfilling the plan" and prefigures the conception of false preferences so ably elaborated by Kuran.[71]

The autonomy of the Politburo diminished rather steadily during the 1930s. With the opposition in the Politburo removed, the famous *kto-kogo* (who [does in] whom) seemed resolved, but questions of who gets what (*kto-chego*) remained burning issues to be decided in, and to some extent by, the Politburo. Both those Politburo members in opposition (Bukharin was removed from the Politburo in April 1929, Tomsky at the Sixteenth Party Congress June/July 1930, and Rykov in December 1930) and Stalin's staunch supporters had nontrivial institutional resources at their disposal. There was enormous overlap in membership in the Politburo and in other key institutions, both party and governmental. Those with governmental positions fought to receive preference for those institutions that were part of their portfolio of responsibilities. (A central theme of Khlevniuk's many publications is that, contrary to Getty's *Origins of the Great Purges*, it is institutional position and role that drove conflict between and among Politburo members in the 1930s rather than a moderate/hardliner divide.)

In addition, the evidence is compelling that Sergo Ordzhonikidze, at least, fought to preserve the autonomy of his institutional base (especially as commissar [minister] for heavy industry from 1932 to 1937), to protect those people within his administrative purview, and retain for the Politburo a role in policy making. In contrast, Lazar Kaganovich, confronted by the challenge of the arrests in his industrial bailiwick and to the Politburo as an institution, took the way out of becoming even more committed to Stalin,[72] seeking the boon Ulysses asked of the Cyclops: to be eaten last.

Needless to say, Kaganovich's acts were to no avail. The erosion of the Politburo as an institutional counterweight to the General Secretary proceeded apace as the 1930s advanced, especially after the Seventeenth Party Congress (January/February 1934) and the assassination of Kirov in December of the same year. We saw above (p. 86 and pp. 91–92) that with the expulsion of the right from the Politburo Stalin began to act unilaterally and at variance with the notion of the Politburo as a collective leadership in 1929–30. If we fast-forward half a dozen years, we see that Stalin was systematically undermining the norms that had set off

---

[71] Timur Kuran treats false preferences as the propensity to express socially acceptable views rather than one's genuine opinions. "Now out of Never: The Element of Surprise in the East European Revolution of 1989," *World Politics*, Vol. 44, No. 1 (October 1991), pp. 7–48 and in a subsequent book, *Private Truths, Public Lies: The Social Consequences of Preference Falsification* (Cambridge, MA: Harvard University Press, 1995).

[72] Khlevniuk, *Politburo*, p. 177.

the Politburo from actions targeted against the masses or, by the mid-1930s, even high Party officials. The rules against the arrest of Politburo members without the permission of the Politburo were ignored, as was the custom of removing a leading figure from his post in the Politburo or Central Committee prior to his arrest.

The meetings of "the fives" and "the sixes" became increasingly the relevant decisional bodies, not the Politburo. Indeed by 1937 this reality had become institutionalized. In a decree adopted in April 1937, at the peak of the purges, the Politburo effectively signed its own death warrant deciding

1. To create a permanent commission of the Politburo, the members of which will be Comrades Stalin, Molotov, Voroshilov, L. Kaganovich, and Yezhov, with the goal of preparing for Politburo [action] and in case of pressing urgency—for determination—of secret matters including foreign policy.

2. To create a permanent commission of the Politburo, the members of which will be Comrades Molotov, Stalin, Chubar', Mikoyan, and L. Kaganovich, with the goal of preparing for Politburo [action] on pressing current economic matters.[73]

As Khlevniuk[74] notes, this resolution effectively legitimized the existing practice of having "a narrow group consisting of Stalin and his closest collaborators" make decisions that were then ratified by the Politburo. Khrushchev tells us that the practice of having quintets, sextets, septets, and novenaries was further institutionalized by a Politburo resolution of October 3, 1946, proposed by Stalin, that

1. The Political Bureau Commission for Foreign Affairs ("Sextet") is to concern itself in the future, in addition to foreign affairs, also with matters of internal construction and domestic policy.

2. The Sextet is to add to its roster the Chairman of the State Commission of Economic Planning of the USSR, Comrade Voznesensky, and is to be known as a Septet.[75]

Khrushchev further tells us that Kliment Voroshilov, "one of the oldest members of our Party" and a long-time member of the Politburo, was "deprived of the right of participation in Political Bureau sessions": "When the Political Bureau was in session and Comrade Voroshilov heard about it, he telephoned each time and asked whether he would

[73] Ibid., pp. 237–38.
[74] Ibid., p. 238.
[75] *Anti-Stalin Campaign*, p. 83.

be allowed to attend. Sometimes Stalin permitted it, but always showed his dissatisfaction."[76] Indeed, the Politburo in the last years of Stalin's tenure as general secretary could not even play the role of an ejectorate, as evidenced by what Khrushchev termed "one of the most unbridled acts of willfulness," namely, Stalin's removing Andrei Andreyev from the Politburo "by unilateral decision."[77]

Moreover, the Politburo, after 1931 composed exclusively of persons closely tied to Stalin, felt the wrath of the purges, especially the Great Purge of 1937–38. Unlike previous purges, these impinged directly on the members of the Politburo. In the next chapter, we discuss how the systematic use of terror was a central feature of Stalin's method of dealing with those who opposed him or might conceivably oppose him at some future date. This, as we will see, applied particularly to kulaks, industrial specialists, nationalities concentrated on the borders, senior military officers, Old Bolsheviks, and attendees of the Seventeenth Party Congress. In the late 1930s it turned out even to apply to those who in 1930 had been Stalin's closest allies in the Politburo.

Stalin's way of intimidating the members of the Politburo was not subtle. Khrushchev certainly has a point when he says that Nikolai Bulganin had told him "'[i]t has happened sometimes that a man goes to Stalin on his invitation as a friend. And when he sits with Stalin, he does not know where he will be sent next, home or to jail.'"[78] Nevertheless, Stalin more typically engaged in a kind of vicious incrementalism. A typical pattern would proceed as follows. Stalin demonstrated his power by having the secret police initially arrest persons who were the Politburo members' second- or third-tier subordinates. These people would typically be induced to confess via some mix of horrific torture and promises that if they confessed, the consequences for them and for their relatives would be less dire. (Spouses and children of "enemies of the people" were almost always arrested.) These confessions would often implicate their superiors who had closer ties to the Politburo member. Some relatives were often purged at this juncture as well. Meanwhile, the Politburo member would typically be transferred to a relatively minor governmental position, downgraded to a mere member of the Central Committee, and his case transmitted to the Party Control Commission. Charges of links to Trotsky, arrest and confession, and death by shooting were the most frequent outcome, though in several instances suicide might be the last step in the process,

[76] Ibid., p. 84.
[77] Ibid.
[78] Ibid., p. 82.

occurring sometimes before the above scenario played out entirely and sometimes before or after being arrested.[79]

Our best documentation of Stalin's salami tactics concerns the way he threatened Sergo Ordzhonikidze by systematically chipping away at the boundaries that separated those whom Ordzhonikidze could protect and those he could not. Ordzhonikidze had been a regional party secretary in the Caucasus soon after the revolution, a member of the Central Committee from 1921 to 1927, a candidate member of the Politburo in 1926, and a member from 1930 on. He also held simultaneously major posts such as being head of the Party Control Commission and, from 1932 on, the people's commissar for heavy industry. Stalin targeted Ordzhonikidze's former cronies, "his" engineers and technicians, including his deputy, Georgy Pyatakov, and his older brother.

Ordzhonikidze's political behavior in the 1930s is vivid testimony to the dictum made famous by Graham Allison a generation ago: "Where you stand depends on where you sit."[80] We have already noted Ordzhonikidze's ability to protect Lominadze in the early 1930s (above, p. 93). In this and other instances, Ordzhonikidze was playing a role typically encountered in Soviet politics, namely a regional party secretary (in this instance a former regional party secretary) providing protection for "his" people with whom he had close personal and career ties. Lominadze (who had earlier weathered charges of being a leftist), however, got caught up in the wave of suspicions prompted by the implications for him and others of the trials (the decisions of which were rendered in January 1935) both of the "Moscow Center" (which included

---

[79] A couple of short CVs are illustrative. The former head of the trade unions, Mikhail Tomsky, committed suicide the day the state prosecutor, Andrei Vyshinsky, included his name among those implicated by Kamenev and Zinoviev in their trial. He had been a member of the Party since 1904, a member of the Central Committee 1919–34, and a member of the Politburo 1922–30. His career trajectory turned downward in 1929 when he became a deputy head of the Supreme Economic Council and the head of the All Union chemical industry association until his death in 1936. From 1932 to 1936 he was also head of the association of state publishing houses. One of the secret police chiefs, N. I. Yezhov, had the following resume: A member of the Party from 1917, he rose meteorically in the mid-1930s. He became a member of the Central Committee and a member of the Party Control Commission. He was appointed deputy head of the latter in 1934 and head from 1935. He then became NKVD Commissar in 1936 and a candidate member of the Politburo in 1937. Each of these later appointments was short-lived: He was replaced as NKVD Commissar in 1938 and became Commissar for Water Transport the same year. He was removed from the Politburo in 1939 and shot February 4, 1940. For useful thumbnail sketches of virtually all the relevant players in Soviet politics in the 1930s, see Khlevniuk et al., *Stalinskoe Politburo*, pp. 259–321, from which the above is drawn.

[80] Graham T. Allison, *Essence of Decision: Explaining the Cuban Missile Crisis* (Boston: Little, Brown, 1971), p. 176.

Zinoviev and Kamenev) as well as the "Leningrad Counterrevolution-ary Zinovievite Group."[81] Each pointed to Lominadze's vulnerability to charges. Lominadze committed suicide to avoid arrest and, minimally, incarceration. Even after Lominadze's death, Ordzhonikidze continued to provide support for his family. His wife actually received a pension from 1935 to 1937, but after Ordzhonikidze's death in 1937 she was ar-rested in 1938 and again in 1950 as the wife of an enemy of the people.[82]

In the Caucasus, Ordzhonikidze had been a hothead and something of a hell-raiser. As head of the CCC, he had been among the most hard-line members of Stalin's inner circle. He was just as protective of his own people as commissar for heavy industry, but "his" people now were a different sort. In that role, he came to recognize the destabiliz-ing and counterproductive nature of mass purges, especially those tar-geted at technical specialists and engineers responsible for generating the industrial output central to the fulfillment of the Five-Year Plans: "a normally functioning People's Commissariat" was "impossible with-out a certain amount of cadre stability."[83] The terror resulted in indus-trial leaders saying openly that the engineers were caught between the proverbial rock and a hard place: They feared being accused of being "saboteurs" on the one hand, and being excessively conservative on the other. As a result, they were increasingly working to rule—"'trying to do everything'" by the book.[84]

Ordzhonikidze strongly and deftly defended the efforts of the engi-neers and termed the existence of widespread sabotage "'nonsense.'"[85] An instructive illustration of how he tried to limit the impact of the charges of sabotage is provided by how he instructed one Professor Galperin to investigate the charges of heavy industry and sabotage in the industrial city of Kemerovo. "'Take into account,'" Ordzhoni-kidze instructed Galperin, "'you're going to a place that was one of the more active centers of sabotage. . . . You must approach the matter as a technician, trying to distinguish conscious sabotage from involuntary mistakes—this is your main task.'"[86]

With these marching orders, Galperin and his committee produced a document that Stalin likely and Molotov certainly considered a

[81] Khlevniuk, *In Stalin's Shadow*, pp. 75–76.

[82] Ibid., p. 77.

[83] Khlevniuk, *Politburo*, p. 170.

[84] Ibid., p. 174. Literally the quote is to do everything according "to the letter of the law (*po bukve zakona*)."

[85] Ibid., p. 175.

[86] Khlevniuk, *In Stalin's Shadow*, p. 131, citing an account published in *Za industrializat-siyu*, February 21, 1937, after Ordzhonikidze's death and before Stalin made it clear that Ordzhonikidze was persona non grata.

whitewash. The latter charged that the forty-five-page report Galperin submitted had said nothing about sabotage "'in spite of the well-known confessions of wreckers such as Norkin, Drobnis, and others, the commission presented the usual sort of conclusion about shortcomings in construction, but missed one point—sabotage.'"[87]

Stalin continued to pressure Ordzhonikidze, this time by targeting a key family member. (It must be reiterated that other Politburo members, even Molotov, had family members arrested.) Ordzhonikidze celebrated his fiftieth birthday in October 1936. It occasioned a nationwide celebration. In what must have been perceived by Ordzhonikidze as a direct threat, the NKVD arrested his older brother, news of which Ordzhonikidze learned on his birthday. According to his wife, he refused to participate in a celebration to honor him, and she attended on her own.[88] In a matter of months after his birthday, Ordzhonikidze committed suicide.

Conclusion

After Trotsky, the Left Opposition, and the Right Opposition had been defeated, it was unlikely, but not inconceivable, that the Politburo circa 1930 could rein in Stalin. This was so even though, after Rykov's ouster, the Politburo was composed entirely of Stalin's supporters and the Central Committee was heavily populated by regional Party secretaries selected by the Secretariat. The regional Party secretaries had experienced the near-civil-war conditions that accompanied collectivization. Not all were completely beholden to Stalin, even though they owed their appointment to him. Many of them, it turned out, could conceivably have been mobilized to support some alteration in Stalin's status had a majority of the Politburo actively favored some discrete way of lessening Stalin's hold over the Party apparatus.

At least some in the Politburo evidently thought in 1930 that the seemingly obsequious step of encouraging Stalin to abandon his dominant role in the Secretariat in favor of doing as Lenin had done, namely, chairing Sovnarkom, the most powerful governmental institution, might be an effective ploy to weaken Stalin and result in something more like collective leadership. As much as the Politburo members

---

[87] Khlevniuk, *In Stalin's Shadow*, p. 131, citing *Voprosy istorii*, No. 8, 1993, at p. 18.

[88] Khlevniuk, *Politburo*, p. 178. While not relevant to the account in the text, Khlevniuk has a quite different read on Lavrenti Beria's role in the undermining of Ordzhonikidze's position than does Robert Tucker in his biography, *Stalin in Power*. Others have built on Tucker's argument to conclude that Stalin had Ordzhonikidze murdered. This is not Tucker's view nor Khlevniuk's, each of whom concludes he committed suicide.

and Stalin himself were subject to the dictator's curse—getting bogged down by having to decide thousands of trivial matters[89]—the likelihood was that Stalin, as the recognized leader, would have gotten even more bogged down by trivia as the chairman of Sovnarkom. This in turn would have increased the Politburo's degrees of freedom—or so, apparently, both members of the Politburo and Stalin concluded. Syrtsov may very well have been correct if he thought that members of the Politburo would support the efforts to limit Stalin's power and to restore the collective leadership that he, Syrtsov, considered normal and desirable, "When the matter becomes somewhat more serious."[90] What he seems to have missed completely was an awareness that the members of the 1930 Politburo faced a collective action problem. All, or virtually all, the Politburo members had to be convinced that all the other Politburo members would act vigorously to rein in Stalin and that all the other Politburo members were convinced each Politburo member would endorse such a move, and so on.

In this respect, Stalin and the Politburo were in a position in 1930 not much different from typical juntas, which constitute a very small ruling group, confronting the perennial dilemma whether the clear leader is to be first among equals or the first above equals.[91]

But, very quickly the situation changed. As we saw, Stalin as general secretary initially acted on his own by preempting the Politburo on a minor issue—how to respond to the deputy finance commissar's letter and by preempting a Politburo commission on a matter of profound implications—calling for the "liquidation of the kulaks as a class," without suffering any costs. By the middle of the decade—after the Seventeenth Party Congress and after the assassination of Kirov—Stalin's unilateral acts become more frequent. Khrushchev, in the secret speech, tells us that "without the approval of the Politbureau" and "on Stalin's initiative" a Central Executive Committee edict was issued that

    I. Investigative agencies are directed to speed up the cases of those accused of the preparation or execution of acts of terror.

    II. Judicial organs are directed not to hold up the execution of death sentences pertaining to [such] crimes in order to consider the possibility of pardon, because the Presidium of the Central Executive

---

[89] Gregory, *The Political Economy*, p. 68. Gregory cites a mind-boggling letter from Kaganovich detailing his activities during the course of two ordinary days at the end of August 1931 that were of sufficient importance to pass on to Stalin (ibid., p. 69) and refers to the table Khlevniuk presents in *Politburo*, pp. 288–91 detailing the number of items discussed in Politburo meetings—about three thousand a year—during the 1930s.

[90] See note 64 above and the relevant text.

[91] Roeder, *Red Sunset*, p. 7.

Committee [of the] USSR does not consider as possible the receiving of petitions of this sort.

III. The organs of the Commissariat of Internal Affairs [NKVD] are directed to execute death sentences against criminals of the above-mentioned category immediately after the passage of sentences.[92]

With this decree, the boundaries between Party members, even Politburo members, and others in the Soviet population lost all meaning. Everyone, with the exception of Stalin and a handful of his closest aides such as Aleksandr Poskrebyshev had become what Bueno de Mesquita et al. term "disenfranchised residents."[93] Bearing in mind that Yevgeniya Ginzburg had it right when she observed that "[t]he year 1937 began for all intents and purposes, . . . on the first of December [1934],"[94] in 1937 and 1938 "any charge . . . could be fitted within the rubric of terrorism. . . . [It was] a term with infinite flexibility."[95] The terror, which had been used to mobilize the largest element in the Soviet population, the peasantry, and then was applied to a second very large category, nationalities that were found in bordering countries as well, now applied to all.

[92] *Anti-Stalin Campaign*, p. 25

[93] Bueno de Mesquita et al., *The Logic of Political Survival*, p. 39. See also Gill, *The Origins of the Stalinist Political System*, pp. 294–96.

[94] Yevgeniya Semenovna Ginzburg, *Journey into the Whirlwind* (New York: Harcourt, Brace, 1967), p. 3.

[95] Gill, *The Origins of the Stalinist Political System*, p. 296.

CHAPTER 4

The Great Purge

THE PRIMARY FOCUS OF the terror shifted by 1935 from the class-based "elimination of the kulak as a class" to the generic "enemy of the people." At the same time, major changes, similarly, took place in incentives, norms, and controls and what the central leadership valued. (Some initial steps in this direction overlap chronologically with the Cultural Revolution.)

These changes were such that Nicholas Timasheff was largely, but not completely, correct when more than half a century ago he maintained that something akin to a Great Retreat had occurred. One recent critic has faulted him for failing to recognize that the goal of constructing socialism[1] never changed. This seems to me tilting at a windmill of the author's own construction. The concept of "retreat" implies a tactical withdrawal and is entirely compatible with unchanged goals. What most certainly happened was that some key bases for mobilization were transformed, often quite dramatically. Rather than mobilize through symbols and institutions that bespoke of Marxism, the regime rediscovered Russia, rejected egalitarianism, adopted measures that had been previously scorned as bourgeois, and strengthened Party and secret police controls in almost every sector of society. But Kenneth Jowitt and Gail Lapidus are right in faulting Timasheff for failing to note the impact of the mobilization and violence of collectivization and the Cultural Revolution which, as it were, paved the way for what Timasheff reported.[2] Moreover, it bears reminding the obvious: that is, the measures taken to provide incentives to those whom the regime favored were coterminous with use of "terror as a system of power."[3] The years after collectivization, the first Five-Year Plan, the famine of

---

[1] Timasheff, *The Great Retreat*; David L. Hoffmann, *Stalinist Values: The Cultural Norms of Soviet Modernity, 1917–1941* (Ithaca, NY: Cornell University Press, 2003). "Socialism in one country" was also taken as an analogous indication that Soviet foreign policy goals had changed. Alexander Dallin was fond of saying that "Socialism in one country at a time" was a more apt description of Soviet foreign policy in the Stalin period.

[2] Lapidus, "Educational Strategies," pp. 78–104, and Jowitt, *New World Disorder: The Leninist Extinction* (Berkeley: University of California Press, 1992).

[3] The title of chap. 13 of Fainsod, *How Russia.*

the winter 1932–33, and the termination of the Cultural Revolution, witnessed dramatic changes in urban life for all. The simultaneity of these major changes and the ghastly purges, most notably in 1937–38, give the mid-1930s a complexity in the regime's relationship to parts of Soviet society—primarily the urban populace and non-Russian nationalities—that is sometimes ignored or misinterpreted. Both the changes and the purges are discussed in this chapter.

The best effort by a cultural historian to capture everyday life in urban Russia in the 1930s is that by Sheila Fitzpatrick, who defines the ambit of her coverage "as everyday interactions that in some way involved the state."[4] This, she says, implies that with that criterion in mind one can largely ignore "topics like friendship, love, and some aspects of leisure and private sociability." She then proceeds to enumerate the topics that do conform to her criterion: "Shopping, traveling, celebrating, telling jokes, finding an apartment, getting an education, securing a job, advancing in one's career, cultivating patrons and connections, marrying and rearing children, writing complaints and denunciations, voting, and trying to steer clear of the secret police."[5] She is correct that all these items do belong on the list. Moreover, she fully appreciates what this implies for our understanding of regime-society relations in the 1930s.

This leaves me puzzled why she asserts that one can largely ignore topics like friendship and love. Sad to relate, the state and the Party were much involved in matters of friendship. I am hard-pressed to explain the distinction she has in mind in including (appropriately) marrying and rearing children but excluding love. Stephen Kotkin and Oleg Kharkhordin have both treated the extent to which mutual surveillance colored friendships and how, in Kharkhordin's words, "networks of friends . . . could subvert the true collectivity of the *kollektiv*."[6]

For Soviet authorities, characteristics of deep friendships raised suspicions. Pressure on individuals was less effective when that person had someone whom he or she could trust with shared confidences regardless of the pressure exerted on such a friend. (This was of course but one of the many ways the regime sought to achieve the atomization that was core to its efforts to convince subjects that the negative views they might have were idiosyncratic.) In the 1930s, the testing of such friendships came largely from the secret police. Bonds between those

---

[4] Fitzpatrick, *Everyday Stalinism*, p. 3.
[5] Ibid.
[6] Oleg Kharkhordin, *The Collective and the Individual in Russia: A Study of Practices* (Berkeley: University of California Press, 1999), especially p. 108; Stephen Kotkin, *Magnetic Mountain: Stalinism as Civilization* (Berkeley: University of California Press, 1995).

with shared experiences in the camps[7] or who refused to betray each other under torture represented extraordinary ties, ones citizens of Western states rarely experience except in foxholes during war time.[8] (The opposite side of the coin, of course, was that the penetration of the society was such that the barriers to interpersonal trust and hence to genuine friendship were very high. Anna did not know whether Sergei was a true friend given that he, Sergei, might be a secret police informant or someone who might well denounce her.[9])

Love, too, was affected by the regime's nearly ubiquitous presence. Perhaps there was no greater symbol of the regime's efforts to establish the principle that loyalty to the Party and the state—"the Fatherland above all"—transcended all other relationships than the effort to glorify Pavlik Morozov. Soviet accounts credited him for denouncing his father and then made him a martyr, alleging that he had been murdered by members of his own family.

The literature agrees that there was a Pavlik Morozov who was murdered, but not on much else. As a reviewer of one recent book about him observes, "We know next to nothing about the little boy who acquired an enormous, nationwide reputation. Beyond that he lived and that he was murdered, every aspect of his story is in doubt. It is not even certain that he in fact committed that act that made him famous or infamous: denouncing his father."[10] What is certain, though, is that he acquired an iconic existence as a result of the regime's effort to make a hero out of someone who had "ratted" on his father as a way of subordinating love for parents to love of the motherland.

Fitzpatrick's own account of marriage and divorce is but one such account[11] that depicts how the interactions of spouses were often fundamentally affected by the regime's presence in their daily lives and

---

[7] One reason for the success of the 1956 Hungarian Revolution was that, while in the camps, major figures in the various noncommunist parties often shared prison cells with leaders from other parties. They became bonded. When an amnesty resulted in their release they resumed their ties with the members of their respective parties and told these people that their cell mates—and, by implication, other noncommunist parties— could be trusted. Civil society was relinked almost over night. Cf. Paul Kecskemeti, *The Unexpected Revolution: Social Forces in the Hungarian Uprising* (Stanford, CA: Stanford University Press, 1961).

[8] In later, less repressive, times, Oleg Kharkhordin points out (*The Collective*, p. 319) communal pressure was used for the same purpose (to more mixed results).

[9] On the duty to denounce under tsarist rule, see A. M. Kleimola, "The Duty to Denounce in Muscovite Russia," *Slavic Review*, Vol. 31, No. 4 (1972), pp. 759–79.

[10] See Peter Kenez's review of Catriona Kelly, *Comrade Pavlik: The Rise and Fall of a Soviet Boy Hero* (London: Granta Books, 2005) in *Slavic Review*, Vol. 65, No. 3 (2006), pp. 610–11 at p. 610.

[11] Among many others, see Yevgeniya Ginzburg, *Journey into the Whirlwind* (New York: Harcourt Brace, 1967).

literally in the rooms of their apartments. Given that persons married to an enemy of the people were often characterized as such themselves, choice of a partner could be affected by an assessment of the probability that person would be incarcerated or shot. Especially for persons married to relatively high-profile spouses, the fact of being married to an enemy of the people could often result in being sent to the camps. ("Smirnov has been found to be an enemy of the people. It is inconceivable that Smirnova could have stayed married to such a man throughout 1920s and into the 1930s if she did not share the same vile beliefs. Q.E.D.") For a larger number, it meant loss of job, loss of apartment, and loss of pension.[12]

As a direct result of the movement into the cities of millions of people who were responding to the logic of collectivization and Five-Year Plans, housing was in short supply in the cities. The regime's coercive practices compounded the experiences of urban dwellers. Fitzpatrick uses multiple examples to describe typical situations. These examples illustrate that in practice, her protestations to the contrary notwithstanding, she considered it appropriate to include love under her rubric of "interactions that in some way involved the state."

One that is particularly telling Fitzpatrick draws from the Harvard Russian Refugee Project. In this instance, the couple had divorced but they continued to live together. They continued to act like man and wife, the divorce notwithstanding. Some major part of the reason for their divorce pertained to the regime's impact on the love lives of its citizens. The female half of the couple told the Harvard Project interviewers that the divorce was, in Fitzpatrick's words, "a calculated survival strategy ('We did it [divorced] so that we would not be responsible for each other. If we had been married when my husband was arrested [in 1938], I would not be sitting here today.')."[13] Among the other examples Fitzpatrick cites, perhaps those that most bring out how the regime's behavior affected the interactions between loved ones are those centering on their reactions to the arrest of a partner or a parent. The narrative accounts we have of such assessments largely concern persons of some distinction and/or social status. (Peasants everywhere rarely write books.) The Harvard Project, summarized by Inkeles and Bauer, by contrast, interviewed persons from across the social structure. They concluded that in general worker and peasant families were more often "rent asunder"[14] by the effect of the overall disruption experienced by Soviet citizens as a result of the tumultuous events of the

---

[12] See, especially, Fitzpatrick, *Everyday Stalinism*, pp. 210–11.

[13] Ibid., p. 141.

[14] Alex Inkeles and Raymond Bauer, *The Soviet Citizen: Daily Life in a Totalitarian Society* (Cambridge, MA: Harvard University Press, 1961), p. 213.

interwar period. But they are a bit unclear when they are generalizing about the effects of the overall disruption and when they are referring to the impact specifically of arrests. They *are* clear that on the whole across social groupings, "individuals from families in which some member had been arrested by the secret police tended more often to report their families drew together."[15]

But the pattern was by no means uniform. Communist Party members sometimes assumed that inasmuch as they were innocent they need not prepare for the possibility of arrest. Consequently, they went off to prison acting as though they would be back the next day after things had been straightened out, only to discover that their innocence was irrelevant. Often, of course, they never returned. The members of the family of someone arrested typically took the stance that *their* father or spouse was innocent, but they were sometimes less sure about the others who were arrested at the same time. Other family members of the arrested were plagued by the thought—having internalized the proposition that the Party could not be wrong—that their partner or father was, or at least might be, guilty. Perhaps the most poignantly painful illustration of this comes from Bonner's account and italicized by Fitzpatrick concerning the younger brother "whose first reaction was to accept his [father's] guilt. 'Look what those enemies of the people are like. . . . *Some of them even pretend to be fathers.'*"[16]

Among ethnic Russians, one of the numerically largest target groups for the Great Purge (or Great Terror; used here interchangeably) was the intelligentsia, with the devastation among subgroups such as the Old Bolsheviks, judges and procurators,[17] and senior military officers obviously greater in percentage terms. But it is part of the complexity of an accounting of the 1930s that by the late 1930s (as exemplified by the career of historian Ye. V. Tarle described above, p. 73n121) that it was an occasionally told story that some members of the intelligentsia, whether prerevolutionary or new Soviet member of the intelligentsia, who were not arrested during the 1937–38 Great Terror, even if they had been repressed previously, found themselves rehabilitated, relatively highly paid, and recognized symbolically. This pattern was part of an overall regime strategy of attempting to co-opt a sizeable sector of the urban population by a partial shift away from the emphasis on the means of production, deferred gratification, and, especially, egalitarianism. Instead, the regime offered the citizenry the prospects of the availability

---

[15] Ibid., p. 213.

[16] Elena Bonner, *Mothers and Daughters* (New York: Knopf, 1992), at p. 317 and cited by Fitzpatrick, *Everyday Stalinism*, p. 213, italics in original.

[17] Solomon, *Soviet Criminal Justice*, pp. 244–52.

of a variety of consumer goods. Of course, their price usually meant that only limited numbers of persons—primarily party and state functionaries, literary and artistic elites, and Stakhanovites—could afford them. Nevertheless, their existence and the legitimacy of consuming them were heavily promoted. If the average Ivan worked even harder and more efficiently, he too might ultimately have the opportunity to partake of the nice things, foods, and events of which cultured[18] people partook.

And being cultured became the "in" thing. Vadim Volkov has described how the content of being cultured evolved during the 1930s. In large part, the effort was initially targeted at overcoming the consequences of the massive move to the cities of about three million persons a year as a result of the first Five-Year Plan. Having taken the boy out of the country, the regime's leadership was bent on taking the country out of the boy. In large part this amounted to conventional urban notions of personal hygiene conceived instrumentally.[19] But the alternative to the "country' they advocated also had many of the superficial trappings of Western modernity[20] and urban Russia before the revolution.[21] Personal hygiene was emphasized. Jackets and ties, as illustrated by the change in the garb worn by Politburo members on formal occasions, replaced the postrevolutionary garb. Restaurants in Moscow that had been closed to citizens at the time of the Cultural Revolution were opened to the public, though with price tags for meals that effectively limited their access to political and cultural elites.

As the previous paragraph implies, not all the items that had been previously condemned as bourgeois were items accessible only to the elite. Most obviously (and appropriately), the campaign for personal hygiene was targeted at the newly arrived peasants. But the regime had other nonelite audiences in mind as well. Rather, Moscow provided substantial facilities that appealed to mass publics. These facilities came with messages, but just as the Great Purge is an essential and devastating aspect of regime-society relations in the mid- and late 1930s, so, too, is the regime's provision of leisure time activities an essential component of its modernization strategy. Media presentations and other events that took advantage of new technologies such as movies,

---

[18] These of course were mores, tastes, and goods that had only recently been savaged as bourgeois. Hoffmann, *Stalinist Values*.

[19] Vadim Volkov, "The Concept of Kul'turnost': Notes on the Stalinist Civilizing Process," in Sheila Fitzpatrick, ed., *Stalinism: New Directions* (London: Routledge, 2000), pp. 210–30.

[20] Vera S. Dunham speaks of the emergence of "middle class values" in Stalin's time. *In Stalin's Time. Middleclass Values in Soviet Fiction* (Durham, NC: Duke University Press, 1990).

[21] Volkov, "The Concept of Kul'turnost'."

long-distance motorized races, and air shows, provided both entertainment and an opportunity for the regime to socialize the broad masses
to an awareness of, and pride in, Soviet achievements. Parks of culture
and rest—the most well known being Gorky Park in Moscow—became
widespread. Physical culture activities—paralleling developments in
Nazi Germany—became equally widespread. S. Frederick Starr, in his
definitive account of *Red and Hot: The Fate of Jazz in the Soviet Union*,[22]
reports that the fox-trot (which had been condemned previously) had
become so popular that "[b]y 1934 many factories were offering fox-
trot lessons free of charge to their workers. One or two days a week
workers could stay for an hour after the end of their shift in order
to be instructed in the latest Western dances by fashionably dressed
women hired by management."[23] Richard Stites reports that, with jazz
triumphant, "[d]ance classes were made mandatory for officers in the
Red Army by its commander, Kliment Voroshilov; he and Vyacheslav
Molotov studied the tango."[24]

Politburo member Anastas Mikoyan is credited with having brought
new products or new methods for producing products to Russian mass
audiences. He did the equivalent of selling refrigerators to Eskimos by
popularizing mass-produced and relatively low-priced ice cream. (He
had been impressed by the technology while visiting the United States.)
He advocated the production of good beer (a goal never accomplished in
Soviet times) and liqueurs as core components of a "happy life." Frank-
furters, which had been condemned as an example of bourgeois taste,
became widespread. To top things off, moreover, Mikoyan staunchly
advocated ketchup, another American product that he targeted to the
Russian mass market.[25] As Stalin said, in an oft-quoted remark, "Life
has become better, comrades; life has become more cheerful."

Well, not exactly. The availability of newly arrived consumer goods
heightened Soviet citizens' awareness and gave them a sense of what
modernity might entail. Hot dogs, beer, ketchup, and ice cream, along
with parks to eat them in, that is, American consumer society, were the
products the availability of which would justify the deferred gratification of the first Five-Year Plan and collectivization. With the achievement of communism, the goods available only to foreigners with hard

---

[22] S. Frederick Starr, *Red and Hot: The Fate of Jazz in the Soviet Union*, 2nd ed. (New York:
Oxford University Press, 1994), p. 111.

[23] For evidence that some Komsomol leaders viewed Western dance music hostilely in
1938, see David L. Hoffmann, *Stalinist Values*, p. 33.

[24] Richard Stites, *Russian Popular Culture: Entertainment and Society since 1900* (Cambridge: Cambridge University Press, 1992), pp. 64–97. The reference to Molotov and
Voroshilov doing the tango is at p. 75.

[25] The above paragraph draws heavily on Fitzpatrick, *Stalin's Peasants*, pp. 90–91.

currency, Party officials, media stars, and Stakhanovites—and usually only in special stores—would ultimately be available to all who were truly industrious and politically correct.

The operative word in the previous sentence, though, was "ultimately." At that time, ideas of "abundance under socialism" and "equality" joined the withering away of the state among those Marxist conceptions that would be achieved dialectically—if at all. As we saw, Stalin had initially justified rendering the withering away of the state as passé by arguing that such an achievement required the initial strengthening of the state and its "organs." So too, equality (*uravnilovka*) came increasingly to be seen as something that would be achieved by intensifying inequality in wages and status symbols with the ordinary worker being relegated to the bottom of the urban wage scale. In her book *In Stalin's Time*,[26] Vera S. Dunham described how the core themes of Soviet novels changed. Put simply (personal conversation with author) what Dunham found was that in the early postrevolutionary years, mothers advised their sons that if they worked hard they could become really good workers. In later novels, by contrast, Soviet mothers told their children, "Stop lying around the house. If you continue to act this way, you're going to grow up to be nothing but an ordinary worker." Data gathered in the Harvard Interview Project indicated that the mothers Dunham described did indeed know best, as Table 4.1 demonstrates. It was difficult by the mid-1930s not to notice the manifest status differentials that resulted in these wage differentials.

Two distinctions were no longer emphasized. These were the distinction between citizens and nonpersons—priests, kulaks, etc.—who had been disenfranchised in the 1918 Russian and 1924 Soviet constitutions and the one between Party and non-Party comrades. The 1936 "Stalin" Constitution declared the country to be divided into two harmonious classes—workers and peasants—and a stratum, the intelligentsia. The latter was now largely composed of persons whose social origins had been worker or peasant. There was an underlying grisly reality—vast numbers of former persons and others who did not fit these categories had been incarcerated, exiled, or killed—that rendered this observation in the Constitution fairly accurate empirically.

So too Stalin blurred the distinction between Party member and non-Party members. Both, for Stalin, could be Bolsheviks. One ominous aspect to this was the implicit message that Old Bolsheviks were not a priori to be treated with deference and that Party membership was no protection from the purges. At the same time, Stalin was also arguing that in contrast to the Cultural Revolution of only a few years previous,

[26] Dunham, *In Stalin's Time*, passim.

Table 4.1 Incomes from Soviet occupational groups, 1940 (annual income in rubles)

Occupation	Less than R4,200 (%)	R4,200 to R6,599 (%)	R6,600 or more (%)	Total (n)
Professional- administrative	8	29	63	115
Semiprofessional	43	37	20	93
White-collar	59	35	7	130
Skilled worker	52	32	15	80
Semiskilled worker	67	26	7	193
Unskilled worker	87	11	2	64

Source: Alex Inkeles and Raymond Bauer, *The Soviet Citizen: Daily Life in a Totalitarian Society* (Cambridge MA: Harvard University Press, 1961), p. 113.
Note: Some rows do not total to 100 percent due to rounding.

persons trained before the October Revolution were no longer to be a priori suspect. He was also signaling the enormous prospects for upper mobility for those who truly bought into the system. In May 1935 Stalin declared, Tucker[27] reports, that "[a] Bolshevik is one who is devoted to the end to the cause of the proletarian revolution. There are many such among nonparty people. Either they haven't had time to enter the party's ranks or they see it as so holy that they want to prepare better to enter the party's ranks. Oftentimes such people, *such comrades* stand even taller than many and many a party member. They are faithful to the grave." Determining in such circumstances who had truly bought into the system must have been quite a trick—and was often as capricious as were the many arrests for no reason. At precisely the same time, early 1935[28] (immediately after the December 1934 murder of Kirov), Stalin and others were stridently urging people to denounce double dealers (*dvurushiki*) who were hiding behind masks—by overfulfilling the plan, by hiding their social origins, by covertly supporting Trotsky while declaring their fidelity to the Party and to Stalin personally. In contemporary parlance, these were people who manifested "false preferences."[29]

In multiple other ways, the message of status inequality with its consequential implications for material benefits became not only pronounced in the mid-1930s but often readily visible. With reason, what Tucker terms the emergence of a new service nobility took place

[27] Stalin, as cited in Tucker, *Stalin in Power*, p. 321, italics added.
[28] Tucker, *Stalin in Power*, p. 307.
[29] Timur Kuran's classic "Now Out of Never," pp. 7–48.

composed of fast risers largely drawn from working class or peasant backgrounds. In the army officer ranks were restored, as were dress uniforms, as was appropriate pomp and circumstance. The people's commissar for defense was now *Marshal* Kliment Voroshilov.[30]

The introduction of ranks in the military was only the beginning. The NKVD also received ranks, ranging, Tucker notes, from sergeant to commissar first rank and wearing pants the color of those of the tsarist secret police.[31] The secret police and the army were scarcely unique in their adoption of uniforms and titles. Fitzpatrick's list is worth reproducing and lends credence to Tucker's reference to a new service nobility: "Titles, ranks, and uniforms were reinstated. In 1934, a government commission recommended that distinctive uniforms be introduced for personnel in civil aviation, waterways and fishing authorities, lumber export, and the polar exploration agency, in addition to those already worn by railroad personnel and militiamen. All uniforms would indicate rank in the same way, by semicircles, circles, pentagons, and stars, and include a greatcoat and field jacket with leather belts at the waist. For managerial . . . personnel, one shoulder strap was to be fastened to the belt."[32]

Then there were the "orders." Some dated from early after the Revolution. They proliferated in the mid-1930s[33] and persisted throughout the communist period. In the mid-1930s one might become a "People's Artist of the Soviet Union" and would always be introduced as such in, for instance, giving a concert. One might receive an Order of Lenin and, from 1939 on, a Stalin prize.[34] These carried with them substantial prize money. There were lesser prizes and orders as well: the Red Banner of Labor, Order of the Sign of Honor, Heroes of Labor, and the like. All

---

[30] Fitzpatrick, *Everyday Stalinism*, p. 108. Fitzpatrick quotes a communist author's diary description of the November 1935 parade in observance of the October Revolution: "Voroshilov received the parade on a marvelous horse in a new marshal's uniform. . . . The troops were also in new uniform. They have got epaulettes, which have not been seen for 18 years. For the junior officer corps, lance-corporals, sergeants, sergeant-majors, stripes have been reintroduced, for the officers, gold epaulettes."

[31] Tucker, *Stalinism*, p. 323 and p. 648 and also cited by Fitzpatrick, *Everyday Stalinism*, p. 108.

[32] Fitzpatrick, *Everyday Stalinism*, p. 107. Fitzpatrick (ibid.) rightly points out that the return to school uniforms implied that there were no visible differences among students. On the other hand, in the late 1930s teachers acquired titles and students found that the pre-revolutionary five marks ranging from very poor to excellent had been restored. Tucker, *Stalinism*, p. 323.

[33] Tucker, *Stalinism*, p. 322.

[34] Timasheff, *The Great Retreat*, p. 319 points out that during World War II, orders named after prerevolutionary heroes such as Aleksandr Suvorov, Mikhail Kutuzov, and Aleksandr Nevsky were introduced to augment those such as the Order of Lenin.

these provided some monthly stipend. According to Shlapentokh, "By 1984, there were 16 national titles for figures in the arts, and 20 types of medals."[35] These markers of status led to known increases in wages.[36] But status also resulted in nonmonetary gains that further stratified the society.[37] Chief of these was access. Top Party and government executives and prize winners alike received access to special stores—where goods were often less expensive than in regular stores or simply were available—and priority access to scarce goods like vacations on the Black Sea and "annual free rail trips, and preferential school admission for one's children."[38]

The efforts to reach out to new elites and to provide entertainment to an even broader public were a major component of regime/society relations in the mid- and late 1930s. The Soviet Constitution had portrayed a harmonious society of workers, peasants, and intelligentsia. Stalin had his own distinctive way of creating a harmonious society of workers, peasants, and intelligentsia. While utilizing material incentives to increase productivity and to conjure images of himself as the beneficent leader, Stalin moved to repress whole categories of people who might conceivably represent a threat either to him or Soviet power. Symbolically, in the mid-1930s subjects of repression were no longer categorized in class terms. Having destroyed "the kulaks as a class," the more generic "enemies of the people" came to justify the repression of a wide range of categories of people. Those who know the history of the period almost automatically think of the Old Bolsheviks in this regard in light of their prominence in the spectacular staged trials that were the most vivid episodes during the Great Purge of 1937–38. But they were in a way a mere subset of the putative or real double dealers who were denounced and/or repressed because they either objectively or subjectively[39] constituted a potential threat to the leadership, which in this instance meant Stalin. A sizeable fraction of those repressed were accused of hiding their real identity, their past, or their links, however tenuous, with others who had been repressed. They were managers of plants with ostensibly successful

---

[35] Vladimir Shlapentokh, *A Totalitarian Society: How the Soviet Union Functioned and How It Collapsed* (Armonk, NY: M.E. Sharpe, 2001), p. 69.

[36] On the broader issue of material incentives, see Joseph Berliner's discussion of premiums, *Factory and Management in the USSR* (Cambridge, MA: Harvard University Press, 1957), especially pp. 27–43.

[37] Mention should be made that for many, especially the typical two-wage-earner professional family, having one or two servants was, as Fitzpatrick reports, "'normal.'" *Everyday Stalinism*, p. 99.

[38] Tucker, *Stalinism*, p. 323.

[39] See Oleg Khlevnyuk, "The Objectives of the Great Terror, 1937–38," in Cooper et al., *Soviet History*, pp. 158–76, on the large number of former members of the CPSU who were potentially available for mobilization against Stalin.

production records who were alleged to be saboteurs. They were people who, whatever their current situation, had or had ostensibly supported Trotsky at some early date. They had been or ostensibly had been, for instance, the child of a priest or other nonperson. This, of course, had the effect of rendering everyone suspect and subject to denunciation, including ultimately the secret police themselves.

The story[40] of the disastrous interaction between the macro-political context created by Stalin and the behavior of individuals pursuing their conception of their own interest is vividly illustrated by what transpired in the rocketry research institute (RNII) and is related in an impressive paper by Asif Siddiqi. RNII was formed out of the merger in September 1933 of two institutes, one located in Moscow populated largely by researchers with primary interests in liquid propellants, the other in Leningrad where the research focus was on solid fuel propellants. Liquid propellants would make possible space exploration, while solid fuel propellants were far more relevant to more immediate military concerns.

The merger was largely accomplished by the efforts of Marshal Mikhail Tukhachevsky. Once the merger occurred, however, the institute was subordinated to the People's Commissariat of Heavy Industry and Tukhachevsky no longer had any formal role in the supervision of the Institute. Civilian supervision notwithstanding, military-relevant researchers, who were pro–solid fuel propellant, dominated the institute. They included the first director, Ivan Kleimenov, a Tukhachevsky protégé. Sergei Korolev, a liquid fuel, outer space proponent became the deputy director, but with little power and little role in rocket design.

An ugly intrainstitute quarrel broke out only months after the institute had been formed. This involved, among other things, Kleimenov cutting off the funding of several research projects of the liquid fuel proponents, especially those that entailed the use of liquid oxygen as opposed to nitric acid. (Siddiqi argues that the dispute over the relative advantages of nitric acid and liquid oxygen "engendered much more acrimony than the one over solids and liquids."[41]) Korolev repeatedly complained about the dominant role of the solid fuel engineers, the result of which was that Kleimenov wrote to the local Party committee seeking Korolev's dismissal. "As a compromise, party functionaries demoted Korolev to a junior position." Korolev wrote to Tukhachevsky complaining about Kleimenov and urging that he be fired. According to Siddiqi,[42] Sergo Ordzhonikidze—whom we have already seen

---

[40] Asif Siddiqi, "The Rockets' Red Glare: Technology, Conflict, and Terror in the Soviet Union," *Technology and Culture*, Vol. 44, No. 3 (July 2003), pp. 470–501.
[41] Ibid., p. 482.
[42] Ibid., p. 480.

protect his subordinates in other settings (above, p. 97)—protected Kleimenov. As often happens in such disputes, many of those in the institute resigned, were forced to resign, or were demoted. Among those fired were two strong liquid oxygen advocates, Leonid Korneyev (who was actually fired twice) and Andrei Kostikov, who had attacked both Kleinmenov and Korolev. Kleinmenov ended all research on liquid oxygen rockets in November 1936.

The purge at the national level thrust itself on the rocket institute. In late May 1937, Tukhachevsky was arrested, tried, and shot. The rocket scientists now became involved in a particularly grisly prisoners' dilemma. Mutual denunciations followed almost immediately after Tukhachevsky's execution. Korneyev wrote Marshal Voroshilov terming "'Kleimenov . . . a saboteur, standing [with] the scum of humanity, extraordinary bastards of the twentieth century such as . . . Tukhachevsky and others.'"[43]

Kleimenov retaliated by writing directly to the NKVD demanding "'investigation and bringing to account'" the efforts of several scientists, including Kostikov and Korneyev, who had "'demanded *the reduction of work on powder rockets and [nitric acid] in favor of strengthening the oxygen sector'*" and who had been led by "a protégé of the executed spy M. N. Tukhachevsky"[44] from outside the institute.

Kostikov responded by writing the local Party committee attacking Kleimenov and others in the institute, accusing them of "incompetence and implicit sabotage."[45] Kleimenov had been on a trade mission to Germany. As happened for many others with foreign contacts, this was taken as evidence that he was a spy. He was arrested in November 1937, tortured severely, and, after a twenty-minute trial, executed on January 10, 1938. In his confession (which he refused to sign), he implicated several others including Korolev who was arrested in June 1938 and sentenced to "ten years imprisonment with five years of 'deprivation of rights.'"[46] Korolev was freed in 1944 and advanced rapidly, and his team launched Sputnik in 1957.

Only in relatively recent years have scholars detailed the extent of the repression of persons members of a diaspora nationalities, the populations of which overlapped Soviet borders and those of some other country or countries. Nothing better illustrates Stalin's general modus operandi in dealing with persons who could conceivably be mobilized against himself and/or the Soviet Union should hostilities break out.[47]

---

[43] Ibid., p. 490. brackets in original.
[44] Ibid., p. 490, italics in original.
[45] Ibid., p. 491.
[46] Ibid., p. 492.
[47] Khlevniuk, "The Objectives of the Great Terror." Also Khlevniuk in David Hoffmann, ed., *Stalinism: The Essential Readings* (Malden, MA: Blackwell, 2003), pp. 99–122.

Whereas in the 1920s, these people had been viewed as possible links with conationals residing abroad in the favorable sense that, as Martin in particular emphasizes,[48] they constituted a piedmont which could serve to recruit their counterparts into supporting union with the Soviet Union or in serving as its supporter in the other country—whether in war or peace.

By the mid-1930s, a profound shift in Stalinist thinking had taken place. The evidence supports the view that much of the driving force for the shift was the increased expectations of war on Stalin's part and the link between that expectation and the possibility that persons in one or another group might side with a state ranged against the Soviet Union. This formulation misses a key theme that served to rationalize the Great Purge, namely, what has been aptly termed a spy mania in the late 1930s.[49] A better formulation would point to Stalin's increasing anxiety during the 1930s about efforts to undermine the territorial integrity of the Soviet state, whether through espionage, through sabotage, or by being available for mobilization by some other power in the event war should break out. This formulation addresses the Soviet leadership's propensity early in the 1930s to define those who would be deported from border areas in national (Ukrainian, Polish, German) terms rather than class (kulaks) terms, a propensity that by late 1935 was entirely defined in ethnically national terms. The deportations initially were linked with an increasingly national assessment of the resistance to collectivization in the Ukraine. This was true in the sense that ethnic Ukrainians were accused of supporting independence for the Ukraine and conspiring with the Polish and German governments to achieve that goal. In addition, ethnic Poles and ethnic Germans were specifically being singled out for deportation, usually to Kazakhstan, from European border zones. As the decade progressed, the fear became that groups, almost all ethnically defined,[50] would side with the enemy, whether the latter be Poland, Germany, and/or Japan. Symbolically, this was signified by labeling individuals members of ethnic groups with a diaspora as "enemies of the people" and such groups as "enemy nations."

---

[48] Martin, *The Affirmative Action Empire.*

[49] James Morris, "The Polish Terror: Spy Mania and Ethnic Cleansing in the Great Terror," *Europe-Asia Studies*, Vol. 56, No. 5 (July 2004), pp. 751–66. Were there spies? Of course there were but surely never and nowhere of the magnitude Stalin portrayed.

[50] The exception that proves the rule were the Kharbintsy, whom the NKVD targeted as a group to be subjected to terror. Martin (*The Affirmative Action Empire*, p. 343) explains that these were persons, almost all ethnic Russians, who had been in Harbin, China, where the headquarters of the Chinese-Manchurian railroad—run by Russians until the mid-1930s—was located. Many of them returned to the Soviet Union after the railroad was sold to the Japanese. They continued to maintain connections with persons in Harbin, which may well be why they became targets of NKVD repression.

Nationality, moreover, was increasingly not defined as something one might choose but rather determined by the nationality of one's parents. Terry Martin has provided us with the best overall account of the gradual shift from class to nationality as the predominant categorization of social entities ostensibly hostile to Soviet power.[51] Whereas at the beginning of the 1930s the enemy had been the kulaks, in 1938 NKVD decrees targeted diaspora nationalities by name and referred specifically to "national operations" as an overall descriptor of activities targeted against ethnic minorities in contradistinction to other "mass operations." NKVD criteria for its activities by 1938 included the arrests, for example, of persons "according to the Polish line." Even clearer, Martin reports, were internal NKVD documents that described that organ's operations as being targeted against "nationalities of foreign governments." This occurred despite the fact that many who were repressed had been born in what was, before the Bolshevik Revolution, Russia in families who had lived for centuries in Russia. Thousands of people found themselves having conversations with the NKVD or other authorities such as one James Morris relates involving Pavel Baranov, a professor at a technical school in Biisk in western Siberia, who was asked, by the local chief of police, "You, it seems, are a foreigner?" to which Baranov replied that he had been born in Warsaw in 1898. For him and thousands others such nuances were lost on the NKVD. He was arrested in early 1938 and never heard from again.[52] According to data contained in KGB files, during the Great Purge nearly 700,000 were executed in 1937–38, of whom almost 250,000 were a part of the "national operations." According to Petrov and Roginsky, of those arrested in the national operations per se almost three-fourths (74 percent) were executed.[53] Martin's summary of Petrov and Roginsky's data: "The national operations made up about a fifth of the total arrests and a third of the total executions during the Great Terror, and arrest in the national operations was much more likely to result in execution."[54]

How the Soviets treated two ethnic groups—the Koreans and the Poles—is especially revealing. If one defines success in terms of the proportion of some population deported, the Korean operation was an impressive success. The deportation of Koreans was ethnic cleansing

---

[51] This paragraph draws heavily on Martin, *The Affirmative Action Empire*, especially chap. 8.

[52] This episode is reported by Morris, "The Polish Terror," p. 751.

[53] N. V. Petrov and A. B. Roginsky, "'Pol'skaya Operatsiya' NKVD 1937–1938 gg.," in A. E. Guryanov, ed., *Repressii protiv Polyakov i Pol'skiskh grazhdan 1937–1938* [Repression against Poles and Polish Citizens] (Moscow: Zvenya, 1997). The book was the first of a series of books supported by Memorial on the repression of nationality groups.

[54] Martin, *The Affirmative Action Empire*, p. 338.

in the most literal sense of the words. In percentage terms, the Korean deportation figures are reminiscent of Soviet election results. In 1937, all (99.6 percent) but approximately 700 of the more than 170,000 ethnic Koreans who were residing at the time in the Far Eastern *krai* were deported to Kazakhstan and Uzbekistan. This, Martin observes, constituted "the first ethnic cleansing of an entire nationality, including communists."[55] Martin cites a revealing statement by the assistant head of the NKVD relevant to the decision to remove virtually all the Koreans from the Far Eastern *krai*. By deporting virtually every Soviet Korean resident from the Far Eastern *krai*, the Soviet regime had minimized the possibility that those left behind would be available for mobilization. As the NKVD official explained, "To leave those few thousand Koreans in the Far Eastern *krai*, when the majority have been deported will be dangerous, since the family ties of all Koreans are very strong. The territorial restrictions on those remaining in the Far East will undoubtedly affect their mood and those groups will become rich soil for the Japanese to work on."[56]

As Martin notes, this observation not only bespeaks a mentality that explains why no effort was made to distinguish among Koreans but also goes a long way to understanding the kind of thought processes that underlay decisions, once someone had been arrested and convicted (often for no reason or for some trivial contact with a foreigner), to regard the spouses, children,[57] sometimes other relatives, and coworkers (especially employees) as also being candidates for being classified as an enemy of the people and as candidates for the gulag.

Much the same rationale appears to have animated the purges of European nationalities as well. We have data for executions by nationality during the Great Terror for the Karelian Autonomous Soviet Socialist Republic, Leningrad oblast, and Odessa oblast. In Karelia, of 11,341 arrested (9,750 of whom were executed), those arrested were overwhelmingly Finns or Karelians. When compared against the proportion of Finns in the population, the number of Finns arrested was extremely high. Specifically, they were fifteen times more likely to be

---

[55] Ibid., p. 334.

[56] Ibid.

[57] See also the telling 1986 exchange between Felix Chuev and Molotov, the English version of which appears in J. Arch Getty and Oleg Naumov, *The Road to Terror: Stalin and the Self-Destruction of the Bolsheviks, 1932–1939* (New Haven, CT: Yale University Press, 1999), p. 487. Chuev asks, "Why did repression fall on wives, children?" to which Molotov responded, "What does it mean, why? They had to be isolated to some degree. Otherwise, they would have spread all kinds of complaints . . . and degeneration to a certain degree" (ibid., p. 487). As they observe, Molotov did not even understand the question. For the Russian version, Chuev, *Sto sorok besed* (Moscow: Terra, 1991), p. 415.

arrested than one would expect from a mere extrapolation of the ethnic makeup of the Autonomous Republic and a stunning forty-five times more likely to be arrested than were ethnic Russians. Karelians were somewhat more likely to be arrested than would be expected by dividing the percentage arrested by the proportion of Karelians in the republic. Ethnic Russians were much less likely to be arrested than one would assume from the proportion of Russians in the Karelian population.[58]

Stalin (and the NKVD head, N. I. Yezhov, even more so) appear to have had a special thing about Poles, especially after the signing of the Polish-German Non-Aggression Pact in early 1934. Estimates cited by Martin[59] indicate that in the Leningrad oblast Poles were thirty times more likely to have been executed during the Great Terror than would be expected by a simple calculation of their size as a proportion of the population of the oblast. Their executions in Odessa were somewhat less as a proportion of the population of the oblast than was the case in Leningrad. Nevertheless, the magnitude (twenty-two times that based on a simple extrapolation) was enormous when compared with the number of Poles in the region.

To these numbers, moreover, it is appropriate to add Belorussians as well. While not classified by Martin as a diaspora nationality, they were seriously overrepresented among those executed in both the Leningrad and the Odessa oblasts. To a certain extent, they appear to have brought on their troubles themselves. Many Catholic Belorussians, Martin observes, "in the 1920s declared themselves to be Poles and sent their children to Polish schools." This act came back to haunt them in the 1930s, when they were arrested during the Polish "operation." "In Belorussia itself, Belorussians made up 47.3 percent of those arrested in the Polish operation (more than the Poles at 42.3 percent)."[60] Having lived as Poles in the Soviet Union, many Belorussians were treated as Poles by the NKVD.

The fear of links abroad extended well beyond those folks whose ethnicity placed them in a category of people the population of which overlapped Soviet borders. Often as a direct result of their professional activities, those who were purged had links abroad or with foreigners from countries that might be a Soviet opponent should war occur. There is disagreement in the literature whether persons in institutions with links to the outside world were more frequently arrested during the Great Purge or whether such institutions or groups of people were simply more visible to the West. Pending an exhaustive evaluation of

---

[58] Martin, *The Affirmative Action*, pp. 426–27.
[59] Ibid. The entire paragraph depends heavily on the two pages by Martin.
[60] Ibid., p. 427.

the data, I side with those who argue that overall foreign connections resulted in disproportionately high purge ratios when compared with analogous institutions or experiences. As we have seen, there is no question about the disproportionate number of persons arrested from some ethnic groups located both in the Soviet Union and in some country bordering on the Soviet Union. At a minimum, in addition, links with foreigners, travels abroad, and other foreign contacts rendered the NKVD's tasks a simpler one in targeting people for arrest.

But foreign contacts were more consequential than that. Thus, Frederick Starr writes, "The one characteristic common to nearly all Soviet jazz musicians purged in 1937 was their prior travel abroad or their close links with foreigners resident in the USSR."[61] Being from abroad or having contact with foreigners applied as well to persons with Party or government ties. Those who were purged included foreign communists (whether abroad or in exile in the Soviet Union),[62] Soviet citizens and others who had been members of the Comintern, officials in the People's Commissariat for International Affairs (Narkomindel), and (ultimately) NKVD agents stationed in Europe. (Few NKVD agents stationed abroad survived the purges.) Even with the NKVD targeting foreign communists residing outside the Soviet Union and bearing in mind the authoritarian political systems of most countries in Central and Eastern Europe during the 1930s, Robert Tucker correctly makes the point that it was safer for foreign communists in their home country than in the Soviet Union. It was not wise for foreign communist leaders to accept invitations to come to Moscow, nor for Soviet diplomats to respond to instructions to return home.[63]

The case of the Polish communists is illustrative. We have already seen how targeted by the NKVD were ethnic Poles possessing Soviet citizenship. Communist Poles from Poland fared worse. Charges were made in 1938 that Poles who had surrendered to the Russians during the Soviet war with Poland in 1920 and remained in Soviet Russia, often rising to important leadership posts, were in fact spies. It strains credulity to imagine that some of those who surrendered in 1920 were inserted in Soviet Russia to be spies almost twenty years down the road, but given the extent to which Polish organizations were penetrated by Soviet agents[64] it may have been that some Polish penetration of Soviet

---

[61] Starr, *Red and Hot*, p. 171.

[62] Perhaps the best single source of the extent of the purges of foreign communists outside the Soviet Union is the Mitrokhin file, which details the many examples of European communists who were assassinated by the NKVD. Christian Andrew and Vasily Mitrokhin, *The Mitrokhin Archive* (London: Allen Lane, 1999 and 2003).

[63] Tucker, *Stalin in Power*, pp. 504–12.

[64] Andrew and Mitrokhin, *Mitrokhin Archive*.

organizations including the Comintern had also taken place. Whatever the case, Stalin dealt with Polish putative double dealers in his characteristic fashion: purge all or virtually all of them. The Polish communist leadership in exile in the Soviet Union was arrested. Most of them were shot and the Polish Communist Party abolished.[65]

Teddy Uldricks has attempted a careful study of the fate of the persons in the Narkomindel (the precursor to the Ministry of Foreign Affairs) as a result of the Great Purge. If we accept his way of counting, Narkomindel's losses at the senior level were roughly comparable to those of the Central Committee elected at the Seventeenth Congress of the CPSU (70 percent) in 1934.[66] By his count, of those who were "commissars, deputy commissars, collegium members, and ambassadors, . . . a minimum of 62 percent . . . fell in the *ezhovshchina*."[67] We can question his use of the term "a minimum." His estimate may be slightly high inasmuch as he counts all those about whom information disappears in 1937 or 1938 as having been purged. This is, however, surely the main reason information about them ceased. But it is at least conceivable some other reason may explain why a few were no longer mentioned in the Soviet press. But even if we have minor caveats about his data, they are surely not far off the mark.

A thought experiment may be of use here, given the absence of absolutely compelling data. Assume a decision maker not troubled with qualms about killing people—a plausible assumption in the case of Stalin, who personally signed the death warrants of thousands. How would such a person regard those with contacts abroad or, in the usual course of events, with foreigners resident in the Soviet Union. He would not know who among those with such contacts would be likely to side with the enemy or under some circumstances be disposed to support his—Stalin's—removal as general secretary. What the gensek would feel comfortable about would be the hypothesis that, as in the case of members of a diaspora nationality or those who had sided with an opposition leader more than a decade ago, on a probabilistic basis such people would be more likely than those who did not have such

[65] Zbigniew K. Brzezinski, *The Soviet Bloc: Unity and Conflict* (Cambridge, MA: Harvard University Press, 1960), p. 96. This experience contributed to the Polish communist leadership after World War II observing the norm that they would not kill each other. An important result of this was that in 1956 during the Polish October Revolution it was possible to identify a communist to lead the country (to wit, Wladyslaw Gomulka) who had been arrested but not shot and who was acceptable to communists and noncommunists alike.

[66] Khrushchev in his secret speech as cited in *The Anti-Stalin Campaign*, pp. 22–23.

[67] Teddy Uldricks, "The Impact of the Great Purges on the People's Commissariat of Foreign Affairs," *Slavic Review*, Vol. 36, No. 2 (June 1977), pp. 187–204 at p. 190.

experiences to harbor views potentially dangerous to him or to the integrity of the Soviet Union. The most efficient way to deal with such people was to treat them all as a cancer on the body politic, rather than waste time and resources endeavoring to develop more refined categories of possible opponents. All (ethnic Poles, Polish communists, jazz musicians, fill in the blank) were presumed guilty and treated as such. Moreover—as in the treatment of a cancer—to be absolutely certain that there would be no recurrence of the putative tumor, the regime cut sharply into the surrounding tissue by arresting spouses, other relatives, acquaintances, and coworkers.

Now let's have a genuine flight of fancy—or horror: Imagine Stalin constructing a regression the outcome variables of which would be whether "to maintain or not Soviet territorial integrity if war goes badly," or "might or might not favor an alternative to Stalin in such circumstances." As the predictor variables in such a regression, a brutally rational calculus would include dummy variables dividing the population into groups with ethnic kinsmen in an adjacent country and those without such links, and people who have had significant experience abroad or in their daily experience with foreigners in the USSR and those who had not. These would go into a model that, along with control variables for sex, age, and proximity to the border, also included variables that dichotomized those Communist Party members (e.g., Old Bolsheviks) who knew Stalin when and those who had only known him as the supreme leader. The model would also sort Party members on whether at some time or other they had been favorably disposed to Trotsky or other key Party members (i.e., Bukharin, Zinoviev, Kamenev). An additional dummy variable would distinguish between those who had merely been Party members at sometime or other and were no longer. Oleg Khlevniuk points out that in February 1937 Georgy Malenkov had reported to Stalin that "'at the present time in the country there number over 1,500,000 former members and candidate members of the party who have been expelled and mechanically dismissed at various times from 1922 onwards."[68] Other candidates for categorization because of their CVs whom Khlevniuk identifies as having been brought up at the February-March Central Committee plenum included former kulaks who had been released from the camps and religious believers. These were not trivial proportions of the population.

As with any dummy variable, many people so coded would not constitute a threat to the regime or to Stalin himself. But he could rationally assume a higher proportion of people classified in that way would constitute such a threat than would be the case for those who had never

[68]Khlevniuk, "The Objectives of the Great Terror," p. 159.

manifested any support for an opposition leader. This suggests a grim rationality to Stalin's propensity to eliminate or render harmless via incarceration or deportation whole categories of people—diaspora nationalities, people with foreign ties of any kind, Old Bolsheviks who more than a decade ago might have flirted with supporting Trotsky—who could conceivably constitute a problem, especially should war break out.[69]

The logic underlying the above implies that an explanation for Stalin's behavior in the 1930s does not require assuming he was maniacal or bereft of his senses.[70] Rather, he wanted to be the unchallenged leader who industrialized rapidly in a way that prepared the country for war. What brought the Great Terror to an end is that the hedonic calculus speculated about in the previous paragraph, while indeed solidifying Stalin's personal power and removing millions of people from the body politic who might have been available for mobilization should the war go badly, ran at cross-purposes with another of Stalin's key goals. I have in mind, of course, the rapid industrialization and militarization of the society in such a way as to have the wherewithal to wage successfully a forthcoming war. In particular, for many people, both civilian and military, the purges undermined conventional expectations about the links between behavior and consequences. If the enemy hid behind overfulfillment of the plan, what was an economic decision maker to do? If an innovation failed, would the entrepreneurial factory manager be accused of sabotage and end up in the gulag? Leading communist officials, notably Khrushchev (after Stalin's death of course), and scholars have agreed that such questions were not rhetorical ones for Soviet citizens, that the purges had in fact impeded growth and the functioning of governmental institutions.

Teddy Uldricks, for instance, specifically links the functioning of Narkomindel in the late 1930s to the purges: "[The] radical displacement of personnel combined with the atmosphere of terror must have brought the normal functioning of Soviet diplomacy to a complete halt."[71] His conclusion about Narkomindel extended to the fighting efficiency of

---

[69] This analysis meshes with the argument advanced by Khlevniuk who refers to the categories in the text above as "biological particulars." I prefer "CV particulars." This subsumes attributes readily obvious on a resume that were not "biological" such as "work experience involving direct contact with foreigners" or "experience abroad" or "formerly member, CPSU." All of these proved to be substantial predictors of whether someone was repressed or not.

[70] E.g., Moshe Lewin, who refers to Stalin's "gloomy personality, with clear paranoid tendencies" in Tucker, *Stalinism*, pp. 111–36 at pp. 130–31 and the corpus of Tucker's works.

[71] Uldricks, "The Impact," p. 192.

the Red Army in the Winter War with Finland 1940–41, to its behavior at the outset of World War II, and to the economy as a whole.

The impact on the Red Army of the Great Purge was devastating. In his memoirs, Khrushchev recalls witnessing an incident at Stalin's dacha where Voroshilov (who headed the Soviet forces in the Winter War) responded to Stalin's criticism by shouting "'You have yourself to blame for all this! . . . You're the one who annihilated the Old Guard of the army; you had our best generals killed!'"[72] In his secret speech, Khrushchev emphasized how the denunciations had undermined discipline: "The policy of large-scale repression against the military cadres led also to undermined military discipline, because for several years officers of all ranks and even soldiers in the Party and Komsomol cells were taught to 'unmask' their superiors as hidden enemies. . . . It is natural that this caused a negative influence on the state of military discipline in the first war period."[73] He also connected Soviet lack of preparedness at the outset of World War II to the treatment of those with experience abroad: "Very grievous consequences, especially in reference to the beginning of the war, followed Stalin's annihilation of many military commanders and political workers during 1937–1941 . . . beginning literally at the company and battalion commander level and extending to the higher military centers; during this time the cadre of leaders who had gained experience in Spain and in the Far East was almost completely liquidated."[74]

And the consequences of the terror extended to the economy as a whole. Thus, Kendall Bailes, while cautioning that the effects of the terror on technical innovation are difficult to gauge, concludes that "even the scanty Soviet statistical sources on [the influence of terror] suggest that terror had an inhibiting effect." Similarly, he cites approvingly the observation of a production engineer interviewed by the Harvard Refugee Project as having said, "[We] were afraid to introduce innovations and rationalization. We often thought that certain methods must be introduced. But usually we did not do it. If an experiment should fail we could be charged with sabotage."[75] More generally, Tucker, citing the Soviet scholar Viktor Danilov, reports that "[t]he Terror had wrought such havoc in the economy that in the critically important coal and steel industry, for example, there was zero growth in 1937–39, and so vital a part of it as the Magnitogorsk works, with only

[72] Nikita Khrushchev, *Khrushchev Remembers* (New York: Little, Brown, 1970), p. 154.

[73] *Anti-Stalin Campaign*, p. 49.

[74] *Anti-Stalin Campaign*, pp. 48–49.

[75] Kendall Bailes, *Technology and Society under Lenin and Stalin: Origins of the Soviet Technical Intelligentsia, 1917–1941* (Princeton, NJ: Princeton University Press, 1978), pp. 353–54.

8 engineers and 66 trained technicians left on its staff, had to rely on 364 mere 'practicals' (workers without special training) to take the places of the qualified people it lacked."[76]

Stalin evidently realized that aggregating his personal power at the expense of the rapid militarization and industrialization requisite to wage a forthcoming war had created havoc. Over a year and a half, beginning in early 1938 and culminating roughly with the Eighteenth Party Congress in 1939, he brought an end to the Great Terror, while leaving in place key laws and decisions that had served to legitimize it and actually tightening up the controls over ordinary Soviet citizens at their workplace. Peter Solomon's book *Soviet Criminal Justice* and the important Soviet documents contained in a volume edited by J. Arch Getty and Oleg V. Naumov provide us with an account of the formal decisions taken at the top to rein in the forces Stalin had unleashed. In part the shift in policy was, naturally enough, accomplished by blaming underlings for having gone too far. Stalin was of course not the first nor the last political leader to deal with the excesses of a policy by employing such a technique. He employed this ploy even though he had manipulated the context in which others operated in such a way that it was rational for subordinates to overfulfill the arrest and execution quotas (*limity*). They did this for precisely the same reasons it was rational for an enterprise director operating under the constraints of a Five-Year Plan to overfulfill the plan. Overfulfilling the quotas for execution of course did not protect NKVD officers from being purged when it proved necessary to find scapegoats, just as we see below (pp. 174–175), many enterprise directors—despite their successes in fulfilling Five-Year Plan—fell victim to the terror in an era when denunciations were the order of the day.

The fundamental steps in the process of closing down the Great Terror were to blame the excesses on the head of the NKVD, Nikolai Yezhov, to mute the calls for vigilance, and to separate criminal and political crimes. The first step in the process came in early 1938. The Central Committee adopted a resolution condemning "'careless, mass expulsions from the party, often leading to arrest.'"[77] The quotas, however, did not stop. On January 31, the Politburo, in a "strictly secret" message, conveyed to the NKVD its proposed quotas for the quarter broken down by regions, which was followed a month later by an instruction increasing the number of arrests in Ukraine by thirty thousand.[78] In

[76] Tucker, *Stalin in Power*, p. 588.

[77] The above quote comes from a Central Committee plenum resolution as cited by Solomon, *Soviet Criminal Justice*, p. 253.

[78] The document is to be found in Getty and Naumov, *Road to Terror*, p. 519.

March, Getty and Naumov assert, "Stalin declined Yezhov's proposal to stage a show trial of 'Polish spies.'"[79] In April the latter was appointed commissar of water transport. This was an ambiguous move on Stalin's part. Taking control of water transport made sense given the NKVD's role in such projects as the construction of the prisoner-built Belomor Canal, but an analogous appointment to his predecessor, G. G. Yagoda, had been a demotion followed by repression.

Dissatisfaction with the NKVD became manifestly clear when the USSR Procuracy (the equivalent of the U.S. Attorney General's office) "issued on June 1 [1938] a major directive on the overhaul (*perestroika* [*sic*]) of its work. The directive told investigators and prosecutors in no uncertain terms 'to quash all unfounded prosecutions that had been started' and 'to cease this practice in the future.'"[80] The regime then proceeded to put teeth into the resolution over the next several months. Criminal charges were brought against overzealous procurators, and a series of highly publicized trials of "slanderers," that is, informers,[81] were conducted.

From Yezhov's point of view, the most ominous development came in late summer when Lavrenti Beria was appointed as his deputy. An even more clear-cut blow to Yezhov personally came in November 1938 when, in an extraordinary document, the Politburo (read: Stalin) issued a decree in which it was reported that the NKVD, among other things, had become penetrated by foreign spies. The decree ordered that the "'NKVD and the procuracy be prohibited from carrying out any mass arrests or mass deportations'" and the "'judicial troikas . . . [were] to be abolished.'"[82] In a matter of days Yezhov resigned as head of the NKVD. Soon thereafter, Beria became its head. Not surprisingly, Yezhov was arrested in 1939 and executed in 1940. Sverdlovsk oblast requested that a raion in the district named Yezhovsk be renamed Molotovsk. At least for the bulk of the Russian Republic,[83] the mass terror, but not the threat thereof,[84] had ended.

Moreover, on December 1, Stalin and Molotov decreed (in the name of the Council of People's Commissars) the restoration of the principle that arrests of Party members had to be cleared by the Party at the

---

[79] Ibid., p. 528.

[80] Solomon, *Soviet Criminal Justice*, p. 254.

[81] For an elaboration of the steps the government took, see ibid., pp. 254–55, on which the above draws heavily.

[82] As cited in Getty and Naumov, *Road to Terror*, p. 535.

[83] Note that this statement explicitly excludes the deportations from the Northern Caucasus, or from the Baltic republics or the western Ukraine, etc.

[84] Solomon, *Soviet Criminal Justice*, pp. 252–59.

relevant level.[85] That, on paper, restored the distinction between the Party and society, which, as we saw in the previous chapter, Stalin had destroyed. This was then followed in January 1939 by a telegram sent by Stalin to police heads and Party officials. In it, he observed that "[t]he application of physical force in the practice of the NKVD, permitted since 1937 by the Central Committee [sic!] has sped up the exposure of enemies of the people. The Central Committee thinks that this method must be applied from now on, as an exception to clear and still dangerous enemies as the correct and expedient one.'"[86] Denunciations of senior officials from below, which had been so detrimental to the military[87] and in heavy industry, were frowned upon. Instead, excesses in this regard were sharply criticized at the 1939 Eighteenth CPSU Congress, the last Congress prior to 1952.[88]

But, as Solomon writes, the cessation of mass operations did not signify the cessation of "contrived political prosecutions."[89] It remained the case (as provided for as a result of the law enunciated on December 1, 1934—the day Kirov was assassinated) that in instances of terrorism a judge acting on his own could sentence someone to be executed. The sentence could then be implemented immediately without appeal. Moreover, it was decided that in cases of wrecking and sabotage (but which now, in principle at least, required that intentionality be demonstrated) the death sentence could continue to be imposed immediately "after the refusal of a petition for pardon."[90]

All things considered, termination of the Great Purge was an initial step away from totalitarianism in large part because the regime thenceforth acted as though preparation for war dominated all other considerations. This observation applies both to years before World War II and as Robert Tucker has pointed out, after that war as well.[91] With collectivization in place and potential rival groupings repressed, mobilization for war trumped political and social mobilization. This had been a clear theme throughout the 1930s and had resulted in the quick termination of the Cultural Revolution. As we have seen, moreover, the incarcera-

---

[85] Ibid., p. 258, citing the relevant document. Solomon refers to "party members and officials." This paragraph draws heavily on Solomon.

[86] Ibid., p. 258, interjection in original.

[87] The overall number of officers executed or imprisoned in 1937–38 was just staggering. For an English-language table summarizing their numbers by rank, see Andrei Kokoshin, *Soviet Strategic Thought, 1917–91* (Cambridge, MA: MIT Press, 1998), p. 43.

[88] Fainsod, *How Russia*, p. 375.

[89] Solomon, *Soviet Criminal Justice*, p. 260.

[90] Ibid.

[91] Tucker, *Stalinism*, pp. 106–7.

tion, deportation, and killing of persons of diaspora nationalities had been prompted in large measure because they might conceivably turn against Stalin and against the Soviet state, a distinction without a difference for Stalin. A similar calculus had informed Stalin's preemptive strike not just against the Old Bolsheviks but others who had been Party members at some time[92] who might, therefore, have a grievance that would render them available for political mobilization by some counterelite. With all these people who might conceivably be enemies rendered harmless, the elements that defined Stalinism from 1939 until his death were in place.

At the level of high politics, Stalin now dominated all the key institutions. This was vividly illustrated immediately before and during World War II. As of May 6, 1941 (the war began for the USSR on June 22), he became the head of Sovnarkom, while continuing as Party general secretary. In the course of the summer 1941 he became the chair of the Supreme Command (Stavka), the chief of the State Defense Council, and the commissar for defense and supreme commander of the Soviet armed forces.[93] His domination of the institutions continued after the war, with it being unclear whether the government, the Party, or the secret police occupied a paramount role. After the war, the duties of the State Defense Council were largely devolved to a Presidium of the Council of Ministers (as Sovnarkom was renamed in March 1946).[94] The pattern of meetings of quintets, sextets, and septets of the Politburo membership persisted. The entire Politburo, continuing the trend noticeable toward the end of the 1930s, rarely met. There was effectively a selectorate of one. Stalin picked and chose whether the Presidium of the Council of Ministers, the Party Politburo, or one of the groups of six or seven would discuss a matter. He unilaterally removed A. A. Andreyev from the Politburo. At the time of the Nineteenth Party Congress in 1952 (the last one having met in 1939), he transformed the Politburo into an enlarged Presidium of the Central Committee and established what amounted to a real Politburo, an institution Roeder depicts as a "shadowy, hand-picked inner working body—the Bureau of the Presidium of the Central Committee."[95]

Stalin's monopoly power over the political elite was replicated by the relationship of the state, the Party, and the secret police to the society. Solomon is careful to point out that the legal basis for the resumption of mass purges was not eliminated in the process of closing down the

[92] Khlevniuk, "The Objectives of the Great Terror."
[93] Nation, Black Earth, pp. 124–25.
[94] Roeder, Red Sunset, p. 55.
[95] Ibid., p. 55.

Great Purge.[96] Doctrinally, too, Stalin continued to insist throughout the period 1939–53 that capitalist encirclement continued to exist even after the Soviet Bloc had been formed during and after World War II, thus perpetuating the basis for justifying mass repression and permanent purge. Moreover, during World War II several small peoples, primarily from the Northern Caucasus—Balkars, Chechens, Ingush, and Karachai Tatars—were designated enemy nations and deported to Central Asia.[97] Thousands of persons from the Baltic states and the seven western districts of the Ukraine were killed, incarcerated, or deported. Many Party officials and cultural figures disappeared as a part of the Leningrad Affair, and the 1953 Doctors' Plot adumbrated the possibility that Stalin was on the verge of launching a major purge when, conveniently for several senior communist officials, he died in March 1953. But the gross abnormality of massive purges, deportations, or incarceration on the scale of events in the 1930s ceased with respect to the bulk of the Soviet Union as it existed before the Molotov-Ribbentrop pact.

The other dimensions of regime-societal relations that had characterized the Soviet system in the late 1930s generally remained in place throughout the years until Stalin's death. Efforts at symbolic mobilization persisted: mere acquiescence by the populace was not accepted. Rather, obligatory voting for single-party candidates and participation in mass events such as the inevitable May Day parades and subbotniks ("voluntary" unremunerated work on weekends) were used to reinforce the belief that everyone understood that everyone (etc.), with the possible exception of a few, unanimously supported the regime and its policies. The central theme of the period was modernization—if by modernization we have in mind large-scale, rapid industrialization. It certainly did not mean large-scale mass consumption or access to contemporary trends in Western art or literature, much less politics.

The glorification of the state—increasingly the *Russian* state—continued. This was accompanied by the adoption of policies vis-à-vis the family at home and in the workforce that were Victorian in content. Large families were encouraged symbolically by recognizing heroine-mothers, though the scarcity of urban housing meant that the encouragement was for urban dwellers almost entirely symbolic. Throughout the 1930s, the trend had been to adopt ever more stringent work laws. As the possibility of war increased, truly oppressive laws governing work attendance and punctuality were adopted, though in practice the workers and the factory managers before, during, and after the

---

[96] Solomon, *Soviet Criminal Justice*, pp. 258–60.

[97] Others, not from the Northern Caucasus, included the Volga Germans and the Crimean Tatars.

war sometimes succeeded in gaming the system. In addition, the trend dating from the mid-1930s toward Party and security force presence in all urban factories and institutes continued. This meant that appointments of institute and enterprise directors were invariably an item on the nomenklatura list at some level of the Party hierarchy.

The presence of a Party cell and the role of Party officials obviously hindered but did not exclude completely scholarly disputes, within the framework of the Party line, in the various institutes of the Academy of Sciences and elsewhere, but it served to severely constrain them. The state, though, was not just an instrument of social control. It also had a near monopoly on goods and services. Sheila Fitzpatrick has emphasized how scarcity became a normal expectation for all Russians. They largely had no alternative to the monopsonistic state as sole supplier for goods and services. Increasingly, the Soviet state provided a wider range of services, often for very low prices, satisfaction for which varied immensely, given that the goods received were what one would expect for such prices. Citizens became increasingly dependent on the state as dominant provider. This doubtless increased a kind of asymmetrically dependent relationship between the society and the regime, whether defined with reference to the Party or the state. What was less certain was whether in the absence of full-blown terror, the regime could continue to pursue the transformative goals that differentiated it from other authoritarian systems; whether the regime could successfully mobilize citizens and the government and Party bureaucracies in pursuit of goals it valued in the absence of large-scale terror. In his last months, Stalin seems to have concluded that in its absence the Soviet Union was drifting—a drift that, as his creation of a counterweight to the Politburo and the "discovery" of the Doctors' Plot demonstrated, he was determined to thwart—in the direction of becoming a normal authoritarian state.

He was right.

CHAPTER 5

From Totalitarianism to Welfare Authoritarianism

IN THIS CHAPTER, we describe the fitful process by which the Soviet political system evolved over almost half a century spanning the period from the closing down (1938–39) of the Great Purge to the end of the Brezhnev era in 1982. In that time frame it went from a system which in 1937–38 (deservedly labeled totalitarian) should be properly located at the tail of the distribution of autocratic states to one that was closer to a normal ("full") authoritarian welfare state.[1]

At the elite level, major and interrelated developments occurred that brought about a modicum of conventional authoritarian politics even during periods such as the years between 1957 when Nikita Khrushchev defeated the Anti-Party Group and his ouster in 1964 in which he was the indisputable (but, as it turned out, scarcely the unchallenged) leader. Both he and Leonid Brezhnev, as George Breslauer shows,[2] generally exercised power over policy throughout their tenure as leaders of the Party. In the course of time, moreover, it became appropriate to speak of the existence of a small selectorate and of the modest norms about the Politburo as a collective decision-making body that had developed.

However, the balance between oligarchic and autocratic propensities within the Politburo fluctuated. The effort and methods Khrushchev and Brezhnev employed to achieve the authority required changed over time as well. Several factors contributed to this evolution. Norms about the consequences of losing in a power struggle changed.[3] For the Soviet leadership the late Stalinist and immediate post-Stalinist periods were a Hobbesian world in which losing a power struggle could be fatal. Slowly, though, the consequences of failed factionalism evolved.

---

[1] Above, pp. 4–6.

[2] George Breslauer, *Khrushchev and Brezhnev as Leaders: Building Authority in Soviet Politics* (London: George Allen & Unwin, 1982).

[3] See, especially, Grey Hodnett, "Succession Contingencies in the Soviet Union," *Problems of Communism*, Vol. 24 (March–April 1975), pp. 1–21. It was Michel Oksenberg who most brought home to me that a great weakness of political science and history was that both were excessively success oriented, the result being far too much attention paid to winners and not enough to the systemic implications of what happens to losers.

Elite turnover was rapid under Khrushchev, but as Jerry Hough[4] and others have pointed out, Central Committee membership came to seem like a life peerage during the Brezhnev era. Ironically, this development implied a status for the Central Committee member analogous to the ordinary Soviet worker who during the Brezhnev era basically had lifetime employment at his or her workplace.[5] By the end of the Brezhnev era, a loser in high politics no longer risked loss of life. Rather he might find himself exiled abroad via a pleasant ambassadorial appointment, forced into retirement, or transferred to a less significant government job but in Moscow. Norms developed as well about the niceties of the way the first or general secretary[6] exercised power over policy and got away with behaviors that were major irritants to the other members of the Politburo/Presidium. As the norm changed concerning the consequences of losing, horizontal linkages among Politburo members intensified and the collective action problems that deterred coalition formation among them were mitigated. This increased the amount of information Politburo/Presidium members had about the views of others, both in the ruling group and among specialists, as well as about facts relevant to key budgetary and policy matters.

This in turn had trickle-down and feedback effects. It provided a climate in which more information was available in open source material to all and even more, on a restricted basis, to the leadership and relevant key subelites. For the members of the Presidium/Politburo it meant that the ploy employed by Stalin of excluding particular Politburo/Presidium members from key subcommittees was less effective as a means of controlling access to information by potentially recalcitrant Politburo/Presidium members. It also became possible for outsiders to ascertain the broad contours of policies, even those about which virtually all information was classified.

It was also no longer a world where the simple dichotomy between intraselectorate (narrowly defined) politics and regime-society relations adequately encompassed the nature of the political system. With the option of a bullet in the back of the head for those who might oppose the regime largely foreclosed in practice, institutionally grounded subelites could and did differentiate themselves and their views from the Party and its views. They also found it in their interest to muster their considerable political resources to assert their claims about the

[4] Jerry Hough, *Soviet Leadership in Transition* (Washington, DC: Brookings Institution, 1980), p. 64.

[5] Walter Connor, *The Accidental Proletariat: Workers, Politics, and Crisis in Gorbachev's Russia* (Princeton, NJ: Princeton University Press, 1991), passim.

[6] Implicit in the concept of "first" was the idea that such a person was first among equals. "General" conveyed the notion that his portfolio was all-inclusive.

allocation of resources and about their role in decision making, even though, to be sure, autonomous interest groups were not tolerated.

Likewise, in the absence of the threat of the ultimate sanction, it turned out that even when the Party state had a near monopoly over jobs and strove to inspire many with an attractive "combat task,"[7] the regime's ability to mobilize the ordinary Soviet citizen for such purposes had diminished. Both Khrushchev and Brezhnev entertained grandiose schemes, those of the former grander than those of the latter. In governing the ordinary citizenry, Brezhnev settled on a bargain[8] with the bulk of Soviet workers that accepted acquiescent, rather than affirmative, behavior on their part and in return provided them with rather egalitarian economic paternalism. What the regime came to expect of the ordinary Soviet citizenry was conformity, not mobilization, and in the years before perestroika it largely succeeded in achieving this. After the Soviet intervention in Hungary in 1956, Janos Kadar's authoritarian slogan was "He who is not against us is with us," in counterpoint to Stalin's "He who is not with us is against us." Brezhnev's approach to regime-society relations paralleled Kadar's. By the time of Brezhnev's death, the ordinary Soviet citizens had more or less bought into this social contract. Those who were least so disposed were precisely the best and the brightest, the key subelites (political leaders and professionals) who were least likely to be mobilized and most prone to nonconforming behavior. In short, by the time of Brezhnev's death reference to regime/society relations had become a shorthand construction that captured some of Soviet reality but scarcely all. It failed to appreciate the more textured interactions characteristic of a "full" authoritarian—as opposed to a totalitarian—dictatorship with a very small selectorate, a small, attentive public somewhat attuned to plural messages emanating from different sources, some subelites whose institutional ties gave them the possibility to articulate claims on resources, and a vast conformist but largely unmobilized mass. Zbigniew Brzezinski's three restraints on elite political power over society: direct, indirect, and natural are relevant here.[9] (They are described above, p. 16.) Of these, the direct remained in place. The indirect were becoming more constrained in their effectiveness in the absence of terror and in the presence of an increasingly educated urban and industrialized population. The natural were becoming increasingly relevant as distinctions between the public and private realms (especially with regard to the family as pri-

---

[7] Jowitt, "Soviet Neotraditionalism," pp. 275–97.

[8] While political theorists have groaned at the application of the term "social contract" to Soviet politics, many who studied the Soviet system found it useful, especially in describing the Brezhnev era.

[9] Brzezinski, *Ideology and Power*, p. 16.

mary socializing agent[10]) became increasingly manifest despite regime efforts to subordinate the citizenry to norms of the various *kollektivy*.

POST–GREAT PURGE LOSERS

In the conclusion to the previous chapter we saw that the steps to closing down the Great Purge were three: blaming the "excesses" on Yezhov, muting the campaign for vigilance, and separating criminal and political crime. On December 1, 1938, Stalin and Molotov decreed (in the name of the Council of People's Commissars) the restoration of the principle that arrests of Party members had to be cleared by the Party at the relevant level.[11]

After World War II ended, Stalin continued to sanction the killing of Politburo members. The Leningrad Affair and the Mingrelian Case took their toll on the leadership of Leningrad, very broadly defined, and wrecked havoc among the leadership of the Georgian region of Mingrelia.[12] It is true that episodes such as the Leningrad Affair paled in comparison to the years 1937 and 1938 and the Great Purge. Nevertheless, Stalin's entourage operated in an environment in which the implicit verb of the famous *kto-kogo* (who-whom) was "to kill."

Moreover, had Stalin lived, almost certainly a purge of greater magnitude than either the Leningrad or Mingrelian events would have taken place. Actions in 1952 and early 1953 had all the attributes of the precursors to a purge. (Soviet leaders had seen these before: the use of signals, institutional shifts, explicit attacks on individuals in restricted audiences, and more muted but pointed attacks in the central press.)

Core to these developments was the "discovery," a couple of months before Stalin's death in March 1953, of a putative "Doctors' Plot" to murder Kremlin leaders. Almost immediately after the 1952 Nineteenth CPSU Congress Stalin decided to expand—and thus dilute—the Politburo composed of twelve members, one of whom was a candidate member, into a Presidium of thirty-six members, of whom eleven were candidate members. (The name reverted to Politburo in 1966.) Stalin's overall strategy seems to have been, by so doing, to reduce the influence

---

[10] See especially Vladimir Shlapentokh, *Public and Private Life of the Soviet People* (New York: Oxford University Press, 1989).

[11] Solomon, *Soviet Criminal Justice*, p. 258.

[12] On the Mingrelian affair, see Robert Conquest, *Power and Policy in the USSR: The Study of Soviet Dynamics* (New York: St. Martin's, 1961), *pp. 130 and 140* and also William Taubman, *Khrushchev: The Man and His Era* (New York: Norton, 2003), p. 221. On the Leningrad case, see Conquest, *Power and Policy*, especially pp. 95–111 and Werner G. Hahn, *Postwar Soviet Politics: The Fall of Zhdanov and the Defeat of Moderation*, 1946–53 (Ithaca, NY: Cornell University Press, 1982).

of those who had served him in the 1930s and to prepare the ground for a new generation of leadership and for the removal of, and perhaps the deaths of, most of a somewhat older generation. "Stalin evidently had plans to finish off the old members of the Political Bureau,"[13] Khrushchev asserted—after Stalin was safely dead of course. Almost certainly, Khrushchev was right at least with respect to eliminating several, though perhaps not all, of the older Politburo members. No reason exists to think that Stalin's basic modus operandi had changed for the better in the fifteen years since 1937–38; usually a good former Politburo member was a dead former Politburo member. Stalin was preparing the ground for removing his prewar Politburo colleagues in what turned out to be his last days.

What added to the anxiety among his lieutenants was that he was probably senile. A core argument of the previous chapter was that a parsimonious explanation of Stalin's behavior did not require incorporating idiosyncratic variables to account for his ghastly behavior in the 1930s. By contrast, the prisms through which Stalin saw the world in 1950–53 were becoming increasingly opaque, ones replete with distortions that are hard to fathom without introducing senility or some other such[14] variable into the account. Kaganovich had long been disregarded and had the disadvantage in the context of the Doctors' Plot of being Jewish. Kliment Voroshilov, Stalin now declared, was a Western spy and wondered out loud, "How did Voroshilov worm his way into the Bureau?"[15] In the first meeting of the Central Committee after the 1952 Nineteenth Party Congress, Stalin launched vicious attacks against Molotov and Mikoyan. These "old workers of our Party" were alleged, Khrushchev said in the secret speech, to be "guilty of some baseless charges. It is not excluded that had Stalin remained at the helm for another several months, Comrades Molotov and Mikoyan would probably not have delivered any speeches at this [the Twentieth] Congress."[16] In his memoirs, Khrushchev[17] was more explicit, "I'm convinced," he wrote, "that if Stalin had lived much longer, Molotov and Mikoyan would have met a disastrous end."

---

[13] Khrushchev's secret speech as contained in *The Anti-Stalin Campaign*, p. 84.

[14] Cf. Khrushchev, *Khrushchev Remembers*, p. 308, where he recalls that "Once Stalin turned to Bulganin and started to say something but couldn't remember his name. Stalin looked at him intently and said, 'You there, what's your name?' 'Bulganin.' 'Of course, Bulganin! That's what I was going to say.'"

[15] Ibid. Khrushchev also asserts that for a decade Stalin had suspected Voroshilov of being an English spy. This is scarcely credible.

[16] *The Anti-Stalin Campaign*, p. 84.

[17] Khrushchev, *Khrushchev Remembers*, p. 310. Also cited in Taubman, *Khrushchev*, p. 218.

Another candidate for removal was Beria. In January 1953, the Doctors' Plot was discovered, which alleged efforts by doctors, mainly Jewish, to murder members of the Soviet leadership. The evidence that he may or may not have been in trouble even prior to the Doctor's Plot is subject to divergent interpretations.[18] My view corresponds with that of Robert Conquest and William Taubman. It is likewise difficult not to conclude that the Mingrelian Case in late 1951 was intended to weaken Beria's power base in Georgia. According to Taubman, Stalin "personally instructed the new police chief, Semyon Ignatiev, not to forget 'the big Mingrelian' "[19]—Beria.

Regardless of one's feeling about the Mingrelian affair, there can be no dispute about the Doctors' Plot. It clearly threatened to be Beria's undoing. The security organs were explicitly attacked in *Pravda* and *Izvestia* for their lack of vigilance in uncovering the plot, even though these putative crimes had been going on for three years. The doctors had allegedly murdered a communist official as early as 1945. In the *Izvestia* account (January 13, 1953) as cited by Conquest, "'The wrecker-doctors were able to function over a considerable period because some of our Soviet organs *and their executives* lost their vigilance and were infected by gullibility.'" *Pravda*, again as cited by Conquest, similarly lamented on the same day that the "'State Security organs [had not uncovered] in good time the wrecking terrorist organization among the doctors. However, these organs should have been especially vigilant.'"[20] Less than two months after the two articles appeared, Stalin died. Almost immediately thereafter, the Doctors' Plot was declared to be a hoax. With that, the prospect of another great purge terminated immediately. At a minimum, Stalin's death lengthened the life expectancy of several members of the core group—Molotov, Mikoyan, probably Voroshilov, maybe Kaganovich.

But not Beria's. Beria may or may not have been more of a threat to Stalin than Stalin to him, but Beria's colleagues clearly perceived him as a threat *to them* both personally and to the collective leadership that had been loudly proclaimed on Stalin's death. In a process that to some extent antedated Stalin's death, after his death a Byzantine exercise in conspiracy, led by Khrushchev (although Malenkov claimed to have led the action against Beria as well[21]), was launched against Beria. He was arrested June 26, 1953, at a meeting of Party and government

---

[18] Taubman has summarized the divergent assessments in *Khrushchev*, p. 706n66.

[19] Ibid., p. 221.

[20] Conquest, *Power and Policy*, p. 188, italics added.

[21] Taubman's survey of the alliances, "re-insurance treaties," and probable duplicity on the part of the Soviet leaders is particularly good. On the competing claims regarding leadership of the coup, Taubman's summary seems decisive: "Molotov, who hated [Khrushchev and Malenkov] . . . , and Mikoyan, who got along with both, confirmed Khrushchev's account." *Khrushchev*, p. 250.

leaders. Six months later, he and many of his cronies were tried and shot. Others in the security forces were tried and executed in 1954.

They had the distinction of being the last key Soviet leaders to receive the ultimate sanction. At the elite level, the norm gradually and fitfully developed that big players who were losers in power struggles were not to be killed. Even in the period during which Roeder argues Khrushchev engaged in directive[22] (one-person) rule—after the 1957 defeat of the Anti-Party Group until his removal October 1964—and when Taubman depicts Khrushchev as "alone at the top," no central leader received what in Stalin's time had often been the end for a major leader in opposition—a bullet in the back of the head.

Conquest marshals some evidence to suggest that Khrushchev tried to ascribe criminal behavior to those members of the Presidium who favored his ouster, but they were not arrested.[23] What Roeder terms "norms governing first tier relations" prevented their indictment. Kaganovich, for one, was petrified that he might be arrested.[24] Khrushchev did, however, get the opportunity to show, however, how acutely mean-spirited he could be in dealing with those who had constituted the Anti-Party Group. Malenkov had already been demoted prior to the Anti-Party Group action. But after the coup failed, he was exiled to manage a hydroelectric station near Ust-Kamenogorsk in northern Kazakhstan and then suffered further indignities ending up in Ekibastuz where, Taubman reports, the "police observed his every move."[25]

On the surface, Molotov was treated somewhat less shabbily. He was named ambassador to Ulan Bator, the capital of Outer Mongolia, a location that gave meaning to the concept "hardship post."[26] He was subsequently sent to Vienna to represent the Soviet Union at the International Atomic Energy Agency.

Khrushchev's malicious punishments were replaced by almost benign acts during the Brezhnev era. In contrast with the turbulence of the Khrushchev era, Brezhnev's major theme was trust in cadres. In a

[22] Roeder, *Red Sunset*, p. 24.

[23] Conquest, *Power and Policy*, pp. 322–24 and seconded by Roeder, *Red Sunset*, pp. 100–101, Richard Lowenthal, "The Revolution Withers Away," *Problems of Communism*, Vol. 14 (January–February 1965), p. 12 and Taubman, *Khrushchev*, p. 369. Roy and Zhores Medvedev, *Khrushchev: The Years in Power* (New York: Columbia University Press, 1976), p. 76 report that the anti-Party group had intended to arrest Khrushchev. (Also cited in Grey Hodnett, "The Pattern of Leadership Politics," in Bialer, ed., *The Domestic Context of Foreign Policy*, p. 91.)

[24] Taubman, *Khrushchev*, p. 369. Conquest, *Power and Policy*, p. 322, points out that some charges were directed solely at Kaganovich.

[25] Taubman, *Khrushchev*, p. 369.

[26] He complained to the Yugoslav ambassador to Moscow, Vel'ko Mićunović, that in Ulan Bator "Even the Foreign Minister is a veterinarian." Taubman, *Khrushchev*, p. 368.

way the "cadres" in "trust in cadres" carried over to those who were no longer cadres but had been removed from a major Party position, whether as a result of opposition to policy or because they had been indiscreet enough to betray the fact that they thought Brezhnev was not an intellectual powerhouse. Removal from key positions often did not even mean punitive exile. Rather it might imply a desirable—not to Outer Mongolia—ambassadorship such as Aleksandr Yakovlev's appointment to Ottawa, and Nikolai Yegorychev's (first secretary of the Moscow City Committee) appointment to Copenhagen. (The latter's first appointment after being removed was in the tractor-making ministry. Still it's mysterious why Harry Gelman speaks of Yegorychev's treatment as "retribution . . . [which] was drastic indeed."[27]) As the Yakovlev example illustrates, such appointments did not preclude returning to key Party posts in Moscow. Yakovlev played an enormous role in the Gorbachev era. Likewise, removal from a key Party position might entail a rather attractive governmental sinecure in Moscow. Such an assignment might be frustrating for an ambitious *apparatchik*, but it also meant the family could remain in Moscow, which considering the alternatives, was a pretty good deal in 1977.[28]

The Reemergence of Normal Authoritarian High Politics

The evolving norm that losers in a power struggle were not to be killed and might not even be exiled or excluded from the Party contributed substantially to a shift in the intensity of high politics over the period 1955–85. With qualification, the Central Committee became once again, as it had been in earliest days of Soviet power, a selectorate, a development in part driven by the fact that backing the wrong horse no longer constituted a life-threatening act. The qualification first: what Roeder termed reciprocal accountability[29] continued to be accomplished by Daniels's circular flow of power.[30] The largest single group of Central Committee members were regional first secretaries who had been appointed by the center or were persons appointed by the regional secretaries, who had themselves been appointed by the center. This usually rendered the Central Committee members beholden to the Party

[27] Harry Gelman, *The Brezhnev Politburo and the Decline of Détente* (Ithaca, NY: Cornell University Press, 1984), p. 53.

[28] T. H. Rigby, "The Soviet Regional Leadership: The Brezhnev Generation," *Slavic Review*, Vol. 37, No. 1 (March 1978), pp. 1–24.

[29] Roeder, *Red Sunset*, p. 57.

[30] Strong, *The Soviet Union under Brezhnev and Kosygin*, p. 20 and cited, inter alia, in Roeder, *Red Sunset*, p. 57.

leadership when the latter was united and in particular to the first or general secretary. As long as the Central Committee members retained their regional positions, they typically retained their membership in the Central Committee as well. Over time the Central Committee constituted itself as the institutional locus of the selectorate in two ways. It ratified, but did not initiate, consensus selections of the Party leadership. It also became the selectorate with the real, not just the formal, capacity to remove the leader when the Presidium was divided.

Roeder provides an excellent thumbnail sketch of the increased relevance of the Central Committee up to and including the ouster of Khrushchev in October 1964.[31] The revivification of the Central Committee as a potential selectorate began almost immediately after Stalin's death. Initially, Malenkov assumed a governmental role (chairman of the Council of Ministers) and was also a Party secretary. This lasted for less than two weeks. His removal from the position of Party secretary was approved by the Central Committee, as was Beria's June 1953 arrest, and Khrushchev's appointment as first (not general) secretary in September 1953. A plenum of the Central Committee was called prior to the removal of Malenkov from his position as chairman of the Council of Ministers in 1955. In 1957, Khrushchev found himself confronted by a majority of the Presidium who voted to remove him from his position as first secretary. When told there was a majority against him and he must resign, Khrushchev refused and is said to have declared, "Arithmetic is arithmetic and politics is politics." Khrushchev, with major assistance from Marshal Georgy Zhukov, turned to the Central Committee to overthrow the Presidium's vote, though by the time the CC meeting actually occurred he had reestablished dominance in the Presidium and controlled the agenda of the session. In 1964, Khrushchev's opponents in the Presidium consulted with the voting members of the Central Committee *prior* to the Presidium meeting at which Khrushchev was pensioned off. These same Central Committee members then approved the decision.

As is often the case, the boundaries defining the norms that governed the range of the leader's unchallenged authority and those that the members of the collective leadership thought constituted the rules of the game overlapped—and were thus matters of contention. Especially after the defeat of the Anti-Party Group, Khrushchev on several instances went beyond what others and in fact he, at times, recognized as usual oligarchic procedures.

After the fact (Taubman observes, "Too little and too late"[32]), for instance, Khrushchev recognized that he had gone too far in distancing

[31] *Red Sunset*, p. 71.
[32] Taubman, *Khrushchev*, p. 367.

himself from the other members of the Presidium when he replaced Nikolai Bulganin as prime minister. He had criticized Stalin for being general secretary and chairman of the Council of Ministers simultaneously and could scarcely defend his doing the same. His assertion that he took on both jobs because he was asked to do so by members of the Presidium rings hollow, especially given that he acknowledged that doing so reflected "a certain weakness on my part—a bug of some sort which was gnawing away at me and undermining my powers of resistance."[33] His comments in *Khrushchev Remembers* testify that he both recognized the procedural norm of consultation with the Presidium members *and* simultaneously maintained that as leader he had the right to act on his own. As Grey Hodnett observed, "One is struck . . . by the counterpoint between the dominant theme of his own personal power and the supporting theme of participation by 'the leadership.'"[34] Both Khrushchev and his colleagues entertained conflicting norms, the latter recognizing his right as leader to have his way while simultaneously grousing about not being consulted.

When he did consult, he generally had his way. His colleagues, especially after he had replaced all those who opposed him in 1957, deferred to him when, as George Breslauer puts it, he pulled rank.[35] They, moreover, continued to face the obvious collective action problem; who would be the first mover when opposition, no longer life-threatening, might still easily be career-ending. So both Khrushchev and his Presidium colleagues entertained contradictory norms, one monocratic, the other oligarchic. Khrushchev entertained simultaneously both visions, the monocratic and the oligarchic. But, he did not face the collective action problem his colleagues faced. He was less deterred from acting on his own in ways designed to reduce the ability of the Presidium to constrain his behavior and to advance his policy agenda than were they who for a long while were deterred from acts to harness his behavior.

Two ways he boxed in the Presidium members were to broaden the audience to whom he targeted his message and to talk about Presidium discussions out of school. He understood that voice is often as useful as vote. Consequently, he resorted to bringing experts, carefully selected, into Central Committee meetings. He was sometimes quite strategic about when he elected to ad lib speeches to the public, the formal text of which the Presidium had approved. (Not always to be sure, sometimes he just ran it.)

---

[33] Khrushchev, *Khrushchev Remembers*, p. 18.

[34] Hodnett strings together many of these contradictory utterances in "Succession Contingencies," p. 2.

[35] Breslauer, *Khrushchev and Brezhnev*.

He also chose to narrow or alter the group with whom he consulted. Once he was chairman of the Council of Ministers, he was in a position to choose whether to take up a matter with the Council of Ministers or with the Presidium, a dodge, as we have seen (above, pp. 17–18 and 127 respectively), Lenin and Stalin had also employed. After he had defeated the Anti-Party Group, moreover, multiple sources indicate he paid increasing attention to a small group of advisers and that he resorted to back channels to execute policy. The Presidium members seemed to have been particularly galled by his use of his son-in-law, Aleksei Adzhubei, as a back channel contact with the West German government, thus circumventing them on a central foreign policy matter.

As the Adzhubei contact with the West Germans illustrates, however, discontent over the observance of procedural norms and disputes over policy are difficult to disentangle, but policy issues certainly played a role.[36] Hodnett's list of "massive policy issues" is terse and to the point: "stagnant agricultural output, declining industrial productivity, administrative chaos, erosion of ideological control, an exposed military-strategic posture, and serious strains within the Communist 'commonwealth'"[37] Many Presidium members were angered by the back channel action, but they also did not wish for the Soviet government to alter its policy to the Federal Republic of Germany—which of course was part of the reason Khrushchev had gone behind their backs. They were humiliated by the Cuban Missile Crisis. (It became known only much later that the reason the Missile Crisis was not listed in the bill of particulars against Khrushchev was the Presidium members were so appalled by what happened that they forbade it being mentioned.) Taubman is quite persuasive, notwithstanding Khrushchev's assertion in his memoirs that the decision to introduce the missiles was "from the outset, worked out in the collective leadership."[38] The introduction of the missiles into Cuba was Khrushchev's project: "Khrushchev led, and his colleagues obediently followed."[39] The combination of failed policy choices and failure to observe oligarchic norms took their toll over time.[40] In an environment where greater information—including clues about what other members of the Presidium thought—was more available than it had been under Stalin, the collective action problem seems to have dissipated over time. Step by step, a Presidium

[36] For an opposing view, see T. H. Rigby, "The Soviet Leadership: Towards a Self-stabilizing Oligarchy," *Soviet Studies*, Vol. 22, No. 2 (October 1970), pp. 167–91 at p. 173.

[37] Hodnett, "Succession Contingencies," p. 4.

[38] Khrushchev, *Khrushchev Remembers*, pp. 498–99, cited by Taubman, *Khrushchev*, p. 541.

[39] Ibid., p. 546.

[40] Hodnett stresses this point. Cf. "The Pattern," p. 92.

consensus seems to have emerged that Khrushchev had to go. This time, moreover, Khrushchev's policy decisions effectively undermined his position with his base in the Central Committee, the core of which was the regional party secretaries. The circular flow of power was far less efficacious as a means by which the First Secretary controlled the bulk of Central Committee members once he had profoundly weakened their power position by bifurcating the Party at the oblast level into agricultural and industrial branches, each headed by a regional Party secretary. (This "harebrained" scheme was almost immediately abandoned after Khrushchev's forced retirement.)

The circumstances under which Brezhnev became first secretary in October 1964 fundamentally shaped the norms that framed his behavior as first secretary. His predecessor had been forced from office. It was an ouster that had been approved by the institution, the Central Committee, that ratified the ejection of his predecessor and had approved the Presidium recommendation that he be made the first secretary. Khrushchev had been ousted. He could be too.

There was more by way of institutionalization of norms during the Brezhnev era than in the Khrushchev era. Some norms strengthened the role of the leader whereas others constrained him. It was clearly agreed at the time of Khrushchev's ouster in October 1964 that henceforth no one would assume both the role of Party first secretary and chairman of the Council of Ministers. In 1966 the Party rules were amended to reestablish the position of general secretary, a post Brezhnev assumed. Subsequently, Brezhnev apparently attempted to become chairman of the Council of Ministers, but to no avail. He did ultimately become the chairman of the Presidium of Supreme Soviet, a nontrivial post given the verbiage in the 1977 Soviet Constitution, which, as Hodnett emphasizes,[41] provided that the Council of Ministers and its Presidium would be subordinate to the Supreme Soviet Presidium.

The creation of the Defense Council of the USSR, to which not all members of the Presidium belonged and which Brezhnev chaired, certainly also strengthened his position. This was especially so after April 1973, when, according to a declassified CIA document,[42] foreign minister Andrei Gromyko, KGB chief Yury Andropov, and defense minister Andrei Grechko who were "participants in Defense Council deliberations" were elevated "to full Politburo membership." This may have contributed to some segmentation of information, with those on the

---

[41] Hodnett, "The Pattern," p. 107.

[42] "Brezhnev's Personal Authority and Collectivity in the Soviet Leadership," www .foia.cia.gov/sites/default/files/document . . . /DOC000049598.pdf, states that the top three members of the Politburo were all members of the Defense Council.

Politburo who were not members of the Defense Council not informed of relevant information.

That said, it is clear that for every Soviet, including members of the Politburo, the amount of information about security matters and foreign policy available, both in open sources[43] and, for instance, translated in classified versions, was far greater after Khrushchev's secret speech in 1956 than it had been previously. I discuss (below, pp. 151–52) the role the publication of Marshal V. D. Sokolovsky's *Voennaya Strategiya* (*Military Strategy*) in 1962 played in an ongoing dialogue within the military and between the military and the political leadership over matters of grand strategy. Here, the point to be made is that its publication, drawing on the figures of the London Institute for Strategic Studies, made it possible for any Soviet citizen—including members of the Party Presidium/Politburo—to be aware of the number, type, and range of the missiles and airplanes that the United States had at its disposal at the outset of the 1960s as well as the U.S. planned operational missile capacity for 1966. Moreover, the publication of *Military Strategy* occurred coterminously with the publication of a raft of major Western works[44] on security matters.[45] This made it theoretically possible (the press runs were small) for Soviet citizens of all sorts to be far more informed about Western security policy and the consequences of nuclear war. (I bought copies of most of these books in a military bookshop in Samarkand in 1966.) The translation on a classified basis of other Western scholarship for the benefit of a more select readership, including

[43] On the recognition of international relations as a discipline, see Zimmerman, *Soviet Perspectives*, chap. 2.

[44] In a two-year time span, 1959–61, Soviet publishing houses (primarily Voenizdat) produced Russian language versions, inter alia, of Klaus Knorr, *The War Potential of Nations* (correctly translated as *Voennyi potentsial gosudarstv*); Pierre Gallois, *Stratégie de l'âge nucléaire*; Henry Kissinger, *Nuclear Weapons and Foreign Policy*; Bernard Brodie, *Strategy in the Missile Age*; Maxwell Taylor, *The Uncertain Trumpet*; and Robert Osgood, *Limited War*. (Zimmerman, *Soviet Perspectives*, p. 52.)

[45] The decision to translate Western books on security matters and make them available to a broader audience sometimes ran afoul of political watchdogs. (Zimmerman, *Soviet Perspectives*, pp. 51–54.) Various dodges were used to avoid sanctions by the censors at Glavlit (the Soviet censorship bureau) or the Central Committee. One such ploy was to balance the text with a mendaciously distorted introduction (which no one was under any obligation to read) by a notoriously hawkish general to accompany the accurate translation of an important work (cf. the introduction and the text of the Russian-language version of Bernard Brodie's *Strategy in the Missile Age* [Moscow: Voenizdat, 1961]). Similarly, politically sensitive materials might be deleted without informing the reader. Thus, a reader of the Russian-language version of Henry Kissinger, *Nuclear Weapons and Foreign Policy* would not have known that the chapter in which Mao was made into something of a strategist had been omitted.

key political and military officials, made it possible for Soviet leaders and specialists to be even more knowledgeable.

In his long tenure as first and then general secretary (1964–82) Brezhnev seems to have truly dominated the Politburo only in the last two years of his life in the way Khrushchev did after 1957, but even in Brezhnev's last two years some oligarchic norms prevailed. These norms largely stemmed from the conditions under which Brezhnev became first secretary in 1964. As we have seen, the most important oligarchic constraint was that no one could be both chairman of the Council of Ministers and Party head. In addition, meetings of the Politburo and the Secretariat were regularized. Brezhnev reported at the Twenty-Fifth Party Congress that the Politburo had had "215 meetings" (see Table 3.2, p. 85, for the frequency of such meetings in the Stalin period) in the interim since the Twenty-Fourth Party Congress and "evidence also suggests that the Politburo is actively consulted, and its consent obtained, in important foreign policy negotiations."[46]

For most of his tenure as Party leader, Brezhnev operated against the backdrop of the norm of stability of cadres.[47] Turnover was on average far less during the Brezhnev era (October 1964–82) than either before or after. Evidently, from Hough's data,[48] while regional Party posts changed infrequently, those in central ministerial positions changed even less often.

Stability of cadres was also the norm from the moment of Khrushchev's ouster until about 1977. There were few changes in the composition of the most senior members of the Presidium during those years. Writing in an article published in 1975, Hodnett noted that between November 1964 and April 1971 only two persons (Kirill Mazurov and Arvid Pelshe) were promoted to full (voting) membership in the Politburo. In this respect "stability of cadres" assured Brezhnev of his position.[49] The one qualification to the proposition about torpor in changes in the Presidium/Politburo concerns the appointment of three full members of the Politburo in 1973 with major foreign policy assignments—Yury Andropov (KGB chairman), Andrei Gromyko (minister of foreign affairs), and Andrei Grechko (minister of defense), the appointments of which presumably served to strengthen Brezhnev's hand in implementing his détente policy.

[46] Hodnett, "The Pattern," p. 101.

[47] Drawing on data provided by John Patrick Willerton, Roeder (*Red Sunset*, p. 107) shows graphically the overall bimodal pattern of turnover (1953–89) with turnover during the Brezhnev era being generally far less than those years before and after his tenure.

[48] Hough, *Soviet Leadership*, p. 64.

[49] Hodnett, "Succession Contingencies," p. 8.

At the same time, for the bulk of Brezhnev's tenure as first/general secretary, the norm of stability of cadres limited his capacity to construct a Politburo the majority of whom were beholden to him for their appointment. For the entire period November 1964 to 1980, persons of some individual standing at the time of Khrushchev's ouster remained members of the Politburo with major responsibilities. In addition to Brezhnev, they included A. N. Kosygin, chairman of the Council of Ministers; Mikhail Suslov, Central Committee secretary for ideology; A. P. Kirilenko, Central Committee secretary for organizational affairs; and, a somewhat lesser light, D. S. Poliansky, Soviet minister of agriculture. In addition, N. V. Podgorny, chairman of the Presidium of the Supreme Soviet, served as a member of the Politburo until he was removed in 1977.

It is widely accepted that Brezhnev tried to have Kosygin removed as chairman of the Council of Ministers in 1969–70 but failed.[50] He then apparently tried a more subtle ploy. In Romania and the German Democratic Republic, there existed State Councils headed by a president who was simultaneously the Party general secretary.[51] Brezhnev proposed the establishment of such a body for the Soviet Union. Had the proposal succeeded, the chairman of the Council of Ministers, Kosygin, would then have reported to Brezhnev as head of the Party. The State Council would have assumed a role in supervising the economy that the Politburo did not have. (Brezhnev later may have accomplished somewhat of the same thing as a result of the constitutional changes described above, p. 141.)

A second norm was to punish defection[52]—efforts by Politburo members (other than Brezhnev) to go outside to mobilize broader constituencies in order to alter Politburo decisions. Roeder quotes an official Party history as follows: "A strict procedure was established in the CPSU Central Committee whereby no important measure and no speech (to be published in the press) by a member of the Presidium or Secretary of the CPSU was undertaken without preliminary group discussion."[53]

Despite the efforts to insulate the Presidium/Politburo from outside influences, Politburo members—Gennady Voronov (agriculture), Petr Shelest (nationality issues), and Aleksandr Shelepin (foreign policy)—defected by taking their case for policy differences to a constituency larger than the Presidium, whether by esoteric communication in the

---

[50] Gelman, *The Brezhnev Politburo*, p. 129; Roeder, *Red Sunset*, p. 109.

[51] John Dornberg, *Brezhnev: The Masks of Power* (New York: Basic Books, 1974), pp. 262–64 and referenced in Roeder, *Red Sunset*, p. 109.

[52] On defection, see Roeder, *Red Sunset*, pp. 108–9 and Gelman, *The Brezhnev Politburo*, pp. 52–54.

[53] Roeder, *Red Sunset*, p. 101.

press or airing differences in the Central Committee. Shelepin, for instance, expressed views in *Krasnaya zvezda* (*Red Star*) that were edited out of *Izvestia* about the significance of American policy in Vietnam for broader dimensions of U.S.-Soviet relations[54] at variance with the consensus views of the Brezhnev-led oligarchy. Shelest was accused of fostering Ukrainian nationalism while Voronov supported the "link" system in agriculture in opposition to Brezhnev's policy of greatly increased spending.[55] The three ultimately paid the price. They were removed from their major positions along with their concomitant membership in the Politburo.

An oligarchic balance prevailed in the Politburo for well more than a decade, even though Brezhnev was clearly "the man." Taking into consideration appointments both to voting and nonvoting members of the Politburo what Hodnett has termed "ethnogeographical" balance prevailed. Shades of American politics: there was "some type of representation accorded to the Western (Baltic and Belorussian), Caucasus, and Central Asian republics and nationalities."[56] Only after thirteen years in office (1977) was Brezhnev able to oust Nikolai Podgorny from his post as chairman of the Presidium of the Supreme Soviet and only in 1980 when Kosygin died and when Brezhnev was obviously in failing health himself, did he control the appointment of the chairman of the Council of Ministers. Kosygin's replacement, N. A. Tikhonov, took positions that, with trivial exceptions, far more closely meshed with Brezhnev's views than had Kosygin's.[57]

So, just as Khrushchev was contradictory about his role and about his interactions with his Party Presidium colleagues, we find that the

[54] Both papers carried Shelepin's speech in their December 10, 1966, numbers. *Izvestia* deleted the italicized passage from the following statement that appeared in *Red Star*. I have italicized the part that conveyed the sense that the worsening international situation was a consequence of a general confrontation of imperialist and revolutionary forces. *Izvestia*'s text implied that the primary reason for the aggravated international tension was the Vietnam War: "As a result of the intensification of the aggressive schemes of the imperialists a serious aggravation the world situation has taken place. *World reaction, headed by the main force of war and aggression — American imperialism — now here, now there kindles the hotbeds of conflict. The imperialists in a number of regions are striving to restore by force the colonial order, to stifle national liberation movement of the people.* The U.S.A. has been waging for several years now a plundering, colonial war against the peoples of Vietnam." Zimmerman, "The Korean and Vietnam Wars," in *Diplomacy of Power: Soviet Armed Forces as a Political Instrument* (Washington, DC: Brookings Institution, 1981), pp. 314–56 at p. 344.

[55] On Shelest, see Grey Hodnett and Peter Potichnyi, "The Ukraine and the Czechoslovak Crisis" (Australian National University Department of Political Science, Occasional Paper No. 6, 1970); on Brezhnev's agricultural policy and Voronov's opposition to it, see Gelman, *The Brezhnev Politburo*, p. 239n24 and the materials cited there.

[56] Hodnett, "The Pattern," p. 98.

[57] Breslauer, *Khrushchev and Brezhnev*, pp. 242–44.

monocratic and oligarchic strands coexisted simultaneously within Brezhnev's Politburo. The former dominated in the last several years of his tenure. But even then some oligarchic norms persisted. These included, crucially, that the posts of general secretary and chairman of the Council of Ministers not be held by the same person; that the Politburo meet routinely about once a week; that some ethnic and/or geographic balance in the Politburo be observed regardless of the preferences of the general secretary and the other members of the Secretariat; that it was inappropriate for members of the Politburo to go outside it to influence policy; and that doing so might result in ouster from that body but would not result in arrest, death, or humiliating exile.

THE SLOW PROCESS OF SOCIETAL REARTICULATION, 1956–1985

Khrushchev tried to accomplish the same kind of political mobilization as Stalin had achieved. But he attempted this task in the absence not only of terror but while affirming that with the formation of the Soviet Bloc, capitalist encirclement no longer existed. (Capitalist encirclement, it will be recalled, had served as the basis for Stalin's argument that the state and its organs of repression were to be strengthened as the country advanced toward communism.)

There were several strands to Khrushchev's vision. In terms of domestic goals he articulated grandiose and appealing schemes: the Virgin Lands scheme for one, and the goal of catching up to and overtaking the United States in the production of consumer goods for another. Globally, he articulated a vision of the manner by which one could persist in believing in the inevitable triumph of communism even though capitalism possessed nuclear weapons and world war threatened not just capitalism but civilization.[58] While repudiating terror, he glorified the *kollektiv* and envisaged vertical and horizontal surveillance as being adequate to achieve the unanimity Stalin had achieved through the systematic use of terror as a means of control.[59] Khrushchev shared with the Stalin of the Great Purges a great concern about the dangers of dissimulation. (As Oleg Kharkhordin notes,[60] Khrushchev himself was a great dissimulator, vividly illustrated by his speech at the Nineteenth Party Congress attacking such people and his putatively secret speech in 1956 at the Twentieth Party Congress.)

---

[58] William Zimmerman, "The Transformation of the Modern Multistate System: The Exhaustion of Communist Alternatives," *Journal of Conflict Resolution*, Vol. 16, No. 3 (September 1972), pp. 303–17.

[59] See especially Kharkhordin, *The Collective*.

[60] Ibid., p. 275.

Like Stalin, Khrushchev and Brezhnev were also great homogeniz-ers. Stalin had homogenized Soviet society by the collectivization of the peasantry and by repressing thousands upon thousands of ethnic minorities on the borderlands of the Soviet Union. Khrushchev's anti-parasite law was similarly intended to homogenize Soviet cities, to cre-ate the impression they were uniformly populated. The law was used to expel idlers—which could mean people without jobs, people working in the second economy, religious or political dissidents, and other more traditional troublemakers—from the central cities, especially ones such as Moscow and Leningrad frequented by Western tourists. Brezhnev emulated Khrushchev's deeds but abandoned the verbiage.[61]

But Stalin—and Fainsod—were right. Terror was the linchpin of the Soviet mobilization system. The purposeful use of the collective, cam-paigns against deviants, and the like all took their toll. But they were not sufficient to prevent the growing articulation of institutionally based interests and the development of a textured social system in which sub-elites with an institutional base could articulate their views about the ambit of politics—who decides—and about everyday politics in the Lasswellian sense: disputes about who gets what, when, and how.[62]

In the absence of terror, *institutionally linked* groupings increasingly asserted a self-awareness of themselves as a group with interests that were somewhat at variance with those of the Party. ("Institutionally linked" is italicized to emphasize the regime's persisting resistance to autonomous groups or groupings.) Other subelites evidenced an awareness of these as a group as well. Moreover, oblast and Repub-lic secretaries, increasingly comfortable that carefully chosen words would not result in their removal, broadened the topics they addressed publicly, especially during the Brezhnev era. In both the Khrushchev and Brezhnev eras it was possible to discern evidence about matters of high policy that throughout the 1930s and 1940s had long been too closely held to be ascertained through open sources. The Soviet Union was becoming less the low-information system that it had been when even the guarded expression of views could be fatal. In the Khrushchev and Brezhnev eras it was more appropriate to speak of a narrow plat-form or a framework—rather than a general line—within which a mod-estly broadened constituency—experts, oblast secretaries and other members of the Central Committee, major military figures—writing in specialized journals could get their policy advocacy on the record. As Milton Lodge noted a generation ago, as early as 1955 the authoritative

[61] Ibid., p. 297 and drawing on Peter Juviler, *Revolutionary Law and Order: Politics and Social Change in the USSR* (New York: Free Press, 1976).
[62] Harold D. Lasswell, *Politics: Who Gets What, When, and How* (New York: P. Smith, 1950).

journal *Kommunist*, after dutifully stating the obligatory ("Marxism-Leninism must be the 'essential' framework within which specialist discussion should take place"), lamented the fact that "scholarly articles 'often' bypass Party formulas and all too frequently attempt 'to reverse fundamental theses of the Party.'"[63]

Equally important, there were changes in the regime's relations to society broadly conceived—the broad masses, as it were. Those who were neither politically active nor politically aware were more conformist but less mobilized. Comparing snapshots of the late Stalin and late Brezhnev periods, the regime would be seen to be less successful in exacting performance in the latter than during the former. Other snapshots taken at the same two times would indicate, similarly, that in the late Brezhnev years, many ordinary Soviet folk had cultivated a handful of horizontal linkages indicative of truly private space of the kind that the Great Purge had been at such great efforts to destroy.

Let me illustrate the specialist-Party dialogue with some pertinent examples about military and foreign policy matters, domains that constitute hard cases—where one would least expect open sources to be informative—and then consider the overall propensity of subelites to differentiate themselves and their views from those of the Party. The first illustrates the ability to generate information about a key Soviet decision, namely the military budget. The second pertains to the efforts of a key component of the Soviet military to stake out its position in the ongoing policy dialogue and to resist efforts by the Party to reserve for itself an exclusive claim as to who decides a major policy matter.

Early on, specialists on Soviet politics recognized that Soviet media utterances were carefully made and made a variety of efforts to sort out the circumstances when the care was prompted by domestic political concerns, attempts to signal foreign elites, and manipulative calculations about how domestic and foreign audiences respond to various symbols. Widespread consensus existed, though, about the published figures for the defense budget: they bore no relation to the actual military budget. The latter was a closely guarded secret. As the Central Intelligence Agency noted, the only statistic published in the state budget for defense was "uninformative because its scope is not defined and its size appears to be manipulated to suit Soviet political purposes."[64]

---

[63] Milton Lodge, "Soviet Elite Participatory Attitudes in the Post-Stalin Period," *American Political Science Review*, Vol. 62, No. 3 (September 1968), p. 828.

[64] Central Intelligence Agency, *Estimated Soviet Defense Spending: Trends and Prospects* (Springfield, VA: National Technical Information Service, 1978), p. 13.

But as I and Glenn Palmer found many years ago,[65] proceeding carefully one could generate links between words and deeds in assessing Soviet military spending. By words here I have in mind the finance minister's annual budget speech to the Supreme Soviet, a speech that represented the authoritative culmination of the political process wherein the budget was determined.[66] The speech was highly formulaic: it mentioned an aggregate number and a list of the ways the Soviet Union had made the world safe for socialism in the past year, often had some unkind words for the United States or imperialism generally, and presented a nonquantitative characterization of the change in the military budget for the next year. Generally, the speech contained a statement of Soviet intentions to the effect that it "must take the necessary measures to strengthen and increase the allocation for defense." In other years, the finance minister merely observed (as he did with reference to 1963) that the USSR found it "necessary to allot part of its national income for strengthening" Soviet defense, while in December 1960 he declared that for 1961 the Soviet Union would "reduce its expenditures" on military spending.[67]

By deeds I have in mind the annual changes in the Soviet military budget during the quarter century 1956–82 (i.e., from Khrushchev's speech to the end of the Brezhnev era) as estimated by various Western sources. We primarily used the ruble-based estimates of Robert Shishko at the RAND Corporation augmented by Miroslav Nincic. Shishko in turn had developed his series by linking estimates by the Stockholm Institute for Peace Research (SIPRI) and materials released by the CIA in 1976. We also compared our estimates with figures based solely on SIPRI data and a series produced by the London Institute for International Strategic Studies.[68]

A first major finding was that what the minister of finance said about Soviet budgetary intentions was not independent of whether he made reference to the United States or to imperialism. In other words, he was addressing two audiences simultaneously: the Soviet attentive

[65] William Zimmerman and Glenn Palmer, "Words and Deeds in Soviet Foreign Policy: The Case of Soviet Military Expenditures," *American Political Science Review*, Vol. 77 (1983), pp. 358–67.

[66] From 1959 to 1982, the minister of finance was the same man (N. F. Garbuzov).

[67] For expenditures for 1963, see *Pravda*, December 11, 1962, as cited in Zimmerman and Palmer, "Words and Deeds," p. 360 and for 1961, *Pravda*, December 21, 1960, as cited in Zimmerman and Palmer, "Words and Deeds," p. 360.

[68] For details, see Zimmerman and Palmer, "Words and Deeds," p. 359. The one Western estimate that qualified our findings was the CIA series published in 1982 employing its broader definition of Soviet defense spending. The CIA itself maintained that *its* narrower "estimates [were] more detailed and precise" (*Estimated Soviet Defense Spending*, as cited in Zimmerman and Palmer, "Words and Deeds," p. 359).

public—largely the Central Committee and specialists—and Western governments and mass opinion. He and his Politburo bosses may have believed it made sense to usually tell the truth but appreciated that there might be circumstances when the rational timing of surprise was appropriate.[69] What we found was that inferences about Soviet spending derived from Soviet statements about U.S. behavior proved a far better predictor of Soviet behavior than would *exclusive* attention to Soviet statements about Soviet intentions with respect to military spending in the forthcoming year. A striking example of this occurred in the December 1960 speech to which reference has already been made in which the minister announced "significant contraction of the Armed Forces and, in connection with that, . . . [a reduction in] its expenditures on their maintenance as well." This was followed by a long tirade on the increase of Western military expenditures over the previous decade. Western estimates were that the Soviet Union increased its budget in 1961 by almost a quarter.

But this example of the strategic timing of surprise was an exceptional one. Using the Shishko-Nincic series we found a striking relation between whether the United States and/or imperialism was mentioned and the "observed" change in Soviet defense expenditures as calculated in the Shishko-Nincic series. In all thirteen instances when reference was made to the United States or imperialism, Shishko and Nincic estimated that there followed an increase in Soviet defense expenditures. It's a mixed bag when no mention is made of the United States. Estimates almost equally divided between decreases (six) and increases (four). Overall, the mean change in years when mention was made of the United States and/ or imperialism estimated in the Shishko-Nincic series was plus 8.3 percent. When no mention was made of the United States, the mean change was *minus* 0.8 percent. Evidently, the old saw should be reversed: if you can't say something bad about somebody, don't say anything at all. We built on that insight to generate a robust model ($r^2 = .78$) accounting for the change in Soviet defense spending on the basis of our content analysis and comparing those estimates with the announced budget change and the results of the Shishko-Nincic model.[70]

We took away from our analysis the strong sense that those who engaged in traditional qualitative ad hoc content analysis and took Soviet words seriously were onto something. As much as the Soviet Union after Stalin's death remained a relatively low-information system, the leadership acted as though it believed it necessary to depict the broad

---

[69] Robert Axelrod and William Zimmerman, "The Soviet Press on Soviet Foreign Policy: A Usually Reliable Source," *British Journal of Political Science*, Vol. 11, No. 2 (April 1981), pp. 183–200.

[70] Zimmerman and Palmer, "Words and Deeds."

contours of the budgetary situation to key domestic elites (while sometimes simultaneously attempting to send deceptive signals to Western
audiences). As Michael Cohen pointed out to us twenty-five years ago,
the only way to make sure that everybody who counts knows that everybody else knows what the broad outlines of a decision are is through
public commitment. That entailed sharing very broad knowledge of the
defense budget—whether it was going to be increased, decreased, or
remain the same—with attentive readers of *Pravda*.

The way in which specialists staked out a claim for having a say
in policy matters was nicely exemplified by the 1962 publication of
Voennaya Strategiya (*Military Strategy*) edited by V. D. Sokolovsky—a
Soviet marshal, Central Committee member, and former chief of the
general staff—and several other generals and colonels.[71] At the time of
its publication it was the most systematic Soviet work on strategy thus
far published. Its central theme was the need for new strategic concepts
to account for the "radically changed" nature of war in the atomic age.[72]
Briefly put, its authors had come to share the views of their Western
counterparts about the nature and conduct of world war in the missile
age, that is, that intercontinental missiles would be decisive.

There was much by way of promotion and self-promotion.[73] But
it turned out not to be an authoritative volume in the traditional Soviet sense. Rather, as Western military specialists quickly recognized,
it was best conceived as an effort by a major segment of the military
establishment to enhance its chances of favorable treatment in the allocation of resources—who gets what—and to increase the scope of the
decision-making competence of the military—who decides who decides. Thomas Wolfe correctly observed that "the volume represents,
in a sense, a point scored for the military side of the argument . . . by
getting the military viewpoint on the record in the form of the first comprehensive exposition of the new doctrine."[74]

---

[71] For English-language versions, see *Military Strategy* (New York: Praeger, 1963) and
Soviet Military Strategy (Englewood Cliffs, NJ: Prentice Hall, 1963).

[72] Stalin and Beria deserve the credit (or blame) for developing atomic and hydrogen
weapons, but prior to their death there had been no open-source appreciation of the strategic implications of the atomic era or details about the consequences of war involving
the use of nuclear weapons. On Stalin's role in the development of nuclear weapons,
David Holloway, *Stalin and the Bomb: The Soviet Union and Atomic Energy, 1939–1956* (New
Haven, CT: Yale University Press, 1994) remains the primary source. Cf. Herbert S. Diner-
stein, *War and the Soviet Union* (New York: Praeger, 1959) on the initial Soviet efforts after
Stalin's death to reconceptualize the nature of war.

[73] For documentation, see Zimmerman, "Sokolovskii [Sokolovsky] and His Critics: A
review," *Journal of Conflict Resolution*, Vol. 8, No. 3 (September 1964), pp. 322–28 and the
sources cited there.

[74] *Soviet Military Strategy*, pp. 33–34.

Two assertions in the first edition in particular bear this out. One pertained to what matters in wartime, the other was almost certainly targeted at Khrushchev himself: "In wartime, strategic considerations often determine policy . . . [and] even acquire decisive significance" and an even more pointed remark that military doctrine—a broader and more political concept than military strategy—is "not thought out or compiled by *a single person or group of persons.*"[75]

High-level Soviet observers also apparently recognized the volume for the challenge that it was to the civilian leadership and to Khrushchev in particular. A second "corrected and enlarged" edition emerged a mere fifteen months after the first. The "corrections" were such as to render the volume more suitable to the political leadership. (A third appeared in 1968.) The second edition was more attuned to Khrushchev's and the Party's views than the first edition had been.

But Sokolovsky and his colleagues did not fold completely. Having made their point in the first edition, the statement that military doctrine was not the product of a single person was dropped. But they continued to resist the contention that "questions of leadership in the preparation of a country for war" be deleted. "Such a proposal," they declared, "is motivated by the notion that military strategy supposedly must concern itself only with the leadership of the armed forces while the preparation of a country with respect to war—this, don't you know, is the affair of politics."[76]

Efforts to circumscribe a broadly based "affair of politics" and to make a case for resource allocation decisions favorable to one or another subelite were extensive in the period between Stalin's death and 1965. In Western scholarship these efforts resulted in a spate of case studies concerning such putative groups as the secret police, the lawyers, and the industrial managers. These were inevitably a bit short analytically as Westerners quarreled over whether the things out there were groups, groupings, or tendencies. But what these papers were capturing was what Franklyn Griffiths called "tendencies of articulation," attentive publics who felt secure enough to express, within clear limits, views that constituted a kind of advocacy or amounted to staking out a claim that they self-identified as a group with views that distinguished themselves from the Party and other interested articulators.

Most acknowledged there were a number of clusterings, with some institutional hook. A major step forward in characterizing the evolving relationship between the Party and key subelites came with two articles by Milton Lodge. His idea was that comparative content analysis of

---

[75] Ibid., p. 104 and p. 130 respectively, italics added.
[76] Sokolovsky, *Voennaya Strategiya*, 2nd ed. (Moscow: Voenizdat, 1963), p. 5.

representative media sources over time would allow us greater purchase as to whether those in the central Party apparatus and among four Soviet subelites (Lodge termed them specialist elites)—the central economic bureaucrats, the military, the literary intelligentsia, and the legal profession—thought of themselves as participating in the policy process, whether they saw that role as increasing in the period between Stalin's death and 1965 and the manner Party relations with specialists had evolved in those years.

What he found was that "1) the specialist elites increasingly manifest a sense of group self consciousness and ascribed group status, and 2) over time the specialist elites develop a distinct set of policy orientations which differentiates them from the Party apparatchiki and challenges the dominance of the apparatchiki in the Soviet political system." That is, to be a group, group self-consciousness must exist and, in the Soviet context, the subelites must think of themselves as being separate from the Party, other elites must perceive them as being a group, and they must have shared values that distinguish them from the holders of other values, most notably the values of the Party apparatus. Drawing on Brzezinski and Huntington's distinction between ideological (Soviet) and instrumental (American) systems, Lodge asked whether, as evidenced in the specialized press, the subelites had become increasingly instrumental over time.

One way to ascertain this was to ask to whom the various elites ascribed the role of socialization. The Party, he found, throughout the years 1952 to 1965, emphasized its role as the primary socializing agent, whereas in the aggregate the specialists were far less so disposed in the years 1959 to 1965 than previously, as Table 5.1 shows.

A second way was to assess the extent to which the elites depicted the Party's role as ideological or instrumental. Each of the subelites attached greater weight to the Party's instrumental role than to its ideological role, whereas the Party gave noticeably greater weight to ideological values. By the same token, Lodge depicted a continuum ranging from (1) "policy making should be the responsibility of the Party leadership solely" to (5) "it should be the domain of specialists solely." The intermediate points were (2) the Party primarily, (3) the Party and the specialists should both participate in the policy-making arena, and (4) the specialists primarily should participate. By his coding for the last year he surveyed (1965) the Party press resulted in a mean score of 2.4, whereas all the subelite media gave responses that placed them somewhere between 3.0 (both the Party and specialists participating) and 4.0 (the specialists primarily), with scores ranging from 3.1 to 3.6. Moreover, on the normative Lasswellian question (who should get what) he found the Party had shifted its priorities over time away from heavy industry

Table 5.1 Elite perceptions of the influence of the party and party organizations, 1952–57 and 1959–65

Organization	1952–57 (%)	1959–65 (%)	Percentage change
Party	69	73	+4
Economic	63	29	−34
Legal	62	19	−43
Military	46	35	−11
Literary	30	19	−11
Specialists overall	50	25	−25

Source: Milton Lodge, " 'Groupism' in the Post-Stalin Period," *Midwest Journal of Political Science*, Vol. 12, No. 3 (August 1968), pp. 330–51 at p. 341.

and military spending to consumerism but had done so *after* the economic, literary, and legal subelites had moved in that direction. Lodge was appropriately cautious. He explicitly recognized that what he was measuring were subelite and Party attitudes, not their behavior. But he was certainly correct in concluding that specialist elites were "no longer transmission belts, [were] at a minimum potential interest groups, and . . . [were] perhaps active participants in the Soviet political system."

EVOLVING ELITE-MASS RELATIONS

This chapter depicts three processes extending over the period from the end of the Great Purge in 1938 to Leonid Brezhnev's death in 1982. In the first part of this chapter we described the slow evolution of norms pertaining to the regime. In the second, we surveyed the gradual development of a more textured relationship involving the regime and institutionally based subelites with the latter emerging more clearly as claimants for resources and for a role in decision making. In this section, we consider trends over the same period in regime-society relations as expectations of a return to terror-based repression diminished and Soviet society became increasingly complex and largely urban industrial. The central argument is that, as the implications of the end of terror as the central instrument of political control became assimilated, the ability of the regime to engage in the mobilized participation that had distinguished it from conventional authoritarian systems diminished but did not dissipate entirely.

When precisely one would date these changes would be a matter of dispute. As we see below, by the end of the Brezhnev era we have trend data that show the ability of the regime to mobilize society to its purposes had diminished in comparison with the late Stalin era. In an important book, Vera Dunham dated the changes to the late Stalin period. Above, page 110, we made reference to Stalin's attacks on dissimulation—those for instance whose treacherous thoughts hid behind overfulfillment of the plan. Dunham argues that Stalin became increasingly concerned with behavior, not thoughts. Her sources were the enormous volume of socialist realism novels published in Stalin's time. In these novels (which of course went through prepublication censorship by Glavlit), the appropriateness of dissimulation was a key theme. Thus, she cites the novel *First and Last*, in which a young naval officer serves the motherland as he sees fit—for which he is rebuked. A higher up and friend "proffers advice, the kind that oils the wheel of any deal." "You should agree with them," he is told, " . . . [t]hat way it will be much more peaceful." The principled young ensign rejects the advice. He is shunned by peers and senior officers alike and becomes the one ensign not promoted to lieutenant junior grade. As Kharkhordin observes, "In the late Stalinist society . . . [t]he ultimate judge . . . is no longer some doctrinal ideal, but the community that imposes standard norms of behavior." One may quarrel with when the emphasis on terror as the primary means of control attenuated. (Readers are cautioned that we are talking about change over time—movement away from an awful base in 1937–38—and that the fear of repression remained considerable. Even as late as the Gorbachev era many Soviet citizens ducked for cover when the famous Nina Andreyeva letter calling for the return to the bad old days was published.)

Moreover, as we have seen, Stalin did not alter the institutional and doctrinal bases for permanent purge. In the late Stalin years mechanisms for mobilized participation other than terror, many of which lasted long after Stalin himself, were marshaled to achieve political support as well. Lists would vary, but all would include the proliferation of kollektivs as a means of social control at most levels of society, the delivery of public goods such as free public education and health care, and Stalin's overt cultivation of Russian nationalism (including the moderation of policies against the Orthodox Church) as having served to alter the bases of the citizenry's support for the regime.

As we stressed at the outset (Introduction, pp. 4–6), in terms of regime-society relations, two key features of traditional, full, authoritarian dictatorships were that they did not attempt to overthrow entirely the notion of a private sphere—especially within the family—and they accepted acquiescence rather than demanded affirmation. The mobilized participation characteristic of the Soviet system in the Stalin period demanded the subordination of the family to the state. In the context of the Great Terror, the regime had considerable success in achieving the kind of penetration of the family in practice exemplified by the Pavlik Morozov story (where the son informs on his father). The strongest exponent of the view that the state-family dynamic altered after Stalin's death is Vladimir Shlapentokh. In a book published in 1989 he wrote that "[s]ince 1953, the Soviet family has gradually emerged as a cohesive unit that confronts the state, rather than serves it."[77] Moreover, he asserted, drawing on survey data from the Vladimir region in the late 1970s, respondents, "asked about the influence of various social factors on them, gave conspicuous priority to the family."[78]

We have better evidence that a secular change occurred in the regime's ability to mobilize its citizenry for its political purposes in the years ranging from Stalin's last years to Brezhnev's last years. Much of this comes from the Soviet Interview Project (SIP). Its investigators interviewed former Soviet citizens who migrated to the United States primarily in 1979 or 1980 and who were asked about their attitudes and behaviors during years immediately before they applied to migrate from the Soviet Union. These former Soviet citizens were overwhelmingly Jewish, relatively more educated than the mean Soviet citizen, and highly urban. Those of us, myself included, who participated in SIP concluded that by controlling for the reasons those interviewed migrated and by focusing on reported behaviors one could derive plausible snapshots about many patterns of political behavior across groups in the Soviet Union (more confidently, in urban areas of the Soviet Union) from sharply discrepant differences in the reported behaviors of groups among those who migrated.

To accomplish the task of assessing the level of, and change in, mobilized participation I categorized the respondents into five categories: (1) political leaders, (2) managers, (3) high-level professionals, (4) low-level professionals and clerical workers, and (5) "others" — which in this highly urban sample largely meant blue-collar workers.[79] I then examined the responses across the groupings to five categories of behaviors relevant to political mobilization. These were (1) election-related behaviors, (2) regime-dominated group behavior, (3) regime-dominated

---

[77] See Vladimir Shlapentokh, *Public and Private Life of the Soviet People: Changing Values in Post-Stalin Russia* (New York: Oxford University Press, 1989), p. 164.

[78] Ibid., p. 167.

[79] A detailed description of the criteria for including respondents in the various categories may be found in Zimmerman, "Mobilized Participation," pp. 334–36. Basic occupation was coded according to the official Soviet system of occupations used in the 1970 census. It should be emphasized that by political leaders I am referring to persons who were two or more steps down from the Politburo or the Council of Ministers but coded as leaders for that census. For more detail, see ibid., p. 334.

media behavior, (4) accessing nonregime media, and (5) mobilization for national security and military preparedness.

Voting was obligatory for Soviet citizens, though in practice some said they only "sometimes" or even "never" voted. Examining only those who played no substantial role in the decision to migrate, we do not detect a statistically significant difference among the five groupings in this respect. (This is likely a result of there only being three political leaders and three managers among forty-seven respondents who said they played no substantial role in the decision to migrate and who reported having never or sometimes not voting.) Comparing the far larger number who said they participated in the decision or that they had made the decision, it was, as Friedgut noted, "exactly the people [the political leaders and the high-level professionals] who should by all criteria, Soviet and non-Soviet alike, be the most active participants in elections"[80] who were relatively prone *not* to vote.

When we examine other aspects of the voting process—being a member of an electoral commission, a canvasser/agitator, or sometimes even a candidate—it is clear that ordinary workers were largely not pressured to participate in such matters. Fewer than 7 percent of the blue-collar workers (those grouped as "others" above") participated as election officials of some kind, whereas a minimum of 15 percent of the remaining respondents did so. Political leaders and high-level professionals did not vote as often as others in the USSR, but it obviously went with the territory that they were more expected to work in elections to soviets. This was probably not an onerous task, especially since in practice only a small percentage of them actually did so.

Likewise, looking at participation in organs such as the people's control or comrades' courts, what is striking is how few people of any sort were mobilized. Only a bit more than one-tenth of those surveyed answered that they went regularly to such meetings—hardly data indicative of a mobilized society. These were among the ways that Party leaders and high-level professionals showed a public face of regime support.

Another domain conventionally associated with political mobilization concerns the media. In the Soviet Union in the late Brezhnev era newspaper readership was very high. Political leaders and high-level professionals (and to a lesser extent managers) paid more attention to the news in the newspapers and on television than did low-level professionals and blue-collar workers. All three higher-level groupings were much more likely to devote their attention to news rather than

[80] Theodore Friedgut, *Political Participation in the USSR* (Princeton, NJ: Princeton University Press, 1979), p. 118.

to variety programs on domestic radio than were the low-level professionals or blue-collar workers.

But domestic radio was only one source of information for urban
Soviet citizens in the late 1970s and early 1980s. Political leaders and
high-level professionals were far more likely to read *samizdat* than were
managers or low-level professionals, who were in turn much more
likely to read it than were the proletariat. Those who were better educated and more politicized were also the people, primarily, who filled
the stadiums to hear Yegeny Yevtushenko and other poets and who
made up small groups (usually of two or three[81]) that were nested in
larger groups who cared intensely about some cultural and increasingly political non-Soviet themes.[82]

Political leaders, managers, and high-level professionals were also
substantially more likely to listen to foreign radio than were low-level
professionals and blue-collar workers. Viewing the system as characterized by mobilized participation would lead us to expect that all Soviet
citizens would be equally disinclined to gain access to nonregime media
sources. If the regime cared primarily to mobilize subelites, it would be
those with responsible positions who would be most deterred from foreign radio listenership. In practice, the situation was quite the reverse.
There were clear differences across the board in foreign radio listenership on the part of those who professed considerable interest in politics. Nevertheless, role in the system was also a major predictor. Almost
all (96 percent) who were political leaders reported listening to foreign
radio, and more than nine out of ten high-level professionals and managers said so as well whereas 80 percent of the low-level professionals
and 77 percent of the workers in the sample reported having listened
to foreign radio. These figures comport more with a vision of the Soviet
Union at the end of the Brezhnev era as a conventional, "full," modern
dictatorship. In such a system, those behaving at variance with regime
norms were evidencing the *social* mobilization that Karl Deutsch depicted as a consequence of modernization along with some routinized
behaviors characteristic of the mobilized participation associated with
traditional assumptions about the Soviet political system.

Donna Bahry, moreover, produced a remarkable comparison of the
overall patterns of political behavior on the part of those in the SIP sample and a survey by Russell Dalton of political participation in the erstwhile Federal Republic of Germany.[83]

---

[81]On the use of triads by those experiencing Nazi and/or Soviet occupation during
World War II, see Keith Darden, *Enduring Occupation* (forthcoming).

[82]Kharkhordin, *The Collective*, pp. 312–14.

[83]Donna Bahry, "Politics, Generations, and Change in the USSR," in Millar, *Politics,
Work, and Daily Life*, p. 70.

Table 5.2 Efforts to avoid military service by occupational category, 1965–80

	Occupational grouping				
	Political leaders	Managers	High-level professionals	Low-level professionals	Blue-collar workers
Made effort to avoid (n)	29% (4)	33% (3)	24% (32)	12% (7)	17% (22)

Source: William Zimmerman, "Mobilized Participation and the Nature of the Soviet Dictatorship," in James R. Millar, ed., Politics, Work, and Daily Life in the USSR: A Survey of Former Soviet Citizens (Cambridge: Cambridge University Press, 1987), pp. 332–53 at p. 344.

While the parallels are not exact, the item-by-item percentages were remarkably comparable and constituted strong evidence that by the end of the Brezhnev era urban Russians were evidencing attitudes somewhat analogous to urban dwellers in North American or European cities and behaving in ways more evocative of social mobilization rather than the political mobilization of the Stalin era.

In a similar vein, consider a fifth domain where the regime's capacity to mobilize can be assessed: namely, preparedness and national security. Stalin maintained that "permanently operating factors" gave Soviet-type mobilization systems an advantage over capitalist states in their capacity to mobilize its resources for the purposes of fighting a World War II–type war. Should this be the case, it would translate into high conscription rates and considerable effective attention to civil defense.

Table 5.2 depicts efforts to avoid military service across the five occupational categories: political leaders, managers, high-level professionals, low-level professionals, and ordinary workers.

The numbers are small and the statistical difference among the categories not significant. Nevertheless, the pattern is what we have come to expect from the instances of mobilization considered in the past few pages, to wit, it was the political leaders, the managers, and the high-level professionals who tried to avoid military service whereas the low-level professionals and the ordinary workers were far less so inclined.

What about civil defense? Here the hackneyed "Compared to what?" is appropriate. Those who during the Cold War worried about the relative civil defense preparedness of the United States and the Soviet Union would probably have been disturbed to learn that approximately two out of five (41 percent) in the sample remembered the location of the civil defense shelter closest to their place of work or school. Similarly, during the two years before they applied to migrate from the Soviet Union a bit more than a quarter of the SIP respondents said they had gone to a shelter (29 percent) and 8 percent of them reported that there was an evacuation drill in which they and/or others in their workplace or school had to leave town temporarily. By comparison with experiences in most other countries—excluding presumably Switzerland and Sweden—these figures were high and evidence of greater mobilization for national security than was the case for the United States.

Those who were more relaxed about civil defense as a threat would have noted in rebuttal that three-fifths did not even know the location of the shelter nearest their place of employment, that about three-fourths of them had not been in a shelter in the last two years before they applied for emigration from the Soviet Union, and that in that same period more than 90 percent had not had an evacuation drill in which people left town. Once again, those least mobilized were the blue-collar workers.

Considering all five categories of behavior, there were areas where participation was relatively homogeneous across occupational groups—regular attendance at people's militia and comrades' courts—but there were no domains where mobilization was unambiguously high and fundamentally homogeneous across groups. Indeed, the political sub-elites evidenced the kind of mobilization to politics one would expect of such people everywhere, but their behavior was a severe challenge to viewing the Soviet Union during the late Brezhnev era as politically mobilized.

It was exactly those with political careers and the high-level professionals who were more likely to engage in behavior incongruent with regime-induced mobilization. They were less likely to vote, more likely to read *samizdat*, more prone to listen to foreign radio, and more likely to endeavor to avoid military service. As Bahry observed,[84] it was those who were "reds" or "experts" who were most likely to engage in behaviors that indicated they had not been mobilized exclusively by the political system. To understand their behavior, we do not reference the classical totalitarian theorists, we read the literature on the change in attitudes and behaviors that accompany industrialization and urbanization.

Those who most engaged in regime-conforming behaviors were the blue-collar workers. They conformed more, but they were generally mobilized less: they read Soviet newspapers far less, they participated in election administration and in work committees less, they were less likely to know the nearest civil defense location. They led lives that were relatively less affected by the political system or by sources that offered contrary political visions. For them, the Soviet Union was a

[84] Ibid.

normal authoritarian system where, in Brezhnev's words, it was possible "to breathe easily, work well, and live tranquilly."[85]

DOCUMENTING CHANGE OVER TIME

Almost inevitably, surveys are snapshots. As such, individual surveys are of limited value as a source for evidence of change over time. Nevertheless, some readily identifiable behaviors occur at more or less the same time for all persons or for some class of persons such as males. Usually, for instance, first jobs occur at about the same time for most people. In the Soviet Union, the state both provided and controlled education. Given that, one indicator of the regime's ability to harness its resources to its purposes in a society is the extent to which educational experience and training have a bearing on the first job an individual gets. If the political system had effectively penetrated society, one could reasonably assume that a substantial proportion of its citizens would typically work at a specialty that bore on their training. Table 5.3[86] supports the proposition that from the late Stalin period through 1976, with the exception of World War II (which we can readily explain by pressing regime needs), that was the case. In the last five years of the Brezhnev era, however, the pattern changed. Only half the respondents whose first job occurred in that period took a first job in a specialty for which they had been trained.

The same cross-temporal trend may be observed when we compare the propensity to work the system across time. *Blat vyshe chem Stalin* (pull is above Stalin) used to be the standard refrain, but under Stalin there was little room for *blat* at least at the early stages of a career. When we asked, "Did you use *blat* or *protektsiya* to get your first job?" the response pattern was almost monotonic. Before World War II one respondent in seven (14 percent) indicated he or she had, while in the last years of the Brezhnev era half (51 percent) said they had. (Controlling for the respondent's role in the decision to migrate does not affect the result; the pattern, though not the frequencies, is the same regardless.)

Further evidence that the SIP had tapped a systemic phenomenon pertained to military service—which is after all a critical indicator of a

---

[85] Breslauer, *Khrushchev and Brezhnev*, p. 192, citing the English translation in Leo Gruliow et al., eds. *Current Soviet Policies VI: The Documentary Record of the 24th Congress of the Communist Party of the Soviet Union* (Columbus, OH: AAASS, 1973), p. 119.

[86] Zimmerman, "Mobilized Participation," pp. 348 and 350. Among those whose first job occurred in 1976–81, it did not matter whether they observed Rosh Hashanah (54%), played no significant role in the decision to migrate (50%), shared in that decision (51%), or made that decision (48%).

Table 5.3 Experience in obtaining first job

	I	II
1936–40	76% (67)	14% (7)
1941–45	52% (38)	11% (5)
1946–50	70% (71)	20% (13)
1951–55	73% (103)	26% (17)
1956–60	74% (151)	35% (44)
1961–65	72% (194)	33% (38)
1966–70	76% (277)	32% (42)
1971–75	75% (333)	44% (61)
1976–81	50% (168)	51% (29)

Source: William Zimmerman, "Mobilized Participation and the Nature of the Soviet Dictatorship," in James R. Millar, ed., *Politics, Work, and Daily Life in the USSR: A Survey of Former Soviet Citizens* (Cambridge: Cambridge University Press, 1987), pp. 332–53 at pp. 348 and 350.

Note: I = Worked at specialty for first job; II = Used *blat* or *protektsiya* to obtain first job.

regime's ability to harness its citizenry to its purposes (Table 5.4). Getting people to serve is a crucial indicator of both military and political mobilization.[87] The same monotonic pattern over time was observed, as was noted pertaining to the resort to *blat* or *protektsiya*. No one interviewed said they tried to avoid military service in the 1930s, whereas by the end of the Brezhnev era 30 percent reported having tried.

To summarize, absent Jowitt's "social combat" task and absent the political use of terror, task mobilization had given way to "political capitalism."[88] By the end of the Brezhnev era, the mobilization system propelled by the fuel of social transformation and terror had been succeeded by a more conventional authoritarian political system lubricated by the grease of *blat* and *protektsiya*. It was one where there were some modest norms for behavior within the Politburo and where the distinction between being a Party member and not had been restored. It was also one where the complexity of a heavily militarized, urbanized industrial system—what Zbigniew Brzezinski in distinguishing between totalitarian and authoritarian systems years ago had termed "the indirect restraints that stem from the pluralistic character of all

[87] Zimmerman, "Mobilized Participation," p. 352. Also William Zimmerman and Michael L. Berbaum, "Soviet Military Manpower Policy in the Brezhnev Era: Regime Goals, Social Origins and 'Working the System,'" *Europe-Asia Studies*, Vol. 45, No. 2 (1993), pp. 281–302. For the late 1980s, see Solnick, *Stealing the State*, and Odom, *The Collapse of the Soviet Military*.

[88] Jowitt, *New World Disorder*, p. 144.

Table 5.4 Percentage of respondents who said they tried to avoid military service

Time period	Percentage saying tried to avoid
Stalin (1930–40)	0% (0)
World War II (1941–45)	6% (7)
Late Stalin (1946–52)	7% (6)
Early Khrushchev (1953–59)	9% (13)
Late Khrushchev (1960–64)	15% (13)
Early Brezhnev (1965–69)	16% (21)
Middle Brezhnev (1970–75)	26% (30)
Late Brezhnev (1976–80)	30% (16)

Source: William Zimmerman, "Mobilized Participation and the Nature of the Soviet Dictatorship," in James R. Millar, ed., *Politics, Work, and Daily Life in the USSR: A Survey of Former Soviet Citizens* (Cambridge: Cambridge University Press, 1987), pp. 332–53 at pp. 348 and 350.

large-scale societies—"[89] resulted in *state* institutions central figures of which articulated claims for resources.

Finally, it was a system that many people thought they could, and did, work,[90] where for many what Brzezinski termed "the natural restraints . . . [including] kinship structure, and particularly the primary social unit, the family"[91] took on real meaning in defining boundaries between their private and public spheres. In such a system, "reds" and "experts," while subject to repression, sometimes severe, were increasingly attentive to non-Soviet sources of information and increasingly prone to engage in behaviors anathematic to the regime's conventional expectations.

[89] Brzezinski, *Ideology and Power*, p. 16 and the table above.
[90] Wayne Di Franceisco and Zvi Gitelman, "Soviet Political Culture and 'Covert Participation' in Policy Implementation," *American Political Science Review*, Vol. 78, No. 3 (September 1984), pp. 603–21.
[91] Brzezinski, *Ideology and Power*, p. 16.

CHAPTER 6

Uncertainty and "Democratization"

THE EVOLUTION OF POST-BREZHNEVIAN
POLITICS, 1982–1991

THE PREVIOUS CHAPTER ARGUED that during Khrushchev's and Brezhnev's tenures in office a slow evolution of norms had occurred at the level of high politics. These norms constrained the actions of both the general secretary and the remaining members of the Politburo. More than anything else, the implicit concordat among them was grounded in a mutual understanding that failed political opposition would not result in death to the loser. But in Brezhnev's case, the circumstances under which he replaced Nikita Khrushchev constrained his behavior as well.

Brezhnev died in 1982. I am tempted to treat Yury Andropov and Konstantin Chernenko as the answers to a trivia question. (Who were the Soviet general secretaries in the interim between Brezhnev's death and Mikhail Gorbachev's selection as general secretary in March 1985?) But Martin Malia[1] was correct to observe that Brezhnev's last years and the interregnum following his death and preceding the Gorbachev appointment are important in understanding the high politics that resulted in the latter's selection as general secretary. In part, the impact these years had was simply a matter of natural attrition. Key figures died who had been major players in Soviet politics for decades. (The most important of these were Kosygin, who died in 1980; the long time Party ideologist Mikhail Suslov, who died, as did Brezhnev, in 1982; and Dmitry Ustinov, the minister of defense and Politburo member, who died in December 1984.) But Andropov also took an active role in providing a milieu in which Gorbachev could emerge as the consensus choice as general secretary. In a move that much diminished the prospects that the head of the Moscow Party organization, Viktor Grishin, would become general secretary, Andropov campaigned vigorously against corruption. Moreover, he also cultivated the minds of some smart Soviet intellectuals and

---

[1] Malia, *The Soviet Tragedy*, pp. 407–9.

encouraged them to assess the implications of the palpable Soviet malaise. The most well known of these efforts was Tatyana Zaslavskaya's *Novosibirsk Report*, written in 1983 and leaked to the West in 1984. It was a thoroughgoing critique of the failures of central planning and a vivid depiction of working-class dissatisfaction. ("They pretend to pay us and we pretend to work.") But Andropov reached out to others as well.[2] Moreover, he made a point of familiarizing Gorbachev (a full member of the Politburo in 1980) with the intellectuals he, Andropov, "had gathered around himself throughout his career"[3] and took other steps (described in many accounts[4]) to position Gorbachev in such a way in the near future that he could emerge as someone around whom a majority of the Politburo could coalesce.

Equally important, Andropov abandoned Brezhnev's "trust in cadres" policy. Only 5 of the, at that juncture, 156 oblast first secretaries were replaced in the meta-stable five-year period 1976–81. Andropov appointed Yegor Ligachev to oversee cadre appointments. During the former's brief tenure as general secretary, 33 regional first secretaries were replaced.[5] Given Ligachev's "puritan"[6] disposition, this doubtless meshed well with Andropov's anticorruption policies. But it also likely increased the number of regional Party secretaries members who, as members of the Central Committee, were available for mobilization for Gorbachev and against Grishin or Leningrad Party chief Grigory Romanov on the death of Konstantin Chernenko, only a year after Andropov's death.

Even Chernenko's brief tenure as general secretary is part of the story of Gorbachev's emergence as general secretary. Yegor Ligachev is quite clear that Chernenko had "displayed some character" when he insisted that the substantially younger and more dynamic Gorbachev "chair the meetings of the Central Committee Secretariat," thus assuming "the unofficial second-ranking post in the highest Party authority."[7] Despite Chernenko's replacement of Andropov, moreover, Ligachev continued to appoint and court various regional Party secretaries while

[2] A prime example was Georgy Arbatov, *The System: An Insider's Life in Soviet Politics* (New York: Times Books, 1993). More generally, see Archie Brown, *The Gorbachev Factor* (New York: Oxford University Press, 1996).

[3] Malia, *The Soviet Tragedy*, p. 408.

[4] Breslauer, *Gorbachev and Yeltsin*, pp. 41 and 47; Richard Sakwa, *Gorbachev and His Reforms, 1985–1990* (New York: Prentice Hall, 1990), p. 6; Brown, *The Gorbachev Factor*, especially p. 47.

[5] Sakwa, *Gorbachev*, p. 11.

[6] Both Breslauer (*Gorbachev and Yeltsin*, p. 31) and Brown (*The Gorbachev Factor*, p. 66) use this term to describe him.

[7] Yegor Ligachev, *Inside Gorbachev's Kremlin* (New York: Pantheon, 1993), pp. 30 and 31.

conveying quite clearly that "only Gorbachev was worthy of occupying the highest post of general secretary of the Central Committee of the Communist Party."[8] Chernenko's frail health was common knowledge among the members of the Politburo inasmuch as Gorbachev had to chair meetings of the Politburo when Chernenko could not attend—as was often the case—though it was taboo, Ligachev reports, to mention Chernenko's health in Central Committee offices or in public.

Acting both strategically and out of necessity, Gorbachev assumed an increasing number of highly visible tasks and increasingly made clear, both by his public behavior and his utterances to a closed audience, his differences from the Brezhnev carryovers in the Politburo. His actions in December 1984 were readily recognizable as a form of electioneering. (Grishin was doing much the same thing by frequent appearances in public along with Chernenko, though Chernenko's health severely limited his ability to do so.) Particularly important in this regard were the trip he and his wife took to Great Britain where he met with Prime Minister Margaret Thatcher and a speech he gave to a closed Party conference on ideology, both of which took place that December. The trip to Britain gave him some legitimacy in the West.[9] But the speech to a closed Party conference was more important politically.

It is partly a commentary on how little Soviet politics had changed since Khrushchev's ouster in 1964 that George Breslauer has characterized the speech as "the most radical single speech by a leading member of the Politburo since Khrushchev."[10] In it, Gorbachev articulated an amorphous vision of what he would do if the Politburo decided to select him as general secretary and how different his administration would be from a Grishin or a Romanov one. But as Breslauer's enumerations indicated, it was clear enough, containing all the buzzwords that came subsequently to constitute the Gorbachev program: "*perestroika, glasnost, reforma, demokratizatsiya,* the 'human factor,' and the need for cadres to 'trust' people and 'respect their intellect.'"[11] Short on

---

[8] Ibid., p. 56. Ligachev subsequently opposed Gorbachev but at this juncture was strongly committed to him. See also Brown, *The Gorbachev Factor,* especially p. 74 where this quote is cited and also more generally pp. 69–88.

[9] After their meeting, Mrs. Thatcher remarked famously that Gorbachev was someone with whom the West "could do business." (Less well remembered is that in almost the same breath she had nice words for Chernenko as well.) Gorbachev had previously gone to Canada in 1983 where he spent considerable time with the then Soviet ambassador Aleksandr Yakovlev. Yakovlev, of course, became Gorbachev's closest adviser when he became general secretary.

[10] Breslauer, *Gorbachev and Yeltsin,* p. 48.

[11] Ibid., p. 49.

specifics, it represented a clear challenge to the Brezhnev consensus—and was recognized as such by other members of the Politburo. Roeder is skeptical[12] whether the speech was as portentous as subsequent writers have made it. He is right to warn against reading history backward, but what bears emphasizing is that the members of the Politburo took it very seriously. Chernenko in fact suggested Gorbachev not give the speech, a suggestion the latter rejected. *Pravda* then proceeded to publish a redacted version from which the most novel passages had been excised. Finally, somehow he contrived to have it published as a small brochure with a *tirazh* (print run) of an even hundred thousand.[13]

Within a matter of months Chernenko died. Generally, as we have seen, when a Politburo or similar type institution presents a united front to one like a Central Committee, the latter's role is usually limited to being approbatory, though consultation to make sure the Politburo's decision will fly with the Central Committee is often politically astute. When such consultations indicate the smaller group's choice may not be ratified, executive committees may adjust their recommendations to ensure that the larger body, in this instance, the Central Committee, does not actually assume its legitimate role but merely ratifies yet again the Politburo's time-honored practice. "Better to choose a secondary option that the larger body will ratify without hesitation than expand the selectorate" has been the usual pattern.

But accounts in both Yeltsin's and Ligachev's autobiographies suggest that it was somewhat arbitrary whether or not to view the selectorate as limited to the Politburo and Secretariat members. The evidence strongly indicates that the Central Committee was prepared to play its usual role as ratifier, if and only if the Politburo got it right, "even though it was normal practice for the Central Committee to accept whatever the Politburo recommended."[14] At a minimum, getting it right meant *not* bringing to them a recommendation that Grishin or Romanov become general secretary. It most probably did mean bringing (and doing it promptly) a recommendation that Gorbachev become general secretary.

We know that the context in which the decision was taken was one in which many senior party secretaries were adamantly opposed to Grishin or Romanov, one where there had been an influx of new secretaries in Andropov's brief tenure as general secretary, where the military played no role at all in the decision to select Gorbachev, and where

[12] Roeder, *Red Sunset*, p. 222.

[13] The last three sentences of the above paragraph come from Brown, *The Gorbachev Factor*, pp. 78–79.

[14] Brown, *The Gorbachev Factor*, p. 81; Breslauer, *Gorbachev and Yeltsin*, p. 41.

there was a widespread sense, especially (but not exclusively) among the under-seventy set, that things had to change.[15]

It is not a stretch to imagine a counterfactual account in which the Politburo, certainly a Politburo some members of which expressed reservations, but perhaps even a Politburo in which all the voting members went along, would have found the Central Committee in effect playing the role of a selectorate. I say "in effect" because the deference norm might have been too strong to result in the Central Committee unambiguously rejecting the Politburo's recommendation. Instead, in this counterfactual world, the Central Committee would have conveyed to the Politburo the message that its members reassemble, reconsider their position—and get their recommendation right this time.

This counterfactual, I would add, is relatively plausible as cᵒ ᵤnter-factuals go. As Ligachev said about the actual events, "the question of who would become *gensek* was far from predetermined."[16] Gorbachev's December speech had indicated he had become a serious candidate. His strongest supporter, though, was Ligachev, a member of the Secretariat but not of the Politburo. If Chernenko had died a few months earlier or Ustinov had lived a few months longer, Ustinov would have been a Politburo member and the military could have played a substantial role, as it did in preventing Khrushchev's ouster in 1957.[17] Chernenko's death might easily have been timed less favorably for Gorbachev's chances, even continuing to assume that Gorbachev had immediately called a meeting and other members had not been successful in achieving a delay of a meeting the only agenda item of which would be, "Who is to be general secretary?"[18] A hastily called meeting would have precluded Dinmukhaned Kunaev, the first secretary of Kazakhstan, from attending unless he happened to be in Moscow. It is, though, easy to imagine a hypothetical version of events in which Vitaly Vorotnikov was not snowbound in Yugoslavia or in which Vladimir Shcherbitsky, the Ukrainian first secretary, was not in San Francisco.[19]

[15] Breslauer, *Gorbachev and Yeltsin*, p. 41 compares 1985 to 1953 and notes "a widespread sense within the Politburo and Central Committee that things could not continue in the old way." See also, ibid., p. 42n3 for several publications illustrating the general sense of malaise among high Party officials.

[16] Ligachev, *Inside Gorbachev's Kremlin*, p. 69.

[17] It is Ligachev's view that Ustinov would have backed Gorbachev. Ibid., p. 77.

[18] Strictly speaking, there was a second item, namely who would chair the Funeral Commission.

[19] On the whereabouts of Kunaev, Shcherbitsky, and Vorotnikov, see Brown, *The Gorbachev Factor*, pp. 84–85. Jack F. Matlock relates that Shcherbitsky traveled part of the way back to Moscow "courtesy of the U.S. Air Force, which flew him from San Francisco to New York, where an Aeroflot plane was sent for him." *Autopsy on an Empire: The American Ambassador's Account of the Collapse of the Soviet Union* (New York: Random House, 1995), p. 45. Matlock does not indicate whether the pilot was instructed to make haste slowly.

Ligachev's and Yeltsin's accounts diverge somewhat, though not as much as Ligachev's snide remarks about Yeltsin and the view from Smolensk being better would indicate. In Yeltsin's account,

[i]t was the plenum of the central committee which decided who was to be general secretary. Practically all the participants in that plenum, including many senior, experienced first secretaries, considered that Grishin's candidacy was unacceptable, that it would have meant the immediate end of both the party and the country. . . .

A large group of first secretaries concurred in the view that of all the Politbureau members, the man to be promoted to the post of general secretary had to be Gorbachov [Gorbachev]. He was the most energetic, the best educated and the most suitable from the point of view of age. We decided to put our weight behind him. We conferred with several Politbureau members, including Ligachov.[20] Our position coincided with his, because he was as afraid of Grishin as we were. Once it had become clear that this was also the majority view, we decided that if any other candidate were to be put forward—Grishin, Romanov, or anyone else—we would oppose him en bloc. And defeat him.

Evidently the discussions within the Politbureau followed along these lines. Those Politbureau members who attended that session were aware of our firm intention, and Gromyko, too, supported this point of view. He it was who spoke at the plenum, proposing Gorbachov as the Politbureau's candidate. Grishin and his supporters did not dare to risk making a move; they realized that their chances were slim (or rather, to be precise, zero), and therefore Gorbachov's candidacy was put forward without any complications or problems.[21]

In Ligachev's version—unlike Yeltsin's account—the fact that Andrei Gromyko had decided for Gorbachev and that he was willing to speak—and did—in advocacy of Gorbachev both at the Politburo's second session and at the Central Committee plenum was of great significance.[22] In Ligachev's reading, Gromyko's strong statement in the second Politburo meeting effectively precluded those with reservations from entering their objections. No one other than Gromyko spoke at the Central Committee plenum.

Ligachev's narrative of the events outside the Politburo, however, basically meshes with Yeltsin's concerning what transpired in the

---

[20] Ligachev quotes this passage from Yeltsin's book and correctly points out that at that juncture he was a member of the secretariat and not yet a member of the Politbureau.

[21] Boris Yeltsin, *Against the Grain* (London: Jonathan Cape, 1990), pp. 112–13.

[22] "I can say with assurance that Gromyko's speech caught [some of the Politburo members] by surprise. . . . I can still say with absolute certainty that there were people in the Politburo who clearly did not approve of Gorbachev's nomination and understood that they would have to resign." Ligachev, *Inside Gorbachev's Kremlin*, p. 76.

twenty four hours after Chernenko's March 11 death. According to Ligachev,[23] "Some[24] of the first secretaries told me that if necessary they were prepared to speak at the Central Committee plenum in support of Gorbachev. And not just based on their own opinion, but also on behalf of a whole group of secretaries and Central Committee members. A kind of initiative group emerged spontaneously." Both accounts make clear that the Politburo's right to nominate its own chair presupposed it choosing Gorbachev. For decades, the reality of Soviet high politics was that the Party rules, which specified that the Central Committee selected the general secretary, had been honored pro forma except when the Politburo was divided. In 1985, the norm that the Politburo had the right to select its own chair was honored pro forma; the reality, though, was that it alone was no longer *the* selectorate.[25]

Scholars, East and West, agree that the Gorbachev era began with a short-lived Andropov-like puritanism. Malia rightly observes that the initial public rationale for the proposed domestic economic changes was the need to change internally in order to compete internationally. Scholars, East and West, equally emphasize that all the ingredients of Gorbachev's policies were to be found in the four buzzwords, *reforma, perestroika, glasnost,* and *demokratizatsiya,* that were core to his December 1994 speech. What exactly these terms implied was not, however, clear. Were they, for instance, instruments or goals in themselves? And were they sufficiently vague that persons, including Gorbachev himself, could infuse them with various interpretations as the need for change became more manifest and as the evolving politics required?

NORMAL SOVIET HIGH POLITICS

In order to change policies, Gorbachev had to articulate a message,[26] but he also had to change the cast of characters. Writing in 1990 John Gooding maintained that Gorbachev's policies were intended "to strengthen rather than to undermine the position of the Communist party."[27] (To be fair, he also observed that if Gorbachev "gets his way

---

[23] Ibid., p. 75.

[24] Ligachev told Gorbachev that "about fifteen to twenty" provincial secretaries had been to see him. Ibid.

[25] Brown, asserts the "selection of Gorbachev was no exception" to the usual practice that the "real choice was made by the Politburo—or even an inner circle within it" (*The Gorbachev Factor,* p. 84), but his narrative makes it clear that the Central Committee's pro forma role in this instance was premised on the Politburo selecting Gorbachev.

[26] Breslauer, *Gorbachev and Yeltsin,* is particularly good on this part of the story.

[27] John Gooding, "Gorbachev and Democracy," *Soviet Studies,* Vol. 42, No. 2 (April 1990), pp. 195–231 at p. 195.

the Soviet Union will become a more normal and a more enlightened country to live in."[28]) Hough, similarly, in an article also published in 1990, asserted that Gorbachev had "engaged in a very methodical and ruthless consolidation of power."[29] Judging, as he was, Gorbachev's moves against traditional notions of Soviet high politics with their concomitant attention to the interaction between the general secretary, the other secretaries, and the Politburo, there was much to be said for Hough's assertion. A jaundiced eye out for Gorbachev's self-enhancing proclivities was always appropriate even when he was attempting to engage in what Roeder terms "*constitutional politics*," when "actors seek to advance their causes by changing the rules themselves," rather than what he labels "*normal politics*," "in which political actors use existing rules to advance their causes."[30]

For Gorbachev did engage in normal high politics — and quite effectively. Once he became general secretary he moved swiftly against the Politburo and Secretariat members who were carryovers, usually from the Brezhnev era. Writing in 1986 it would have been difficult to specify the means whereby Gorbachev was not engaged in the conventional patterns general secretaries had taken in prior times. From the perspective of normal Soviet high politics what was remarkable in the first year or so of Gorbachev's assumption of the role as general secretary was not his democratic instincts but the alacrity with which he changed the composition of the leadership. Brown correctly notes that "[b]y the time he had completed one year as General Secretary, Gorbachev had presided over by far the largest turnover in the top leadership team ever to be effected so early in the incumbency of any Soviet party leader."[31]

He quickly transformed the composition of the Politburo and the Secretariat. "In Gorbachev's first year five plenary sessions of the CC were held and some twenty-three people changed their posts in the Politburo and Secretariat."[32] Grigory Romanov was ousted in July 1985 and replaced by Lev Zaikov. Andrei Gromyko (who nominated Gorbachev, as we saw above) was kicked upstairs in the same month to become president of the Presidium of the Supreme Soviet and replaced by Eduard Shevardnadze as foreign minister.[33] Nikolai Tikhonov (who

[28] Ibid.

[29] Jerry Hough, "Gorbachev's Endgame," *World Policy Journal*, Vol. 7, No. 4 (Fall 1990), pp. 639–72 at p. 639.

[30] Roeder, *Red Sunset*, p. 22, italics in original.

[31] Archie Brown, ed. *Political Leadership in the Soviet Union* (London: Macmillan with St. Anthony's College, 1989), p. 193.

[32] Ibid.

[33] Roeder (*Red Sunset*, p. 112) interprets this as evidence of a balanced Politburo thwarting Gorbachev who had only a year before said it was appropriate for the general secretary to hold both positions. Given how many other personnel changes Gorbachev

was eighty and had been chairman of the Council of Ministers since Kosygin's death in 1980) retired in September. Grishin was unceremoniously removed from his post as first secretary of the Moscow City Committee in December 1985—and in February 1986 his membership in the Politburo—and replaced by Boris Yeltsin.[34]

The Central Committee was also subject to rapid turnover from the very beginning of Gorbachev's tenure as general secretary. Again, as in the case of the Politburo and Secretariat, a reading of changes in the Central Committee as normal Soviet high politics was a plausible construction of what transpired during the years 1985 to 1988. The figures vary but converge on the message. Brown reports that "whereas new members of the Central Committee accounted for 28 percent of Brezhnev's Central Committee elected in 1981, they made up 44 percent of those elected in 1986. . . . [Of these,] complete newcomers . . . constituted 41 out of 319 full members in 1981 and 95 out of 307 in 1986."[35] By Sakwa's reasoning, similarly, "Under Brezhnev about 90 percent of living CC members were re-elected every five years, whereas on 5 March 1986 only 60 percent of full members were re-elected and twenty-three candidates of 1981 became full members."[36] By Robert Kaiser's count, "Of the 307 voting members of the Central Committee elected near the end of Gorbachev's first year, 131 were new."[37]

Even as late as 1989, traditional job-slot criteria played a determinative role in the composition of the Central Committee. Initially, Gorbachev tried to remove Central Committee members at a Party Conference (the first such Conference since before World War II), only to be rebuffed by those who invoked the norm that Party rules specified that Central Committee members could be removed only at a Party Congress. Gorbachev then succeeded in persuading seventy-four voting members of the Central Committee, all of whom had retired from the jobs that almost automatically implied membership in the committee, to request at a Central Committee plenum that they be allowed to retire.

---

made in his first year, I am dubious. A parsimonious explanation is that Gorbachev was trying to make it difficult for Gromyko to have a large say in foreign policy matters while simultaneously rewarding him with a symbolic but relatively harmless position in appreciation of his support a brief few months before. On the need for Gorbachev to be tactful toward Gromyko, see Brown, *Political Leadership*, p. 190. Twenty-five years later, Gorbachev was still citing Gromyko as someone in the old guard who recognized the need for fundamental change. (*New York Times*, March 14, 2010.)

[34] For a detailed description, see Timothy J. Colton, *Moscow: Governing the Socialist Metropolis* (Cambridge, MA: Belknap, 1995), pp. 571–72.

[35] Brown in Brown, *Political Leadership*, p. 191.

[36] Sakwa, *Gorbachev*, p. 12.

[37] Robert G. Kaiser, *Why Gorbachev Happened* (New York: Simon & Schuster, 1991), p. 115.

The requests were granted. (Brown, archly, observes that "Stalin's solution to the presence of potential enemies on the Central Committee had been to have them arrested and shot; Khrushchev replaced them at Party Congresses; Gorbachev became the first Soviet leader to *persuade* large numbers of Central Committee members to retire in between Congresses."[38]) And they were large numbers: the seventy-four voting members who retired—the so-called "dead souls"—constituted almost one-third of the Central Committee. Their departure, to be replaced by others, reduced the likelihood that the Central Committee might remove Gorbachev, a possibility that conventional Sovietological analysis would have thought inconceivable in light of the fact that "[o]nly 26 percent of the 1990 Central Committee members had even been among the 5,000 delegates to the 27th Party Congress in 1986. Gorbachev had achieved a replacement of the political elite virtually as complete as Stalin had between 1937 and 1939."[39]

While unlikely, such a development was not impossible. One could make the case, as did Jerry Hough, that the changes in 1986 were "certainly" evidence that Gorbachev "took all the usual steps of a Soviet general secretary to consolidate power. He removed members of the old elite—those who were beholden to Leonid Brezhnev—at the fastest pace of any general secretary in history. He methodically placed men who seemed beholden to him in key power positions."[40]

Hough's argument works reasonably well in describing personnel changes in the Politburo[41] but does not convince with regard to the Central Committee. It is doubtful whether those "elected in 1986 . . . were presumably Gorbachev supporters"[42]—at least not for long. Kaiser was right to remind us that it was Ligachev who was the cadres secretary. It was he "[who picked] most of the new men" in 1986.[43] Those he selected may well have been enthusiastic for the version of Gorbachev that Ligachev had in mind when he had urged Gorbachev on the regional Party secretaries. But it does not seem likely that extrapolating forward there would have been much reason to assume they continued to support him in 1990–91. Similarly, Kaiser was correct in wondering whether, in light of Gorbachev's policies in the interven-

---

[38] Brown, *The Gorbachev Factor*, p. 187, italics in original.

[39] Hough, "Gorbachev's Endgame," p. 660. It is worth belaboring the obvious: the folks ousted in 1986 were not shot, nor did they disappear into the camps.

[40] Ibid., p. 647.

[41] Though Brown argues that after the Twenty-Eighth Congress Gorbachev "still did not give [him] a majority of genuine supporters within" either in the Central Committee or the Politburo (*The Gorbachev Factor*, p. 177).

[42] Hough, "Gorbachev's Endgame," p. 660.

[43] Kaiser, *Why Gorbachev Happened*, p. 115.

ing years between 1986 and 1990 whether in 1990–91 they favored the "Gorbachev enthusiasts or [the] radical reformers."[44] Ligachev didn't— and Gorbachev himself observed to his aide, Anatoly Chernyaev, in May 1990 that "'70 percent of the apparatus of the Central Committee and of the Central Committee itself are against me and hate me.'"[45] A year later, he resigned as general secretary at a Central Committee meeting where he had been severely criticized. After a brief recess, a vote was taken and his resignation was rejected.[46]

CONSTITUTIONAL POLITICS

Gorbachev's moves to implement his policies and to enhance his power position were not limited to normal politics. The key buzzwords of these years—perestroika, demokratizatsiya, reforma, and glasnost— required confronting, as Roeder notes, "the Soviet polity with issues well beyond the realm of 'normal' politics."[47] Rather, especially during the three-year period 1988–90, Gorbachev launched multiple overlapping efforts to alter the rules of the game. He did this both to enhance his power position *and* to change the system. Key among these were attempts to transform and then supplant Party institutions, create and empower the office of the presidency, and enlarge the selectorate. The effects of these efforts were to shift the power of the Party to the state and to set in train measures that fundamentally altered the selectorate and, if fully implemented, would have resulted in a Soviet Union with a nearly universal selectorate. The achievement of that goal was to have occurred in 1995, conveniently after Gorbachev had served a first term as president, having been elected to that office by the Congress of People's Deputies in 1990. But that presupposed the continued existence of the Soviet Union. It ceased to exist on December 25, 1991, after the failed August putsch and the agreement by the respective presidents of Russia, the Ukraine, and Belarus that they were going to replace the USSR with a Commonwealth of Independent States.

Gorbachev's undermining of the key Party institutions was coupled with the simultaneous creation of new governmental organizations, notably the establishment of a Congress of People's Deputies and the

[44] Ibid.
[45] As cited by Brown, *The Gorbachev Factor*, p. 196. For the original see A. S. Chernyaev, *Shest' let s Gorbachevym* (Moscow: Progress, 1993), p. 345. An English-language version of Gorbachev's interactions with Chernyaev is *My Six Years with Gorbachev* (University Park: Pennsylvania State University Press, 2000).
[46] Kaiser, *Why Gorbachev Happened*, p. 411.
[47] Roeder, *Red Sunset*, p. 212.

transformation of the symbolic chairmanship of the Presidium of the Supreme Soviet into a powerful presidency.

The gutting of the Secretariat was exquisitely handled. In August 1988, Gorbachev recommended the elimination of the branch economic departments of the Central Committee. In October the number of such departments was reduced from twenty to nine. For a year or two the Secretariat effectively ceased to operate as an institution. As Ligachev summarized what transpired, "The creation of commissions automatically buried the Secretariat. This was a very serious violation of the Party's bylaws, unprecedented in recent decades. . . . No one made any mention of eliminating Secretariat meetings or seemed to be attacking them. The commissions were established, and the Secretariat's meetings simply ended of their own accord."[48] The creation of the commissions coupled with the development of the governmental institutions of the presidency and the greatly enhanced role, at least on paper, of the legislative branch held forth the prospect that the ministries would no longer be involved in the kind of reciprocal accountability of which Roeder has written so eloquently. Instead, they would be replaced "with sovereign delegation in which bureaucrats were accountable to policymakers [in the executive or legislative governmental branches] who in turn were accountable to a selectorate independent of the bureaucracy."[49]

The Central Committee was also weakened. The Party rules concerning the selection of the general secretary were changed at the Twenty-Eighth Party Congress. No longer would the Central Committee have the right to select or reject the general secretary. Instead, that would be the prerogative of the Party Congress. As Hough observes, "This ended the danger that [Gorbachev] might be removed by the Central Committee."[50] The Congress dutifully reelected him at the same Congress. He received 3,411 votes, and his opponent, Teiumuraz Avaliani, a leader in the 1989 coal miners' strike in Siberia,[51] received 501 votes.

Even without elaborating on the shift of power from the Party to governmental institutions, the selectorate had in effect been expanded

---

[48] Ligachev, *Inside Gorbachev's Kremlin*, pp. 109–10. The Secretariat resumed meeting after the Twenty-Eighth CPSU Congress in 1990. Ligachev also asserts (p. 111) that "The cessation of the Secretariat meetings also undermined the principle of collective leadership."

[49] Roeder, *Red Sunset*, p. 220.

[50] Hough, "Gorbachev's Endgame," p. 659.

[51] Kaiser, *Why Gorbachev Happened*, p. 354n. On the workers' strikes, see especially Stephen Crowley, *Hot Coal, Cold Steel: Russian and Ukrainian Workers from the End of the Soviet Union to the Post-Communist Transformations* (Ann Arbor: University of Michigan Press, 1997).

by several orders of magnitude—from the dozen members of the Politburo to the roughly 4,700 Party members selected to attend the Congress. In addition, there were efforts to achieve some democratization of the selection of the attendees to the Congress. No decision on how the attendees would be selected was reached at the February 1990 Central Committee plenum. Failing agreement, the buck was passed to the regional Party units; they were charged to establish their own regulations. Of the 164 such units, 135 employed some kind of putatively competitive candidacies to select the attendees, though Roeder reports that Gorbachev himself said the Party secretaries continued to dominate the selection process.[52]

The third Party institution to suffer serious weakening was the Politburo itself. To describe the emasculation of the Politburo serves as a segue to depicting the overall shift in power from the Party to the state institutions, most notably the creation of a powerful presidency. Once the epitome of monolithic unity, the Politburo was expanded in 1990 to twenty-five members, fifteen of whom were the republic first secretaries. A half century ago Richard Pipes wrote his classic volume on the formation of the Soviet Union.[53] In it, he had noted that one might at least make a case that the governmental institutions were structured in such a way that the Soviet Union might be depicted as a federation. The Party, though, was unambiguously hierarchical. It was where the real power had resided. If the Politburo were the key locus of decision making, the inclusion of representatives from each of the fifteen republics would have been a telling point in trying to ascertain whether the Soviet Union had become a federation. But the Politburo was no longer where the action was nor where the key players were (other, of course, than Gorbachev himself).

The key players were members of the newly created Presidential Council (many having resigned from the Politburo in July 1990) made up "in the first instance, of the Chair of the Supreme Soviet (Lukyanov was elected to this post), the Prime Minister (Ryzhkov), the Minister of Foreign Affairs (Shevardnadze), the Minister of Defense (Dmitry Yazov), the Ministry of the Interior (Vadim Bakatin), the head of the KGB (Kryuchkov) and the head of the State Planning Commission ([Yury] Maslyukov)."[54] In addition to these members who were appointed by virtue of their office, Gorbachev filled out the Council with a mélange of people of his own choosing including his two closest

---

[52] Roeder, *Red Sunset*, p. 216.

[53] Richard Pipes, *The Formation of the Soviet Union: Communism and Nationalism, 1917–1923* (New York: Atheneum, 1978).

[54] Sakwa, *Gorbachev*, pp. 162–63.

advisors (other than Shevardnadze), Aleksandr Yakovlev and Vadim Medvedev, along with several others ranging from Yevgeny Primakov, who in 1990 was the chair of the Council of the Union of the Supreme Soviet, and Valery Boldin, at that time the head of the Central Committee's General Department (and soon thereafter the president's chief of staff) to the Kirghiz author Chingiz Aitmatov and a distinguished physicist, Yury Osipian.[55]

The Presidential Council was but an aspect of Gorbachev's effort to create an imperial presidency while retaining his position as general secretary of the Party. (He resigned as general secretary only after the failed coup d'état in August 1991.) Brown rightly describes the Presidential Council as "in essence an advisory body to the President."[56] Its existence was brief. It was abolished in November 1990 as Gorbachev sought to assuage his hard-line critics,[57] who were, ostensibly, pressing for the further strengthening of the presidency.

What they probably had in mind was for Gorbachev to use the resources available to the president to implement policies that would exacerbate his relations with the intellectuals and non-Russian nationalists. Hough enumerates a litany of the powers of the president:

> The president would not only appoint the chairman of the Council of Ministers, head the defense council, and conduct foreign and defense policy, but would also have the power to issue decrees (*ukazy*), in his own name. Theoretically, these are subject to Supreme Soviet approval, but in practice Gorbachev has been independently issuing sweeping decrees on a wide range of domestic policy questions. . . .
>
> While the legal powers of the new president are impressive, they are not very different from the de facto powers of the old general secretary.[58]

On the basis of this enumeration, Hough argued that Gorbachev was "consolidating his dictatorial power" and that "by the fall of 1990, Gorbachev had achieved virtually absolute power within the central government of the Soviet Union."[59]

Hough's list of Gorbachev's powers as president is unexceptional and a caution against disregarding Gorbachev's proclivities to position himself as the median "voter." Twenty-five years later, Gorbachev was still positioning himself in the center—ascribing "most of the blame" to "the radicals [who] pushed us to move faster, the conservatives [who]

---

[55] Ibid.; Brown, *The Gorbachev Factor*, pp. 208–9.
[56] Brown, *The Gorbachev Factor*, p. 208; Hough, "Gorbachev's Endgame," p. 659.
[57] Brown, *The Gorbachev Factor*, p. 275.
[58] Hough, "Gorbachev's Endgame," p. 659.
[59] Ibid., pp. 654 and 661–62, respectively.

stepped on our toes."[60] Gorbachev himself noted that if he were simply a power maximizer he could have done that by gaining control over the Politburo in his guise as general secretary: "The general secretary of the Central Committee of the Communist Party of the Soviet Union was a dictator with no equal in the world. Nobody had more power than he. . . . So what did I want to start all this for?"[61]

The problem is that Hough failed to take into account the extent to which, in Roeder's terms, constitutional changes had transpired in the years 1985 to 1990. In an article published in 1990—a year before the collapse of the Soviet Union—Hough scoffed at Seweryn Bialer for predicting, in an article also published in 1990, its "imminent collapse." Likewise, he charged a large group of Western scholars and Russian democrats of having a "profound misunderstanding of the Soviet Union" and of "grossly [exaggerating] the severity of the Soviet Union's problems."[62]

These comments about Hough's article are not offered in order to single him out for overestimating the resilience of the Soviet Union to external and internal shocks—to some degree or other this is a charge that could be directed against a raft of distinguished, card-carrying Soviet specialists.[63] Through a prism that assumed an absence of systemic change and Soviet politics as usual, the fact was that Gorbachev was disentangling himself from Politburo and Central Committee constraints and deferring the direct election of the president until 1995.

This was certainly fuel for some cynicism about the mix of Gorbachev's aspirations. But, by 1990 such a prism shaped by prior experience was no longer the only appropriate modality for assessing Gorbachev's behavior. Besides the multiple fundamental changes in domestic and foreign policy he had wrought, for our purposes what was determinative was that he was bent on altering fundamentally the link between the president and the president's selectorate. Carried out to the end, the process, which would have involved having the president elected by the adult population, would no longer have any of the attributes of reciprocal accountability. No longer would the Soviet political minuet be one in which (1) comrade Ivanov, the general secretary of the CPSU, would select from the all-union nomenklatura

[60] *New York Times*, March 13, 2010.

[61] As cited in Kaiser, *Why Gorbachev Happened*, p. 376.

[62] "Hough, "Gorbachev's Endgame," p. 642. The phrase "imminent collapse" appears at p. 640. For Bialer's articles in 1990, see "The Passing of the Soviet Order?," *Survival*, Vol. 32, No. 2 (March–April 1990), pp. 107–20 to which Hough refers and also "Is Socialism Dead?," *Bulletin of the American Academy of Arts and Sciences*, Vol. 44, No. 2 (November 1990), pp. 19–29.

[63] Shoon Kathleen Murray, *Anchors Against Change: American Opinion Leaders' Beliefs after the Cold War* (Ann Arbor: University of Michigan Press, 1996).

regional party secretaries and leading governmental officials who (given their positions) would (2) in turn automatically become members of the Central Committee and (3) in their guise as members of the Central Committee then ratify the recommendation—ostensibly from the Politburo—that Comrade Ivanov be renewed as general secretary of the CPSU. Instead, the relation between the president and the legislature would be "embedded within an overall hierarchical political order of popular sovereignty."[64]

Governmental administrators would in this scheme be accountable to policy makers. The latter in turn would be accountable to citizens who were not bureaucrats. A much enlarged selectorate would emerge. Initially, it was to consist of two legislatures at the national level, the Congress of People's Deputies and the Supreme Soviet, the members of which would themselves mostly be selected by popular vote. In theory at least, implemented fully in 2005, the bulk of the citizenry constituting the selectorate as such would select the president, who would control the administrative bureaucracy. In this sense the hierarchical relationship between leader and led would be inverted: it would be the citizenry who exercised sovereignty by selecting the leader.[65]

Even the changes that had already taken place were by no means trivial. Readers do need to keep in mind that one-third of those selected as members of the Congress were not elected at large. Rather, they were chosen to represent various "public organizations." These ranged from one hundred each for the CPSU and the All Union Council of Trade Unions to thirty for the All-Union Academy of Sciences and one each for the All-Union Society of Philatelists and the All-Union Society for the Struggle for Sobriety.[66] True to form, the CPSU selected one hundred nominees for its one hundred positions as a public organization, thus demonstrating that the expectation of unanimity and the absence of risk remained a typical mode of operation for it as an organization.

But the election of the remaining two-thirds of the Congress was testimony to the countermobilization of mass publics that had taken place during the Gorbachev era. This in turn was a consequence of the opening up of the media,[67] many of the archives, and the borders; along with

---

[64] Roeder, *Red Sunset*, p. 92.

[65] Ibid., passim.

[66] Michael E. Urban, *More Power to the Soviets: The Democratic Revolution in the USSR* (Aldershot: Edward Elgar, 1990), p. 93. As a stamp collector, I received some satisfaction knowing that philatelists were accorded the same weight in the Congress as those determined to achieve sobriety among Russians.

[67] To paraphrase a Soviet economist, Revold Entov, who was visiting Ann Arbor at the time, Soviet newspapers, he said, were better than the *New York Times* and the *Washington Post*: "You read them to find out what happened yesterday. We read Soviet newspapers to find out what happened" during the last half century.

the vast proliferation of spontaneously organized, mission-oriented groups operating independently of Party controls (the *neformaly*). Unlike Gorbachev and many other high Party officials included as Party designees, those Party officials who had to battle in the constituency trenches for a position in the Congress often found it an unpleasant and career-threatening experience[68]—not directly because they had been defeated in their run for a seat in the Congress of People's Deputies but because their defeat, when it occurred, was often followed by dismissal or resignation from their Party post. Even though the adult population did not directly select the first president of the USSR, its role in the March 1989 election as the cohort selecting many deputies who did constitute the selectorate was substantial.

The election in March 1989 was the first genuine nationwide election of any consequence since the vote for the Constituent Assembly immediately after the Bolshevik seizure of power in 1917 (above, pp. 15–16). By and large those regional Party secretaries who lost came from Moscow and areas to the north of it.[69] The two capitals (Moscow and Leningrad), the Baltic Republics, and Moldavia were particularly noteworthy in their propensity to reject regional Party secretaries.[70] More generally, the cities were more mobilized against the Party leaders than were the rural areas. Outside Moscow and Leningrad, of the *gorkom* (city) secretaries who ran, only four of eighteen won. Similarly, only four of thirteen secretaries of city *raikom* (district) committees won, whereas slightly more than half (twenty-two of forty) of the leaders of rural raikoms were elected.[71] The story in the two capitals was dramatic and witness to how perestroika had succeeded in broadening the social composition of the selectorate. In Moscow, Boris Yeltsin had become something of a cult figure among intellectuals and Muscovite residents more generally by making known his opposition to Ligachev and the latter's narrow construction of perestroika.[72] He, Yeltsin, had

[68] It was also unpleasant for many who chose to compete against Party officials. The "dirty tricks" used in a vain attempt to thwart Boris Yeltsin's effort to be elected a member of the Congress have been amply documented. For a vivid account of the consequences one outspoken welder experienced as a result of his agreeing to run for deputy, see Kaiser, *Why Gorbachev Happened*, pp. 256–57.

[69] V. A. Kolosov et al., *Vesna 89: Geografiya i anatomiya parlamentskikh vyborov* (Moscow: Progress, 1990), p. 75. This volume is far and away the most detailed description of the March 1989 election results of which I am aware.

[70] Ibid., p. 83.

[71] Ibid., p. 78.

[72] His clash with Ligachev (and with Gorbachev) and his violation of norms concerning keeping disputes between Politburo members within a narrow circle, his ouster from the Politburo, and the rarity of his return to "big" politics have been thoroughly treated in multiple sources. See Timothy J. Colton, *Yeltsin: A Life* (New York: Basic Books, 2008),

been forced to resign as first secretary of the Moscow City Committee in a round of criticism and self-criticism reminiscent of times past. He seized the opportunity to redeem himself and to return to the public eye by running for election to the Congress of People's Deputies. In the largest single district in the country, Moscow district 2 (district 1 was reserved for Lenin), he received 89 percent of the votes cast, whereas the mayor of Moscow was defeated. In Leningrad, the Party leadership was thoroughly trounced. The Leningrad *obkom* secretary ran unopposed and still lost. (To vote against required crossing out the person's name.) The *gorkom* secretary received 15 percent of the vote. Four other leading Party figures were defeated.

Nationally, roughly one oblast first secretary in five ($n = 33$) was defeated even though many ran unopposed. In response to these developments, Gorbachev made clear his view that elections in which Party officials lost represented signals about individual Party leaders that constituted valuable information, and were a part of "'a normal process, a democratic one, that we must not regard as some kind of tragedy.'"[73] Indeed, he observed, the elections were part of an overall process of systemic change that included the introduction of competitive elections, "new methods of economic management . . . [and] the revival of the soviets. . . . This," he said, "is why we started everything in the first place—so a human being can feel normal, can feel good, in a socialist state. So that he will feel above all like a human being."[74]

Needless to say, there was a certain hollowness to Gorbachev's rhetoric in that the wheels had been well greased for his elevation to the presidency. A jaded view of Gorbachev's maneuverings would emphasize that for all his utterances about democracy, he did not face the uncertainty that characterizes truly competitive, honest elections and which would have presumably been a key feature of the 1995 Soviet elections had the Soviet Union not collapsed. He had been one of the one hundred identified by the Party to represent the Party as a social organization. Unlike Yeltsin, who as we shall see (below, p. 199) was elected president of Russia by the entire Russian adult population, Gorbachev was not chosen president, nor even as a deputy, by popular vote. Rather, he was selected president by a vote of the Congress of People's Deputies, the composition of which by design, political craftiness, and some outright fraud was intended to minimize uncertainty.

---

especially pp. 153–73; Colton, *Moscow*, pp. 581–83; Roeder, *Red Sunset*, p. 216; Breslauer, *Gorbachev and Yeltsin*, especially pp. 118–20; Brown, *The Gorbachev Factor*, pp. 110–11; Kaiser, *Why Gorbachev Happened*, pp. 179–86; Yeltsin, *Against the Grain*, pp. 140–56.

[73] This paragraph draws heavily on Urban, *More Power to the Soviets*, p. 112; the quote from Gorbachev is cited in ibid., p. 115.

[74] Cited by Kaiser, *Why Gorbachev Happened*, p. 276.

Even so, his selection was a far cry from the 99.44 percent pure "Ivory Snow" elections of the Stalin era or the rigged 2008 presidential election. With the migration of effective power from the Central Committee and Politburo to the presidency, the Supreme Soviet, and the newly created Congress of People's Deputies, the matter of who would select the Soviet leadership had become one of serious contention. It was no surprise that, once the decision had been made that for this initial election the president of the USSR would be chosen by the Congress, it was Gorbachev who was elected as the first and, as it turned out, only president of the USSR. What was remarkable, and indicative of the altered relationship between the selectorate and the selected, was that Gorbachev, who needed an absolute majority of the members of the Congress to be chosen president, received only 59 percent of the votes cast. No opponent was nominated, but Gorbachev received 1,329 votes in favor, 495 against, and 420 abstentions.[75]

The Failed Ejectorate

As the former American ambassador to the Soviet Union, Jack F. Matlock, points out, the public bath (*banya*) often plays the role in Russian politics and business that smoked-filled rooms once played in American politics.[76] It is a place where conspiracies are launched and deals are made. Such was the case on August 17, 1991, when Vladimir Kryuchkov (the head of the KGB since 1988) invited several powerful personages to join him at a KGB bathhouse in Moscow. Those who attended included Valentin Pavlov (the Soviet prime minister since January 1991) and Dmitry Yazov (whom Gorbachev had appointed defense minister in 1987).

Their actions came against a backdrop of developments of historic magnitude. In the two years prior to August 1991 the Soviet Union had experienced the "loss" of Eastern Europe; a food crisis, especially in the major cities; a collapse in oil prices; major labor unrest on the part of the coal miners;[77] and dramatic articulations of republic-level demands for sovereignty from the Baltic Republics, republics in the southern Caucasus, and Russia itself. To top things off, a treaty transforming the Union of Soviet Socialist Republics into a confederation titled the Union of Soviet *Sovereign* Republics was to be signed on August 20.[78] Kryuchkov, Pav-

[75] Kaiser, *Why Gorbachev Happened*, p. 327; Sakwa, *Gorbachev*, p. 162.

[76] Matlock, *Autopsy on an Empire*, p. 579.

[77] Crowley, *Hot Coal, Cold Steel*.

[78] On the so-called 9 + 1 agreement, see Mark R. Beissinger, *Nationalist Mobilization and the Collapse of the Soviet State* (Cambridge: Cambridge University Press, 2002), especially pp. 422–25.

lov, and Yazov all became members of the soon-to-be-created and self-styled State Committee for the State of Emergency in the USSR (GKChP). They were joined at the banya by Oleg Shenin, the Central Committee secretary for cadres, Valery Boldin,[79] Gorbachev's chief of staff (who had been with Gorbachev since 1981), and Oleg Baklanov, the Central Committee secretary responsible for ties to the defense industry. Out of their discussions and Kryuchkov's earlier efforts, a plan emerged.

Kryuchkov had been planning for months before the banya meeting to have a state of emergency declared. His staff members had made detailed preparations up to and including "names of people to be arrested and the phones to be tapped."[80] He had also been meeting with many of the relevant members of Roeder's iron triangle (the party apparatus, heavy industry, and the armed forces including the secret police[81]) for several months, largely to grouse about the diminishing role of the Party and the danger that peace might break out between East and West. Among those participating in these discussions were Boldin, Yasov, and Baklanov.

The plan, such as it was, had three components. First, a "temporary" State Committee for the State of Emergency in the USSR was to be established. It would, as its name implied, declare a state of emergency throughout the entire country. The coup was to take place (and did) two days after the banya assemblage. Its duration would, ostensibly, be limited in theory to six months. The cast of characters of the committee included six persons who obviously belonged by virtue of traditional job-slot criteria. All of them would almost certainly have been (or had been at one time) members of the CPSU Politburo or the Party Secretariat in the days prior to Gorbachev's weakening of those institutions. These were Pavlov, the prime minister; Kryuchkov, the KGB head; Yazov, the defense minister; Boris Pugo, the minister of internal affairs; and Baklanov, a Central Committee secretary, whose portfolio included the defense industry. By the same token, the sixth member of what became known disparagingly as the gang of eight was Gennady Yanayev, the vice president. The vice presidency was a recent innovation, having been established at Gorbachev's urging only at the beginning of 1991. Yanayev was the first person designated vice president.

---

[79] Familiarity breeds contempt. It turns out Boldin really did not like Gorbachev and liked his wife even less. For a brief review of Boldin's *Ten Years That Shook the World* (New York: Basic Books, 1994) see Robert Legvold's review in the July/August 1995 issue of *Foreign Affairs* (Vol. 74, No. 4, pp. 149–50).

[80] Kaiser, *Why Gorbachev Happened*, p. 423. For detailed and revealing excerpts from the testimony both of the conspirators and Gorbachev himself, see V. G. Stepankov and E. K. Lisov, *Kremlevskii zagovor* (Moscow: Izdatel'stvo 'Ogonek', 1992).

[81] Roeder, *Red Sunset*, passim.

Yanayev's appointment was not welcomed by members of the Congress of People's Deputies, who failed to render a majority in favor in the first round of voting but did so on Gorbachev's appeal. Gorbachev subsequently rued (and had reason to rue) that he had pressured the deputies to approve Yanayev as vice president.

The other two were evidently selected to a large extent to symbolize that the committee had the support of key civilian sectors of the economy. They were Vasily Starodubtsev, the head of the Peasants' Union (in actuality a group supporting collective farms), and Aleksandr Tizyakov (representing defense-oriented state industries).[82] In the minds of the other members of the GKChP, its legitimacy would be enhanced by enlarging its membership with a person claiming to speak for the peasantry but favoring the perpetuation of peasant serfdom and by adding yet another person from Roeder's iron triangle to the committee in addition to the minister of defense, the KGB head, and the minister of internal affairs.

Neither Starodubtsev nor Tirzyakov was a token participant. Starodubtsev's Lenin kolkhoz was a poster child for the collective farm system in general. He had also been mightily threatened by the events of the previous two years. When Yeltsin ran for president of Russia he received 76 percent of the vote in Starodubtsev's region.[83] Tizyakov, it was subsequently reported, was obsessed with the idea of removing Gorbachev and devoted enormous effort prior to the creation of the junta to planning the steps it would take to ensure the coup would succeed.[84] Though Kryuchkov was the main organizer of the coup, it was to Tizyakov "the idea belonged of creating the GKChP as the highest organ of power."[85]

The second element in the plan, which was prompted in part by a perceived need to achieve a modicum of legitimacy, entailed sending a group of key officials to meet with Gorbachev at his summer vacation residence. They included Valery Boldin, Gorbachev's main staff assistant once he became general secretary; Oleg Baklanov, a member of the national Defense Council; General Valentin Varennikov, the deputy minister of defense; a party secretary, Oleg Shenin; and the eponymously named General Vyacheslav Generalov of the KGB.[86] Their

---

[82] Brown, *The Gorbachev Factor*, p. 296.

[83] Stepankov and Lisov, *Kremlevskii*, p. 127.

[84] On his obsessive planning of the steps to be taken once the coup had occurred, see ibid., p. 130.

[85] Ibid., p. 129. See also Beissinger, *Nationalist Mobilization*, pp. 368–69.

[86] Gorbachev's "visitors" are enumerated in many places. See, for instance, Stuart Loory and Ann Imse, *Seven Days That Shook the World* (Atlanta, GA: Turner, 1991). They were accompanied by Yury Plekhanov, whose responsibilities involved the protection of Soviet leaders.

task would be to persuade Gorbachev that he must resign and yield power to Yanayev, who would serve as acting president. Until that happened he, his family, and his closest associates would be rendered incommunicado and powerless to act. To lend credence to their threat, the telephone connections to his residence in Crimea were severed and the areas—land and sea—around the vacation spot were reenforced militarily. The legitimacy of his resignation would be ratified by an Anatoly Lukyanov–led Supreme Soviet. The GKChP's cover story was to be that Gorbachev was unable to perform his duties because of unspecified health reasons. And indeed, without obtaining Gorbachev's agreement or a physician's assessment, the junta issued a statement declaring that Yanayev had become acting president owing to Gorbachev's "inability to fulfill the responsibilities of President of the USSR for health reasons."[87] Had Gorbachev yielded to his visitors' demands he would have returned to Moscow but in a role subordinate to the GKChP. Tirzyakov was quite explicit that whoever would be president, his task would be "only to fulfill the will"[88] of the emergency committee. But we will never know. Gorbachev turned the visitors down cold. In two and a half days the coup had collapsed.

The third part of the plan was to coordinate the actions of those with the instruments of violence—the army, the KGB, and the militia—to maintain order.[89] Like the Bolsheviks in 1917, the initial effort was to seize power in Moscow and Leningrad. In his biography of Yeltsin, Colton inventoried the troops that were to be mobilized to seize the capital.[90] They included, initially, tanks and other armored vehicles and manpower from the Red Army's Taman Motorized Rifle Division, the Kantemirov Tank Division, and the Twenty-Seventh Brigade of the KGB's *spetsnaz* (special forces). A day later, "troops from the MVD's Dzerzhinskaya Motor Rifle Division, paratroops from Tula and Ryazan, and units of the Vetebskaya Division of the KGB"[91] arrived in Moscow. In his biography of Yeltsin, Colton states "the eight principals inundated Moscow with armor (about 750 tanks and vehicles) and troops"[92] and, in his book on Moscow, quotes Yeltsin (who once the coup began had holed up in the Russian White House) after the fact as having acknowledged that the building "'could have been stormed by

[87] Stepankov and Lisov, *Kremlevskii*, p. 92. The statement was signed by Yanayev, Pavlov, and Baklanov.
[88] Ibid., p. 130.
[89] For useful accounts see Matlock, *Autopsy*; Kaiser, *Why Gorbachev Happened*, pp. 420–30.
[90] Colton, *Yeltsin*, p. 196.
[91] Colton, *Moscow*, pp. 648–49.
[92] Colton, *Moscow*, p.196.

a single company.'"[93] In theory, the troops mobilized could engender the real muscle that would induce mass compliance in Moscow and Leningrad to the GKChP's orders, which would in turn be followed, as the committee's name implied, by the implementation of a state of emergency throughout the country including, as Beissinger notes, "presidential rule in the Baltic republics, Moldova, Georgia, and key cities of Russia."[94]

Had normal Soviet politics applied, the plan might have worked. I say this notwithstanding the absence of a clear leader, with the possible exception of Kryuchkov (Yanayev was hopeless) among the GKChP, the inebriation of members of the committee at crucial moments during its brief existence, and the failure to execute the most obvious steps immediately on their announcement of the creation of the committee (the failure to arrest Yeltsin and other key leaders,[95] the failure to achieve a true monopoly over the key means of communication). In these respects and others, the Russian coup effort paled in comparison with General Wojtech Jaruzelski's seizure of power in Poland in December 1981.[96] Assuming Soviet citizens faced the kind of collective action problem the atomization of the Soviet public had traditionally engendered and assuming the troops would unquestioningly follow orders—as Soviet leaders would reasonably presume they would—the forces mobilized were quite adequate to the task.

But Soviet politics had changed in profound ways. The junta launched the coup because they were alarmed by what was going on. Indeed, the timing of the coup was driven by the plan to sign the 9+1 agreement August 20. That agreement would have transformed the USSR into a Union of Sovereign States. The members of the committee were scarcely motivated by a disinterested concern for the future of the country. Kryuchkov had bugged a meeting involving Gorbachev, Yeltsin, and Nursultan Nazarbayev (president of Kazakhstan at the time), at which the three had agreed that after the signing of the 9+1 agreement Nazarbayev would become prime minister in lieu of Pavlov, and Yazov and Kryuchkov would be replaced. Even so, the plotters seemed not to have understood fully the institutional and behavioral changes in train. (They weren't the only ones. The U.S. ambassador, Jack Matlock, is sharply critical of the senior George

---

[93] Colton, *Moscow*, p. 649.

[94] Beissinger, *Nationalist Mobilization*, p. 426.

[95] Remnick reports that the GKChP had ordered 250,000 handcuffs and 300,000 arrest forms, though only a handful of persons were actually arrested. David Remnick, *Lenin's Tomb: The Last Days of the Soviet Empire* (New York: Random House, 1993), p. 453.

[96] For a comparison, see especially ibid., p. 452.

Bush for initially acting as though the coup would succeed.[97]) They certainly failed to take measures appropriate to the task at hand in light of these changes.

What the junta hoped to achieve was a return to the status quo ante perestroika—authoritarian Brezhnevism—a political system closer to Levitsky and Way's "full" authoritarianism than to the totalitarianism of the Stalin era—by employing the means that had been effective *before* the changes that occurred during perestroika, measures that were far less effective in an environment in which Soviet, and Moscow mass publics especially, were increasingly being transformed from subjects into citizens. As Beissinger has observed, "The Brezhnevian regime of repression was extremely efficient, but . . . Brezhnev generally did not rely on severe violence to marginalize challenges. Rather, the predictable, consistent, and efficient application of low level and moderate coercion proved extremely effective."[98] When the state has a reputation for repressing demonstrations most of the time, the propensity for large-scale mass action in the streets diminishes substantially. On this score the Brezhnev regime was rather successful: In Beissinger's calculus, two-thirds (67 percent) of the demonstrations exceeding a hundred people entailed some repression. There existed a kind of equilibrium: the demonstrations were generally small, the predictability of the regime's actions relatively high, and the level of sanctions against the demonstrators fairly low—limited for instance to severe beatings rather than long jail sentences or deaths.

Such was the kind of authoritarian rule to which the junta aspired, the good old days when the Politburo or a Politburo-type organization served as the selectorate and chose one from among its membership as the national leader, when challenges to the regime were considered literally irrational—when "the psychological prison became the symbol of the regime's efforts to infuse a sense of normalcy around loyalty to the existing order,"[99] when modest shows of force were usually sufficient to deter mass actions from getting out of hand. Vice President Yanayev gave voice to the wishes for quieter and more repressive times at his August 19 press conference when he observed,

---

[97] Matlock, *Autopsy*, p. 588. He also remembers that when he "was interviewed on ABC's *Nightline* on August 19 . . . every other commentator . . . implied that it was foolish to think that the KGB and army could not maintain control if they wished. (Ibid., p. 604.) George Breslauer pointed out to me that on CNN that evening Gary Kasparov had predicted the coup would fail within a week—which exasperated Jeanne Kirkpatrick, who was also on the same program.

[98] Beissinger, *Nationalist Mobilization*, p. 334.

[99] Ibid., p. 70.

An uncontrollable situation, in which there are no clearly defined spheres of authority, has come about in the country. All this cannot help but cause widespread discontent among the population. A real threat of the disintegration of the country and the breakup of our single economic space, our single space of civil rights, our single defense and our single foreign policy has also come about.

Under these conditions, normal life is impossible. In many parts of the USSR, blood is being shed as a result of clashes between nationalities, and the breakup of the USSR would have very grave consequences, not only domestic but also international consequences. Under these conditions, we have no other choice but to take resolute measures to halt the country's slide toward a catastrophe.[100]

There was some basis to the expectation that a show of force would be sufficient to assume effective control. It had been only three years since the February 1988 publication in *Sovetskaya Rossiya* of the infamous reactionary letter by Nina Andreyeva. The evidence from that episode suggested that much of the populace would acquiesce to any power move from on high. Kaiser relates that those around Gorbachev were extremely ill at ease: "We were all cowards," he reports one of Gorbachev's supporters as having said.[101] William and Jane Taubman were in Moscow at the time the letter was published. They describe how many of the intellectuals (but not all) with whom they were in close contact similarly ducked for cover until Yakovlev's rejoinder was published in *Pravda*.[102]

But as events were to show in August 1991, they *were* behind. Remnick reports that after the fact Gorbachev had argued that if the Emergency Committee "'had acted twelve or eighteen months earlier the way they did in August it [the coup] would have come off.'"[103] Gorbachev may have been right in this particular assessment, his stunning obtuseness about the coup and the significance of its failure for the "socialist path" notwithstanding. An implication of his counterfactual history is that the coup would have been successful had the halfhearted but bloody attempted coup in Vilnius, Lithuania (January 1991) been either more effectual or not attempted at all, if the multiple

[100] *Pravda*, August 20, 1991, as translated by the *Current Digest of the Post-Soviet Press*, Vol. 43, No. 33 (September 18, 1991), pp. 11–13, dlib.eastview.com/sources/article.jsp?id =13537887.

[101] Kaiser, *Why Gorbachev Happened*, p. 211.

[102] William Taubman and Jane Taubman, *Moscow Spring* (New York: Summit Books, 1989).

[103] Remnick, *Lenin's Tomb*, p. 498.

1991 Moscow mass demonstrations had not occurred, and had Yeltsin not been elected president of Russia (June 1991).

With the issue whether Gorbachev would continue as president on the table, the players were not just the junta leaders and those in the armed forces who would follow the junta's orders. The players had changed. There was a Congress of People's Deputies, two-thirds of whom had been elected in national elections. There were two presidents, the Soviet president, Gorbachev, ensconced and encircled in the Crimea, and the Russian president, Yeltsin, who had been acting increasingly like a head of state, one who had controlling access to Russia's enormous natural resources. That president had come to Moscow almost immediately after the announcement of the takeover by the Emergency Committee. There he was ensconced and soon encircled in the White House. Not only were there now two Moscows. In the physical and increasingly the institutional sense, even two Kremlins existed side by side. After Yeltsin's inauguration, a month after his June 1991 election, "Gorbachev approved rooms in the Kremlin for Yeltsin. They were in Building No. 14 across a cobblestone square from Gorbachev's lair in Building No. 1."[104] The analogue with the dual power in Petrograd on the eve of the October Revolution was obvious. It became even more manifest when one augments the emergence of Russian institutions autonomous from or virtually autonomous from Soviet institutions with how accustomed to going into the streets citizens in the two capitals had become by August 1991.

With minor qualifications, the implementation of the planned takeover never extended even to Leningrad, much less to the rest of the country. In Leningrad, the mayor, Anatoly Sobchak, condemned the coup on Leningrad television (which was available in many cities across the country) and convinced the regional military commander, Viktor Samsonov, of the unwisdom of sending troops into Leningrad where vast mass demonstrations against the coup took place in Palace Square.

Moscow was where the drama played out. Neither the junta nor the considerable armed forces there turned out to be capable of playing the role of an ejectorate. Normal Soviet politics had been premised on both the de-participation and mobilized participation of mass publics.[105] De-participation was *de rigueur* in the sense that autonomous behavior independent of Party dictates was prohibited. Mobilized participation was also the norm.[106] Mere acquiescence was considered unacceptable. The populace was expected to show its support for the regime

[104] Colton, *Yeltsin*, p. 194.
[105] Roeder, *Red Sunset*, pp. 42 ff.
[106] Zimmerman, "Mobilized Participation," pp. 332–53.

by voting in favor of the regime's candidates, marching in May Day parades and the like. Institutions such as these contributed to creating acute collective action problems, ones that enhanced the regime's ability to atomize the society and to mobilize the citizenry for more grandiose and substantive purposes.[107] This of course was something students of Soviet politics knew long before formalizations of collective action problems became fashionable in the social sciences.

One of Mark Beissinger's achievements was to augment an understanding of the collective action problem with the demonstration that from the regime's perspective it takes far more resources to control a large crowd than a small one. The relation is curvilinear, not merely linear.[108] Mere differences in the size of the protest matter. Small numbers of unarmed protesters in the streets are at the mercy of the wielders of violence, whether the latter be the secret police, the military, or putatively private security providers, whereas the latter often have far better things to do with their time than confront a really large crowd even if that crowd is unarmed or anomic.

By August 1991 both de-participation and regime-induced mobilized participation were things of the past for a sizeable fraction of Muscovites. Leadership and horizontal linkages are two of the most obvious ways to overcome the collective action problem. In Yeltsin they had a leader who by the time of the coup had already begun to outdistance Gorbachev in the Russian public's favor. His response to the coup was of legendary proportions: the single most iconic image of the events related to the coup occurred when he came out of the White House and clambered on a tank, whereupon, in an act that was either genuinely brave or thoroughly stupid, or both, he proceeded in no uncertain terms to denounce the coup before about fifty people gathered around the tank. That number increased exponentially as people in Moscow became aware of the speech, which was broadcast on CNN and could be seen by Muscovites with a "simple antenna."[109]

Equally important, in Moscow mass demonstrations had become a regular occurrence during 1991. A crowd estimated at four hundred thousand turned out on February 22, 1991, to show support for Yeltsin and to demand that Gorbachev resign. The next day (Red Army Day) a counterdemonstration ranging in the tens of thousands took place. Two weeks later (March 10) the leading prodemocracy organization, Democratic Russia, mobilized a demonstration of well in excess of a hundred thousand. Once again, the demonstration called for support of Yeltsin

[107] Kuran, "Now Out of Never," pp. 7–48.
[108] Beissinger, *Nationalist Mobilization*.
[109] Loory and Imse, *Seven Days*, p. 235.

and for Gorbachev's resignation. Another two weeks passed. Despite Gorbachev's efforts to ban demonstrations in Moscow and his introduction of troops there to maintain order, another crowd estimated at two hundred thousand took to the streets to show support for Yeltsin.[110] As a result, when the coup occurred, hundreds of thousands of Muscovites had had the experience of taking to the streets—and probably knew personally others who had also taken to the streets during calendar 1991.

In several very large demonstrations in 1991 there had been little or no repression. In the Brezhnev era (above, p. 187), two-thirds of all protests had resulted in repression. That number dropped to fewer than one-third in the first two years of the Gorbachev era and decreased further after the events in Tbilisi in 1989.[111] Experience with previous protests affects mobilization patterns. Prior experience conveys to the dissenters some sense of what the limits are. It may also provide information about the propensity of others to protest, which then feeds back on a dissenter's proclivity to protest. The combination of Muscovites' experience in the street and Yeltsin's leadership trivialized the collective action problem in August 1991. Those in the street were brave, but few thought they were committing suicide. But the guns and tanks in the streets of Moscow remained a serious problem.

The leaders of the junta seem to have expected that the troops they had mobilized would be the cohesive force the Red Army had always been in coping with disturbances in the satellites or on the periphery of the Soviet Union. Those disposed to protest are particularly likely to be deterred when the potential protesters are not cohesive and when the state's forces are. The morale of the armed forces will be a function of the extent to which they empathize or identify with their leaders and with the potential protesters. The cohesiveness of the protesters will also be affected by the same factors—the effectiveness and visibility of their leadership, morale, and the ability to co-opt the opposition. While the armed forces had been willing to repress the Afghans, Georgians, and Balts, the reputational costs for the military had been high. The coup leaders seem not to have tumbled to the possibility that some of the officer corps who had seen action in Georgia or the Baltic republics might be less, not more, prone to resort to violence. An even larger number of the officer corps as a whole were less enthusiastic about the idea of firing on ethnic Russians, especially women, than they had been in recent actions against Afghans, Georgians, or Lithuanians. In the event, some generals, most notably the head of the air force, General Yevgeny

---

[110] The estimates referenced in this paragraph all come from Beissinger, *Nationalist Mobilization*, pp. 421–27.

[111] Ibid., pp. 347–53.

Shaposhnikov, quickly joined the Russian side. Others switched as well. Still more played a double game. Midlevel officers gave the orders they received very careful attention but never executed them while secretly communicating with Yeltsin's aides in the White House. There were mutinies in the KGB with key units refusing to fight. Tank units changed sides. Within the GKChP, the defense minister was among the committee members most disposed to avoid bloodshed.

By the same token, the incentive to protest is low when there are severe information asymmetries so that the political leadership by virtue of its control over the means of communication thwarts the efforts of potential protesters to ascertain whether substantially large numbers are protesting elsewhere. Lenin and Trotsky had seized the telephones and the telegraph. The media seizure in 1991 was far less secure. Foreigners, myself included, continued to receive email messages. The foreign news organizations continued to transmit materials. Some opposition radio stations, most notably Ekho Moskvy, continued to broadcast intermittently. Yeltsin's speech was broadcast on CNN, which, as noted above (p. 190), Muscovites could watch easily. Even the major national television channels, while reading all the decrees emanating from the Emergency Committee, provided relatively balanced accounts. A young TV reporter, Sergei Medvedev, cleverly construed an assignment for the 9:00 P.M. *Vremya* program *Moscow Today* to show "how 'life is going on as normal,'" which, as Remnick observes, was basically the case: "Much of Moscow, like nearly all of the rest of the country, did seem normal," as license to include clips of the White House and the unforgettable picture of Yeltsin on a tank.[112] The opposition newspapers had been ordered shut down, but a pooled *samizdat* paper, the *Obshchaya gazeta*, appeared. The government paper, *Izvestia*, was divided: the printers demanded that Yeltsin's statements be published and the editor, Nikolai Yefimov, ordered them to do as they were told. In the end, they published both the statements of the Emergency Committee *and* Yeltsin's appeal to resist the coup. The Emergency Committee's declarations appeared on page 1 and Yeltsin's appeal on page 2.

Aside from personal power considerations (which, as we have seen, were considerable for several members of the committee, given that their jobs were on the line), the Emergency Committee had been formed to restore order, to prevent the dissolution of the Soviet Union, and to create a situation in which a Politburo-type organization backed by Soviet armed forces would determine who would lead the country. Its members did not, however, act as if they understood the magnitude of

[112] Remnick, *Lenin's Tomb*, p. 473.

the changes that had occurred nor the extent to which the Gorbachev-initiated processes were no longer ones that Gorbachev controlled. The members of the Congress of People's Deputies—those who directly chose Gorbachev to be president—were a mere handful when compared to the emerging selectorate, the Soviet adult population. But they were far larger in number than the members of the Politburo and the Central Committee. And two-thirds of them had been chosen by a newly enfranchised selectorate of the adult Soviet population.

The leaders of the GKChP sought to restore a situation across the Soviet Union that had characterized that country for most of the period dating from the days immediately after the very first days of the October Revolution. They hoped to restore the certainty of selection that one associates with "full" authoritarian systems generally and particularly with the practices observed by the Soviet leadership. Very likely they deluded themselves. Short of armed intervention, Ukraine was not going to remain in such a Soviet Union. Nor were several smaller republics—notably the Baltic republics but possibly Moldavia (current-day Moldova) or one or more south Caucasian republics as well. But the Soviet Union the Emergency Committee sought to govern was already a shell of its former self. They sought to seize power from the wrong president. The formal collapse of the Soviet Union occurred in December 1991 but by August 1991 the preeminent president in Moscow was Yeltsin. He occupied that position because he took two risks. He had risked the uncertainty that accompanies free elections. This resulted in the legitimacy that accompanied having been elected by a selectorate embracing the adult Russian population. He then risked far more than electoral defeat by demanding in the most dramatic manner possible that Gorbachev be restored to power. In the capital cities Yeltsin's nationally defined selectorate—nationally defined here meaning Russian, no longer Soviet—reaffirmed their support for him and what he had come to stand for by demanding that his chief rival be restored to his legally selected position as president of the Soviet Union.

Gorbachev's aspiration had been to achieve, under his tutelage, a socialist Soviet Union that would be his conception of a normal country. He could neither abandon the idea that such a country would be under his tutelage (at least until 1995, when ostensibly there would be a national referendum to elect the Soviet president) nor abandon the idea that the country would be one country and socialist. When he returned to Moscow from the Crimea, he was restored to his position as president, but of a shell of a country that was rapidly fragmenting, especially once Ukraine declared its independence on August 24. Even the illusion of its existence was dissipated when the leaders of Ukraine, Russia, and Belarus signed the Belovezhye Forest Accord in December

1991, formally declaring the end of the Soviet Union. The GKChP had tried and failed to eject Mikhail Gorbachev from his position as president of the USSR. The three leaders of the Ukraine, Russia, and Belarus, in a manner akin to the birthday party game of musical chairs, succeeded in ousting him by eliminating the Soviet Union of which he was the first and only president.

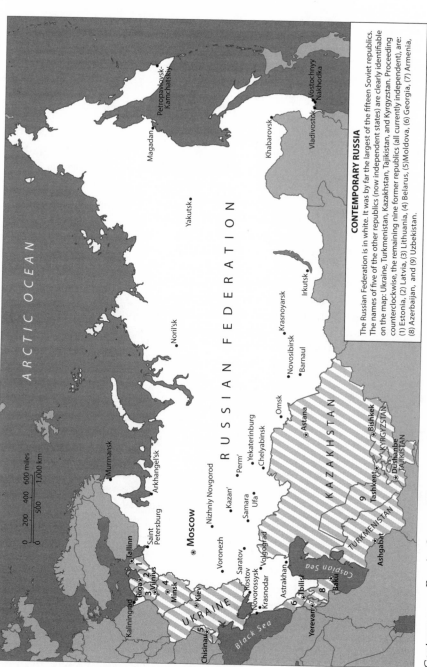

Contemporary Russia. *Source:* "The World Factbook," (Washington, DC: Central Intelligence Agency, 2013), www.cia
.gov/library/publications/the-world-factbook/index.html.

CONTEMPORARY RUSSIA

The Russian Federation is in white. It was by far the largest of the fifteen Soviet republics. The names of five of the other republics (now independent states) are clearly identifiable on the map: Ukraine, Turkmenistan, Kazakhstan, Tajikistan, and Kyrgyzstan. Proceeding counterclockwise, the remaining nine former republics (all currently independent), are: (1) Estonia, (2) Latvia, (3) Lithuania, (4) Belarus, (5)Moldova, (6) Georgia, (7) Armenia, (8) Azerbaijan, and (9) Uzbekistan.

CHAPTER 7

Democratizing Russia, 1991–1997

AT THE TIME THE SOVIET UNION COLLAPSED,[1] Boris Yeltsin and Mikhail Gorbachev had similar perspectives on some key issues and approaches to politics notwithstanding their many differences. For one thing, they both sought to create a normal country. It was Gorbachev's rationale for all that he had introduced: it was, he told the Central Committee, "why we started everything in the first place—so a human being can feel normal, can feel good, in a socialist state."[2] The importance Yeltsin attached to having Russia become a normal country—"to be like the rest," as we noted at the outset—was so great that he titled the first chapter of his *Struggle for Russia*, "A Normal Country."[3]

Both, moreover, had some conception of the West in mind when they expressed this desire. By the time the Soviet Union collapsed both Yeltsin and Gorbachev had become self-described social democrats. Their conceptions of what being a social democrat entailed differed considerably. Gorbachev's remarks on his return from the Crimea after the August coup revealed that almost to the very end of the Soviet Union he maintained that the Party could serve as the medium for accomplishing the transition to social democracy. Though he said he had Sweden in mind,[4] his obtuse reluctance to abandon the idea that the Party could still be a democratizing force suggests that he had not really grasped what Western social democracy entailed.

We can take Yeltsin at his word that he had become a social democrat. But his visceral enthusiasm for markets suggests that Colton is bang on in observing that "[i]f Yeltsin was a social democrat at all, it was more in the stamp of Tony Blair of Britain, Felipe Gonzalez of Spain or Gerhard Schröder of Germany than of the left-wing statists of interwar and postwar Europe."[5] Yeltsin's conception of social or socialist democracy attached greater weight to "democracy" and far less to "socialist." (He

[1] Breslauer, *Gorbachev and Yeltsin*; Chernyaev, *My Six Years With Gorbachev*; Kaiser, *Why Gorbachev Happened*; Brown, *The Gorbachev Factor*.
[2] Kaiser, *Why Gorbachev Happened*, p. 276.
[3] Yeltsin, *The Struggle for Russia*, pp. 3–14 at p. 3.
[4] According to BBC correspondent John Simpson, as cited in Colton, *Yeltsin*, p. 218.
[5] Ibid., p. 222.

had been one of those insisting that "sovereign" replace "socialist" in the name for a political entity involving all fifteen republics that would have succeeded the USSR, had the latter remained a single country.) Colton reports a telling interchange between Yeltsin and the BBC correspondent John Simpson. To the latter's question, "Gorbachev . . . was talking about Swedish social democracy; that is his model. . . . Is your model, Yeltsin's model . . . the model of François Mitterand's France, or John Major's Britain, or the United States, or Japan, or Spain, or Germany?" Yeltsin answered, "I would take everything together; I would take the best from each system and introduce it in Russia." Congratulated on having given a politic answer, Simpson prodded him, saying he had to have "some kind of notion," to which Yeltsin opined, "You cannot just take a model and install it ready made. Maybe create a new model, but take something from the Swedish model, and why not take a piece from the Japanese model—an interesting piece—and from the French, too, especially as regards the parliamentary aspect? And in the United States, where they have 200 years of democracy . . . they have a definite framework for this democracy, and that's interesting, too."[6]

Gorbachev and Yeltsin each confronted similar institutional contexts. Russia was the only republic that followed the Soviet Union's lead by creating the institution of a powerful president coupled with a two-tiered parliament: a Congress of People's Deputies charged with the task, a la the American electoral college, of selecting a Supreme Soviet, and a Supreme Soviet. Each president had obtained the right to issue decrees having the effect of law, Yeltsin achieving this right conditionally in November 1991. Each had far-reaching, transformative goals domestically. Each believed himself indispensible to the accomplishment of these goals. Each found Soviet (perhaps more precisely in Yeltsin's case, Soviet-type) institutions impediments to the achievement of these goals. And both emasculated these institutions in order to have their way. Both had problems with the uncertainty of contested elections. Gorbachev, as we saw, in 1990 deferred a possible moment of truth until 1995, whereas Yeltsin in 1993 promised to advance the timing of presidential elections to 1994 and then reneged.

Democratizing Elections, 1993–1999

The nonincarcerated adult population of the Russian Republic had served as the selectorate that overwhelmingly chose Yeltsin as the president of the Russian Republic in June 1991. The legitimacy that

[6] Ibid., pp. 218–19.

accompanied being chosen by the populace as president was augmented by his actions in thwarting the August 1991 GKChP coup and defending Gorbachev's status as president of the USSR. But, it turned out, the institutional ambiguity characteristic of dual power had not been eliminated with the collapse of the Soviet Union. True enough, the Soviet legislative and executive branches were no longer. In the immediate aftermath of the August 1991 putsch, the *Soviet* Congress of People's Deputies acquiesced in its own demise: "The congress adopted a resolution suspending itself and transferring executive power to a new State Council, which was to govern until a new constitution could be adopted. A vestigial USSR Supreme Soviet continued to function, but it was in a dubious twilight zone of constitutional and political legitimacy since neither Russia nor the other republics recognized its decisions as having legal force."[7] And then in December of that year the office of the presidency of the USSR evaporated with the disappearance of that country.

Not all Soviet institutions and procedural modes, however, ceased to exist. Certainly, Yeltsin's behavior suggested strong analogues between the Russian presidency, to which he was elected while the USSR continued to exist, and Gorbachev's presidency of the Soviet Union. Yeltsin quickly began to emulate Gorbachev in asserting the ambit of the presidency, in this instance, the Russian presidency. In the immediate afterglow of the failed coup attempt by the GKChP—prior, that is, to the collapse of the Soviet Union—the Russian Congress of People's Deputies in November 1991 granted Yeltsin the temporary decree-granting powers that Gorbachev had had as USSR president.

In addition, the 1977 Brezhnev Soviet Constitution, as modified by Gorbachev's 1990 institutional innovations and the parallel 1978 Russian Constitution, continued to be treated as the fundamental legal framework. No Russian Constitution was adopted in the immediate aftermath of the collapse of the Soviet Union. The Soviet-era Russian Constitution, with "all the usual Soviet attributes,"[8] served as the default document.

---

[7] Thomas F. Remington, *The Russian Parliament: Institutional Evolution in a Transitional Regime, 1989–1999* (New Haven CT: Yale University Press, 2001), p. 45. Whether the Congress had voted to continue its existence until a new constitution was agreed upon is illustrative of the pervasive institutional ambiguity, as the quote in the text from Remington suggests. Accounts vary. Gorbachev, for instance, says the USSR Supreme Soviet was to continue to function pending the adoption of a new Constitution but then says that the first act of business of the State Council was to recognize the independence of the Baltic states. Gorbachev, *Memoirs: Mikhail Gorbachev* (New York: Doubleday, 1995), pp. 648–51. Yeltsin asserts that Gorbachev at the podium insisted that "if the Congress didn't dissolve itself, it would be disbanded" and that "the proposal for a Council of Heads of State went through without a hitch." Yeltsin, *The Struggle for Russia*, p. 109.

[8] Victor Sheinis, "The Constitution," in McFaul et al., *Between Dictatorship and Democracy*, p. 57.

Moreover, while the *Soviet* Congress of People's Deputies had acquiesced in its own termination in the aftermath of the failed August 1991 putsch, the *Russian* institutional expressions of the Brezhnev era as amended on Gorbachev's initiative continued to exist, most notably the Russian Congress of People's Deputies. Like Yeltsin, its members had been chosen in a way that engendered a republic-wide and vote-based legitimacy. That legitimacy differed from Yeltsin's only in that they had been elected in 1990 and the latter had been elected president in June 1991. In the sense that the presidency was premised on a division between the executive and the legislative branches, it was novel against the backdrop of Soviet history. The Russian Congress of People's Deputies, like its Soviet counterpart, by contrast, had been meant to italicize its throwback character as an institutional return to Leninist norms. The approach to governance by the Congress and the Supreme Soviet was not premised on the expectation of a separation of legislative and executive power but rather on an assumption of legislative pre-eminence vis-à-vis the executive, both the president and the government. Moreover, as became evident within a year after the collapse of the Soviet Union, its leadership and the bulk of its members took seriously the slogan, "All power to the Soviets."[9] This ran directly at variance with Yeltsin's vision of the president as key decision maker with a permanently and nearly unlimited mandate to transform the economy. What the Supreme Soviet had granted while the memory of Yeltsin on a Soviet tank was fresh in everyone's memories, its members refused to extend in December 1992. Consequently, the parliament and the president, each with valid claims to legitimacy, were soon at loggerheads—*dual power* once again, this time involving the two key institutions of the Russian Federation. Each branch of government had legitimate claims to rule, but each also based that claim by reference to institutions that had been created by a state that no longer existed.[10]

While the two sides disagreed about almost every manner of substance and the key question of who decides, each agreed that an acceptable means of resolving the dispute was by a nationwide referendum. McFaul notes that "both sides feared a new direct election, but both

---

[9] John Lowenhardt, *The Reincarnation of Russia: Struggling with the Legacy of Communism, 1990–1994* (Durham, NC: Duke University Press, 1995), especially pp. 127–28; Eugene Huskey, *Presidential Power in Russia* (Armonk, NY: M.E. Sharpe, 1999), especially pp. 163–82.

[10] In foreign affairs the Russian Federation assumed the legal obligations and benefits (most notably, becoming a permanent member of the UN Security Council) of the USSR. In bilateral relations Russia has largely attempted to have its cake and eat it too, asserting that the Soviet Union had imposed communist rule on Eastern Europe and the Baltic states while Russia had liberated these states from Nazi dominance.

were also eager to secure a new popular mandate."[11] Each proposed questions to be addressed in a public referendum. Not surprisingly, they were formulated strategically, but at least each recognized the legitimacy of referenda as recourses to dispute resolution.

After much haggling, the referendum—which was not binding—took place in April 1993. Those who would have been the selectorate had there been a presidential election rather than a referendum largely endorsed Yeltsin and Yeltsin's policies. Asked whether they trusted Yeltsin, 59 percent answered in the affirmative. A bare majority (53 percent) approved "of the socioeconomic policy conducted by the Russian president and by the Russian government since 1992." This was a surprise given the severe economic dislocations resulting from the introduction of economic reforms and the inflationary policies of Viktor Gerashchenko, head of the Central Bank. Just fewer than half (49.5 percent) "supported early presidential elections,"[12] whereas two-thirds (67 percent) called for a new parliamentary election prior to the date scheduled.[13]

But in practice neither side was willing to move forward without attempting to sandbag the moves of the other. The controversy persisted throughout the summer. Finally, on September 21 Yeltsin issued Resolution 1400. It disbanded the parliament and declared that elections would be held in mid-December. (A telling indicator of the extent to which Yeltsin was governing unilaterally is the number of the resolution.) The Congress and particularly the chairman of the Supreme Soviet, Ruslan Khasbulatov, responded vigorously.[14] It voted to impeach Yeltsin. It declared the vice president, Aleksandr Rutskoi, to be president. Hundreds of its members decamped to the same White House out of which Yeltsin had emerged in August 1991 to declare that putsch illegal. This time Yeltsin was on the outside of the White House.

A standoff ensued, lasting several days. Apparently, an agreement to conduct joint elections in early 1994 was almost achieved.[15] But this drama did not result in what Russians, emulating Hollywood, term a

[11] Michael McFaul and Nikolai Petrov in McFaul et al., *Between Dictatorship and Democracy*, p. 34.

[12] Ibid., p. 35. On the same page McFaul and Petrov reproduce the English-language version of all four questions.

[13] For a summary of the issues raised concerning the way the votes were counted, see Timothy J. Colton and Jerry F. Hough eds., *Growing Pains: Russian Democracy and the Election of 1993* (Washington, DC: Brookings Institution, 1998), p. 31n8. Particularly at issue was the denominator to be employed, i.e., whether invalid ballots were to be included.

[14] For a depiction of the resources Khasbulatov as chairman of the Supreme Soviet had at his disposal, see Thomas F. Remington, "Ménage à Trois: The End of Soviet Parliamentarism," in Jeffrey W. Hahn, ed., *Democratization in Russia: The Development of Legislative Institutions* (Armonk, NY: M.E. Sharpe, 1996), pp. 106–40, especially pp. 120–23.

[15] Colton and Hough, *Growing Pains*, pp. 6–7 citing an interview by Valery Zorkin, the Supreme Court head, published in *Nezavisimaya gazeta*, November 12, 1993.

kheppi-end. No consensus was achieved. Instead, on October 3, demonstrators supportive of Rutskoi attacked the Moscow mayor's office (adjacent to the White House) and the television station, Ostankino. Recourse was taken to the ultimate ejectorate: Yeltsin responded by browbeating key units of the military (troops who sided with Yeltsin insisted on receiving written orders before acting) into attacking the White House, killing, by official count, 187[16] and arresting approximately 30.[17]

What followed was a founding election[18] *of sorts* that took place on December 12, 1993. "Of sorts" is italicized intentionally. Michael Urban has correctly emphasized that the "December 1993 [election should be seen in many ways] as a replication of late-Soviet electoral practices," as he terms it, "democracy by design."[19] Colton refers to it as "an engineered founding election." In the aftermath of his clash with the Congress of People's Deputies, Yeltsin was nearly as averse to uncertainty as Gorbachev had been in the last years of Soviet power. Yeltsin had promised in September that the presidential election would be moved up to June 1994. He reneged on that promise in November 1993. Instead, he announced that the presidential election would take place as scheduled in 1996. He and his team employed numerous measures to reduce the uncertainty of truly contested elections and to increase the probability of results favorable to those in power through the selective employment of, and disregard for, electoral rules.[20]

More generally, as Urban notes, the elections were competitive, but they were also ones "conducted within frameworks drafted and imposed by only *one* of the contending parties."[21] It was not a pacted transition.[22] Instead, it makes far more sense to borrow, as does Michael

---

[16] Colton, *Yeltsin*, p. 279.

[17] Lowenhardt, *The Reincarnation of Russia*, p. 138.

[18] On founding elections in general, see Guillermo O'Donnell and Philippe C. Schmitter, *Transitions from Authoritarian Rule: Tentative Conclusions about Uncertain Democracies* (Baltimore: Johns Hopkins University Press, 1986).

[19] Michael Urban, "December 1993 as a Replication of Late-Soviet Electoral Practices," *Post-Soviet Affairs*, Vol. 10, No. 2 (April–June 1994), pp. 127 and 129.

[20] Ibid., passim; Colton in Colton and Hough, *Growing Pains*, pp. 7–11. They also document the extent to which various governmental agencies were acting at cross-purposes with each other as well as how quickly Yeltsin backpedaled from many of the more draconic measures instituted in the first month after the seizure of the White House.

[21] Urban, "December 1993," p. 128, italics in original.

[22] Ibid.; Colton, "Introduction," in Colton and Hough, *Growing Pains*, especially pp. 7–16. On pacted transitions, see Adam Przeworski, *Latin Democracy and the Market: Political and Economic Reforms in Eastern Europe and America* (Cambridge: Cambridge University Press, 1991). For a critique, see the many publications by Michael McFaul, notably *Russia's Unfinished Revolution: Political Change from Gorbachev to Putin* (Ithaca, NY: Cornell University Press, 2001); McFaul et al., *Between Dictatorship and Democracy*; and McFaul, "The Fourth Wave of Democracy and Dictatorship: Noncooperative Transitions in the Post Communist World," *World Politics*, Vol. 54, No. 2 (January 2002), pp. 212–44.

McFaul, from an intellectual tradition in the literature on world politics that equates hierarchy and inequality—and not equilibrium among the parties—with stability. The December election was one in which Yeltsin, having outmuscled the Congress, sought to institutionalize that victory by obtaining public approval for a superpresidential constitution as a result of which the "president of Russia [would have] just as many powers as he needs to carry out his role in reforming the country"[23] and would be only modestly constrained by a legislature's ability to rein in his behavior.

I italicized "of sorts." But it *was* a founding election, adopting a minimalist definition of the prerequisites for such an election is that the relevant actors accept its results as defining the rules of the game and that the inevitable errors and putative fraud do not substantially distort the overall results. From an overall systemic perspective, Yeltsin accomplished what he set out to achieve. Almost three-fifths (58 percent) of those the Central Electoral Commission (CEC) reported as voting favored the Constitution. Not the entire spectrum of Russian political parties was allowed to participate,[24] but a diverse range of thirteen parties did. The reported results of the vote for the Constitution and the votes for representatives to the newly created parliament are compatible with an interpretation that emphasizes both errors and putative fraud. They do not at all indicate that the reported aggregate results had been centrally determined. The biggest surprise of the election was that Vladimir Zhirinovsky's soi-disant Liberal Democratic Party (LDPR) received far and away the largest number of the party-list votes (22.9 percent), half again as many (15.5 percent) as received by candidates of the ostensible party of power, Russia's Choice. This result may have been partly explained by local fraud, but, as Colton observes, it is difficult to tell a story in which "scattered bureaucrats could have distorted the returns time after time to privilege Yeltsin's constitution [and also] . . . shunt votes to the LDPR, for which few had the slightest affinity."[25]

In addition, it is important to emphasize the extent to which the behavior of the Communist Party of the Russian Federation (KPRF) (which received 12.4 percent of the party-list votes), and its rural partner, the Agrarian Party of Russia (7.9 percent), contributed to legitimating Yeltsin's preferred outcome with respect to the Constitution. While they scarcely participated as equals—the KPRF had initially

[23] *Izvestia*, November 16, 1993, as cited in Colton, *Yeltsin*, p. 280.

[24] Some parties, such as the Russian Communist Workers' Party and the Russian Officers Union, which had been involved in the October clashes, were proscribed. Others, with an average of 107,000 ostensible signatures (Colton, in Colton and Hough, *Growing Pains*, p. 17), were determined by the CEC not to have obtained the requisite 100,000 signatures.

[25] Colton, in Colton and Hough, *Growing Pains*, p. 26.

been banned in the immediate aftermath of the storming of the White House—they did decide to participate in the election and they acquiesced in the results. Both actions served to legitimate the Constitution and signaled the KPRF's willingness to accept the rules of the game[26]— and the expectations of its leaders that their candidate would successfully compete in the forthcoming presidential election, an expectation that as late as early 1996 seemed well founded.

In short, for those of a teleological bent, the stunning results in December 1993 favoring the role the LDPR would have in the Duma and the strenuous efforts of the KPRF and the Agrarian Party to defeat Yeltsin's Constitution contributed dialectically to the acceptance of a superpresidential constitution. Given that the CEC had said that a majority had endorsed the Constitution and that the major players, whatever their views of Yeltsin, had acted as though they accepted the rules of the game, Yeltsin and his successors could act in many domains with only modest but genuine checks and balances while invoking the Constitution for legitimacy. Moreover, the 1993 Constitution has persisted to this writing (2013) as the legal instrument to invoke when Russian political actors either decide to act legitimately or are required to by circumstances.[27]

The 1993 Constitution clearly tilted the distribution of power in favor of the executive and the president in particular. But the Duma that the new Constitution created was not powerless if the actors involved operated within the framework of that law. How this had consequences for elite political behavior when laws are obeyed was illustrated by early actions of the newly created Duma. In the aftermath of Yeltsin's 1993 victory, the Duma amnestied Rutskoi, Khasbulatov, and fourteen others from the erstwhile Supreme Soviet and those who had been a part of the August 1991 putsch as well.[28] Aleksei Kazannik, whom Yeltsin had appointed as general prosecutor, concluded that the Duma's actions were legal under Article 103 of the new Constitution, ordered those amnestied freed, and then resigned. After some posturing

---

[26] McFaul and Petrov, "Elections," in McFaul et al., *Between Dictatorship and Democracy*, p. 37; McFaul, *Russia's Unfinished Revolution*, especially pp. 239–40.

[27] Richard Sakwa, "The Dual State in Russia," *Post-Soviet Affairs*, Vol. 26, No. 3 (July–September 2010), pp. 185–206.

[28] Colton, *Yeltsin*, p. 282. To top it off, "all members of the 1990–93 Supreme Soviet were permitted to keep the housing that had been assigned them." Ibid. A useful article that compares the treatment of losers among the Russian political elite across time is Olga Kryshtanovskaya, "Has Beens: Trends of Downward Mobility of the Russian Elite," *Russian Social Science Review*, Vol. 46, No. 2 (March–April 2005), pp. 4–51. It appeared originally as a two part article in *Obshchestvennye nauki i sovremennost'*, 2003, No. 5, pp. 33–39 and No. 6, pp. 62–77.

and threats, Yeltsin acquiesced, suggesting that a constitutional order might be emerging.[29]

Likewise, with the results of the voting for the Duma as backdrop, the ability to engineer and design elections seemed more problematic than the enthusiasts for electoral engineering had assumed. Yeltsin had clearly bought some time by reneging on his promise to call presidential elections before 1996. He had also increased his degrees of freedom by ramming through his constitution. But the absence of certainty in the 1993 elections and the feistiness of the post–December 1993 parliament, the efforts of Yeltsin's electoral "engineers" and Constitution "designers" notwithstanding, brought home to Yeltsin and his entourage that 1996 was not too far away and with it the uncertainty that characterizes the function that elections perform in democracies and competitive authoritarian systems.[30] And, as we see in the following section, such was the case.

The 1996 Presidential Election

Students of electoral democracies would have recognized the 1996 Russian presidential election. As is the case in many countries, Russian presidential elections have an initial round. If no one gains a majority of the votes cast for candidates, a second round between the first and second place vote-getters takes place.[31] The election had its rough edges in actions by key players, their supporters, and the folks charged with ensuring the openness and fairness of the election. The election had its flaws and outright fraud to boot. Mr. Dooley (a Peter Finley Dunne character) famously observed about American political campaigns that "Politics ain't beanbag." This insight transfers to the 1996 Russian presidential election.

Still, Russia in 1996 and especially the presidential election come off fairly well when compared to the decade that followed and other post-Soviet countries (much less so, East European countries) at that juncture, when we scrutinize what the regime did and did not do to shape the outcome of the election, and when we examine whether the populace

---

[29] McFaul, *Russia's Unfinished Revolution*, p. 238 and Colton, *Yeltsin*, p. 282.

[30] On democracies, see McFaul and Petrov, "Elections," p. 40. On competitive authoritarian systems, see Levitsky and Way, *Competitive Authoritarianism*, especially pp. 16ff.

[31] Until mid-2006, Russian elections provided voters with the opportunity to cast a vote against all. According to the CEC, 4.8 percent voted against both Yeltsin and Zyuganov in the second round of the 1996 presidential election. For a description of how this option affected some elections, see Derek S. Hutcheson, "Disengaged or Disenchanted? The Vote 'Against All' in Post-communist Russia," *Journal of Communist Studies and Transition Politics*, Vol. 20, No. 1 (2004), pp. 98–121.

was able to perform its role as a selectorate—whether they were citizens or subjects (for Bueno de Mesquita et al., disenfranchised residents).[32] Clearly, Russia was in a country in transition. Many thought they knew the direction it was headed. Considered as a data point along a continuum that included the 1989, 1990, and 1991 Soviet votes and the 1993 and 1995 Russian votes, 1996 could be seen as a part of a process that might appropriately be labeled as democratization. Mikhail Myagkov, Peter Ordeshook, and Alexander Sobyanin conclude their 1997 article tracing the evolution of the Russian electorate from 1991 to 1996 by observing how future elections might yield different coalitions than had been in play in securing Yeltsin's 1996 victory by observing, "This, of course, is how it should be in a democracy."[33] Seen as a data point for subsequent elections, the best claim that can be made is that it exemplified competitive authoritarianism at its most promising but one that was not borne out as the sequence of presidential elections 2000, 2004, and 2008 bore witness.

Within well less than a decade, the democratic tide of which 1996 and the 1996 presidential election in particular seemed to exemplify had clearly ebbed. Individual scholars and the producers of aggregate assessments both took note of the changes. Two of the best analysts of that period, Timothy Colton and Michael McFaul, noted the turn toward authoritarianism in articles published early in the new century. In an important paper devoted in considerable measure to Russia, McFaul's 2002 *World Politics*[34] article rebutted the notion that the formerly communist states were part of a third wave of democratization.[35] Instead, he argued, they were best thought of as a fourth wave of democracy *and* dictatorship. Colton, who had published *Transitional Citizens* in 2000, observed in a Festschrift for Archie Brown published in 2005 that it was "especially painful to realize . . . that Russia . . . has significantly regressed and is by standard measures[36] further removed from being governed democratically than it was in the beginning of the 1990s."[37]

---

[32] "Subjects obey. Citizens choose." Timothy Colton, *Transitional Citizens: Voters and What Influences Them in the New Russia* (Cambridge, MA: Harvard University Press, 2000), p. vii; Bueno de Mesquita et al., *The Logic of Political Survival*, p. 39.

[33] Mikhail Myagkov, Peter Ordeshook, and Alexander Sobyanin, "The Russian Electorate, 1991–1996," *Post-Soviet Affairs*, Vol. 13, No. 2 (April–June 1997), pp. 134–66 at p. 165. See, in addition, Myagkov, Ordeshook, and Dimitri Shakin, *The Forensics of Election Fraud: Russia and Ukraine* (Cambridge: Cambridge Univrsity Press, 2009).

[34] McFaul, "The Fourth Wave of Democracy."

[35] The classic argument for such a third wave is of course Samuel P. Huntington, *The Third Wave: Democratization in the Late Twentieth Century* (Norman: University of Oklahoma Press, 1991).

[36] By which he primarily means Freedom House's annual assessments.

[37] Timothy J. Colton, "Putin and the Attenuation of Russian Democracy," in Alex Pravda, ed., *Leading Russia: Putin in Perspective* (Oxford: Oxford University Press, 2005), pp. 103–18 at pp. 103–4.

It's appropriate to view the 1996 presidential election from both top-down and bottom-up perspectives. The central "takeaway" with respect to the government is that the election took place. Beyond that, the tactics employed to secure Yeltsin's reelection, while in some respects doubtless illegal, were ones that one encounters in competitive authoritarian elections the world around. From the vantage point of both the regime and its citizenry, the election was reasonably—the reasons for the qualification are addressed below—fair and perceived that way by Russian citizens and some outside analysts. In addition, it was a referendum on the political economic system broadly conceived—including Russia's orientation to the outside world.[38] Yeltsin and his supporters managed to frame the central question in the election as a binary choice between communism and democracy. This was not an artificially constructed framing. There was a "there" there. The Duma had passed a nonbinding resolution "to annul the Belovezh agreements of 1991"— which, as Yeltsin himself notes, "essentially . . . [would have had the effect of] resurrecting the former Soviet Union."[39]

Moreover, the regime's actions notwithstanding, Russian citizens manifested three key attributes central to a functioning democracy. They were reasonably well informed about the major candidates and those candidates' broad-gauged policy orientations. They evidenced reasonably coherent notions about the 1996 candidates, their priorities, and the matters they would most effectively address as president. Russian voters resonated to this framing in their voting behavior. If one knew what political system—defined broadly to include the political economy overall and broad dispositions about Russia's orientation to the international system—respondents in 1996 considered most suitable for Russia, one could with great confidence predict how most of them voted in the runoff between Yeltsin and Zyuganov.

REGIME BEHAVIOR

Yeltsin and his coterie were divided as to whether to have the elections or put them off as Yeltsin had done in 1993. We know fairly much about the within-Kremlin dynamics of the decision not to postpone the presidential election, but it is important to place them in a somewhat larger context. The December 1995 Duma election did take place. Everyone who counted politically, including some who had either refused to

[38] I elaborate on that point in *The Russian People and Foreign Policy: Russian Elite and Mass Perspectives, 1993–2000* (Princeton, NJ: Princeton University Press, 2002), especially pp. 131–38.
[39] Yeltsin, *Midnight Diaries* (New York: Public Affairs, 2000), p. 25.

participate or been forbidden to participate, in the 1993 elections participated. This contributed to an institutional environment in which the political costs of postponing the 1995 Duma election would have been far greater than if it had not been postponed. It took place despite the fact that many important public figures, including the speaker of the Federation Council (the upper house of parliament), members of the Duma, some Russian bankers, and some regional heads of administration had called for postponing it. Moreover, that it took place was of considerable symbolic significance. As Michael McFaul emphasizes, "[It] was the first election in Russia to be held in accordance with a law that had been approved by an elected parliament and an elected executive." This evidence of "repetition and routinization" provided an important institutional setting in which the decision to conduct the presidential elections would be made.[40]

Equally important as background to the decision to conduct the 1996 presidential election were the realities[41] and/or perception of the economic situation and that the KPRF had used the interim between the December 1993 and December 1995 to become a nationwide party with grassroots organizations locally "in every city, town, village, and kolkhoz in Russia."[42]

At the time of the 1995 Duma elections (these assessments did not alter significantly during the entire electoral cycle), Russian citizens generally perceived the economy overall and their particular family situation as being poor or very poor and not likely to improve soon. Professor Colton and I conducted a three-wave survey in 1995–96 (before and after the Duma election and after the presidential election). Before the Duma election roughly 11 percent of the respondents who gave an answer said their material circumstances had improved or improved greatly in the past year. About three-fifths (62 percent) said their situation had worsened or worsened severely. There was great uncertainty about the coming year. Three in ten respondents were uncertain as to the future, and 28 percent thought their material situation would worsen or worsen sharply in the next year, with an additional quarter of the total number of respondents (23 percent) saying their material situation would remain the same in the coming year.

The communists had reason to be optimistic about their prospects in the presidential election. It was not a promising setting for an incumbent. This was clearly manifest in the polls: Yeltsin's approval

[40]The citations, and more generally this paragraph, are taken from McFaul, *Russia's Unfinished Revolution*, p. 288.

[41]Shleifer and Treisman, "A Normal Country," pp. 22–26, argue persuasively that indicators of energy consumption suggest the economic decline was less onerous than widely believed.

[42]McFaul, *Russia's Unfinished Revolution*, p. 283.

ratings were in single digits. In his biography of Yeltsin, Colton quotes as "typical" Yegor Gaidar's remark in February 1996 that "'[n]o matter how you arrange the possible coalitions, it is hard to imagine that the president will win.'"[43] Small wonder that some power-maximizing members of Yeltsin's coalition, especially those without some normative commitment to democracy, might conclude that postponing the presidential election was less risky than going ahead with the election as scheduled inasmuch as it was an election that Yeltsin could not possibly win. Other, equally rational, persons around Yeltsin viewed the prospect of postponement as fraught with danger.

Yeltsin announced his decision to run in December 1995. "We must win the elections," he declared, "in order to quickly begin to live freely and with dignity as do all normal people in normal countries. "[44] He formed a campaign committee headed by the first deputy prime minister, Oleg Soskovets, in mid-January 1996.

Given the seemingly minuscule prospects of his winning, readers will not be surprised that the brave words in his speech were not initially matched with deeds. In fact he waffled. In March, he came within a hair's breadth of endorsing and implementing plans to postpone the election for two years, banning the KPRF, and closing the Duma. The primary advocates of postponing the election were Soskovets and Aleksandr Korzhakov, an erstwhile bodyguard for Yeltsin who had become one of the half dozen most powerful people in the Kremlin. Korzhakov's overt rationale to Yeltsin was straightforward, though he had a far larger agenda as well. (He wanted to replace the prime minister, Vladimir Chernomyrdin, with Soskovets, who would then become heir apparent to the heart-attack-prone Yeltsin.) Yeltsin reports Korzhakov saying to him, "'It is senseless to struggle when you have a 3-percent approval rating, Boris Nikolaievich. . . . If we lose time with all these electoral games, then what?'"[45]

By his own account, Yeltsin decided to postpone the election. He instructed his staff to prepare the requisite documents. The decision, however, was never implemented. An interesting coalition successfully persuaded him to reconsider. In his *Midnight Diaries*, he gives greatest credit to his daughter, Tatyana Dyachenko, and to Anatoly Chubais. The latter had been appointed head of an analytical group to assess the effects of various efforts to mobilize the voters. Chubais told Yeltsin

[43] As cited in Colton, *Yeltsin*, p. 351.

[44] Yu. M. Baturin et al., *Epokha Yeltsina: Ocherki politicheskoi istorii* (Moscow: Vagrius, 2001), p. 554. Baturin is an interesting person. He was the presidential assistant for legal and security policy under Yeltsin and subsequently a cosmonaut.

[45] As cited in Yeltsin, *Midnight Diaries*, p. 23.

bluntly that "It's a crazy idea to get rid of the Communists this way. The Communist ideology is in people's heads. A presidential decree can't put new heads on people. When we build a normal, strong, wealthy country, only then will we put an end to communism. The elections cannot be postponed."[46] In *Midnight Diaries*, the Russian president wrote, "To this day, I am grateful to Anatoly Borisovich Chubais and to Tanya [Dyachenko, Yeltsin's daughter], that at that moment [when he was on the verge of postponing the election] another voice was heard, and I, who possessed enormous power and strength, became ashamed before those who believed in me."[47]

I am prepared to accept Yeltsin's assertion that his daughter and Chubais tipped the balance in the direction of not postponing the election, but their intervention has to be seen as part of larger cluster of serious players who made it clear that in their judgment postponing the election was folly. As a comment on the way the world had changed, there was the president of the United States, Bill Clinton, who weighed in with a letter to Yeltsin. He had been prompted to do so by Yegor Gaidar, through the good offices of the U.S. ambassador to Moscow. (Gaidar, it will be recalled, was the principal implementer of "shock therapy.") Moscow heavyweights opposing postponement included Chernomyrdin, the prime minister; the mayor of Moscow, Yury Luzhkov; Anatoly Kulikov (the minister of the interior); Sergei Shakrai (at that juncture a Duma deputy); Viktor Ilyushin (a presidential assistant); and others.

While Yeltsin's daughter appealed to Yeltsin's better side and exemplified the young intellectuals who constituted the core of Yeltsin's social base, Kulikov's strong opposition constituted a useful dash of realism. Yeltsin acknowledges that he was surprised by Kulikov's strong expression of opposition. Kulikov was indeed particularly forceful in his opposition. He mobilized additional important opponents of postponing the election (Vladimir Toumanov, the chair of the Constitutional Court, and Yury Skuratov, the prosecutor general) and brought them along to a meeting with Yeltsin.[48] Moreover, he did not back down despite Yeltsin's abuse. Perhaps most important, he invoked the possible role of the ultimate ejectorate should the selectorate not have the opportunity to express a judgment through legal means. According to Yeltsin, Kulikov emphasized that "[t]he Communist Party . . . controlled the

[46] Ibid., p. 25.

[47] Ibid. Colton, *Yeltsin*, p. 566n53 cites Peter Reddaway and Dmitri Glinski, *The Tragedy of Russia's Reforms: Market Bolshevism against Democracy* (Washington, DC: U.S. Institute of Peace, 2001), p. 513 as having said that Yeltsin "had no qualms about throwing the constitution out the window" and notes that "he did have such qualms, and he acted on them." As the text above makes clear, Colton was right.

[48] Colton, *Yeltsin*, pp. 356–57.

local, legislative, or representative branch of government in more than half of the regions of Russia. The Party could get people out on the streets. He couldn't vouch for all of his subordinates in such a situation. What would we do if some police units were for the president and others against him? Would we fight?"[49] In short, when lobbied directly by the president of the United States, the minister of internal affairs, the prime minister of Russia, the nation's two most influential economists, major legal figures, several other key advisers, and his daughter, and confronted by what must have been seen a direct challenge by the Duma, Yeltsin did the right thing. He decided not to postpone the election. What Yeltsin would have done had the Duma not renounced the December 1991 Belovezhye Forest Accord in mid-March 1996,[50] only a few days before he decided not to postpone the election, remains an unanswerable counterfactual.

Once Yeltsin had committed himself to campaigning full bore, Chubais took over the main tasks of running the campaign. As a result, Soskovets was first marginalized and then in June he and Korzhakov were fired.[51] Chubais and his group provided an immediate boost to the campaign. Few elements in the vast repertoire of democratic electioneering were not put in play. The most conspicuous by its absence was that Yeltsin did not associate himself with a particular party. Several reasons have been advanced for Yeltsin's behavior. He was certainly not alone in his aversion to the term "party," which for many Russians was evocative of the Communist Party. As a result, many of the forty-three parties on the 1995 Duma ballot were not called "parties" but rather something else, usually "blocs" or "movements." Compared with Western democracies or OECD-coded midlevel economies considered free or partly free by Freedom House, this was rather unlike most conventional presidential campaigns, though one might draw analogues to other "fathers of their country" such as George Washington and Charles de Gaulle.

What differentiated Yeltsin from other Russian candidates for president in 1996 was not so much the aversion to labels. Rather, it was that Yeltsin chose to be above party even though he had initially endorsed at least one[52] clear-cut party of power, Our Home is Russia, something of

---

[49] Yeltsin, *Midnight Diaries*, p. 24.

[50] Baturin et al., *Epokha Yeltsina*, p. 558: Those who opposed postponement of the election "were unintentionally helped by the Duma."

[51] For details of the scandal that proved the last straw prior to the removal of Soskovets and Korzhakov, see Colton, *Yeltsin*, pp. 371–72.

[52] The waffle is intended to indicate that I am aware he also initially supported the Ivan Rybkin bloc. That may have been counterproductive, but in any event it "never really got off the ground." McFaul, *Russia's Unfinished Revolution*, p. 282.

a precursor to the United Russia of 2010–11. With no help from Yeltsin, it mobilized the support of thirty-six governors in the December 1995 Duma elections but nevertheless fared poorly in those elections, obtaining less than 11 percent of the vote. There was in addition a second party of power, the Ivan Rybkin Bloc, which did even worse, receiving less than 1 percent of the 1995 vote. Colton's explanation is that Yeltsin did not want to be constrained by being a member of a party,[53] an attribute he shared with both Gorbachev and Vladimir Putin, the latter being head of, but not a member of, United Russia.

Otherwise, all the other elements — good and bad — of late-twentieth-century Schumpeterian democracy and competitive authoritarianism were manifested. The same kind of broad coalition that had urged Yeltsin to resist the temptation to postpone the election rendered enormous financial support — by common recognition well in excess of spending limits. They also made abundantly clear their support for Yeltsin via symbolic gestures. Western leaders and institutions ponied up. The IMF provided a $10.2 billion grant that was specifically targeted at increased social spending and the payment of wage arrears. As Reuters observed, unnecessarily, "[t]he move is expected to be helpful to President Boris N. Yeltsin in the presidential election in June."[54] Other, equally unsubtle, gestures came from the World Bank, the president of which on May 23 in Moscow announced a $500 million project for the coal industry, declaring, Colton notes, "with a straight face," "The timing of the loan is purely coincidental."[55]

Other support from foreign leaders came in the form of major decisions deferred until after the election, active public endorsements, and meetings of important leaders including Yeltsin that gave him the opportunity to be seen as being presidential. President Clinton agreed to defer NATO expansion until after the election. Chancellor Helmut Kohl gave Yeltsin probably the most explicit endorsement. A G7 meeting in Russia was prolonged by a day entirely in order to provide Yeltsin photo opportunities with the world's leaders.[56]

Many of the nouveau riche oligarchs, including "arch rivals Vladimir Gusinsky from Most Bank and Boris Berezovsky of Logovaz,"[57] pledged their financial support to Yeltsin but conditioned it on the appointment of Chubais to run the campaign. Good old fashioned pork was distributed as Yeltsin toured the country campaigning. Colton has

[53] Colton, *Yeltsin*, p. 350.
[54] As cited in Zimmerman, *The Russian People*, p. 137.
[55] As cited in Colton, *Yeltsin*, p. 363.
[56] This paragraph draws heavily on Colton, *Yeltsin*, p. 363.
[57] McFaul, *Russia's Unfinished Revolution*, p. 293.

a particularly delicious example of a typical Yeltsin day on the hustings as reported by a *New York Times* reporter: "President Boris N. Yeltsin was in a beneficent, spendthrift mood on the campaign trail today. He promised a Tatar leader he met on the street $50,000 to open a new Muslim cultural center here [in Yaroslavl]. He visited a convent of the Russian Orthodox Church and gave $10,000 from the treasury to help cover housekeeping costs. . . . He even vowed to have a telephone installed for a woman who complained that she had been waiting for telephone service for eight years."[58] This story was repeated in multiple variations and locations. Likewise, Prime Minister Chernomyrdin instructed the bureaucracy to employ their access to governmental funds to enhance Yeltsin's chances. There were allotments for almost everyone: single mothers and diabetics, aerospace contractors, rural folk, and small businesses. He raised pensions for the elderly and veterans. He provided funds to cover unpaid back wages and for those pauperized by the 1992 inflation and authorized wage increases for teachers and industrial workers.[59] An end to conscription was also promised.

The Yeltsin team made a mockery of the stipulation that the media should devote equal attention to the various candidates. The three largest television networks, ORT, NTV, and RTR, all supported Yeltsin's bid for reelection. This was important since far more Russian voters paid (and continue to pay) attention to the news on television than to radio or newspapers.[60] Especially in the second-round runoff between Yeltsin and Zyuganov, both the state-owned and privately owned television stations gave greater and more favorable attention to Yeltsin. The already fuzzy line between state and commercial television was blurred further when Igor Malashenko, president of NTV, joined the Chubais group and became charged with the task of handling the links between the campaign and the various television channels.[61] Yeltsin himself contributed to the disproportionate attention showed to him on TV by moving from region to region on an almost daily basis and by playing to the crowds in ways that appealed as well to television

---

[58] Colton, *Yeltsin*, p. 369. For expansions on the same point, see ibid., p. 370.

[59] I have amalgamated the lists from Colton, *Yeltsin*, p. 367 and McFaul, *Russia's Unfinished Revolution*, p. 295. The lists vary some but make the same point.

[60] Zimmerman, *The Russian People*, p. 23; Sarah Oates and Laura Roselle, "Russian Elections and TV News: Comparison of Campaign News on State-Controlled and Commercial Television Channels," *Harvard International Journal of Press/Politics*, Vol. 5, No. 2 (2000), pp. 30–51.

[61] Oates and Roselle, "Russian Elections," p. 39; Baturin et al., *Epokha Yeltsina*, p. 503 notes that before 1996 NTV had limited number of hours of air time but that after its "powerful support" of Yeltsin it received the right to broadcast twenty-four hours a day on channel 4.

audiences. Chubais had made a profound impression on Yeltsin by showing him two photos, one taken in 1991, the other in April 1996. The contrast was sharp. In 1991 Yeltsin was surrounded by enthusiastic supporters, whereas the April 1996 photo showed "a powerful wall of the backs of heads and the torsos of security forces and somewhere far off a sullen crowd."[62] Yeltsin got the point. Russians witnessed a new old Yeltsin who was "one of us" to augment the Yeltsin who had been acting presidential by meeting with the leaders of the world. He was particularly active in late May and the first half of June, shaking hands, kissing babies, dancing the twist in Ufa,[63] and appearing in one city after another, peregrinations that made for natural news stories. In late June, his health became a serious impediment to campaigning, having his fourth heart attack on June 26. Malashenko, who knew the seriousness of the episode, kept the information out of the news. In an interview, he told Colton straight-out, he "preferred the corpse of Yeltsin" to a living Zyuganov.[64]

Not all Yeltsin's actions as president amounted to doling out dollars (at this juncture dollars were the usual way of doing business) and gallivanting around the country kissing babies. In particular, he managed in April 1996 to launch a peace initiative for the First Chechen War, a war that was enormously unpopular[65] and an embarrassment to the Russian military as well. (In the Colton/Zimmerman 1995/96 survey only 11 percent of those responding agreed or strongly agreed with the statement that it was right to use force in Chechnya). The Chubais team members were convinced he could not win the election with the war on. In the same month he signed an agreement with Belarus to create a Community of Sovereign Republics.[66] That agreement soon ran afoul of divergent conceptions of what the implementation of the agreement between two states would entail, but in the short run it provided an opportunity for a really nice ceremony.

While Yeltsin's publicity and pork barrel efforts had an impact, his initial more strategic moves were not capped with success. Soskovets persuaded him that he should picture himself as a "communist and nationalist."[67] This did not generate much enthusiasm from the public. When the Chubais team took over the campaign, Yeltsin pursued

[62] Baturin et al., *Epokha Yeltsina*, p. 565.

[63] Colton, *Yeltsin*, p. 368.

[64] The interview is reported in ibid., p. 372.

[65] Baturin et al., *Epokha Yeltsina*, p. 548.

[66] McFaul, *Russia's Unfinished Revolution*, p. 256. David Rivera, who was living in Moscow at the time, reports that "the dominant interpretation there" was that it was an effort "to divert nationalist votes away from Zyuganov." (Personal communication.)

[67] Ibid., p. 293.

a more successful three-pronged strategy. Their polling indicated that the greater the turnout, the better Yeltsin's chances were of securing votes, so they pushed hard to increase the turnout. (Yeltsin writes with pride that his Russian survey researchers obtained better results than did the French counterparts in predicting the French presidential election.) These efforts included a television campaign to turn out the vote and cleverly changing the date the vote for which the second round was scheduled from a Sunday in the summer, when affluent citizens from, for instance, the two capitals would most likely be at their dachas, to a Wednesday when they would most likely be in their apartments.[68]

Second, he abandoned the effort to outbid Zyuganov on nationalist or communist dimensions. Instead, Yeltsin altered the pitch of his campaign to emphasize that the danger of civil war would be minimized if he continued as president and framed the choice in the election itself as a referendum on democracy versus communism. (As McFaul puts it, "yet another referendum on communism."[69]) The fear of civil war was considerable among the mass public. (In the Colton/Zimmerman survey, 44 percent, when interviewed after the election, said that if their candidate had lost, civil war would have been the result.) The effort to frame the choice as democracy versus communism also struck a resonant chord. It was an entirely believable framing of the issue given how well organized the KPRF had become; the vote in the second round of the 1996 presidential election was in fact perceived as a referendum on the political system, and people voted accordingly.

Third, he moved to build a coalition that would secure him a majority in the second round after he had obtained a plurality of voters in the first round. The three candidates in the first round who were closest to Yeltsin (35 percent) and Zyuganov (32 percent) were General Aleksandr Lebed (14.5 percent), Grigory Yavlinsky (7 percent), and Vladimir Zhirinovsky (6 percent). No other candidate obtained more than 1 percent of the vote.

Yeltsin's pollsters concluded—correctly—that Zhirinovsky's votes were a lost cause and that appealing to Zhirinovsky overtly would be counterproductive. What Yeltsin hoped for from Zhirinovsky was a "tacit endorsement." He got it: "[Zhirinovsky] in a dramatic and emotional press conference . . . ridiculed Zyuganov and his allies [charging they were not] nationalists . . . [but] unreformed communists."[70] By contrast, Yeltsin and his team attempted to persuade Yavlinsky to support him and were willing to deal. Yavlinsky, however, demanded more

[68] McFaul, *Russia's Unfinished Revolution*, p. 299.
[69] Ibid., p. 293.
[70] Ibid., p. 299. McFaul attended the press conference.

than Yeltsin was ready to concede. Surprisingly, these discussions were initiated well before the first round of voting took place at a time when Yeltsin's poll numbers were actually lower than Yavlinsky's.[71] Among the conditions Yavlinsky insisted on that Yeltsin found unacceptable was that Chernomyrdin be removed as prime minister. Yeltsin correctly assumed that in the second round he would get the bulk of the votes of those who voted for Yavlinsky in the first round regardless, so the main strategic goal was to ensure that Yavlinsky did not finish second in round 1.

The candidate whose support mattered most was General Aleksandr Lebed. The polls indicated that he would take votes from Zyuganov but that many of his supporters would vote for Yeltsin in the second round. He received financial support from the Yeltsin camp in the first round. Two days after the first vote, he was appointed assistant to the president for national security and secretary of the Security Council "with newly expanded powers over the Ministry of Defense and the Ministry of Internal Affairs respectively."[72] Pavel Grachev was removed as minister of defense and replaced by a quite senior general, Igor Rodionov. Survey results showed these were widely supported moves. The coalition with Lebed virtually cinched Yeltsin's election.

It was, moreover, an election the results of which were only marginally affected by fraud and ballot box stuffing. What there was occurred "on both sides."[73] Yeltsin and his team had worried about the rural vote. His team were particularly worried about the communists stuffing ballots in the countryside in the Red Belt (an area largely consisting of regions below the fifty-fifth parallel), where substantial majorities had voted for Zyuganov. To combat this, Yeltsin's staff sent busloads of young people into the countryside to ensure against the falsification of ballots, a successful effort and one, in the case of the second round, the effectiveness of which "the Communists only recognized mid-day on election day."[74] There were few egregious cases of Soviet-style turnout, if by egregious we have in mind the "Ivory Snow" elections we rightly associate with the Soviet era (Table 7.1). A handful of raions—four out of five in rural republic areas—reported near unanimous turnout, but none of these reported near unanimous voting for Yeltsin.

The Electoral Commissions in the republics were somewhat more zealous in reporting ostensible turnout than were their counterparts in the oblasts, but this translated into only four raions reporting votes

---

[71] Baturin et al., *Epokha Yeltsina*, p. 570.
[72] McFaul, *Russia's Unfinished Revolution*, p. 298.
[73] Baturin et al., *Epokha Yeltsina*, p. 573.
[74] Ibid.

Table 7.1 High turnout and high vote for Yeltsin, second round, July 1996 presidential election

High turnout in raions by number of raions	99% or more	90% or more	80% or more
In republics	4	75	189
In oblasts	1	5	170
Overall	5	80	359
High vote for Yeltsin in raions by number of raions	99% or more	90% or more	80% or more
In republics	0	4	36
In oblasts	0	0	20
Overall	0	4	56

Notes: Oblasts here refer to all nonrepublics. I am indebted to Kirill Kalinin for these data, which he gathered from the Central Electoral Commission reports.

of 90 percent or more in Yeltsin's favor. Where the bias with regard to turnout shows up pertains to the republics several of which reported high turnout in their raions. The CEC reported that of the eighty instances where 90 percent or higher turnout was reported, seventy-five occurred in raions in the republics (Table 7.1). Myagkov et al. show that among the oblasts (i.e., excluding votes from republics), turnout reported for both rounds of the 1996 election was distributed normally, with the clustering around the mean for all raions in oblasts.[75] Some distortion, however, is observable when the turnout figures for republics are displayed. There the results were skewed in the direction of higher turnout than expected. Importantly, Myagkov et al. conclude, "In 1996, it was Yel'tsin's main challenger, Zyuganov, who most often gained from turnout."[76]

Extraordinary—and scarcely credible—shifts in voting behavior between the first and second rounds did take place in Tatarstan and Dagestan. In those republics in some raions the difference in the votes cast for Yeltsin and Zyuganov in the first and second round (*tur*) requires, as Myagkov et al. put it, either an explanation that invokes fraud as a major variable or a belief in fairy tales. The leaders of these republics evidently concluded after the first round that they had bet on the wrong horse. Contrary to their prior expectations, after the first

[75] Mikhail Myagkov et al., "Fraud or Fairytales: Russia and Ukraine's Electoral Experience," *Post-Soviet Affairs*, Vol. 21, No. 2 (April–June 2005), p. 97.

[76] Ibid., p. 105.

round they concluded Yeltsin was going to win in the second round. They likely conveyed this message to the relevant republic Electoral Commissions, who in turn instructed the raion Electoral Committees to adjust accordingly—which in a handful of instances they did. This is illustrated by data reported by Myagkov et al., who remark, "It is almost as if the candidates' names have been transposed between rounds."[77] Thus, in one of the Dagestan raions where the shift was very large, Yeltsin ostensibly received about 5,300 votes and Zyuganov about five times that number in round 1. In round 2, by contrast, Yeltsin was reported as having received 23,350 votes, while Zyuganov's reported vote total had diminished to slightly in excess of 12,000 votes. In another Dagestan raion it was reported that Yeltsin received a bit more than 1,200 votes in round 1 whereas Zyuganov was alleged to have received almost 18,000 votes. In the second round, Yeltsin received somewhat more than 11,200 votes, while Zyuganov was reported as having received under 10,000 votes. A raion in Tatarstan probably took the prize for least believable result. In that raion, the regional CEC announced that in the first round Yeltsin had received some 7,400 votes and Zyuganov somewhat less than 11,000 votes. They then proceeded to claim that in the second round Zyuganov's vote total had diminished to about 1,400 votes and that Yeltsin's vote total had jumped to almost 21,800 votes.[78]

Myagkov et al.[79] also show that the turnout in the republics was skewed in such a way that in addition to the clustering at the mean an additional hump may be seen at about 90 percent turnout. But not even all republics manifested sharply visible skewedness in their reported turnout figures. Of the twenty-one republics, only three were ranked in the top 15 regions by turnout in the first round and five in the second. As we see in subsequent chapters, the skewedness of the data for turnout in 1996 paled with that for subsequent presidential elections.

In sum, in 1996 the Yeltsin regime employed a mixture of mass media monopolization, some old fashioned barnstorming on Yeltsin's part, spending somewhere between $100 to $500 million (sums far in excess of the roughly $3 million allowed legally),[80] appearing to be doing something to get out of the mess in Chechnya, some clever coalition building, and effectively recasting the electoral choice in a dichotomous fashion as one between democracy and communist dictatorship. Taken

[77] Ibid., p. 95.
[78] See ibid., on which this paragraph relies heavily.
[79] Ibid., p. 98.
[80] Michael McFaul, *Russia's 1996 Presidential Election: The End of Polarized Politics* (Stanford, CA: Hoover Institution Press, 1997), p. 13.

together, what had seemed almost impossible in January 1996 by the summer of that year had become an unsurprising result. "A bit before 5:00 a.m. [the day after the second round election] it became clear that B. Yeltsin was winning and fully deserved to win."[81] The surveys had shown Yeltsin with a rating in single digits in January. Yeltsin's pollster, Aleksandr Oslon, had 13 percent saying they would vote for Yeltsin on March 1 with Zyuganov obtaining 19 percent. His results showed the two of them effectively tied in mid-April and on May 4. On May 11 his survey showed Yeltsin ahead 28 to 24 percent for Zyuganov, with the remainder divided among the many other candidates. By June 11, twice as many (36 percent vs 18 percent) said they would vote for Yeltsin as said they would vote for Zyuganov.[82] Although the election nearly killed him (not hyperbole), Yeltsin was the clear winner. There was hanky-panky on both sides to be sure, but not such as to affect the outcome. Zyuganov himself recognized this. The CEC reported 53.8 percent voted for Yeltsin and 40.3 percent for Zyuganov over all. These results and the results of a post–presidential election survey based on a national sample Colton and I conducted were within a percentage point of each other.

Much that was not conducive to democracy characterized the 1995–96 electoral cycle. In violation of electoral laws, the mass media, television especially, were overwhelmingly supportive of Yeltsin. Ballot box stuffing was rife in parts of Dagestan and Tatarstan. The amounts, public and private, Yeltsin spent on the electoral campaign were clearly in violation of the law. Warts and all, however, the 1996 presidential election contrasted sharply with the subsequent presidential elections of the first decade of the twenty-first century. The range of candidates in the first round largely embraced the spectrum of political views in the country. With the exception of a few raions in republics, the votes were counted freely and fairly. Faced with a dichotomous choice—democracy versus communism—the Russian citizenry—ostensibly the selectorate—knew enough to differentiate among leaders and the domains in which the latter would likely prove effective. Freedom House scores of threes and fours (partially free) on political rights in the mid-1990s were more apt for Russia than according it the ones and twos it awards to states with genuinely free and fair elections. That said, extrapolations from the experience of the 1996 presidential election to the prospects of future elections with less rough edges were sufficiently

[81] Baturin et al., *Epokha Yeltsina*, p. 573.
[82] The data in the paragraph are drawn from Colton, *Yeltsin*, p. 362. He in turn cites the in-house bulletin published by the Public Opinion Foundation, a complete run of which Colton had received from Oslon (*Yeltsin*, p. 566n70).

plausible as to warrant envisaging them as part of a process labeled "democratization" with its teleological implications.[83]

Sad to relate, as we see in the next two chapters, the case for making claims that Russia was in train to become a normal democratic country attenuated rather steadily after the 1996 election. The uncertainty that characterizes elections in democracies and competitive authoritarian regimes had almost entirely dissipated. Instead by 2008, presidential elections had become reduced to the "façade status" Levitsky and Way associate with 'full" authoritarianism.[84] Indeed, by 2008 when Dmitry Medvedev was selected (by Putin) to serve as his replacement as president, it was not at all out of line to term what transpired an "election-type event." Moreover, there were some ways the 2012 presidential election resembled the 2008 election, the most striking being that a single person, Putin, had once again positioned himself as though he thought he constituted the selectorate. However, the reaction to Putin's announcement that he and Medvedev had "castled" was sufficiently adverse as to generate the possibility of actions by an ejectorate composed largely of urban Muscovites or at least by a selectorate sufficiently empowered that they could possibly affect the outcome of the first round in the March 2012 presidential election.

[83] Michael McFaul and Nikolai Petrov, "Elections," p. 26: "The 1995–1997 electoral cycle . . . may have been the most competitive and consequential in Russia's brief democratic history."

[84] Levitsky and Way, *Competitive Authoritarianism*, especially p. 13.

CHAPTER 8

The Demise of Schumpeterian Democracy, the Return to Certainty, and Normal ("Full") Authoritarianism, 1998–2008

THE OBVIOUS TELEOLOGICAL extrapolation for Russia epitomized by the shift over time by Freedom House from sixes and sevens (unfree) on political rights prior to perestroika in Soviet times to the three (partly free) on the same rights in 1996 implied by reference to "transitional democracies" did not occur. Over the past quarter century there has been a proliferation of characterizations of the Russian political system. In depicting the mid-1990s I think immediately of a range of labels: competitive authoritarianism (Steven Levitsky and Lucan Way[1]), an electoral democracy (Michael McFaul[2] drawing on Adam Przeworski and Larry Diamond), one that was "partly free" (Freedom House), or simply a democracy (Myagkov et al.[3]). While there are those who would dissent, most specialists, whatever the labels they employ, share three things in common in their assessment of the first twenty years of the post-Soviet Russian political system.

First, their judgments and topics for inquiry reveal that they (and I) have been much influenced either directly or indirectly (usually via Robert Dahl) by Joseph Schumpeter's minimalist understanding of what democracy entails in *Capitalism, Socialism, and Democracy*.

Schumpeter analogized democracy to the market. In his terms, democracy involves an "institutional arrangement for arriving at political decisions in which individuals acquire the power to decide by means of a competitive struggle for the people's vote." In his minimalist conception, such an arrangement does not exclude some "unfair" or "fraudulent" competition, but it does imply "free competition among would-be leaders for the vote of the electorate" and "on principle at

[1] Levitsky and Way, *Competitive Authoritarianism* and the typology I have laid out in the introduction.

[2] "This process of electing leaders must occur under certain or fixed rules, but with uncertain outcomes that cannot be reversed." McFaul et al., "Introduction," p. 2.

[3] Myagkov et al., "The Russian Electorate," p. 165. Cf. Myagkov et al., "Fraud or Fairytales."

least, everyone is free to compete for political leadership by presenting himself to the electorate. . . . In particular, it will normally mean a considerable amount of freedom of the press" at least as concerned the possibility of having a variety of views reach mass publics—those whom he referred to as "the people."[4]

Second, whether or not scholars accept Levitsky and Way's categorization of political systems, most scholars[5] would agree with their summary description of the Russian political scene in the mid-1990s. As noted in the Introduction (above, pp. 4–6), Levitsky and Way make a fundamental distinction between competitive authoritarianism and full-blown authoritarianism. Competitive authoritarianism in their reading is characterized by the presence of core democratic institutions which "exist and are meaningful, but [are] systematically violated in favor of [the] incumbent." Elections are "widely viewed as [the] primary route to power," and there is some uncertainty about the outcome. In such a setting, there exists "major [legal] opposition" that "can compete openly, but is significantly disadvantaged by incumbent abuse." In full authoritarianism, core democratic institutions are either "non-existent or reduced to façade status," elections "are not viewed as a viable route to power," and "major opposition [is] banned, or largely underground or in exile."[6]

Against that as background, most would agree with Levitsky and Way's characterization of the Russian political scene in the mid-1990s, namely that "the regime was quite open in the early and mid-1990s. Elections were highly competitive, the legislature wielded considerable power, and private mass media—most notably Vladimir Gusinsky's NTV—regularly criticized Yeltsin and provided a platform for opposition."[7]

Third, standard measures of the Russian political system have been adjusted to account for changes in the direction away from democracy over the past decade or so as have been the assessments of most scholars who have been responding both to the changes in Russian aggregate assessments and to well-known events. Briefly put, over the decade

---

[4]Schumpeter, *Capitalism, Socialism*, pp. 269, 285, and 271–72. To be clear: I have in mind chap. 22, which is excellent, not his discussion of citizenship in chap. 20, which is less helpful.

[5]Not all scholars ever had a relatively benign assessment of the 1996 presidential election. Among the sharpest critics were Steven Rosefielde and Stefan Hedlund, *Russia since 1980: Wrestling with Westernization* (Cambridge: Cambridge University Press, 2009) and Reddaway and Glinski, *The Tragedy*.

[6]All the quotes in the above paragraph are from Levitsky and Way, *Competitive Authoritarianism*, p. 13.

[7]Ibid., p. 191.

2000 forward the competitiveness in Russian elections steadily dissipated, leaving nothing but façades with no serious prospects of being a path to power for a major opposition figure. (This pattern is replicated for other, lesser, positions as well.) Instead, in the period between the 1996 Yeltsin electoral victory and 2008 when Dmitry Medvedev was selected (by Vladimir Putin) to replace the latter as president, presidential elections became decreasingly open, decreasingly competitive, and increasingly meaningless. By even the most generous reckoning, the size of the selectorate decreased precipitously between 1996 and 2008. In practice, the 2008 selectorate consisted of one person, as in much of Stalin's Soviet Union. Likewise, between 2000 and 2008 there was a trend to manifestly bogus voter turnout reports, a trend that spread from the republics to the oblasts.[8]

These developments have to be placed in the context of other, often highly publicized events over the decade following Putin's first election in 2000. Lists would vary but most would include selective enforcement of tax laws, which resulted in the incarceration of major oligarchs or their flight from the country; the dangers for journalists of political reporting; the legislation passed in the aftermath of the September 2004 hostage crisis in Beslan (a small town in the North Caucasus) eliminating the election of governors and representatives to the Federal Assembly; the overwhelming disparity in the coverage of various candidates on television; and the exclusion of potential candidates with national name recognition from running for office.[9]

It is against the background of these events that the Freedom House and the World Bank scores altered in a direction away from democracy. What had been for Freedom House a three on political rights in 1996 became a six by the time Medvedev was selected president in 2008. Using all countries as the comparison set, Russia's ranking on the World Bank's Voice and Accountability scale, which had been in the thirty-ninth percentile in 1996, dropped to the twenty-second percentile in 2009 and 2010 and the twenty-third (22.5) percentile for 2011. Similarly, its governance score (based on a computation of distance from the overall mean) for Voice and Accountability decreased by half a standard deviation during the same time span. In 1996, the Russian Federation's governance score for Voice and Accountability was only a third (−0.32) of a standard deviation from the overall mean. By 2009, the score on the same measure was effectively a full standard deviation

---

[8] Evgeniya Lukinova et al. "Metastasized Fraud in Russia's Presidential Election," *Europe-Asia Studies*, Vol. 63, No. 4 (June 2011), pp. 603–21.

[9] We focus in this chapter on potential presidential candidates. The phenomenon was scarcely limited to thwarting candidates for the presidency.

(−0.96) from the mean for all countries and only marginally closer to the mean in 2011 (−0.94).[10]

These shifts in the aggregate quantitative assessments were paralleled by shifts in the assessments of most of the Western scholars who at the turn of the century had taken a relatively benign view of Russia in the 1990s. Those who modified their views included Mikhail Myagkov et al., Steven Fish, Timothy Colton, and Michael McFaul, all of whom were reacting to trends in Russian political behavior.[11] In each instance, the modifications were in the same direction as the change in quantitative indicators.

We treat these developments in more detail in this chapter. Here, it suffices to present brief synopses of the three presidential elections subsequent to 1996 and prior to 2012. In the 2000 presidential election the Central Electoral Commission (CEC) reported that Vladimir Putin obtained more than a majority (53 percent) in the first round. A core democratic institution—presidential elections—existed and was "meaningful but systematically violated" in favor of Putin, Yeltsin's designated heir apparent. The 2004 election was no contest. Potentially serious candidates, including the KPRF leader Gennady Zyuganov, did not participate. Putin obtained 71 percent of the vote as reported by the CEC. The 2008 ratification of Putin's selection of Medvedev completed the trend away from competition. The uncertainty that characterizes democratic elections and, to a lesser degree, competitive authoritarian regimes had almost entirely dissipated. The only possible candidates who might have constituted "major opposition", Garry Kasparov, the former world chess champion, and Mikhail Kasyanov, a former prime minister,[12] were disqualified. This left only Zyuganov, Zhirinovsky,

---

[10] See info.worldbank.org/governance/wgi/index.asp#home.

[11] Compare, for instance, the articles by Myagkov et al., "The Russian Electorate," and Myagkov et al., "Fraud or Fairytales," pp. 91–132; Steven Fish, *Democracy from Scratch* (Princeton, NJ: Princeton University Press, 1995) and *Democracy Derailed in Russia: The Failure of Open Politics* (Princeton, NJ: Princeton University Press, 2005). Among those who had favorably evaluated Russia's political behavior in the mid-1990s who commented on the nondemocratic tendencies in Russia in the first decade of the twenty-first century, cf. Colton, *Transitional Citizens* and "Putin and the Attenuation of Russian Democracy," 103–18; the trend in the writings by Michael McFaul, e.g., *Russia's Unfinished Revolution*; (Masha Lipman, first author) "Putin and the Media," in Dale Herspring, ed., *Putin's Russia: Past Perfect, Future Uncertain* (Lanham, MD: Rowman & Littlefield, 2003), pp. 63–84; (with Nikolai Petrov and Andrei Ryabov) *Between Dictatorship and Democracy*; (with Kathryn Stoner-Weiss) "The Myth of the Authoritarian Model," *Foreign Affairs*, Vol. 87, No. 1 (January–February 2008), pp. 68–84.

[12] John P. Willerton, "Semi-Presidentialism and the Evolving Executive," in Stephen White et al., *Developments in Russian Politics 7* (New York: Palgrave Macmillan, 2010), pp. 20–42 at p. 26. Maria-Luiza Tirmaste, "Central Electoral Commission Rejects Mikhail

and Andrei Bogdanov as the opposition candidates, a troika appropriately dismissed as "a has-been, a clown, and a nobody."[13] In Levitsky
and Way's terms, Russia by 2008 had become a "full" authoritarian
regime.[14]

THE 2000 ELECTION

Putin was the fourth prime minister Yeltsin had successfully appointed
over the course of seventeen months. Yeltsin had proposed prime ministers on five occasions; he failed in his effort to reappoint Chernomyrdin.
He repeatedly encountered serious resistance by the Duma. In practice,
the 1998 Duma probably did not have the muscle or the political skill to
be an ejectorate vis-à-vis the president himself. With respect to the choice
of the prime minister, though, it was the selectorate. Each time Yeltsin
proposed a potential candidate in that year and a half stretch he was
obliged to keep that in mind. His first candidate was Sergei Kiriyenko.
He received only 143 votes the first time the Duma voted. (The 1993
"Yeltsin" Constitution had provided that if the Duma rejected the president's nominee three times over a two-week period national elections
would be called to elect a new Duma.) The Duma continued to resist,
with Kiriyenko receiving even fewer votes (115) in the second round.
Combining bluster and bribery,[15] Yeltsin had his way on the third round
of voting. Kiriyenko obtained the necessary votes; Duma members got
their apartments in Moscow or their $5,000 (the rumored amount of-
fered by the Kremlin for those who voted the right way).

Within four months, Kiriyenko was gone. The main intervening variable was the value of the ruble. It lost half its value in two weeks. Yeltsin
nominated Chernomyrdin—a heavyweight, as Yeltsin asserted—again.
Even though Chernomyrdin had been one of the "red directors" in Soviet times, his candidacy was rejected overwhelmingly by the KPRF-
dominated State Duma where he received even fewer votes (94) in the

Kasyanov," *Kommersant*, January 28, 2008, and cited in *Current Digest of the Russian Press*,
Vol. 60, February 19, 2008, p. 6, dlib.eastview.com/browse/doc/20437104.

[13] "Russia's Presidential Election," *Times Online*, February 29, 2008, www.timesonline
.co.uk, as cited in Levitsky and Way, *Competitive Authoritarianism*, p. 200.

[14] They do write in one place (Levitsky and Way, *Competitive Authoritarianism*, p. 186)
that "Russia was a stable competitive authoritarian regime through 2008." From other
places in the text it becomes clear this is surely a slip of the pen.

[15] Yeltsin tasked the head of the Presidential Business Department, one Pavel Borodin,
with tending to the "problems," of those deputies who took a "constructive" approach to
solving the constitutional crisis. "Constructive" in this instance translated into Moscow
apartments and other perks (Colton, *Yeltsin*, p. 410).

first round of voting than Kiriyenko had in either of the two rounds. Chernomyrdin did receive more votes in the second round (138) than Kiriyenko had obtained in the second round but fell short of being approved by almost a hundred votes. Yeltsin realized Chernomyrdin's candidacy was doomed.[16] Yeltsin decided to backtrack rather than risk the possibility that the Duma would pass at least one article of impeachment before he could dissolve it.[17] (Ironically, he faced a problem of his own doing. The 1993 Yeltsin Constitution had explicitly provided that the president could not dissolve the Duma if it had passed a resolution of impeachment.) Instead, he nominated a compromise candidate, Yevgeny Primakov. Primakov had held a range of jobs, including being the director of the Institute of World Economy and International Relations, a candidate member of the Gorbachev Politburo, and minister of foreign affairs. He was one of many Yeltsin appointees with connections to the secret police or the military, the *siloviki*, of whom so much has been made in the Putin era. Primakov formed a kind of coalition cabinet.[18] Yeltsin retreated. His health worsened. But he was not done. His relations with Primakov soured as did his relations with the Duma. Immediately prior to Duma votes on whether to eject him from office, he seized the initiative by removing Primakov and appointing another person as acting prime minister, Sergei Stepashin, who, like Primakov before him, had held major positions in the security forces. Stepashin lasted less than three months. He was succeeded by Vladimir Putin, whom virtually all readers will recognize as yet another person with direct ties to the security forces. As with Stepashin and Primakov, he had the support of the Duma. He was approved in the first round of voting in a close vote that required several members of the KPRF faction to vote in his favor—which they did.

The explanations why Yeltsin selected Putin are many and diverse. Some are more plausible than others. Among the less plausible are those that see Boris Berezovsky as manipulating Yeltsin either directly or indirectly through the latter's daughter (Tatyana Dyachenko) to appoint Putin or that Putin employed compromising material (*kompromat*) against Dyachenko to secure appointment as prime minister and/or the promise of immunity to Yeltsin and his family as a quid pro quo for Yeltsin's resignation in his, Putin's, favor.

Some part of explanations that invoke the putative resignation-for-family immunity quid pro quo may be because Putin's *ukaz* dealing with the particulars of Yeltsin and his family, post-presidency, is easily

---

[16] Boris Yeltsin, *Prezidentskii Marafon* (Moscow: Izdatel'stvo AST, 2000), p. 225.
[17] Colton, *Yeltsin*, pp. 416–17.
[18] Ibid., p. 418.

misread. The target of the various aspects of the text is subject to being confused. The *title* refers both to "the President of the Russian Federation no longer in office"—an awkward circumlocution for Yeltsin—*and* to members of his family. The text's terms vary in the target to whom and when they apply. The family members "residing with him are guaranteed medical service[s] as were granted while he was a President." There are entitlements to the members of the family after his death. The "full immunity from criminal and/or administrative prosecution," however, extends only to Yeltsin. It does *not* refer to his family,[19] much less to The Family—the ostensible Mafia-like group who were centered around Yeltsin.

The arguments about the influence of Berezovsky or other "oligarchs" either directly on Yeltsin or indirectly through his daughter, Tatyana Dyachenko, and the analogous argument that Putin himself had leverage on her run afoul of the direct testimony of the key players. Colton, who interviewed all the principals, reports that it is "his guess . . . Berezovsky's support . . . would for Yeltsin have been the kiss of death to any candidate."[20] On Berezovsky, Yeltsin is terse: "I never liked and do not like Boris Abramovich [Berezovsky]." Again Yeltsin: "There are no mechanisms by which Berezovsky could influence the president."[21] Berezovksy himself reports having had only a handful of conversations with Yeltsin.

Even more farfetched as an explanation for Putin's selection first as premier and then as acting president is the assertion that he "launched a *kompromat* operation against Yeltsin's daughter, which he . . . parlayed into an appointment as acting prime minister and then into the post of acting president,"[22] with the quid pro quo being that Putin would grant immunity to Yeltsin and his family. In saying this, I do not rule out the possibility that Putin launched a kompromat operation against Yeltsin's daughter, Tatyana Dyachenko. (See p. 228, note 34.) Use of kompromat was ubiquitous in Moscow in 1999–2000. But I do question whether, if the use of kompromat by Putin specifically on Yeltsin's daughter happened, it played a role in Yeltsin's decision to select Putin to serve as prime minister and then as acting president. Yeltsin's daughter (in her third interview with Colton) said "that her father did not ask her opinion on the selection of Putin"[23]—which reduces by a lot the possibility

[19] For an English-language version of the decree see the appendix (pp. 100–102) to the chapter by Virginie Coulloudon, "Putin's Anti-corruption Reforms," in Herspring, *Putin's Russia*.
[20] Colton, *Yeltsin*, p. 431.
[21] Yeltsin, *Prezidentskii Marafon*, p. 110.
[22] Rosefielde and Hedlund, *Russia since 1980*, pp. 172–73.
[23] Colton, *Yeltsin*, p. 586n84.

that Yeltsin's decision to appoint Putin as prime minister was driven by considerations of his daughter's well-being.

The argument about a putative quid pro quo—immunity for the family in exchange for appointing Putin acting president—is also on shaky ground. On the basis of his interviews of the principals, Colton reports that Yeltsin "never negotiated over immunity or any aspect of the Putin decree."[24] Moreover, such a decree could have been overturned by the Duma, which indeed supplanted Putin's decree with a statute in February 2001. Most important, as we saw on the previous page, Putin's immunity decree applied only to Yeltsin per se. Finally, Putin's treatment of Yeltsin was consonant with the way he treated others after they had retired or been forced to retire. Despite Putin's behavior vis-à-vis Berezovsky and other oligarchs, it turns out that retributive behavior vis-à-vis persons forced to resign or otherwise removed from governmental positions has generally not been Putin's style. In a country with a history studded with occasions when people removed from office have departed this earth with a bullet in the back of the head, Putin's treatment of losers or retirees has been generally benign, usually involving finding such losers a well-paying lesser job in the provinces.[25]

Conspiracy theory explanations are perhaps more exciting, but in the absence of better evidence than we now have, more humdrum and parsimonious explanations, which have the advantage of meshing with the current evidence, suffice. They tell a plausible story of how someone like Putin became prime minister—though not necessarily Putin himself—and then acting president, how Yeltsin was provided for in retirement, and how Putin achieved the visibility such that if the 2000 election had been squeaky clean he would have ultimately been elected—though not necessarily in the first round—given that the first round (tur) took place in March 2000.

Yeltsin decided to replace Stepashin as prime minister in reaction to his weak response to the resurgence of violence in the North Caucasus and the emergence of an anti- Kremlin coalition headed by Primakov and the then mayor of Moscow, Yury Luzhkov. Their election almost certainly would have had untoward consequences for at least some of those who had made up Yeltsin's winning coalition. The final straw came "when Stepashin did not deal firmly with lobbyists for governmental favors, passing on some of the pressure to Yeltsin himself."[26] (Yeltsin never

---

[24] Ibid., p. 431.
[25] Kryshtanovskaya, "Byvshiye: Tendentsii niskhodiyashchei mobil'nosti rossiiskoi elity," *Obshchestvenniye nauki i sovremennosti*, 2003, No. 5, pp. 33–39 and No. 6, pp. 62–77.
[26] Colton, *Yeltsin*, p. 430.

manifested the degree of commitment to Stepashin[27] that he showed Putin immediately on the latter becoming prime minister. Yeltsin says he wanted to pass on the Crown of Monomakh[28] to Putin.) Colton describes the former as "wishy-washy"[29]; Yeltsin says, "too soft."[30]

Whatever Putin's attributes, he was at this writing (2013) neither wishy-washy nor soft. We know from Yeltsin's writings the kind of person he thought the country needed. Yeltsin's retrospective enumeration of attributes he liked in a leader are revealing even though his experience with the leader to whom he was referring in that enumeration was someone, Nikolai Bordyuzha,[31] with whom Yeltsin quickly became disenchanted. Bordyuzha, Yeltsin wrote, was "a genuinely intellectual military officer whose world view was much closer to the young generation of politicians than to the core of generals."[32] What the country needed, he added, was "an intelligent, democratic, new thinking, but militarily tough, person."[33] To this should be added that in Yeltsin's judgment, Putin had other appealing attributes to boot—relative youth, preciseness in memo writing, clarity of thought, and, in particular, loyalty[34] and the right values. Putin, he wrote, was someone who would "at all costs support democratic freedoms [and] a normal market economy in the country."[35]

In Yeltsin's speech to the nation announcing his decision to appoint yet another prime minister, he emphasized that in his judgment Putin would render "a great service to the country" as prime minister and made it clear that Putin was, at least for the nonce, his preferred candidate as his successor. (Given the political life expectancy of Putin's predecessors as prime minister, Putin had good reason to fear that his appointment was the kiss of death politically. In *First Person: An*

---

[27] On his lack of support, ibid., p. 430 and Reddaway and Glinski, *The Tragedy*, p. 610.

[28] Yeltsin, *Prezidentskii Marafon*, p. 315. The Russian word is *shapka*, literally a cap. In English the cap of Monomakh does not convey the burden of responsibilities implied in the Russian use.

[29] Colton, *Yeltsin*, p. 430.

[30] Yeltsin, *Prezidentskii Marafon*, p. 311.

[31] Sakwa, *Putin*, 2nd ed., p. 18 reports that Bordyuzha had "been described as 'Putin No. 1.'"

[32] Yeltsin, *Prezidentskii Marafon*, p. 253.

[33] Ibid., p. 254.

[34] Putin seems to have been involved in employing compromising material (*kompromat*) by the Kremlin to thwart the efforts by Yury Skuratov to prosecute corruption that might have come uncomfortably close to home. Stephen Blank, "The 18th Brumaire of Vladimir Putin," in Iuri Ra'anan, ed., *Flawed Succession: Russia's Flawed Power Transfer Crises* (Lanham, MD: Lexington Books, 2006), p. 147. In any event, Putin publicly endorsed the truly "scandalous charges" against Skuratov. (Colton, *Yeltsin*, p. 431.)

[35] Yeltsin, *Prezidentskii Marafon*, p. 315.

Astonishingly Frank Self-Portrait he quotes Gennady Seleznev as having said "'Why did they do that to you? They've buried you.' Everybody thought that that was the end for me."[36]) At the same time, Yeltsin implied that Putin was embarking on a probationary period of sorts in which Russian citizens, in good Schumpeterian terms, would have the opportunity to serve as the ultimate selectorate:[37] Russians, Yeltsin declared, "[would] have the opportunity to evaluate his [Putin's] work-related and human qualities." "I want all who go to the polls in July 2000 to believe in him also and make their own choice. I think he has sufficient time to prove himself."[38]

Yeltsin, having recognized the theoretical right of the adult citizenry to serve as the selectorate, moved to reduce the uncertainty that characterizes democracy in ways that fit the label of competitive authoritarianism. "The absence of rotation in the transition from Yeltsin to Putin . . . casts a shadow over the whole process,"[39] Richard Sakwa writes with some justification. Putin's tenure as prime minister was as short as that of his predecessors. The brevity was not, however, because he fell out of favor with Yeltsin. Rather, with Yeltsin's encouragement and the Kremlin's resources, Putin took full advantage of the probationary period to position himself to be Yeltsin's successor.

He greatly aided his own chances of being elected president by acting presidential in many ways, most particularly by becoming involved in the supervision of the Second Chechen War. The resumption of open hostilities in the North Caucasus presented him with an opportunity to reverse the outcome of the vastly unpopular First Chechen War by involving himself directly in the waging of a replay that was widely popular. He took it. The hostilities were of two kinds: (1) an armed incursion by some 2000 guerrillas based in Chechnya into Dagestan where their leader proclaimed the creation of an Islamic Republic of Dagestan and (2) terrorist bombings in Moscow (August 31, September 9, and September 13, 1999) and in two small southern cities, Buynaksk (September 4) and Volgodonsk (September 15).[40]

A determination whether some or all these events were provoked by Russian intelligence agencies probably awaits the opening of the

[36] Vladimir Putin, *First Person: An Astonishingly Frank Self-Portrait* (London: Random House, 2000), p. 139.

[37] As Schumpeter made clear when he wrote of "the primary function of the electorate [being] to produce a government . . . I intended to include in this phrase also the function of evicting it." *Capitalism, Socialism*, p. 272. See also Sakwa, *Putin*, 2nd ed., p. 17.

[38] Yeltsin, *Prezidentskii*, p. 364.

[39] Sakwa, *Putin*, 2nd ed., p. 17.

[40] The above paragraph draws heavily on Sakwa, *Putin*, 2nd ed., p. 21 and the footnotes thereto (pp. 333–34).

230 • Chapter 8

archives, but there has been much speculation in this regard.[41] There would be less were it not for the puzzling events in Ryazan on the night of September 22/23—a week after the bombings in Volgodonsk—where an armed bomb, allegedly a dummy, was found. The FSB maintained it was part of a test exercise.[42] Whatever the impetus, Putin's involvement in the war gave the media ample opportunity to promote his talents and to contrast him to both the enfeebled Yeltsin and the irresolute Stepashin.

Likewise, the Kremlin administration launched a vigorous media campaign along with an equally earnest effort to create a progovernment party, Unity (Yedinstvo), that would compete vigorously in the December 1999 Duma elections, elections that became a kind of primary[43] for the presidential election, which at that juncture was scheduled for July 2000. There were two major opposition parties, the Communist Party of the Russian Federation (KPRF) and Fatherland-All Russia.

The KPRF constituted a substantial bloc of potential voters both in the Duma elections and the presidential election. The government's (and Putin's in particular) real problem, though, was Fatherland-All Russia, a bloc whose leaders were the mayor of Moscow, Yury Luzhkov, and the former prime minister, Yevgeny Primakov. They had managed to gather a substantial number of governors as supporters and bid fair to obtain a large share of the seats in the Duma elections. Unlike 1996, when Yeltsin had been supported by all the major TV networks (above, p. 212), Putin did not have the unanimous backing of all the major TV channels. In particular, NTV, a creation of Vladimir Gusinsky, opposed the Second Chechen War and provided large amounts of time for Fatherland-All Russia and Yabloko. In addition, Moscow's then mayor, Luzhkov, funded TV-Center (channel 3), which, not surprisingly, devoted far more coverage to him than to Putin. Sarah Oates reports that Luzhkov received 37 percent of the coverage in comparison to Putin's 15 percent on channel 3.[44] According to Oates, though, overall Putin re-

---

[41] For an argument that "based on the available evidence the FSB is a much more plausible culprit" for the bombings, see Blank, "The 18th Brumaire," p. 158.

[42] For the conspiracy argument, see Masha Gessen, *The Man without a Face: The Unlikely Rise of Vladimir Putin* (New York: Penguin, 2012). Daniel Treisman, *The Return: Russia's Journey from Gorbachev to Medvedev* (New York: Free Press, 2011), at pp. 97–98, reports, "The Duma refused to investigate the 1999 apartment bombings, and voted to seal all materials concerning the Ryazan incident for seventy five years."

[43] Olga Shvetsova, "Resolving the Problem: The 1999 Parliamentary Election as a Presidential 'Primary,'" in Vicki L. Hesli and William M. Reisinger, eds., *The 1999–2000 Elections in Russia: Their Impact and Legacy* (Cambridge: Cambridge University Press, 2003), pp. 213–31.

[44] Sarah Oates, "Television, Voters, and Development of the 'Broadcast Party,'" in Hesli and Reisinger, *The 1999–2000 Elections in Russia*, pp. 29–50 at p. 45. At p. 29, Oates defines such a party as "a political movement that relies heavily on television for its creation and electoral success—albeit not for its survival."

ceived far more "news coverage during the campaign, close to 50 percent of the total for all national television channels together. . . . Coverage on the major state channels (ORT and RTR [Russian Television and Radio]) continued to be biased in favor of progovernment forces, in this case Putin."[45] (There also were spillover effects for Putin because of the television coverage of Sergei Shoigu, then minister of emergency situations, who led Unity at its outset. Like Putin, he supported the Second Chechen War. He too was highly visible on national television in accounts of the war. When Putin announced he was going to vote for Unity, he mentioned his friendship with Shoigu as one reason why.)

Previous efforts to create "a party of power" had floundered. The most notable failure was Our Home-Russia (Nash dom-Rossiya—which wags immediately dubbed Nash dom-Gazprom), which was created to present a slate of candidates in the 1995 parliamentary elections. Heavily supported by the Kremlin, it received only 10 percent of the vote in the 1995 election. Unity was far more successful. It rapidly gained traction more or less in lockstep with Putin's rise in visibility and breadth of his support.

Table 8.1 shows Putin's rapid trajectory as a potential candidate for president as well as his approval ratings as prime minister. In August 1999 Putin barely appeared over the horizon: only 2 percent expressed the intention to vote for him, though his approval rating as prime minister (31 percent) was considerably higher. By October, one in five (21 percent) declared their intention to vote for him and two-thirds (66 percent) told interviewers they approved of the job he was doing as prime minister. The poll data for November showed him obtaining almost half the votes (45 percent) and his approval rating as prime minister at 78 percent. On November 24, Putin declared that, speaking "as a citizen," he was going to vote for the Unity candidates in the Duma elections. In December, survey results showed him achieving a slight majority (51 percent) against all comers and 79 percent approval ratings.[46] In the second wave (after the parliamentary elections and conducted mostly in January 2000) of the Colton/McFaul 1999/2000 survey, 57 percent of those who said they would vote, said they would vote for Putin against the field. Perhaps even more important, the same survey revealed that in pairwise comparisons—especially relevant should no candidate obtain a majority in the first round, thus requiring a second tur—Putin would easily overwhelm either Primakov or Zyuganov.

---

[45] Ibid., p. 46.

[46] All the figures are from VTsIOM and cited in Timothy J. Colton and Michael Mc-Faul, *Popular Choice and Managed Democracy: The Russian Elections of 1999 and 2000* (Washington, DC: Brookings, 2003), p. 173. The Levada Tsentr website currently provides presidential approval ratings on a monthly basis, beginning with January 2000.

Table 8.1 Putin's growing popularity while prime minister,
August–December 1999

Month 1999	Percentage saying they would vote for Putin for president	Percentage approving Putin's performance as prime minister
August	2	31
September	4	53
October	21	66
November	45	78
December	51	79

Source: All the figures are from VTsIOM (All Russia Center for the Study of Public Opinion) and cited in Timothy J. Colton and Michael McFaul, *Popular Choice and Managed Democracy: The Russian Elections of 1999 and 2000* (Washington, DC: Brookings Institution, 2003), p. 173. The Levada Tsentr website currently provides presidential approval ratings on a monthly basis, beginning with January 2000.

Primakov withdrew in very early February 2000, being paraphrased as having said that to have an election "is senseless, since the future head of state has already has been defined."[47] Zyuganov continued in the presidential race although doomed to second place at best.

One would have had to be prescient in August 1999 to have anticipated the results of the parliamentary election December 19 of that year. They climaxed several months of strategic behavior by the presidents and governors from many of the republics and oblasts. In the late summer 1999 plans were afoot to launch "a pro-Kremlin coalition called Unity . . . led by the Sergei Shoigu, the minister for emergency management."[48] Its founding congress was October 3 of that year.[49] The prior experience with a party of power (Our Home-Russia) had not been encouraging for the Kremlin. The skillful wooing of the governors through the use of administrative resources coupled with active courting by Putin gradually convinced many of the regional leaders, determined to be on the winning side, that the smart money and the bulk of the regional leaders were moving from Luzhkov and Primakov to the party, Unity, that had hitched its star to Putin.[50] After a slow start, the shift in public support for Unity during the month of November was dazzling. Four percent of the public said they would vote for it

[47] Ibid.

[48] Colton, *Yeltsin*, p. 434.

[49] Henry E. Hale, *Why Not Parties in Russia? Democracy, Federalism, and the State* (New York: Cambridge University Press, 2006), p. 82. For a detailed description of the efforts to court the various presidents of republics and governors of oblasts before October, see Shvetsova, "Resolving the Problem," pp. 223–26.

[50] Ibid., p. 223.

in a mass poll released by VTSIOM on November 2 and 8 percent on November 22. Putin's November 24 announcement that he would vote for Unity candidates prompted a cascade[51] of new supporters for Unity. On November 29, 18 percent declared for Unity. In the parliamentary elections on December 19, it received 23 percent of the vote, only a bit less than the KPRF.[52] Fatherland-All Russia obtained just over 13 percent. When coupled with Putin's striking performance rankings, the parliamentary elections had in effect played the role of a primary in an American presidential election.[53]

The clincher for Putin was a master stroke by Yeltsin. Putin's behavior as prime minister convinced Yeltsin that he, Yeltsin, had been right in appointing Putin as prime minister. Yeltsin deftly resigned on New Year's Eve, December 31, 1999. This had two major effects. It made Putin acting president and activated Article 92 of the Constitution. That article provided that in the event of a presidential resignation, an election must occur within ninety days after the resignation rather than in July 2000. It increased enormously the prospects that Putin would win in a general election by shortening the number of days others could campaign, increasing his visibility as the leader of the country, and reducing the amount of time during which Putin's ratings might decrease (they did) from the stellar numbers he manifested at the dawn of the new century.

Assessing the 2000 Presidential Election

By a relatively close amount, Putin won in the first round, securing only slightly more than a majority (52.9 percent, or approximately 39.7 million) of the 75 million votes cast. The election left much to be desired in terms of normative democratic theory. The timing of President Yeltsin's resignation, combined with all the advantages of incumbency and state television, gave the election for many a sense of fait accompli and was reminiscent of Mexican elections before 2000. The tables were certainly tilted toward Putin given that as prime minister and acting president he was a focal point, someone who by his position and his access to the media could rather easily mobilize regional public leaders. But it must be remembered that four others had been prime

---

[51] On cascading, see Susanne Lohmann, "The Dynamics of Informational Cascades: The Monday Demonstrations in Leipzig, East Germany," *World Politics*, Vol. 47, No. 1 (October 1994), pp. 42–101; Beissinger, *Nationalist Mobilization*.

[52] These figures from VTsIOM surveys are taken from Shvetsova, "Resolving the Problem," p. 223.

[53] Ibid., pp. 223–26.

minister in the then very recent past. None of them received the kind of ratings Putin obtained, nor had they succeeded in wrapping themselves around the flag in the way that Putin did. The media advantage was also substantial, though again it should be emphasized that ORT's "vitriolic attacks" on Luzhkov and Primakov were paralleled by NTV's "extraordinary barrage of personal attacks" on Putin.[54]

But for all the vitriol there was enough information disseminated so that Russians could distinguish among the parties and the persons who were most closely associated with them. (The circumlocution is used because Putin never actually joined Unity—nor its successor United Russia for that matter.) Russians, including the respondents to the 1999/2000 Colton/McFaul surveys, had little to go on about Putin's views since he refused to campaign, a traditional ploy for the frontrunner. But when those in the Colton/McFaul sample were interviewed immediately after the December 1999 parliamentary elections they responded that Unity would be most able to deal with the problems associated with Chechnya. Fatherland-All Russia, headed by Primakov, the former minister of foreign affairs and prime minister, was seen as relatively best able to handle foreign affairs though in absolute terms more thought Unity would handle foreign affairs best. A market-oriented party, Yabloko, led by Grigory Yavlinsky, an economist, got higher grades for being able to handle the economy than anything else. The other right-wing party, the weakly backed Union of Right Forces, obtained relatively more support for being able to "defend human rights and democratic freedoms." The KPRF received its best score for being able to deal with the tasks of "securing social guarantees for people."

After the March presidential election, the respondents were surveyed again, this time with the individual candidates in mind. (As noted on p. 232, Primakov withdrew in early February.) Once again the responses substantially reflected the respondents' preferences for individual candidates. Respondents were asked about six policy issues: improving the economy, ensuring social stability, defending rights and freedoms, dealing with Chechnya, representing Russia's interests abroad, and dealing with crime and corruption. On each of the six issues, Putin outpaced all his rivals. There were, though, differences in the response patterns across issues that suggested an aggregate judgment that particular candidates would handle certain dimensions of Russia's problems relatively better than others could. Zyuganov is seen as being relatively more able to ensure social stability. Yavlinsky, the politically liberal economist, is viewed as relatively more able to improve the economy and defend human rights and freedoms. Just as

---

[54] Both quotes are from Sakwa, *Putin*, 2nd ed., p. 20.

Unity had been seen in December 1999 as the party most able to address the problem of Chechnya, Putin ranked especially highly in respondents' assessment of how well he and other candidates would handle the problem. With Primakov out of the race and after three months of serving as acting president, Putin also did particularly well, relatively speaking, in the Russian respondents' assessment of his probable effectiveness in foreign policy.[55]

As we have seen, Putin received strong support from people in all demographic categories and claimed a majority in the first round. There were obvious ways the 2000 election differed from the one in 1996. With Primakov no longer a candidate, however, the issues that drove Russian electoral behavior in 2000 resembled somewhat those in 1996. One purchases a lot of the answer to the question "What predicts Russian voting behavior in the 2000 presidential election?" by combining the respondents' judgment of the political system most suitable for Russia and their estimates of the economy in the coming year into a simple additive scale. Of those who said they considered the present system or Western democracy preferable (a number far fewer in 2000 than in 1996) 95 percent declared they voted for Putin rather than Zyuganov. Two-thirds (66 percent) of those who said they preferred the Soviet system before perestroika reported voting for Zyuganov. Respondents' read on the Russian economy similarly produced classically sociotropic voting patterns:[56] if they answered that the economy would improve or improve significantly, they voted for Putin. The batting average was even higher when the two variables were combined. Zyuganov received almost all the votes of respondents who considered the old Soviet system preferable for Russia and viewed darkly the prospects for the economy. Likewise, if respondents said that the present system or Western democracy was the preferred system for Russia and favorably assessed the near-term economic prospects for Russia, they voted almost unanimously (97 percent) for Putin. Framed by their assessment of the prospects for the economy, Russians once more treated the election as a "democracy versus communism" referendum.[57]

But there was more evidence than there had been in 1996 calling into question the election as measuring up to the minimalist standards of Schumpeterian democracy. Those more benevolently disposed will emphasize, as we have noted, Yeltsin's explicit bow in the direction

[55] This paragraph draws heavily on pp. 142–43 of Zimmerman, *The Russian People*. Sakwa (*Putin*, 2nd ed., chap. 10) lays particular attention to Putin's role in asserting Russia's foreign policy claims.

[56] Donald R. Kinder and D. Roderick Kiewit, "Sociotropic Politics: The American Case," *British Journal of Political Science*, Vol. 11 (1981), pp. 129–61.

[57] Source: Table 4.10 in Zimmerman, *The Russian People*, p. 145.

of recognizing the public's right to vote yea or nay on Putin; Putin's enormous popularity as evidenced by high mass approval of his performance as prime minister and acting president; the fact that, while people projected on Putin their views and hopes, they knew enough about the other candidates in the first round to make decisions that were in the aggregate congruent with the views of the various presidential candidates; and the fact that for the Colton/McFaul survey of a national sample of Russians taken in the month or so after the March 2000 election, 6 percent more people said they voted for Putin than the CEC reported. (The tendency to recall, erroneously, voting for the winner in American presidential elections is a well-known phenomenon.)

They would also note that in the 2000 election only eight raions (out of approximately 2,700) reported Soviet-style electoral turnout of 99 percent or higher. None reported that 99 percent or more had voted for Putin. Of the 114 that the CEC declared to have a 90 percent or higher turnout, 23 reported 90 percent or more voted for Putin, almost all in rural raions in republics.[58]

The con argument would emphasize that Yeltsin once more opted for certainty while talking about elections as facilitating a real choice. Such an argument would mention Primakov's reluctance to run after the December 31 bombshell, the timing of Yeltsin's resignation, and the advantages of incumbency. They would also bemoan the empirical data primarily generated by Myagkov et al. and the empirical and anecdotal evidence mustered by *Moscow Times*. Taken together, the two call into question whether Putin actually received 50 percent plus 1 of the actual votes cast in the first round, whether of the reported 75 million votes cast roughly 2.25 million votes were fraudulently obtained. (No one seriously disputes the proposition that he would have won in a second round; see the pairwise comparison of Putin versus Zyuganov, above p. 231.)

Just as there are multiple ways to skin a cat, there are multiple ways to rig an election. The ones that really mattered in the 2000 presidential election break down into four categories: inflating the turnout at the national level, actions by the central election committees at the regional or raion level, acts at the precinct level that directly augment the vote such as ballot-box stuffing, and explicit forms of intimidation. I discuss these in turn. Some of the elements in a calculus that downgrade Putin's vote total were ones that involved clearly fraudulent behavior. Others are less certain and subject to plural interpretations.

One that was clearly fraudulent and that would play a large part in putting together the case that Putin received fewer than half of the

[58] Data gathered from the CEC and calculated by Kalinin.

valid votes cast pertains to the gains from turnout that Putin obtained in the March 2000 presidential election when compared to the vote for Unity in the December 1999 election. Needless to say, not all increases in turnout are fraudulent. They can stem from mobilization efforts or the salience of different elections. One reason I consider the 1996 presidential election—to repeat: warts and all—to more approximate a democratic election by Schumpeterian criteria than were the 2000, 2004, and 2008 presidential elections is that, as we saw above (p. 216), Myagkov et al. found that in 1996 Zyuganov had actually gained more from turnout, especially in the first round, than did Yeltsin. Given all the "administrative resources" available and utilized, this is a rather striking finding.

By contrast, Zyuganov was at a real disadvantage in 2000: "In 2000, the edge was Putin's by a factor of 4 to 1" and often by huge percentages.[59] This is an important figure because one of the biggest problems with the CEC's turnout figures concerned the difference in the number of eligible voters at the time of the December 1999 Duma election and the March 2000 presidential vote. In the intervening three months an additional 1.3 million eligible voters were added to the electoral rolls. Accepting that the gain from turnout calculated by Myagkov et al. is as they assert, a sizeable fraction of the surplus in excess of the 50 percent plus 1 Putin obtained is accounted for by this one factor.

This jump in the number of eligible voters would in many countries be easily explicable by the difference in interest in a presidential and a legislative election. In the Russian instance, however, that cannot be taken seriously as an explanation for the gap since by law all citizens are automatically registered on their eighteenth birthday. Consequently, to reject the fraudulent voting argument for this jump in turnout one has to resort to explanations that turn on some combination of a childbirth surge in 1982–83, the ending of the war in Chechnya, a massive amnesty of prisoners from December 1999 to March 2000, and/or mass in-migration from December 1999 to March 2000.[60]

To be sure, many (but scarcely hundreds of thousands) Russian citizens did in fact have their eighteenth birthday in the three months intervening between the Duma and the presidential elections. But the argument for an increase in the birthrate in 1982–83 was, frankly,

[59] Myagkov et al., "Fraud or Fairytales," p. 105.

[60] What follows draws heavily on the articles about the 2000 election published in the *Moscow Times* and the relevant pages in Fish, *Democracy Derailed*, especially pp. 39–52. The relevant articles may be accessed at dlib.eastview.com/browse/doc 228188 through 228203. They are also available via Eastview: Russian Central Newspapers (UDB_COM Moscow Times, The, and then by date) and online at the paper's archive. Most list Yevegeniya Borisova as the author.

preposterous. No surge in births took place in 1982–83. Rather, as the *Moscow News* articles noted, according to Russia's State Statistics Committee (Goskomstat), the population decreased by more than 800,000 people in 1999 and by another 235,000 (largely, deaths over births) in the first quarter of 2000. *Moscow Times* then made the obvious point that new births were irrelevant to the voting pool, so that the decrease in the pool of eligible voters had to be larger than the figures for decreases in the overall population. It goes on to note that arguments invoking other possible sources of increased population—jail releases and net immigration—do not withstand scrutiny either. Justice Ministry data were cited to the effect that in fact there had been a 38,000-person increase nationally in the number of prisoners incarcerated in the first quarter of 2000. According to Goskomstat, a modest increase—slightly more than 50,000—in the net flow of migrants (immigrants minus emigrants) did occur. Nevertheless, one cannot tell a story in which the number of eligible voters increased between December 1999 and March 2000. Small wonder the *Moscow Times* found it easy to identify senior American and Russian demographers[61] who were dismissive of rationales offered by the CEC for the augmented turnout.[62] It also becomes easier to explain why in 2000 "Putin won 108 percent of Yedinstvo's 1999 votes, or approximately 1.25 million votes from some unknown source."[63]

Turnout in some republics was abnormally high. Myagkov et al. have graphed the distribution of reported turnout for 1996 and 2000 republics[64] at the *raion* level. Were there no distortions in the turnout patterns, one would expect to observe a normal bell-shaped curve. Using the rather shaky CEC data they show skewed clustering to the right of the overall mean for the republics. That hump reflects the fact that in the March 2000 election ten of the top fifteen regions by turnout were republics,[65] several of which were notoriously unreconstructed carryovers from Soviet times.[66]

There was less turnout distortion in the case of the oblasts in 2000, though the KPRF candidate, Zyuganov, did complain vigorously about

[61] Murray Feshbach (Georgetown University), Yevgeny Andrei (Russian Institute of National Economic Forecasting), and Irina Rakhmaninova (Goskomstat).

[62] The paragraph above draws heavily from Yevgeniya Borisova, "Baby Boom or Dead Souls," *Moscow News* and reproduced in LexisNexis Academic and the discussion of the articles in *Moscow News* by Fish, *Democracy Derailed*, pp. 33–52.

[63] Myagkov et al., "Fraud or Fairytales," p. 108.

[64] Ibid., p. 98.

[65] Ibid., p. 106.

[66] See the discussion in Myagkov et al., ibid., on Tatarstan, Dagestan, and Chechnya. On Kabardino-Balkariya, see Zimmerman, "A Return to False Preferences" (unpublished manuscript).

several oblasts. Saratov in particular came under close scrutiny by *Moscow Times*. As in the case of Dagestan, the tinkering with the protocols (the reports of the votes cast forwarded from the precinct to the regional electoral commissions) largely took place at the regional level.[67] In contrast with Tatarstan and Dagestan, however, the communists and the reporters from the *Moscow Times* were operating with relatively good data in the case of Saratov and the falsification was small. In 2000 the region was made up of 1,815 polling stations. The KPRF had access to the protocols from 1,520 stations. Of these, the communists identified "direct fraud at 138 polling stations," which, it was alleged, resulted in Putin obtaining "an extra 11,779 votes in Saratov." Since there were almost 1.525 million votes cast, the deduction of about 12,000 votes would have had a trivial bearing on Putin's total vote for Saratov.

Chechnya represents another obvious example where the decisions to jigger the results were taken at a level higher than the precinct, most likely at the republic center or perhaps even higher. Unlike Saratov where we have a rough indication of the votes Putin probably received, there is almost no basis for having confidence in the results reported by the regional CEC, to wit, that Putin received very slightly more than half the votes—50.04 percent[68] cast. One suspects the number reported was going to be slightly above 50 percent regardless of the behavior of those residing in Chechnya at the time of the presidential election. No credence should be attached to this number, as the reporters for the *Moscow Times* point out. Even the credulous official international observers from the Organization for Security and Cooperation in Europe had no confidence in the putative voting results announced for that beleaguered republic. It warrants recalling that three months before the March 2000 presidential election no vote for the Duma occurred in Chechnya because of the war with which Putin was actively associated. When the Chechens voted for president in March the republic was still under martial law. There were no observers, foreign or domestic, monitoring the polls. Fish observes ironically that the reported "outcome, if accurate, represented either a magnificent spirit of forgiveness or an intriguing display of masochism on the part of people whose homes had been decimated by a military campaign

[67] But not entirely. See, for instance, the complaint from fifty-five residents of a small village in Yershovsky raion and eighteen signers from an even smaller village alleging that more of them had voted for Zyuganov than the local protocols had declared. For both the information in this footnote and the paragraph in the text, see Yevgeniya Borisova, "Saratov," *Moscow Times*, September 9, 2000, and reproduced in LexisNexis Academic.

[68] The figure, 50.6 percent, first appears in Borisova "And the Winner Is. . . ." I treated as the denominator the sum of those ballots in stationary boxes and those in mobile boxes (i.e., those carried to people in hospitals or stay-at-homes), as reported by the CEC. Those ballots in mobile boxes were easy targets for electoral abuse.

associated closely with Putin himself."[69] The announced results should be given little credence. What the 50.04 percent figure reported by the CEC does do is it meshes well with the hypothesis that leaders at various levels received instructions about their goals with respect to the number of votes cast (by 2008 [below, figures 8.1 and 8.2, pp. 264–65] the evidence for this had become overwhelming) and/or cast for Putin.

The key fraudulent acts also took place in the regional center in Dagestan. Here, however, we are more able to estimate (with a large error term to be sure) the gap between the turnout and the vote reported for Putin, on the one hand, and the nonfraudulent figures on the other than in the case of Chechnya. Indeed, Dagestan represents an important element in the brief against the proposition that Putin would have received more than a majority of the votes in the first round of the presidential election nationally had all the players been dealing from the top of the deck. In their econometric analysis, Myagkov et al. place Dagestan in between Tatarstan and Baskortostan as a contributor to Putin's increase in votes as a function of ostensible increases in turnout.[70]

Likewise, the attention devoted to Dagestan by the *Moscow Times* was well founded. Dagestan ranked tenth of Russia's regions in the March presidential election in reported overall turnout, having been forty-seventh for the December 1999 parliamentary elections. Much of that increment seems to have come from augmenting the precinct-level protocols at the raion or republic level. Reporters for the *Times* succeeded in examining the protocol copies from 245 (16 percent) of Dagestan's 1,550 precincts. They found that Putin's vote had been over-reported by roughly 87,000 votes. Extrapolating, this would imply that Putin was credited for about 550,000 votes in Dagestan that he did not receive.[71] Precincts 876 and 903 are illustrative of the boosts provided Putin, the decrease for Zyuganov, and the complete dismissal of votes for the minor candidates. The republic electoral commission awarded Putin 3,535 votes in precinct 876, whereas, according to Fish, the protocol copy showed Putin to have registered 1,070 votes. Zyuganov in the protocol copy was credited with 689 votes, a number reduced in the official, republic, report to 258. The other candidates received a smattering of votes in the protocol reports but none in the final version. Likewise, for precinct 903, Putin went from 480 on the protocol copy to 1,830 votes in the republic version, while on the protocol copy,

[69] "And the Winner Is . . . ," *Moscow Times*, September 9, 2000, cited in LexisNexis Academic and reproduced in Fish, *Democracy Derailed*, p. 40.

[70] Myagkov et al., "Fraud or Fairytales," p. 104. Their estimates are based on the computation of a voter/turnout times eligible voters (V/TE) ratio. They detail their computations for Bashkortostan in 2004 but merely report their findings for 2000.

[71] Fish, *Democracy Derailed*, pp. 34–35.

Zyuganov received 401 votes and the other candidates a handful. In the republic-wide official enumeration, the latter received no votes at all and Zyuganov, 80.[72]

Almost as striking as the amount of fraud in Dagestan at the republic level was the obviousness of the fraudulent reports. The table in Fish[73] drawn from the investigations by reporters from the *Moscow Times* shows the results from ten precincts after the results had been massaged by the republic CEC. Fish's table brings home dramatically the propensity at the republic level to credit the minority candidates with no (zero) votes. Precincts 852, 855, 896, 899, and 903 record no votes at all for the minority candidates, though precincts 896 and 903 were each acknowledged to have received four votes "against all" candidates (an innovation eliminated in 2006). The cavalier manner in which Zyuganov's vote total was reduced was also readily apparent. Precincts 842, 852, 855, and 858 decreased his vote total by 300, 400, 500, and 750, respectively.

Tatarstan constitutes another republic where the vote for Putin was enhanced substantially in 2000. It is more hierarchically structured than Dagestan. Whereas in the case of Dagestan, the ballot stuffing and vote enhancing occurred primarily in the regional center, Tatarstan was a place where the distortions came primarily at the precinct level where the protocols were generated.[74] The message had gotten out to the precinct leaders. *Moscow Times* reports an interview in a local newspaper by Rashid Khamadeev, the mayor of Naberezhnye Chelny, a small town 125 miles east of the republic capital, Kazan. He reported that the president of Tatarstan, Mintimer Shaimiev, in view of the fact that Primakov was not running, had pressed local leaders to urge people to vote for Putin, adding, "Of course if [a local leader] does not desire to do so, he may refuse. But after the elections I have a great desire to analyze the quality of work of each [local leader]. We . . . will see how each leader worked—in whose favor? Is it worth it to keep him in his post?"[75]

One major opportunity for wholesale fraudulent behavior in Tatarstan stemmed from the printing of duplicate ballots. The KPRF alleged that "hundreds of thousands of duplicate ballots had been printed at the Kazan Polygraph-Printing Combine on Ulitsa Baumana [Bauman St.] in Kazan." While I worry about some charges that came from KPRF officials, considering the source, or because competing hypotheses are readily available, the specificity of this particular charge

---

[72] Ibid., pp. 36–38.

[73] Ibid.

[74] The same was true for Bashkortostan. For examples, see Fish, *Democracy Derailed*, p. 40, citing the *Moscow Times* articles.

[75] "And the Winner Is. . . ."

creates an air of plausibility about it, especially given the behavior of the secret police in response to the KPRF's complaints. The secret police were notified and an FSB officer came to investigate. He contacted the person who had made the charge. So far, so good. Instead of inspecting the printing press, however, the KGB officer asked the informant to identify his source—thus presumably implying that the malefactor was the informant, not the producers of excess ballots.

Good old fashioned ballot stuffing came in for its share of affecting the vote count in places like Tatarstan. For Tatarstan, we have the testimony of Yabloko poll observers from adjacent precincts who reported being pushed out of the room in which the local vote officials were counting ballots. The *Moscow Times* reports multiple examples of similar actions in its special report, both in Tatarstan and elsewhere.[76] But here again we run up against the problem of generalizability. It seems to have happened with considerable frequency in a republic like Tatarstan. The extent to which it occurred within Tatarstan, much less in other republics, is problematic inasmuch as much of the ballot stuffing very likely occurred in precincts, notably rural, where observers for parties other than United Russia were few and far between and where one might reasonably expect high percentage votes for the Putin in an honest election.

To these examples of fraud of the sort that one might plausibly invoke to build a case for extrapolating to the republic in which the fraud occurred, the *Moscow Times* account of the 2000 election also adds a range of other episodes that augmented the voting for Putin. These almost certainly happened, but the incidence of which is again impossible to ascertain with the data available. Persons knowledgeable about late-nineteenth- and early-twentieth-century American urban politics will recognize many of them; others were more novel. Thus, in Kazan observers noted an especially anomalous list of residents of an apartment: it was recorded that a couple was living there with three elderly people, all born in 1901. It turned out, of course, that these were the small children of the couple. More innovative was the propensity of apartment buildings to grow in size overnight. Again in Kazan, one Alkat Zaripov happened to note that "on the form where we all sign and give our passport details" his apartment building had been enlarged from its actual 180 apartments to 209 rental units and that the building adjacent with 108 apartments had instantaneously increased to a one containing 125 apartments.

<hr />

[76] In Tatarstan, www.themoscowtimes.com/print/news/article/tatarstan/258956.html, pp. 1–2 and www.themoscowtimes.com/news/article/and-the-winner-is—-part-2/258956 .html, pp. 4 and 5. Elsewhere: ibid., p. 5.

Perhaps the most ominous action from the perspective of locating Russia in 2000 along a continuum ranging from democracy to some hybrid genre such as competitive authoritarianism to full authoritarianism was the intimidation of voters. Russia is, of course, by no means the first country where local government officials have had conveyed to them the proposition that a link existed between the turnout in their district and their long-term employment chances.

But ominous threats of this type extended to a far wider range of people. As a generalization, proportionately more rural residents were likely more threatened than were urban dwellers. The circumstances in 2000 were particularly propitious for such threats, given the state of the collective farms in many areas: "For years now, collective farms in Tatarstan, Bashkortostan, Kursk, Mordoviya and Dagestan . . . have been failing to pay wages on time, and instead have paid in goods produced at the farms. . . . These goods are a survival kit for villagers."[77]

It is thus not surprising to learn that in Mordoviya the head of the collective farm told villagers in the small town of Permievo that "if they vote for Zyuganov" he "would find out—and they would not get tractors for sowing, or wood, or food. . . . The villagers, most of whom are old women, of course got frightened and voted for Putin."[78] A somewhat similar situation occurred in Saratov. There the local officials received much the same threats as their counterparts had received in Mordoviya. The *Moscow Times* reported that a local KPRF branch head, Nikolai Lukovenko, had complained that the administration officials were told that if Putin did not win in their regions "they may as well not show up at work March 27." They were also told "their regions [would] not get fuel for agricultural needs."[79]

But such threats were not limited to government officials and villagers. The *Moscow Times* cites examples of "local government [officials] leaning on factory directors, school principals, hospital administrators and farm chiefs, who in turn bullied their employees and others dependent on them. Those reluctant to vote 'correctly' report being threatened with losing their jobs, being evicted or being denied their right to state support such as pensions."[80]

How widespread this intimidation was is difficult to assess on the basis of the accounts related by the *Moscow Times* reporters. One way, though, to tease out additional evidence is to explore the data generated

[77] "And the Winner Is. . . ."

[78] Ibid.

[79] Ibid., p. 1. For a similar saga in Kaliningrad, see www.themoscowtimes.com/news /article/kaliningrad/258959.html, p. 2.

[80] "And the Winner Is. . . ."

by the 2000 Colton/McFaul survey. Two of the republics, Tatarstan and Kabardino-Balkariya, and three of the other regions (Primorsky krai, Saratov, and Nizhny Novgorod) about which Zyuganov formally complained were in the Colton/McFaul sample. The survey did not ask directly whether the respondents were intimidated by either the leading political figure in the region or the administrator at their workplace. Rather, it only asked whether the respondents were heavily influenced in their decision to vote by the views of the enterprise administrator or by the governor or president of the region; "heavily influenced" does not necessarily equate with "intimidated," though they very likely correlate.

What I think is legitimate is to report the following. The three nonrepublic regions about which Zyuganov complained did not differ substantially from the other nonrepublic regions in the sample. In both instances, a large proportion of respondents report that their enterprise administrator or the regional governor played no role in their decision to vote. The proportions reporting they voted for Putin who assert that neither the regional governor nor their enterprise administrator played any role in their decision to vote approximates (59 percent) the proportion reporting they had voted for Putin in the survey (59 percent) and the amount the CEC reported were cast for Putin (53 percent) versus the field. Similarly, the distribution of the remaining responses—those saying they had been influenced by the regional governor or the enterprise administrator for those regions about which Zyuganov complained and the balance of the nonrepublic sample—was rather similar. In both those nonrepublic regions, about which Zyuganov complained and the remaining nonrepublic regions, respondents increasingly reported having voted for Putin the greater they responded that their enterprise administrator or their governor influenced their decision to vote.

Where I am most disposed to regard "influence in the decision to vote" as a proxy for were "intimidated by" concerns the respondents in the republic subsamples. The response patterns in the republics differ fundamentally from those in the remainder of the sample. In both republics those who responded that they were heavily influenced by the preferences of the president of the republic (40 percent of the respondents; $n = 28$) and/or the administrator at their workplace (35 percent; $n = 19$) *unanimously* reported having voted for Putin. (All but three [governor] or two [administrator] of the remaining respondents said they were not influenced at all.) By way of comparison 8 percent of the respondents in the balance of the survey reported being heavily influenced by the views of the leader of their region and voting for Putin, whereas 4 percent said the same about the administrator at their workplace. When respondents turn out to have been four or five times more likely to assert they were "strongly influenced" by a regional leader or an enterprise administrator and report having voted unanimously for a candidate, it is difficult not to conjure a whiff of intimidation in the air.

THE 2004 AND 2008 ELECTIONS

As we have seen, in Schumpeterian terms, democracy involves an "institutional arrangement for arriving at political decisions in which individuals acquire the power to decide by means of a competitive struggle for the people's vote."[81] In Schumpeter's minimalist conception, such an arrangement does not exclude some "'unfair' or 'fraudulent' competition or restraint of trade,"[82] but it does imply "free competition among would-be leaders for the vote of the electorate" and "on principle at least, . . . it will normally mean a considerable amount of freedom of the press."[83] As someone who analogized democracy to the market, Schumpeter would similarly have viewed the monopolistic position over the bulk of the television channels that Putin had obtained prior to the 2004 election as precluding "a considerable amount of freedom of the press," at least as concerned the possibility of a variety of views reaching mass publics.

In this section I argue that the 2004 election is best viewed as a data point along a negatively sloped regression line that begins with the 1996 election, extends through the 2000 and 2004 elections, and continues through the 2008 election.[84] The 2000 election was covered in the previous section. The 2008 elections would be easy to code for Schumpeter. It would have been unambiguously viewed as authoritarian in view of the monopoly position that United Russia had assumed over the course of the three presidential elections 2000–2008; the duopolist Putin-Medvedev tandem, which precluded a situation in which "on principle at least, everyone is free to compete for political leadership"; and the analogously monopolistic position over the bulk of the television channels that are incompatible with "a considerable amount of freedom of the press."[85] The ways that the 2011–12 electoral cycle does and does not represent a continuation of the trend observed across the three elections, 2000 to 2008, are then discussed as a precursor to the next chapter, which discusses the 2011–12 electoral cycle, and the conclusion.

---

[81] Schumpeter, *Capitalism, Socialism*, p. 269.

[82] Ibid., p. 271.

[83] Ibid., pp. 285 and 272, respectively.

[84] Good coverage of the 2003–4 electoral cycle may be found in Vladimir Gelman ed., *Tretii elektoralnyi tsikl v Rossii, 2003–2004 gody* (St. Petersburg: European University Press, 2007).

[85] Ibid., pp. 271–72.

Whether a democratic project was central in Putin's thinking in his first term and extending through the 2004 election is a closer call than those following the 2004 election and running up to and including the egregiously fraudulent 2008 election. Given their interpretation of the 2000–2004 events, some specialists have interpreted Putin's behavior in that time period as having a strong democratic thrust. Robert Horvath, in an important 2011 article, dates the turn toward authoritarianism as coming after the 2004 election. It is his view that "[o]nly during 2005–2007 . . . did the Putin regime circumscribe Russia's public sphere,"[86] and he quotes Richard Sakwa favorably for having asserted in 2004 that what Putin was doing was "to transform the democratic capitalist project from a state of emergency into an everyday part of Russian normality."[87]

Sakwa in turn based his characterization of Putin as the defender of democracy largely on several important statements the latter made in the early years of his tenure in office. Of these, his statements attending the discussion of the 2001 Law on Political Parties were among the most compelling. Those looking for evidence that Putin was a democrat could find it in utterances bearing on that law. These emanated in the first years of his administration and implied that he—as did Gorbachev and Yeltsin—endorsed the proposition that multiparty democracy—with its attendant expectation of a national adult selectorate—was a key aspect in his vision for Russia: "During Putin's first term, amid the horrors of the Second Chechen War and terrorist atrocities in Russian cities," Horvath writes, "the Kremlin remained committed to the liberal democratic project."[88] In justifying the Law on Parties adopted in 2001, for instance, Putin, in his 2000 State of the Nation speech, asserted that "[a]gainst the background of centuries-old traditions of parliamentarianism and multi-party systems in other countries, the shortcomings of our party system are particularly noticeable. . . . A strong government is interested in strong rivals. Only in conditions of political competition is serious dialogue possible on the development of our state."[89]

Putin returned to the same theme after the Law on Parties had been adopted in the summer 2001: "If there are—de facto—two, three, and

---

[86] Robert Horvath, "Putin's 'Preventive Counter-Revolution': Post-Soviet Authoritarianism and the Spectre of Velvet Revolution," *Europe-Asia Studies*, Vol. 63, No. 1 (January 2011), pp. 1–25 at p. 1. For a view that the colored revolutions were taken more seriously, see Peter Duncan, "Russia, the West and the 2007–2008 Electoral Cycle: Did the Kremlin Really Fear a Coloured Revolution," *Europe-Asia Studies*, Vol. 65, No. 1 (January 2013), pp. 1–25.

[87] Sakwa, *Putin*, 1st ed., p. 40.

[88] Horvath, "Putin's 'Preventive Counter-Revolution,'" p. 1.

[89] As cited in Kenneth Wilson, "Party-System Development under Putin," *Post-Soviet Affairs*, Vol. 22, No. 4 (October–December 2006), pp. 314–48 at p. 315.

four-party systems in developed, civilized countries, why does [ ] there have to be 350 or 5000 in Russia? . . . This leads to a situation in which the population cannot orient itself politically. It leads to a situation in which people choose not between ideologies and programmes but between individuals and personalities. And it will always be like this in Russia, *if we don't construct a normal political base.*"[90]

Sakwa's views had modified by the publication of the second (2008) edition of his biography of Putin. What should be noted in this context, however, is that even the first (2004) edition was more nuanced in his assessment of Putin's orientation to democracy than Horvath implies. In it, Sakwa picked up on the fact that for Putin themes of patriotism, statism, social solidarity, and the greatness of Russia[91] were also central to his message. This led Sakwa to write in 2004—while continuing to emphasize Putin's democratic disposition—that "Putin's politics of normality and a 'return to normalcy' [were] accompanied by disturbing overtones of 'normalisation,' the term used to describe the pacification of Czechoslovakia following the Soviet invasion in 1968,"[92] a statement he modified in the 2008 edition by appending the observation that "Putin wanted normality, but the methods employed gave rise to elements of normalisation."[93]

But the "methods employed" were Putin's methods. Putin's behavior in the years 2000 to 2004 meshed more with patriotism, statism, social solidarity, and the greatness of Russia than with the deference to Western models of the party system or democracy more generally. Indeed, it was in the realm of political behavior that the authoritarian strands were most noticeable. As noted above (p. 223, note 11) several scholars who in the first years of the twenty-first century had taken a benign view of the Russian leadership's behavior had by 2004–5 discerned the trend to authoritarianism. They did so in part because of their recognition of the disjuncture between Putin's words and deeds. Fundamentally, verbiage aside, Putin was bent on bringing to heel those groups whose resources were such as to be able to resist him and his policies, to encourage the development of a strong single party (United Russia), to utilize a virtual press monopoly to mobilize electoral support, and to ensure electoral preeminence largely by inflating electoral turnout cum run-of-the-mill fraud.

A succinct statement of this view is advanced by Olga Kryshtanovskaya and Stephen White in their "The Sovietization of Russian

[90] Ibid., p. 342, italics added.
[91] These are drawn from Putin's "Russia at the Turn of the Millennium" speech as cited by Sakwa (*Putin*, 1st ed., p. 46) and were italicized by Sakwa.
[92] Sakwa, *Putin*, 1st ed., p. 42, 2nd ed. p. 49.
[93] Ibid.

Politics." They argue that "soon after Putin and his team had come to power, the main objective was formulated: to restore the effectiveness of state power in all spheres of life. This meant eliminating [the alternative] centers of power that had begun to compete with the Kremlin for resources and political influence. The governors were a potential danger in this connection. . . . So were [the members of] the Duma, and the oligarchs who had come to think of themselves as all-powerful, and the independent media, opposition parties, and public organizations. . . . They were dealt with one by one."[94]

As will we. The decision in December 2004, in the aftermath of the September 2004 Beslan incident, to eliminate the election of the governors has a prehistory that extends across the Putin era. Indeed, as Kryshtanovskaya and White point out, the initial steps in bringing them to heel occurred almost immediately after the 2000 presidential election.[95] In a matter of six months several major shifts in the macropolitical distribution of power relations were implemented.

Putin set out systematically to put an end to the pervasive asymmetrical regionalism—as a result of which half of the country's regions had special deals with Moscow—to which Yeltsin had resorted in order to hold the country together in the 1990s.[96] Structurally, seven federal districts were established, each headed by presidential envoys (*polpredy*). The seven districts overlapped with the Ministry of Interior districts[97]—and not, for instance, with the economic regions of the country. Of the first seven presidential envoys, five were or had been senior military or security officers. While the charge to the envoys was somewhat vague, their overall mission was clear: they were to monitor the application of federal laws and to oversee the federal agencies in the respective districts. Concomitant with this development, "the branches of key federal agencies (notably the Prosecutors' Office, the Federal Security Service, the Ministry of Interior, and the Tax Inspectorate) were themselves reorganized around these federal districts."[98] This went a long way in the direction of reducing the dependence of the federal agencies on the local governors. In addition, Putin moved to harmonize federal and regional legislation, the latter in many instances having become quite out

[94] Kryshtanovskaya and White, "The Sovietization of Russian Politics," p. 284.

[95] Ibid., p. 286.

[96] Daniel Treisman, "Deciphering Russia's Federal Finance: Fiscal Appeasement in 1995 and 1996," *Europe-Asia Studies*, Vol. 50, No. 5 (July 1998), pp. 893–906.

[97] Nikolai Petrov and Darrell Slider, "Putin and the Regions," in Herspring, *Putin's Russia*, pp. 203–24 at p. 210.

[98] Neil Melvin, "Putin's Reform of the Russian Federation," in Alex Pravda, ed., *Leading Russia: Putin in Perspective* (New York: Oxford University Press, 2005), pp. 203–27 at p. 209.

of line with the former. Some of the legislation adopted in the Yeltsin years amounted to the creation of a Russian confederation.

Similarly, he moved to reduce the tangible resources at the disposal of the various regional leaders and to make clear that their bailiwicks were subordinate to federal law. A major step in the first direction was to alter the tax code and to increase the effectiveness with which taxes were collected. At the beginning of Putin's term in office,[99] not all regions in Russia even had federal tax offices in them. Putin put an end to this. He also reformed the tax code—a measure that "ensured that governors could retain only 30 percent of the consolidated regional budget, whereas they had previously retained 60–70 percent."[100] The governors were further limited by their loss of the power to appoint directors of state-owned regional media,[101] though this mattered less as the governors increasingly supported United Russia and Putin.

The second important way by which Putin sought to minimize the governors' ability to constrain Putin's behavior was to push through a bill in the Duma that allowed Moscow to remove governors (and the local legislatures) for violating the federal constitution. The result was that, even before Putin's actions in the aftermath of the Beslan tragedy, the federal government agencies were more a presence in the regions than they had been previously and the politically relevant resources available to the governors had been diminished.

Despite the reduction, however, the governors continued to have resources that could be, and in the 2003 and subsequent legislative elections were, harnessed for Moscow's purposes. They had name recognition, which they parlayed into votes as the locomotives (*paravozi*) at the head of United Russia ballots in the Duma elections.[102] Using data from the 2004 Colton/Hale survey, Olesya Tkacheva found that, while respondents were not prone to evaluate governors or parties as being very influential, they were more likely to so evaluate governors than they were political parties.[103]

In December 2001 Unity and the Fatherland party headed by Moscow's mayor, Yury Luzhkov, merged to create United Russia. After

[99] Ibid., p. 210.

[100] Ibid.

[101] Andrew Konitzer, *Voting for Russia's Governors* (Washington, DC: Woodrow Wilson Press, 2005), pp. 4–5.

[102] Olesya Tkacheva, "Federalism and Democratic Consolidation and Beyond" (University of Michigan dissertation, 2009), p. 11. Tkacheva terms such folks "poster children." Given their name recognition, they contributed to United Russia's vote total, but then almost invariably declined to serve, thus allowing someone further down the list in a PR system to gain membership in the Duma.

[103] Ibid., p. 14.

that, the governors found it even more in their interest to choose United Russia as the party to which they proffered their support and membership, whether because it offered them far greater prospects of staying in office, because it gave them enhanced opportunities to collect rents from the center, or because they were threatened by the selective employment of kompromat.

From a Russia-wide perspective, the more important development vis-à-vis the governors was their emasculation as a national force, the influence of which had been considerable in the 1999 legislative and 2000 presidential elections. A key step in reducing their influence both on their respective home grounds and as substantial factors on the national political scene was the creation of the seven intermediate federal districts to which mention has already been made. As early as August 2000, the Duma, at Putin's behest, altered the composition of the Federation Council. No longer were the governors automatically members of the upper house. Instead, senators were appointed by the regional legislatures. The effect was to reduce substantially the national visibility of the regional governors and to diminish correspondingly the role of the Federation Council as an institution: "Governors disappeared from the television screens, and sessions of the Federation Council lost the coverage they had previously enjoyed."[104]

The Duma, similarly, lost its ability to thwart the plans of the president. Readers will remember Yeltsin's problems with the Duma (above, pp. 199–203). Such was not the case for Putin. He, by contrast, succeeded in implementing an enormous agenda right from the start of his tenure in office.[105] This success persisted through the period up to and including the Medvedev presidency. One element at the outset of his tenure in office was very skillful deal making involving the party of power—Unity—and the other parties in the Duma, including initially an extraordinary coalition between Unity and the KPRF, which cut the other parties out of leadership positions in the Duma.[106] The KPRF was in turn muscled out of its committee chairmanships in April 2002. In the period prior to the December 2003 legislative election, the Kremlin was highly successful in crafting coalitions to address specific issues on an ad hoc basis involving United Russia and various other parties in the Duma.

---

[104] Kryshtanovskaya and White, "The Sovietization of Russian Politics," p. 287.

[105] Thomas F. Remington, "Putin, the Duma, and Political Parties," in Herspring, *Putin's Russia*, pp. 39–62 at p. 41, for a suggestive and quite long list of the economic reforms the Duma enacted during Putin's first term in office.

[106] Ibid., pp. 46–47; Paul Chaisty, "Majority Control and Executive Dominance: Parliament-President Relations in Putin's Russia," in Pravda, *Leading Russia*, pp. 119–37.

A second involved several "procedural innovations" that facilitated presidential "control over the internal activities of the legislature."[107] These included the use of "zero readings" as a method of reconciling differences between the views of the administration and the leaders of United Russia prior to the official first, second, and third readings.[108]

By the December 2003 Duma election the need for coalition building involving United Russia and other parties (but not within United Russia) had been reduced substantially as national-level politicians benefited from Putin's enormous popularity. Politicians at all levels sought to ride into office on his coattails, with the result that after that election United Russia had slightly more than 300 of the 450 total seats in the Duma. An important institutional innovation, increasing the minimum number of members of the Duma required to form a so-called deputy "group" from thirty-five to fifty-five,[109] further altered the incentives for individuals to join United Russia, as did the proliferation of deputy chairs of the Duma.

The latter institutional innovation was but one example of what Thomas Remington terms the "political logic of an authoritarian dominant party system."[110] In such a system, the leader has two alternative paths to ensuring the compliance of his followers: repression and revenue sharing. Some coercion is necessary, but as Remington, following Dahl and Levitsky and Way, points out, "coercion is . . . costly and potentially risky."[111] Revenue sharing is also costly but, when combined with a modicum of selective coercion and intimidation, can be very effective as a means of ensuring the compliance of elites, if there is enough revenue to share both with them and with mass publics. Where Russia has an advantage over many authoritarian regimes lies in its abundance of natural resources, notably oil and gas. Where Putin had an advantage over his predecessor was that, during his administration, gas and oil prices were at historically high prices (though with nontrivial price fluctuations) sufficient to fund "a giant patronage machine" and to generate a "steady stream of revenues to preserve the loyalty of a national network of public officials,"[112] including members of the Duma.

---

[107] Ibid., p. 126. Chaisty notes the parallels between this development and that of the British House of Commons as described by Gary Cox in *The Efficient Secret* (Cambridge: Cambridge University Press, 1987).

[108] Chaisty, "Majority Control," p. 127.

[109] Ibid., p. 124.

[110] Thomas Remington, "Patronage and the Party of Power: President-parliament Relations under Vladimir Putin," *Europe-Asia Studies*, Vol. 60, No. 6 (2008), pp. 959–87 at p. 960.

[111] Ibid.

[112] Ibid.

The third category of opponents whom Putin overwhelmed were the (in)famous oligarchs. He dealt with them quickly after his inauguration. There are many accounts of Putin's interaction with individual oligarchs.[113] Putin clearly had little problem with very rich people continuing to make lots of money assuming they observed what amounted to a set of ground rules, basically, as long as their wealth was not channeled into politically relevant activities nor involved control over a major media source. The implicit deal, if there was one,[114] was that the oligarchs could keep their money if they did not engage in politics. Putin's main targets were Vladimir Gusinsky, Boris Berezovsky, and Mikhail Khodorkovsky, though there were others as well.[115]

Whether there was a deal or not, the media instruments that Gusinsky and Berezovsky controlled did not limit their criticism of Putin. Gusinsky owned NTV as well as *Itogi* (a Russian partnership with Newsweek) and *Segodnya* (a daily newspaper) and was the first to come under attack. NTV had opposed the First Chechen War and persisted in criticizing the second one as well.[116] Identifying with the successful conduct of the latter had been one of the major ways Putin had generated national visibility and favorable public evaluation. A range of resources were employed to bring Gusinsky down. He was arrested in June 2000. Although the charges were dropped, he fled to Spain. Armed security guards stormed the TV channel headquarters in April 2001 and in the same month *Segodnya* was forced to shut down.[117]

Boris Berezovsky was next in line. Tompson argues that Berezovsky and Gusinsky differed in one key respect. "Gusinsky was punished for opposing Putin" whereas "Putin had no interest in appearing beholden

---

[113] Sakwa discusses Vladimir Gusinsky on pp. 144–51 in the 2nd edition of *Putin*; Boris Berezovsky at pp. 145–53; and Mikhail Khodorkovsky at pp. 146–47 and 174–75. McFaul et al. treat Gusinsky in *Between Dictatorship and Democracy* at pp. 181–83 and 185–90, Berezovsky at pp. 182–85, and Khordokovsky at pp. 294–329. Kryshtanovskaya and White have brief but useful discussions of Putin's relations with Gusinsky, "The Sovietization of Russian Politics," pp. 287, Berezovsky, p. 288, and Khodorkovsky, p. 288.

[114] William Tompson, "Putin and the Oligarchs," in Pravda, *Leading Russia*, pp. 185–86: "The tacit understanding was never formalized in any way, and it is not clear from contemporary reports of the meeting [between the oligarchs and Putin] what, if anything, either side promised the other" and p. 194: The bargain "was both unwritten and unequal. . . ."

[115] Platon Lebedev of Yukos, Oleg Deripaska of Russian Aluminum, Roman Abramovich (Sibneft), and Vladimir Potanin (Norilsk Nickel) all came under scrutiny in some fashion. (Sakwa, *Putin*, 2nd ed., p. 147.)

[116] Kryshtanovskaya and White, "The Sovietization of Russian Politics," p. 287.

[117] Ibid., p. 287. Putin was clever not to leave his fingerprints on the instruments being used, for instance, against Gusinsky. Thus, he criticized Gusinsky's arrest. Gusinsky was released after four days, but the court cases proceeded. He ultimately found himself faced with a choice between criminal charges or migration. He migrated. Tompson, "Putin and the Oligarchs," passim.

to the ambitious and unpopular Berezovsky. . . . [The result was that] Gusinsky was punished for opposing Putin, Berezovsky for having aided him."[118] What they had in common—and what the other oligarchs concluded (correctly) differentiated them from the experience of others—was that they had extensive influence over media (Berezovsky had 49 percent control over the major television channel ORT), used those media to advance their *political* goals rather than merely to protect their businesses and wealth and were highly visible. By the summer 2000 Berezovsky was living in exile in Great Britain.

The Kremlin then went after Khodorkovsky.[119] His resources were not limited to his leadership of the major oil firm Yukos. They far exceeded those of your run-of-the-mill oligarchs; he challenged Putin's views publicly, he had "provided substantial financial support to at least two opposition parties," and he "had hinted at future political ambitions of his own."[120] The attacks on Yukos and Khodorkovsky, probably not accidentally, overlapped with the 2003 legislative and 2004 presidential elections. After a lengthy trial, he was tried for fraud and tax evasion and imprisoned for eight years in May 2005.[121] Putin's message to the wealthy businessmen was clear: "my way or the highway," or as Kryshtanovskaya and White expressed it less colloquially, "Any attempt to engage in politics would be swiftly terminated. . . . Businessmen had either to accept the new rules of the game or to leave the country."[122]

Much of the attack on the oligarchs was prompted by Putin's discomfort with mass media that were not controlled by the state. As in Putin's advocacy of multiparty democracy, one could point to text by Putin in the early years of his presidency about the media that harmonized with a recognition that a free press was core to a democratic system. Thus, Sakwa reports President Putin in July 2000 saying, in a speech to the Federal Assembly, that "without truly free media Russian democracy will not survive, and we will not succeed in building a civil society."[123] This, Sakwa characterizes as an example of Putin's "post-Sovietism" and contrasts it with utterances at the same time about the media that were "neo-Soviet." Thus, Putin charged that the media often generate presentations that promote "'the political and commercial interests of

[118] Ibid., p. 186.
[119] Ibid., p. 192.
[120] Ibid.
[121] Kryshtanovskaya and White, "The Sovietization of Russian Politics," p. 288. In 2010, Khodorkovsky was tried again and his sentence lengthened considerably.
[122] Ibid., p. 288. After ten years in prison, in December 2013 Khodorkovsky accepted these rules of the game, was pardoned, and departed for, initially, Germany.
[123] Sakwa, *Putin*, 2nd ed., pp. 151–52.

their owners,'" behavior that resulted in "'mass disinformation'" and "'a means of struggling against the state.'"[124]

For most Russians, television was (and remains) the key source for information about political events. The Hale et al. survey found that "only 49 percent of our respondents had conversations about politics in the seven days prior to the survey, but 88 percent had watched a daily television news program during that period."[125] Given the importance of television as a source of information for the majority of ordinary folks, it would have been crucial, if there were going to be serious opposition to Putin, for television to serve as a source of alternative leader perspectives as well as alternative reads about the economic situation in the country. This did not happen. Rather, the key to Putin's moves in the early years of his tenure in office was to control the media, most notably television, and to demonstrate that it was folly to oppose him. With the intimidation of the most powerful potential sources of support for an opposition candidate either in emigration or incarcerated, United Russia in a position to call the shots in the Duma after the December 2003 elections, and the mass media fully in control by the Kremlin, the leaders of the major parties other than United Russia decided to pass on the opportunity to compete in the presidential election.

They might have chosen that option even in the absence of the fundamental shift in the distribution of power between the Kremlin and what had been key forces in Russian politics, 2000–2004, described in the past few pages. The leaders of parties other than United Russia[126] also had to take into consideration that Putin and his handlers had a good product to advertise and good news to share. Putin himself was youthful and vigorous. His successes in Chechnya and in foreign policy generally[127] reinforced a general sense that he was the best prepared among the candidates to handle a range of issues.[128] In addition, there were favorable developments to report about the economy. That news was largely driven by the jump in world oil prices. Even though few people thought themselves beneficiaries of the improvement in the

[124] Ibid., pp. 151–52.

[125] Henry Hale et al., "Putin and the 'Delegative Democracy' Trap: Evidence from Russia's 2003–04 Elections," *Post-Soviet Affairs*, Vol. 20, No. 4 (October–December 2004), pp. 285–319 at p. 311.

[126] In the 2003 Duma election three small parties were also supported by the Kremlin: Motherland (Rodina), the Party of Life, and the Pensioners' Party.

[127] On Putin's foreign policy and the positive effects it had among Russians, see especially Sakwa, *Putin*, 2nd ed., especially chap. 10.

[128] Hale et al., "Putin and the 'Delegative Democracy,'" p. 307.

economy,[129] the prospect of better times ahead if Putin continued as president was a factor that enhanced his appeal.[130]

With all this working for him, Putin was elected overwhelmingly. The CEC reported he had received 72 percent of the vote. In lieu of the KPRF leader, Gennady Zyuganov, Nikolai Kharitonov was chosen to run on the KPRF ticket. He received 14 percent of the vote. Hale et al. point out that no other candidate received more than 5 percent of the vote,[131] not even Oleg Malyshkin (Zhirinovsky's bodyguard), who substituted for Zhirinovsky, the head of the Liberal Democratic Party.

As we have seen, the distribution of resources—money, media monopoly, and mass mobilization—shifted heavily in Putin's favor. And still Putin behaved as though the electoral victory needed to be assured. He fostered a climate in which several local leaders, especially in republics, felt it behooved themselves to ensure he achieved an overwhelming victory in their region. In 1996 Zyuganov actually had had a turnout advantage. In 2000, Putin had a four-to-one advantage in the proportion of regions where "a one percent increase in turnout gives a candidate an additional 0.25 [or greater] over and above what he would [have] received as a reflection of his 'normal' share."[132] In 2004 *all* of the regions where one of the candidates obtained a 25 percent or higher boost in votes from abnormally high turnout favored Putin.[133]

A consequence of this was that raions in a handful of oblasts reported figures evocative of Soviet times and a larger number reported heavier than normal turnout. Myagkov et al. demonstrate that, in contrast to 2000, overreporting on the part of some oblasts in 2004 resulted in a modest skewing to the right of aggregate evaluations of oblasts: "the exaggerated right tail . . . suggests the possibility of an artificially inflated turnout in at least some [oblast] election districts."[134] But, as in previous instances, it was the republics where the distortions both in turnout and in reported votes for Putin were far and away the largest. Republic turnout was more skewed to the right in 2004 than it had been in 1996 and 2000. The CEC reported four raions in which, ostensibly, there had been a 99 percent or greater turnout in 1996 but no instances in which Yeltsin received 99 percent or more votes. In 2000

---

[129] In the Hale et al. survey (ibid., p. 308)—and presumably in the country as a whole—regardless how they reported having voted, only a fifth (20 percent) of the respondents answered that their "own family's economic situation had improved over the last 12 months."

[130] Ibid., p. 307.

[131] Ibid., p. 292.

[132] Myagkov et al., "Fraud or Fairytales," p. 105.

[133] Ibid.

[134] Ibid., p. 99.

the CEC reported eight (seven of them in the republics) regions where the turnout reported was 99 percent or higher and no instances of Putin receiving 99 percent or higher. For 2004, the CEC reported that of the nation's total of 35 raiony that had turnout totals that were Soviet in nature—i.e., 99 percent or higher—32 were in republics. Of these, Putin received a vote of 99 percent or greater in 17.[135] Heading the pack, as it were, was Nurlatinsky raion in Tatarstan. According to the CEC, there had been "19,109 registered voters in 2004, of whom 19,052 voted. . . . Of those, 19,012 voted for Putin."[136]

"Full" Authoritarianism: The 2008 Election

We noted in the previous section that during President Putin's first term there were precursors to the extensive changes in an authoritarian direction that transpired during the years 2005 to 2007, years when, in Horvath's words "the democratic process [was reduced] to an empty ritual."[137] In attempting to explain that shift to authoritarianism, Horvath has well documented the Russian leadership's ostensible alarm at the colored revolutions. Much of this was in response to events on Russia's borders, both in the southern Caucasus and even more so in Ukraine[138] where the "Orange Revolution" resulted (for a time) in a strongly pro-Western government, despite "the Putin regime's blatant efforts to influence the outcome of the Ukrainian presidential election."[139]

The fact that these precursors predated the Orange Revolution weakens the argument that the changes were overwhelmingly driven by the Russian leaders' putative alarm at the colored revolutions: "Even before Putin's important speech [in the aftermath of the Beslan tragedy] it had been clear that changes were going to be proposed in the election laws."[140] Nevertheless, Horvath's point is well taken. The leadership was worried about the possible spread of the disease of the colored revolutions to Russia.[141] The colored revolutions did have Western support

---

[135] Figures computed by my research assistant, Kirill Kalinin, on the basis of CEC data.

[136] Myagkov et al., "Fraud or Fairytales," p. 102.

[137] Horvath, "Putin's 'Preventive Counter-Revolution,'" p. 1.

[138] Adrian Karatnycky, "Ukraine's Orange Revolution," *Foreign Affairs*, Vol. 84, No. 2 (March–April 2005), pp. 35–52.

[139] Horvath, "Putin's 'Preventive Counter-Revolution,'" p. 6.

[140] Stephen White and Olga Kryshtanovskaya, "Changing the Russian Electoral System: Inside the Black Box," *Europe-Asia Studies*, Vol. 63, No. 4 (June 2011), pp. 557–78 at p. 557.

[141] For a view of repression in Putin's Russia in which the colored revolutions plays a more modest role, see Graeme B. Robertson, "Managing Society: Protest, Civil Society, and Regime in Putin's Russia," *Slavic Review*, Vol. 68, No. 3 (Fall 2009), pp. 528–47.

and they did encourage activists in Russia. They also made it much easier for the regime to utilize opportune moments to alter the political rules of the game by linking events in Russia to external support.[142]

The most vivid example of this was Putin's opportunistic treatment of the Beslan tragedy, which he used to introduce several institutional changes, all of which strengthened the Kremlin's hand vis-à-vis other political actors, especially in the regions. He proposed several centralizing actions, only one of which—"the establishment of a special federal commission on the North Caucasus—[dealt] directly . . . with the problems of which Beslan was a symptom."[143] From the perspective of the political system as a whole, the key proposal was to eliminate the direct election of the regional governors.[144] (Prior to the restoration of the election of the governors in the spring 2012, the last governor elected was in February 2005.) Other moves were targeted at the party system—to make it more difficult to form new parties that were not sponsored by the regime,[145] and to constrain some highly visible individuals. The measures adopted by the end of calendar 2006 included amending the law on political parties so that to be recognized as a party a group must have a minimum of fifty thousand persons; requiring that participation as a party in the Duma necessitated a minimum of 7 percent instead of 5 percent; the minimum threshold of 50 percent turnout for national elections was eliminated, as was "none of the above" as an option for the voter; single member districts were eliminated; and parties that had even a single member convicted of extremism could be denied the right to compete.[146]

These measures, when taken together, further stacked the deck against those elites who sought to challenge Putin. As it turned out, however, the initial threat to regime stability after Putin's reelection came from pensioners who were distraught over the government's

---

[142] Horvath cites a conversation that Valery Solovei had with one of "the Kremlin's intellectual mouthpieces" who privately admitted that the "crisis situation in the country is [a result] of the actions of the regime itself, and not from abroad.'" Horvath, "Putin's 'Preventive Counter-Revolution,'" pp. 21–22.

[143] Sakwa, *Putin*, 2nd ed., p. 141; Wilson, "Party-System Development," pp. 337–41.

[144] Kryshtanovskaya and White, "The Sovietization of Russian Politics," p. 286. For diverging views of how strategic Putin had been in using the Beslan crisis to further his centralist aspirations, compare Kryshtanovskaya and White, "The Sovietization of Russian Politics," p. 286 and Sakwa, *Putin*, 2nd ed., p. 142.

[145] An example of a party created with the Kremlin's blessing was Rodina (Motherland), the leaders of which initially were Dmitry Rogozin and Sergei Glazyev. Its main purpose initially seems to have been to draw votes away from the KPRF. Other "Kremlin projects" included the Party of Life, the Party of Pensioners, and the People's Party. Wilson, "Party-System Development," p. 331.

[146] Sakwa, *Putin*, 2nd ed., p. 122.

efforts to monetarize social welfare benefits. (The in-kind benefits were largely carryovers from the Soviet era.) The pensioners went into the streets in many large cities—St. Petersburg, Samara, Saratov, Kazan, Ulan-Ude—[147] demanding the restoration of in-kind social benefits. What began as a protest over economic decisions quickly took on political overtones. The latter, moreover, were not only demands targeted at the government and specifically at the three economically liberal ministers—the minister of public health and social development Mikhail Zurabov, the finance minister Aleksei Kudrin, and the minister of finance German Gref. Rather, they were also directed specifically at Putin himself: "Across the country, protesters chanted 'Down with Putin' and held banners demanding his resignation."[148]

Moreover, the groups and institutions who sided with the pensioners spoke for large segments of the population that taken together—had they been fully mobilized—might have constituted an ejectorate were it not that the regime quickly backed off from its market-oriented liberal policies. The opposition came from across the political spectrum, but the protest in the streets of various cities was nowhere near the magnitude of the protests in Moscow against the putsch in 1991 or the Moscow demonstrations targeted in response to the Duma elections and at Putin in December 2011. (The pensioner protests do not seem to have involved many more than ten thousand participants in any one city, a pittance when compared with the December 2011 protests in Moscow or the numbers who went into the street in support of Yeltsin in the run-up to the collapse of the Soviet Union.[149]) The Russian Orthodox Church, in the person of Patriarch Aleksei II of Moscow and All Rus, declared that monetarization did "not embody the principles of fairness" and asserted that "under no circumstances should reforms take away people's ability to use transportation and communications, to keep their homes, and to have access to health care and medicines."[150]

Representatives from the military chimed in. The Air Force commander in chief, Vladimir Mikhailov, declared that "[t]he entry into force of the new benefits law hits hardest at young officers, whose pay is meager enough as is."[151] The police responded quickly: "in order to

---

[147] "Pensioners Have Lost Faith in a Benevolent Government," *Current Digest of the Russian Press* [*CDRP*], Vol. 57, No. 5 (March 2, 2005), p. 9 citing *Nezavisimaya gazeta*, February 1, 2005. Eastview.com/browse/doc/13771878.

[148] Horvath, "Putin's 'Preventive Counter-Revolution,'" p. 8, citing A. Levina in *Novaya gazeta*, January 24, 2005, p. 9.

[149] Beissinger, *Nationalist Mobilization*, passim.

[150] "Church Renounces the State," *CDRP*, Vol. 57, No. 1 (February 2, 2005), p. 5 and citing *Kommersant*, January 14, 2005, p. 1, dlib.eastview.com/browse/doc/13771860.

[151] Ibid., pp. 1–2.

head off wholesale resignations among policemen, officials are hastily giving them raises."[152]

They were not alone. Trade union representatives from St. Petersburg and Leningrad oblast joined together to protest the elimination of in-kind subsidies. The "coordinating committee for joint actions . . . [adopted] a resolution . . . calling for preparations for mass protests against monetization." "Even," *Kommersant* observed, "the press secretary of the pro-government Federation of Independent Trade Unions . . . , Andrey Baranov, said that 'the replacement of benefits with cash impacts not only pensioners, but all working people,' and so we 'should expect to see protests more serious than these demonstrations by pensioners.'"[153]

Where these "more serious protests" might have come from were small political parties and their offshoots. Rogozin's Rodina (Motherland) took advantage of the situation to establish itself as a genuine political party independent of Moscow rather than a Kremlin-project nationalist party the chief goal of which was to weaken the KPRF. Rogozin, in particular, was not above warning Putin that "'an aggravation of the situation in the country . . . [would] develop according to the scenario rehearsed in neighbouring countries,'"[154] escalating the stakes by demanding "'the restoration of freedom of speech, the restoration of human rights and freedoms and the opportunity to express one's views openly without censorship,'"[155] and encouraging resort to the streets. Both Rodina and Yabloko had youth groups they could mobilize for such a purpose; Young Yabloko was a particular concern because its leader, Ilya Yashin, had spent time in Kyiv during the Orange Revolution and was of the view that "'[s]treet politics is the only thing we have left.'"[156]

The Putin administration's reaction to this coalescence of views among the church, the police, the military, two minor parties, and youth organizations implicitly recognized that these groups taken together could amount to an ejectorate. Its reaction was twofold. On the substantive matter of replacing the in-kind payments, it caved almost immediately.[157] Following Putin's instructions, Minister of Public

---

[152] "Baton of Protest," *CDRP*, Vol. 57, No. 1 (February 2, 2005), citing German Petelin in *Novyye Izvestia*, January 13, 2005, p. 6, dlib.eastview.com/browse/doc/13771834.

[153] "Church Renounces," p. 2.

[154] As cited by Horvath, "Putin's 'Preventive Counter-Revolution,'" p. 9.

[155] Ibid.

[156] Ibid., p. 12.

[157] "Public Transit Runs over Monetarization," *CDRP*, Vol. 57, No. 3 (February 16, 2005), pp. 4–5, citing Vadim Visloguzov, "Ministers Draft Plan to Defuse Crisis, Pushing Regions to Sell Pensioners Cheap Transit Passes, They Admit Offer Is Retreat from Monetization," *Kommersant*, January 20, 2005, p. 3. dlib.eastview.com/browse/doc/13771818.

Health and Social Development Zurabov and Finance Minister Kudrin proposed to the various regional governors that the federal government would assist them in covering the costs of continuing the policy of in-kind transportation costs. The governors in turn would sell passes to those people eligible via national criteria or regional rules. Zurabov and Kudrin recognized their proposal constituted a "clear retreat"[158] and Kudrin acknowledged that "[i]t will not be possible to switch over to market-based, break-even transportation fares right away. Our task is to start out by replacing one means of subsidizing public transportation with another means and, in the process, to move away from providing benefits in a nontargeted manner."[159]

Other steps that increased the regime's ability to control the streets followed. One was the creation of a youth organization, Nashi (Ours). Nashi bears some resemblance to the erstwhile Komsomol, replete with commissars. It was assigned two major tasks,[160] the first being to channel youth into support for the regime and away from contact with harmful (foreign) influences, the second being to be prepared as a group to deny the street to more democratic youth organizations. In the cruder sense of denying the street that task has in practice generally been assumed by smaller units including the fans of the soccer team Spartak who have roughed up members of more democratic youth organizations. In the broader sense, members of Nashi have been successfully demonstrative in their support for Putin in ways that would be apparent to all, East and West. Robertson reports Vladimir Frolov of the Fund for Effective Politics as having said that "'[i]f push comes to shove, *Nashi's* job will be to occupy every public square in front of every public building of importance,' so that 'CNN would have a nice picture with the Kremlin in the background.'"[161] (Illustrating the role with which Nashi was tasked, in the run-up to the 2012 election Nashi announced on February 21, 2012, "that 20,000 of its activists [would] patrol Moscow's streets on election day to ensure that the opposition does not 'destabilize the situation' or—and this is the real point—'cast doubts on the election results.'"[162])

[158] Ibid., p. 4.

[159] Ibid.

[160] For an argument that *Nashi*, despite its ties to Putin, has become increasingly independent, see Maya Atwal, "Evaluating *Nashi*: Sustainability: Autonomy, Agency, and Activism," *Europe-Asia Studies*, Vol. 61, No. 5 (2009), pp. 743–58.

[161] Robertson, "Managing Society," pp. 543–44. The Power Vertical (Brian Whitmore), "Can the Decembrist Uprising lead to a Moscow Spring?," www.rferl.org/...can__the _decembrist_uprising...2441726. Readers also may access the Whitmore article by using the RFE/RL Russia archive with the keywords "power," "vertical," and "Decembrist."

[162] The Power Vertical, "Can the Decembrist Uprising?"

Another instrument the regime concocted to resist external influence and to criticize those organizations who had benefited from Western largesse was the doctrine of sovereign democracy. Close to an oxymoron, sovereign democracy was a clever slogan. Democracy, the content of which was unspecified, was a good word that seemed to promise that Russia would become a normal Western state. Sovereign, by contrast, symbolized Russia's determination to limit the impact of Western aid that might provide the wherewithal for some nongovernmental organizations to mobilize Russians in such a way that they might challenge the stability of which Putin was so enamored and might ultimately result in Russia adopting dangerous new practices that would weaken his hold on power. In the simplest version of this narrative,[163] the colored revolutions were ultimately a product of the State Department and the CIA working hand in glove with the Soros and other Western foundations. A more subtle statement was that by Vladislav Surkov (a deputy prime minister who left the government in May 2013) who defined "sovereign democracy as a model of political life in which the governing authorities, their agencies and their actions are chosen, formed and guided solely by the Russian [rossiiskaya] nation in all its diversity and unity, the interests of achieving material well-being, freedom and justice for all of the citizens, social groups and peoples that make it up."[164]

A third string in Putin's bow was the effort to harness the NGOs and to restrict or outlaw several of the smaller political parties. Prior to their strengthening in the spring 2012, the laws on NGOs were subject to plural interpretation and could be used both to control and encourage the institutions about which the laws refer.[165] In 2012, the laws on NGOs were revised to oblige those with political goals and foreign

[163] Horvath, "Putin's 'Preventive Counter-Revolution,'" p. 22 "The-blame-it-on-the-Americans" theme is one to which Putin has returned time and again. A recent instance of such charges is his blaming the then American Secretary of State Hilary Clinton of inspiring the December 2011 protest and his explicit invocation of sovereign democracy in a speech in the Moscow region. *JRL*, No. 3 (February 22, 2012).

[164] Pavel Dulman, "Nation-Preserving Methods of Democracy," *CDRP*, Vol. 58, No. 47 (December 20, 2006), pp. 6–7. Stephen White points out that the concept of sovereign democracy was not universally endorsed by Russian elites. Medvedev, whom Putin was soon to select as the presidential candidate, was not enthusiastic about the concept and declared in 2006 that he preferred to speak of "'genuine democracy' or of 'democracy within a comprehensive state sovereignty'" and worried about the impressions it might cause, especially abroad. White, *Understanding Russian Politics* (New York: Cambridge University Press, 2011), p. 360. White also reports that in January 2007 Medvedev said that his differences with Surkov had been "terminological" (ibid., p. 362). In 2007, Putin was describing sovereign democracy as a "'controversial term'" garbling Russia's foreign policy and its internal politics. (Ibid.)

[165] Jo Crotty, "Making a Difference? NGOs and Civil Society Development in Russia," *Europe-Asia Studies*, Vol. 61, No. 1 (2009), pp. 85–108.

financing to declare themselves foreign agents. But even before the 2008 presidential election the Kremlin was "literally capable of licensing civil society activity."[166]

This pattern applied to the law on parties as well. In the case of parties the prospects for those that were not safely ensconced in the Fifth Duma (those ensconced were United Russia, the KPRF, LDPR, and Just Russia) were severely constrained by the rule that two million valid signatures be gathered in a brief time period and that not more than 5 percent of the requisite signatures be invalid. (This rule was drastically revised in the spring 2012; see below, p. 285.) As in the case of the NGOs, the rule was implemented selectively. The result was that Andrei Bogdanov, head of the Democratic Party of Russia, was the one person on the ballot from a party that did not have members in the Fifth Duma. Bogdanov's candidacy, Igor Romanov reports, was sanctioned by the CEC in order to be certain that his presence on the ballot would "keep the election from falling through"[167] should the others withdraw. Others were less fortunate. The Pensioners' Party leader, Valery Gartung, was denied access to the hall where party delegates were meeting. Rogozin was pressured to resign from Rodina (Motherland). Mikhail Kasyanov, the former prime minister, was unable to satisfy the CEC that he had gathered the required 2 million legitimate signatures with no more than 5 percent invalid in the brief time span allotted. He produced 2 million signatures, but 13 percent were ruled invalid.[168]

Schumpeter would not have been pleased. The selective application of the law on parties effectively precluded the "free competition among would-be leaders for the vote of the electorate" which would result in a situation in which theoretically "on principle at least, everyone [would be] . . . free to compete for political leadership by presenting himself to the electorate" and "normally . . . a considerable amount of freedom of the press."[169]

Neither of these elements—free competition among would-be leaders and a free press—were present in the 2008 presidential election. Their absence alone would have sufficed to view the presidential election as neither free nor fair. But two other factors were novel. In combination they substantiated Michael McFaul's assertion that the 2008

[166] Robertson, "Managing Society," p. 541.

[167] "Lucky Stiff!," CDRP, Vol. 60, No. 3 (February 12, 2008), p. 10, dlib.eastview.com /browse/doc/20437158, citing Igor Romanov, Nezavisimaya gazeta, January 25, 2008, p. 1. Also, Richard Sakwa, The Crisis of Russian Democracy: The Dual State, Factionalism, and the Medvedev Succession (Cambridge: Cambridge University Press, 2011), p. 279.

[168] Sakwa, The Crisis, pp. 275–80 and Horvath, "Putin's 'Preventive Counter-Revolution,'" pp. 17–20.

[169] Schumpeter, Capitalism, Socialism (, pp. 269, 285, and 271–72.

presidential election was "'the least competitive election in Russia's post-communist history.'"[170] One pertained to the selectorate, the other the dramatic change in the pattern of turnout distortion.

With respect to the selectorate, Putin resorted to a master stroke that simultaneously reduced its size to its theoretical minimum — one, himself — while not attempting to circumvent the Russian constitution — which quite explicitly precluded persons from serving more than two successive terms as president. In a manner evocative of the Soviet era and Daniels's circular flow of power, Putin selected Medvedev as his successor as president. Medvedev, in turn, selected Putin to serve as prime minister. (Medvedev may have agreed early on that the latter would once again be president in 2012.[171] The case for this is discussed below, pp. 267–274.) This "tandem democracy" did not produce an adverse reaction on the part of key elements in the public and indeed seemed acceptable to large segments for whom one or the other leader resonated relatively well. Only in September 2011, when the two announced that Putin would be the candidate for president in March 2012, that Medvedev would assume the post of prime minister, *and* that allegedly this had been decided upon in 2007, did one group, the urban middle class, react adversely.

The other novel factor concerned the diffusion of turnout distortion. Scholars who analyze electoral results are generally reticent, in the absence of a plethora of smoking guns, to maintain with complete confidence that an election was fraudulent. The 2008 results were, however, an easy call. One would have been suspicious merely on learning the results announced by the CEC for Medvedev. They were too convenient for him and for Putin. Medvedev received, the CEC announced, 70.3 percent of the overall vote. It was an amount (1) nicely situating him slightly below the amount the CEC had reported for Putin (71.3 percent) in 2004 and (2) large enough to create the sense in the Russian public that, even if there had been some fraud, Medvedev would have won in the first round regardless. But what was the most convincing evidence of fraud concerned the turnout. The most obvious evidence of bogus balloting in 2008 was where it occurred as it had for years: in the republics. Figure 8.1, which shows the presidential turnout for the republics, brings this out vividly; the Soviet-style turnout in the republics corresponds to the pattern in those regions observed in previous Duma

---

[170] As cited by Jim Nichol, "Russia's March 2008 Presidential Election: Outcome and Implications," *CRS Report for Congress*, March 13, 2008, p. 3.

[171] "Putin to Run for President as Medvedev Bows Out," *CDRP*, Vol. 63, No. 39 (September 26, 2011), citing Nikita Girin, "The Congress of Victors," *Novaya gazeta*, September 26, 2011, pp. 3–4, /dlib.eastview.com/browse/doc/26165119. The *Novaya gazeta* headline was intentionally evocative of the Seventeenth CPSU Congress in 1934.

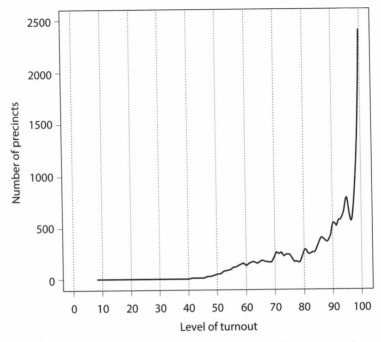

Figure 8.1 Reported turnout by precinct, republics 2008. The computations were done by my research assistant, Kirill Kalinin (Kkalinin@umich.edu). Earlier versions of Figures 8.1 and 8.2 (p. 265) first appeared in Mebane and Kalinin, "Comparative Election Fraud," presented at the American Political Science Association meeting, Toronto, September 2009. Reprinted with permission of the senior author.

and presidential elections. Given the centralized nature of the regimes in most of the republics and the subsidies most republics receive from the federal government, such transparently bogus behavior—evocative of the Soviet past—was not surprising.

What was novel was that the disease of turnout falsification had, in the felicitous phrase of Evgeniya Lukinova et al., begun to metastasize throughout the body politic.[172] Figure 8.2, with its obvious peaks at multiples of ten (60, 70, . . . 100) and less pronounced peaks for turnout figures divisible only by five and not ten at the precinct level in the oblasts, constitutes vivid testimony to the extent to which the disease of falsification had spread throughout the system by March 2008.

[172] Lukinova et al. "Metastasized Fraud," pp. 603–21.

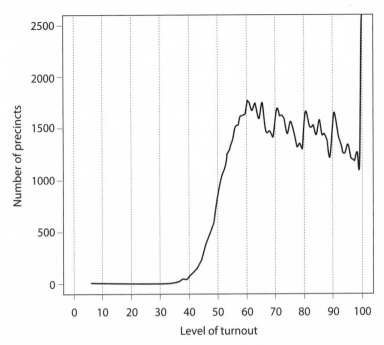

Figure 8.2 Reported turnout by precinct, oblasts 2008.

The most plausible explanation for these extraordinary results is that people at the precinct level were told that these were their goals and they delivered. They were likely oblivious to, or possibly contemptuous of, how the aggregation of their reported results would be construed by people outside the "power vertical." The lesser lights charged with reporting turnout in their precincts grasped that it was in their interest to report having "fulfilled" the plan, while all the survey data showed that the mass public, in the absence of alternatives, was at a minimum content with the Putin-Medvedev tandem.[173]

What upset the equilibrium came three years after the 2008 presidential election when in September 2011 Putin and Medvedev announced that (1) Putin was going to be the presidential candidate in March 2012, that (2) Medvedev would become the prime minister, *and* that (3) agreement to proceed in that fashion had been decided upon in 2007. Unlike

[173] Richard Rose and William Mishler, "How do Electors Respond to an 'Unfair' Election? The Experience of Russians," *Post-Soviet Affairs*, Vol. 25, No. 2 (April–June 2009), pp. 118–36.

the response to Putin's selection of Medvedev as presidential candidate and Medvedev's appointment of Putin as prime minister, which
did not engender a reaction of any magnitude, the combination of the
three produced a sharp and adverse reaction both against the ruling
party, United Russia, and against the prospects of Putin continuing as
the dominant figure in Russian politics. As we see in the next chapter,
politics returned to Russia in the winter 2011–12. For the time being at
least Russia was no longer the full authoritarian system it had become
by the 2008 presidential election. Rather than a selectorate of one, it enlarged dramatically. There were even signs that both Putin and his opponents, the vastly asymmetrical power positions of the two notwithstanding, envisaged the possibility an ejectorate might emerge. For the
near future at least, the political system took on attributes, following
Levitsky and Way,[174] best described as a competitive authoritarian regime, one where those in power had at least some restless nights prior
to the counting of the ballots.

[174]Levitsky and Way, *Competitive Authoritarianism*, p. 12.

CHAPTER 9

The Return of Uncertainty?

THE 2011–2012 ELECTORAL CYCLE

RUSSIA CONTINUES TO SURPRISE. Extrapolations to the 2011–12 electoral cycle from the previous three elections would have been substantially off target. As the previous chapter showed, each of the 2000, 2004, and 2008 elections was progressively more authoritarian and less uncertain than its predecessor. Putin and Medvedev's announcement (September 24, 2011) that they were going to switch places ("castle," *rokirovka)* after the March 2012 election with Prime Minister Putin becoming president and President Medvedev becoming prime minister seemed a harbinger of continued "full"-blown authoritarianism,[1] with a selectorate of one or, at the most, two and an absence of uncertainty concerning the outcome of the presidential election.

Events proved otherwise. From the fully authoritarian system it had been at the time of the 2003–4 and 2007–8 electoral cycles, Russia was transformed—for the time being—into a competitive authoritarian system: some legal major opposition parties (with others excluded from participation) coupled with an uneven playing field and some uncertainty as to the outcome of the election both in the case of United Russia in the December 2011 Duma election and for Putin in the March 2012 presidential election.[2] Many Russians rejected the effort by Putin and Medvedev to impose again the one- or conceivably two-member selectorate that had characterized the political system at the time of the 2008 presidential election. Instead, near universal suffrage obtained. External influences were substantial. They were even larger in the mind and rhetoric of Vladimir Putin. The return to competitive authoritarianism in the winter 2011–12 is the subject of this chapter. (Brief coverage of the events immediately following Putin's resumption of the presidency is provided in the conclusion.)

The 2011–12 electoral cycle was more complicated and less predictable than its predecessors. Using the results announced by the Central

---

[1] Levitsky and Way, *Competitive Authoritarianism,* especially pp. 12–13.

[2] Ibid., and the expanded typology in the introduction to this volume, pp. 4–6.

Electoral Commission (CEC), United Russia failed to obtain even a majority, much less an overwhelming majority, in the December 2011 Duma election. Even so, there was a widespread belief that the results announced by the CEC were bogus. This fueled large rallies, primarily in Moscow, in the interim between that election and the March presidential election. A result of those rallies was that the Kremlin tolerated the presence of many poll watchers and introduced huge numbers of electronic monitoring devices at the polling booths for the March 2012 presidential election. Evidently inferring that they had not mobilized resources sufficient to counter the opposition's strategy for the Duma election, the Kremlin set out full bore[3] to ensure Putin achieved more than 50 percent in the presidential election. They succeeded. But along the way, Putin had to confront the fact that, despite the Kremlin's resources of money, media dominance, and political muscle, it was not a foregone conclusion he would achieve a majority in the first round.

How did it come about that United Russia received less than a majority of the votes and that as late a month before the presidential election, Putin gave voice to doubts whether he would obtain a majority in the first round of the election?

THE TANDEM GETS A FLAT

One of the premier Russian students of Russian politics, Vladimir Gelman, gives Putin and Medvedev a five plus (A+) for coming up with the idea of a tandem in which Putin, constitutionally precluded from serving a third consecutive term as president in 2008, assumed the role of prime minister and Medvedev became the president.

Nothing fails like success; the strategy worked much less well the second time around. The decision by Putin and Medvedev to "castle" with Putin assuming the presidency in 2012 and Medvedev in turn appointed prime minister after the 2012 presidential election was not received with exultation except by United Russia diehards. Medvedev's September 24, 2011, announcement that Putin would be United Russia's candidate for president in 2012 was received sufficiently warmly at the United Russia party congress that Medvedev observed that "[t]his applause spares me the need to explain what experience and authority Vladimir Putin possesses."[4] Not surprisingly, the UR congress attendees endorsed Putin's candidacy. Most accounts report that the

---

[3] Gelman, "Treshchiny v stene," p. 95.
[4] CNN, "Russia's Medvedev Backs Putin for Another Presidential Run," http://www.cnn.com/2011/09/24/world/europe/russia-putin.

decision was unanimous, though the BBC reporter Artem Krechetnikov wrote that "52 of the 639 delegates did not take part in the secret ballot, four spoiled their ballot, and one person . . . even voted against."[5]

It played considerably less well among other important cohorts, most particularly the Moscow urban class and literary figures. Mikhail Prokhorov, an oligarch turned presidential candidate, nailed it when, in an interview with *Spiegel Online*, he observed "[t]hat [the castling] was cynical. It really angered people. The creative class then said: Wait a minute, we earn the taxes and so we earn respect and demand respect. People no longer remain silent when decisions are taken over their heads."[6]

To some extent the tandem brought it on themselves by their arrogance and by asserting that the decision to switch roles had been made years before the 2012 presidential election. I and others (e.g., Brian Whitmore, Tatyana Stanovaya) incline to the view that the firm decision to switch was actually made within a year of the September 24 announcement, not during the 2007–8 electoral cycle.

Putin and Medvedev made two mistakes in telling the Russian public of their intention to continue the tandem. The first, and more minor one, was to announce that Putin was going to be president again. This was hardly a surprise. The second was to announce in *September 2011* that the decision to castle in 2012 had been made at the time, four years before, when he and Medvedev had agreed that the latter would become president in 2008 and he prime minister. Then, after Medvedev had served a term, the two would switch places yet again. It was easy to imagine this might continue well into the twenty-first century. Krechetnikov, writing the day after the September 24, 2011, announcement, reported that "a number of experts had long assumed that the members of the tandem had agreed between themselves to castle forever." Krechetnikov himself allowed as how that "[i]f a social explosion does not occur, then the tenure of the leaders of 21st century Russia, like the pre-revolutionary monarchs and in the USSR, will be defined by biology and not politics."[7]

In the absence of relevant memoirs or other firm documentation, however, it seems dubious to assume that a definitive decision about 2012 was taken at the time of the 2008 election—very likely "an informal contract"[8] but not something ironclad. Instead, it seems more plausible

---

[5] Artem Krechetnikov, "Medvedev opredelilsya, k ch'ei partii on prenadlezhit," www.bbc.co.uk/russian/russia/2011/09/110924_putin_medvedev_shuffle.shtml, p. 2.

[6] Spiegel online, "Interview with Putin Challenger Prokhorov: 'In the Worst Case There'll Be Civil War,'" www.spiegel.de/international/world/interview-with-putin-challenger—prokhorov-in-the-worst-case-there-ll-be-civil-war-a-812309.html.

[7] "Medvedev opredelilsya . . ." www.bbc.co.uk/russian/russia/2011/9/110924_putin_medved-shuffle.shtml, p. 1

[8] Gelman, "Treshchiny v stene," p. 98.

to assume that the definitive decision was not taken until well after the 2008 election and that Tatyana Stanovaya is right to assert that "'Putin began to think seriously about his return approximately two years after Medvedev's election, seeing the inordinate activity, and even the pressure of Medvedev.'"[9] There is, however, evidence in both directions.

One piece of evidence that those who accept the argument that Medvedev and Putin had agreed at the very beginning that Medvedev would serve only one term and Putin would then replace him came soon after Medvedev was elected. Fairly early in his tenure he took a step that made it easier and more attractive for Putin to resume the presidency at the end of Medvedev's first term. That step was to elongate the term of the president from four years to six years. This meant it would be possible for Putin to serve, assuming Medvedev served out his four-year term, until 2024. Medvedev advanced this proposal in his inaugural address half a year (November 5, 2008) after his election in March. It came, Treisman tells us, as a surprise to Medvedev's staff and occurred a "day after Medvedev had had a long private talk with Putin."[10]

It was not, moreover, an idea that originated with Medvedev. The newspaper *Vedomosti*, citing "unidentified Kremlin sources," reported that in 2007, while Putin was still president, Vladislav Surkov, at that juncture the first deputy chief of staff, had pushed to extend the term of office. "'This was not Medvedev's improvisation, the reform was thought up under Vladimir Putin [by Surkov, who envisaged] the election of a successor who would carry out the necessary constitutional changes and unpopular social reforms so that Putin could return to the Kremlin for a longer term.'"[11] And "Kremlin critics" said this was exactly what Medvedev had done: "The extension of the presidential term from four to six years [was] part of a scheme to return powerful former President Vladimir Putin to his old job."[12]

This suggests there may have been some broad understanding at the time of the 2008 election about what would happen in 2012, but does not necessarily imply an explicit agreement. Assuming the matter came up in a meeting between the two members of the tandem, my intuition is that the conversation was something like Putin's celebrated meeting with the oligarchs who were told what the rules of the game

---

[9] As cited in Brian Whitmore, "The Essence of Decision," *RFE*, October 18, 2011, p. 2.

[10] Treisman, *The Return*, p. 159.

[11] *Vedomosti*, November 7, 2008, as cited in Brian Whitmore, "Is Medvedev Preparing Putin's Return to the Presidency?," *RFE*, November 11, 2008, pp. 1–2 and cited at www.rferl.content/Is_Medvedev_Preparing_Putins_Return_To_the_Presidency/.1348061.html.

[12] Brian Whitmore, "Longer Presidential Term in Russia Closer to Reality," *RFE*, November 19, 2008, p. 1, www.rferl.org/content/Russia_Lawmakers_Approve_Longer_Presidential_Term/1350636.hml.

were (Chapter 8, p. 253). The overwhelming majority of them got the message, but a handful did not. Likewise, Medvedev probably understood full well what Putin's wishes were but likely did not think he, Medvedev, was violating the essence of their understanding of his role if he explored how receptive the public would be to his being reelected president as long as he did not challenge Putin's overall preeminence. If this is so, it is scarcely the first time that the signal was clearer to the signaler than to its recipient.

The case for believing the decision came in the run-up to the 2011–12 electoral cycle and was not cast in stone at the time of Medvedev's election in March 2008 turns largely on the behavior of the tandem in 2010–11, though Medvedev's accounts in the fall 2011 contribute as well. For Putin the matter had been decided "several years ago." Medvedev's remarks about the decision that he would not be a candidate for reelection and that Putin would be the candidate for president in 2012 were less precise. In one depiction, they "actually discussed this possibility [of reversing roles in 2012] when the tandem had just been formed."[13] In another, a decision was reached to undertake the switching of roles after a "sufficiently long analysis."[14]

To the outsider, Putin and Medvedev seemed to be campaigning in the months before the September 2011 "castling" announcement. Putin set out to reassure himself and his constituency that he still had the attributes that had contributed to his initial election as president in 2000. His constituency needed to be reassured.

Respondents to Levada-Center surveys had consistently identified the fact that being "business-like, industrious, energetic" was Putin's strongest feature when asked to choose from a long list of favorable attributes. In February 2008, 62 percent of the respondents selected those three features as his strongest points. In September 2011 and April 2012, the grouping of these three continued to be perceived as the most apt descriptors of Putin's strong points. The number of people attributing these descriptors to him, however, had decreased to 46 percent in September 2011 and to 39 percent by April 2012.[15]

Putin chose to emphasize what had stood him in good stead early on. He resorted to the behavior that had differentiated him from Yeltsin. Stunts such as a jaunt through Siberia in a yellow Lada and scuba diving for (planted) buried amphoras were vintage Putin. (Readers may

---

[13] www.russiatoday.com, September 25, 2011, *Johnson's Newsletter* 172, No. 13, September 25, 2011.

[14] www.rferl.org/content/putin_medvedev_2012_decision/24363764.html, p. 1.

[15] Lev Gudkov, *Prezidentskiye vybory v Rossii 2012 goda: post-elektoralnyi analiz* (Moscow: Levada-Center, 2012), p. 6.

wish to view a YouTube clip of Putin's peregrinations across Siberia in which what appear to be ordinary workers are watching Putin pass by. The parade includes a second yellow Lada, multiple other cars, SUVs, vans, and campers and a flat bed truck carrying yet a third yellow Lada that had evidently broken down.[16]) They smacked of reassuring himself and his constituency that he was still the young, energetic Putin who deserved to lead the country yet again. Viktor Titov's comments at a roundtable at Moscow University's Department of Sociology and Psychology of Politics[17] suggest these stunts had become rather stale: "At first, emphasis was made on his [Putin's] assets—a real macho, dependable, charismatic, strong-willed, and so on. . . . But now twelve years after, Russians are no longer blind to his liabilities as well. It means promises that were never kept, absence of control over his subordinates, the deterioration of living standards."

Similarly, Brian Whitmore marshals several of Medvedev's 2010–11 acts that suggested he was campaigning for something by acting presidential. One of these was his housecleaning of the governors, the most well known of whom was the mayor of Moscow, Yury Luzhkov, an action some suggested was "the opening shot in a . . . battle between . . . [Putin and Medvedev] over which will be the establishment candidate for president" in 2012.[18] A second was the publication of a major call for liberalization emanating from the Institute for Contemporary Development, of which Medvedev was the chairman of the Board of Trustees. It reads like a campaign document. A third was Medvedev's order in March 2011 that government officials withdraw from the boards of various state corporations. What may have been a final straw for Putin also came that March when Medvedev and Putin publicly clashed over the appropriateness of seeing the NATO bombings of Libya, in Putin's phrase, as "a medieval appeal for a crusade."[19] It is worth noting that in the speech that provoked Medvedev's rejoinder to Putin, the latter was careful to emphasize that this kind of decision was not on his turf, that this was the purview of the president— and then to observe, "But if you're interested in my personal opinion, I have one, of course."[20]

[16] "Putin edet na kalina, odna uzhe slomana," YouTube.

[17] As cited in www.rferl.org/content/putins_winter_of_ discontent/2497812.html.

[18] Fred Weir, "Mayor Luzhkov Ouster: Sign of Crack in Putin-Medvedev Unity?," *Christian Science Monitor*, September 28, 2010, www.csmonitor.com/World/Europe/2010/0928/Mayor-Luzhkov-ouster-sign-of-crack-in-Putin-Medvedev-unity.

[19] "Putin, Medvedev Clash over Libya Intervention," *CDRP*, Vol. 63, No. 12, pp. 5–8 at p. 5, citing Vladimir Solovyov et al., *Kommersant*, March 22, 2011, dlib.eastview.com/browse/doc/24741093, p. 1.

[20] Ibid.

This was not the first time the two had diverged in their assessments while Medvedev was President. (Note for instance the divergent public views on Eduard Limonov and Mikhail Kasyanov.[21]) But Medvedev's rapid and strong reaction—"'It is absolutely inexcusable to use expressions that, in effect, lead to a clash of civilizations-such as "crusades" and so forth'"[22]—suggests something substantially over and above the foreign- and domestic-audience targeting that several Russian commentators[23] insisted explained the differences between Putin's and Medvedev's assessments.

One Russian scholar who did not accept the argument that the Putin and Medvedev were simply targeting different audiences was Igor Bunin, president of the Center for Political Technologies in Moscow. He advances a plausible interpretation of their behavior vis-à-vis NATO's action against Libya that assumes the decision to castle had not been cast in stone at that juncture. He argues that Putin was attempting "to test the strength of the president's position. 'Had Medvedev allowed [Putin] [Bunin's brackets] to step on his [Medvedev's] turf and issue instructions to him, a broader campaign would have followed. . . . Everyone would have jumped on the offensive.' . . . Putin wanted to test the president's ability to defend the perimeter of his authority. . . . And Medvedev . . . 'responded very harshly, albeit without naming names. *He responded like a commander-in-chief.'*"[24]

This assertiveness contrasted with prior foreign and domestic policy choices where Medvedev had deferred to Putin. It may have been precisely Medvedev's acting presidential that contributed to Putin's determination to run again. (An important interim step was Putin's announcement in May 2011 that he was creating an amorphous umbrella party, the All Russian People's Front, which at some time in the not-too-distant future[25] may well replace United Russia as Putin's party and as the leading party.) If Medvedev were to continue acting like a

---

[21] Sergei Anisimov, *Izvestia*, January 11, 2011, "Is Russia at a Political Crossroads," *CDRP*, Vol. 63, No. 1 (January 1, 2011), p. 6, dlib.eastview.com/browse/doc24219739. It can also be found at dlib.eastview.com/searchresults/article.jsp?art=0&id=24219739. Limonov is the founder of the National Bolshevik Party. Kasyanov was prime minister in the beginning of the Putin era.

[22] "Putin, Medvedev Clash," p. 2

[23] E.g., Olga Kryshtanovskaya and Nikolai Petrov as cited by Aleksandra Samarina, *Nezavisimaya gazeta*, March 23, 2011, p. 1, and translated by *CDRP*, Vol. 63, No. 12 (March 21, 2011), p. 7, dlib.eastview.com/searchresults/article.jsp?art=2&id=24741093.

[24] Ibid., p. 7, dlib.eastview.com/searchresults/article.jsp?art=2&id=24741093, italics added.

[25] See in particular, Aleksandra Samarina and Iva Rodin, "Field Exercises of the All-Russia People's Front," *Nezavisimaya gazeta*, March 29, 2013, p. 1 and reproduced in *CDRP*, Vol. 65, No. 1: "Vladimir Putin is creating a coalition of party structures before the

president, it was remotely possible that he might have extended the range of his actions to its constitutional limits by replacing the prime minister. In plural interviews,[26] Gleb Pavlovsky (who had been a presidential adviser until April 2011) asserted that members of Putin's team had frightened "'Putin with the myth that Medvedev was preparing to remove him. And [they frightened] Medvedev [with the rumor] that Putin would more or less move regiments to Moscow if that happened.'"

UNITED RUSSIA COMES A CROPPER

Needless to say, regiments were not moved. Medvedev nominated Putin to serve as the presidential candidate under the United Russia banner, a nomination that was endorsed overwhelmingly by UR. The fix was in. What had become standard issue on the basis of previous elections was repeated, perhaps somewhat lackadaisically. The elimination in 2006 of the "against all" vote as an option made it easier for United Russia to secure a majority. Parties that might have constituted genuine opposition parties were excluded on technicalities. Administrative resources, media domination, the carousel (the practice of moving busloads of voters from poll place to poll place), mobilizing military units and persons in homes for the elderly, and intimidation of employees all were employed as in previous elections.[27]

But this time the reported outcome in the Duma elections was dramatically at variance with the results of previous Duma or presidential elections in the Putin era. In the summer 2011 it had been widely believed that come December United Russia would obtain the supermajority it had achieved in 2007[28] and that this would be the precursor to the reelection of Putin as president. Not the December 2011 Duma

---

2016 [Duma] elections in order to present the electorate with a spectrum of ideological platforms able to win the sympathy of the population."

[26] One was to the British *The Guardian* in March 2012 and a second with Yevgeniya Albats in the Moscow *New Times* in early April 2012. The quote (including the brackets) is taken from Brian Whitmore "The Unraveling: The Tandem's Slow Death," *The Power Vertical*, April 2, 2012, p. 2, www.rfe.org/content/how_the_tandem_disintegrated/24535389.html.

[27] The above paraphrases, with less passion, a paragraph from an article by Yulia Latynina, a commentator for *Novaya gazeta*: "The majority of the people who voted against the Swindlers and Thieves Party (United Russia) has not read Navalny's blog," en.novayagazeta.ru/columns/50110.html.

[28] Henry E. Hale, "Putin Machine Sputters: First Impressions of the 2011 Duma Election," *Russian Analytical Digest*, No. 106 (December 2011), p. 1; Gelman, "Treshchiny v stene," p. 94.

election. Instead, the CEC reported that United Russia had not even received a majority of the votes (49.3 percent), a far cry from the votes necessary to achieve a constitutional majority and from the votes (64.3 percent) UR had received in 2007.

Moreover, the figures for United Russia were high.[29] Anatoly Karlin, in a broad survey of approaches to the study of voting behavior in the December election, reproduces a graph generated by a mathematician, Maxim Pshenichnikov, that is comparable to the graph reproduced in on p. 265 for the 2008 oblast turnout in the presidential election.[30] As Karlin notes, "[F]rom about the 60% turnout point, . . . there begin to appear consistent peaks at 'convenient' intervals of 5%, as if the polling stations with 70%, 75%, 80%, 90% and 100% turnout were working to targets!"[31]—as they almost certainly were. Karlin and the mathematician, Sergei Kuznetsov, point out that some of these peaks can be explained by reference to number theory. However, they also recognize that "the fat tail and some of the 5% intervals . . . *cannot* be explained by number theory—e.g. 65%, 70%, 85%, 90%, 95%" and that "this means a lot of fraud probably did happen."[32] How much was "a lot of fraud" is difficult to say with great certainty. Subject to further research, Karlin's estimate of 5 to 7 percent seems defensible. He considers a wide variety of analytic approaches and takes into account the exit polls, even the best of which were suspect because of high refusal rates. This would imply that neither the argument by the CEC that there was no fraud nor estimates that Golos endorsed that placed the distortion at approximately 15 percent withstand serious scrutiny.

The castling ploy and the emergence of Aleksei Navalny as a major protagonist are often pointed to in Russian journalistic accounts as being key to the outcome of the December 2011 Duma election and the post-Duma election protests that took place largely in Moscow during the interim between the Duma election and the March 4 presidential election. Both warrant special consideration in telling the story of the results of the December Duma election and the postelection protests, but they need to be placed in a broader context. That concerns the changing economy from 2007 to early 2012, the changing assessment of Putin's performance in that time frame, the pervasive mass perception of corruption and illegal and unpunished behavior on the part of

---

[29] Ibid., p. 95.

[30] The two differ in that the graph on p. 265 tapped turnout in the 2008 presidential rather than in the Duma election and covered only oblasts.

[31] Anatoly Karlin, "Measuring Churov's Beard: The Mathematics of Russian Election Fraud," p. 4, www.darussophile.com/2011/12/measuring-churovs-beard.

[32] Ibid., p. 12, italics in original.

Table 9.1 Respondents' overall assessment of the situation in Russia in 2000, 2010, and 2011

When surveyed	11/2007 (%)	11/2010 (%)	12/2011 (%)
Response category			
Growth and development	38	24	18
Stabilization	31	29	32
Reduced growth and stagnation	21	32	36
Difficult to say	10	15	14

Source: L.D. Gudkov et al., *Rossiiskiye parlamentskiye vybory: elektoralnyi protsess pri avtoritarnom rezhime* (Moscow: Levada-Center, 2012), p. 5.

Note: N = 1,600.

the rich and powerful, the ambivalent role of the mass media, and the evolving role of the Internet and its spinoffs. Each is an important part of the story.

Both the change in the economy and the declining assessment of Putin's performance are well documented on the basis of well-regarded national surveys. In national samples collected by the Levada-Center from late 2007 onward general support for the leadership diminished steadily both before and after September 2011. This showed up in Levada-Center's monthly national surveys of 1,600 Russian respondents. In them, Russians were asked how they would characterize the then current situation in Russia. Would they view it as one of "growth and development, stabilization, or reduced growth and stagnation." Table 9.1 compares the responses in November 2007, November 2010, and December 2011 to a question calling on respondents to give an overall evaluation of the situation in Russia.

In the run-up to the December 2007 Duma election, slightly more than two-thirds (69 percent) of the respondents viewed the situation at the time surveyed as one either of stability or of growth and development. Only one in five (21 percent) termed it one of reduced growth and stagnation. In the immediate aftermath of the December 2011 Duma election slightly more than two-thirds (68 percent) of the respondents characterized the situation as either stabilization or reduced growth and stagnation. Fewer than one in five (18 percent) described conditions as one of growth and development. Similarly, to the standard question posed by Levada-Center in its monthly surveys "Do you approve of the activities of Vladimir Putin in his position as prime minister?" a steady and nearly monotonic decrease was discernible over the time period October 2010 to January 2012. Slightly more than three-quarters (77 percent) gave Putin good grades for his performance in October 2010. In February 2011 his rating, while still high, had dropped to 73 percent and to 69 percent by June. This dropped to 66 percent in October and had reached 64 percent in January 2012.[33]

The pervasiveness of perceptions of corruption by people with only tangential or third hand awareness of Navalny's efforts to diffuse information of such behavior has been strongly emphasized by Yulia Latynina.[34] For such people, they had often not known, Latynina observed, about the scandalous incident on Lenin Prospect in Moscow when the car of Lukoil vice president Anatoly Barkov ran over two women obstetricians, one thirty-six, the other seventy-two, and suffered no penalty nor about Gelendzhik, a palace ostensibly built for Putin out of public funds. They or someone close to them had, though, had personal experience with analogous injustices—a "relative run over by a bureaucrat" with no resulting punishment or who "had had their property taken away and were unable to obtain justice."[35]

This seems plausible in light of Russia's rankings on Transparency International's various relevant scales. Its Global Corruption Barometer found that a quarter (26 percent) of those Russians interviewed reported having paid a bribe in 2010. When asked whether during the period "2007–2010 their government's anti-corruption efforts have increased, stayed the same, or decreased," 53 percent said they had increased, 39 percent said they had stayed the same, and 8 percent said they had decreased. This perception notwithstanding, only one in five surveyed (19 percent) termed "the government's efforts to fight corruption" effective. Of the remainder, 28 percent said the efforts were neither effective nor ineffective and 53 percent termed these efforts ineffective. Globally, Russia ranked 143rd out of 183 overall in 2011, 123rd out of 142 on judicial independence in 2011–12, and 28th of the 28 wealthiest and most influential countries in the world on a Bribe Payer's Index for 2011.

That said, there was little public evidence of discontent in the immediate aftermath of the castling announcement and prior to the Duma election. Yavlinsky reported that after the United Russia congress, "the number of people who [wanted] to work with me and Yabloko rose sharply."[36] A more visible exception came not from the urban middle

[33] Levada-tsentr, *Indeksy*, September 2013.

[34] Latynina, "The Majority of the People," p. 9.

[35] Ibid.

[36] The Yavlinsky interview is accessible by googling "Change is Only Possible if There is an Alternative" or by accessing rfe/rl Russia and searching Yavlinsky, change, possible.

class but at a martial arts match in November at the Olympic Stadium in Moscow where Putin was introduced at the end of the fight. Quite contrary to his previous experiences with audiences having the demographics of the attendees at a martial arts match in Moscow, he was roundly whistled (booed).[37]

In the two months immediately following the September 24 castling announcement, the behavior of the distinguished author Boris Akunin was more typical and illustrates the discontent and dilemma of an important member of Moscow's urban middle class and literati who was reluctant to act prior to the Duma election. In this Akunin probably stands as a place marker for many other Muscovites. Grumbling about what had happened, Akunin and his wife initially acted as though they had no means whereby they could effectively express their views in Russia. Akunin, his wife, and, it turned out, thousands of others, were available for mobilization but were apprehensive about the consequences of being a first mover. For Akunin and his wife, the weeks that followed the September 24 announcement were, Akunin reports, "one of the most depressing periods of my life."[38]

Feeling powerless, his wife opted for exit.[39] "'That's it.'" she declared, "'We need to leave. I don't want to spend the rest of my life in the country of Mister Dobby.'" Akunin, who was skeptical of the effectiveness of street protests, took the position that "'This is not his [Putin's] country. Let's wait some more.'" "There will be a social eruption. People are not idiots, they will not agree to this castling move."[40] Akunin was right: something did occur that had the flavor of a social eruption, and Akunin played a major part in those rallies that were forthcoming in the months subsequent to the Duma election.

Here is where the relative diversity of the media in conjunction with the Internet and its spinoffs—LiveJournal, Facebook, YouTube—combined to ease the standard collective action problem that unorganized citizens face in dealing with an authoritarian system that dominates the media. Giving voice to the discontent was easier to do in a competitive authoritarian system than it had been in Russia's fullblown authoritarian system circa 2008.[41] The Kremlin struck quickly to delete the booing incident from the television news coverage. From the regime's perspective the media coverage was exactly wrong. The Krem-

[37] Hale, "Putin Machine Sputters," p. 3.

[38] "Let's Not Rush to Win in Russia," *New York Times*, January 20, 2012, op-ed section.

[39] Albert O. Hirschman, *Exit, Voice, and Loyalty* (Cambridge, MA: Harvard University Press, 1970).

[40] "Let's Not Rush to Win."

[41] Gelman addresses this as part of his overall theme that UR was not sufficiently "monolithic," "Treshchiny v stene," p. 96

lin was in a position to excise the booing incident from the television news, but "internet users actively discussed the spontaneous auditory assault on the prime minister."[42]

Still, the Kremlin could not or did not control television to the degree it had in other years. Television was less monolithic during the Duma election and in covering the protest rallies than it had been in previous electoral cycles. This was in part because some elements in the media were taking their cues from Medvedev's advocacy of modernization. As one television official put it (correctly), there had been "an increase in pluralism on television . . . for the past 18 months or so, in case someone has not noticed."[43]

Henry Hale was one of those who did notice. He reports that Rossiya 1, a state-owned channel, not only scheduled debates among various party leaders (as in previous campaigns, Putin and Medvedev refused to participate) at sensible times, ones "when people would actually watch them (at 10:50 p.m. between popular shows on weekdays), but broadcast them live . . . and even advertised them as being dramatic events worth watching."[44] Similarly, the television coverage of the anti-Putin rallies after the Duma election, while selectively reported, conveyed some of what was transpiring. As the *Moscow Times* reported, "Since [the] mass 'protests' broke out after December's State Duma elections, the channels have surprised people by covering the rallies, sometimes with uncharacteristic fairness."[45]

At the same time, pressure was placed on those who in someone's judgment had "gone too far." Ekho Moskvy was pressed to alter the composition of its governing board.[46] The erstwhile socialite turned democratic advocate, Kseniya Sobchak,[47] had her television program,

---

[42] Christopher Walker and Robert Orttung, "Russia's Revolution Won't Be Televised," *Radio Free Europe*, November 30, 2011.

[43] Aleksandr Melman, "The Great Television Revolution," *Moskovsky Komsomolets*, February 1, 2012, cited in *JRL*, No. 19 (February 2, 2012), No. 20 quoting Anton Khrekov, an author of the NTVshniki talk show.

[44] Hale, "Putin Machine Sputters," p. 4.

[45] Nikolaus von Twickel, "Media Thaw's Staying Power Hotly Debated," *Moscow Times*, No. 4844, March 16, 2012.

[46] Cited in http://eastview.com/browse/doc26762954. "On March 29, 2012, the Ekho Moskvy Board of Directors removed Editor in Chief Aleksei Venediktov, First Deputy Editor in Chief, First Deputy in Chief Vladimir Varfolomeyev, and independent directors Yevgeny Yasin and Aleksandr Makovskiy from the station's governing body. This action has ensured that it will be easier to remove Venediktov if the Kremlin decided on such a course of action." Robert W. Orttung and Christopher Walker, "Putin and Russia's Crippled Media," *Russian Analytical Digest*, No. 123 (February 21, 2013), pp. 2–5 at p. 4.

[47] Andrew Meir, "The Stiletto in Putin's Side," *New York Times Magazine*, July 8, 2012, pp. 16–19, is an English-language account of Ms. Sobchak's peregrinations.

Gosdep (short for State Department), canceled ostensibly because her audience was not interested in politics when she scheduled Aleksei Navalny as her guest on a forthcoming show. (The online and cable TV Dozhd picked it up.) From contacts in the Russian Far East, the long-time commentator, Vladimir Pozner, learned that a taped interview with Navalny had been excised prior to its being shown in his Moscow time slot.

Nevertheless, the proliferation of persons who had access to electronic media helped diffuse information about protest activities after the Duma election and increase the number of folks who thought it had been neither free nor fair. While television remained the dominant source for information about the elections and the rallies that were sandwiched between the two elections of the 2011–12 cycle, what was new was the burgeoning of the Internet.[48] From 2000 to 2012 the number of daily users of the Internet went from 3.1 million to approximately 52 to 54 million, or almost two-fifths of the Russian population.[49] Those under thirty-five were especially likely to say that the Internet was an important source of information—more than radio and newspapers but still less than television. The Internet, blogs, and social networking contributed heavily to facilitating the mobilization of Russians in the aftermath of the Duma election. Thousands participated in rallies, most notably on December 10, December 24, and February 4 (a month prior to the presidential election). The turnout estimates vary tremendously, with police saying about 36,000 had turned out for the February 4 rally and organizers claiming that more than 120,000 had attended. If we take as a rule of thumb that the "real" participation in events of this kind is the sum of the estimates of the organizers and the police divided by two, the online portal Lenta.ru's estimate of from 50,000 to 60,000 was probably not too far off.[50] Whatever, no one would dispute that a lot of people turned out in cold weather (−19°C = +2°F), primarily in response to the widespread perception that the Duma election had been neither free nor fair and exasperation at the Putin/Medvedev switch.

Which brings us to Aleksei Navalny. The part of his impact that was best known—prior to the 2013 Moscow Mayoral election—was his articulation of a strategy and a slogan, both of which produced results, though the slogan was to a substantial extent successful largely because

[48] Olesya Tkacheva, "Fighting Electoral Fraud in the 2011 Russian Election with Internet and Social Media," in Tkacheva et al., eds., *Internet Freedom and Political Space* (Santa Monica, CA: RAND, 2013).

[49] Tkacheva, "Fighting Electoral Fraud," pp. 124–125.

[50] Anna Arutunyan, "Protest Stays Festive, Tandem Leaderless," *Moscow News,* February 6, 2012, cited in *JRL,* No. 22 (February 7, 2012), No. 27.

Table 9.2 Duma votes 2011 and 2007 compared (Central Election
Commission data)

Party	2011 (%)	2007 (%)
Communist Party of the Russian Federation	19.2	11.6
Liberal Democratic Party	11.7	8.1
Fair Russia	13.2	7.7
Yabloko	3.4	1.6
United Russia	49.3	64.3

Sources: For 2011 and 2007 distribution of Duma votes by party, see "Final Result of the Duma Election, 4 December 2011," www.russiavotes.org/duma/duma_today.php, drawing on the official figures of the Central Electoral Commission (http://www.vybory .izbirkom.ru).

many Russians were primed for the message. The strategy contributed to important electoral consequences in the Duma election. The slogan legitimated opposition to, and indeed scorn for, the dominant party, United Russia. His strategy was simple, to form what Gelman terms a "negative consensus,"[51] and had the strong advantage of appealing to nationalists, democrats, liberals, and leftists, many of whom have a well-deserved reputation for being unable or unwilling to talk to, much less collaborate with, persons of a different ideological bent. Navalny did not have that problem. As he put it, he would accept the support of "nationalists, liberals, leftists, greens, vegetarians, Martians."[52] He urged people to vote for any party other than United Russia, but to vote rather than stay at home or submit invalid ballots. This strategic calculus benefited all the conventional parties other than United Russia (Table 9.2). According to CEC reports, the Communist Party of the Russian Federation received almost twice as many votes in 2011 as it did in 2007 (19.2 percent vs. 11.6 percent). Zhirinovsky's Liberal Democratic Party increased modestly (11.7 percent) over its 8 percent in 2007. Fair Russia nearly doubled its vote total (13.2 percent in 2011 vs. 7.7 percent in 2007) and Yabloko doubled its vote from 1.6 percent in 2007 to 3.4 percent in 2011. As we noted previously, the CEC reported that United Russia received 49.3 percent of the vote in 2011. This represented a sharp decrease over the 64.3 percent the CEC said it had received in 2007.

The slogan was even simpler. United Russia, Navalny declared, was the "Party of Swindlers and Thieves (*partiya zhulikov i vorov*)." Regardless whether the person learned the slogan directly from a blog or picked it up second- or thirdhand, the label stuck, in large part because

[51] Gelman, "Treshchiny v stene," p. 104.
[52] Ellen Barry, "Rousing Russia with a Phrase," *New York Times*, December 9, 2011.

Table 9.3 Do you agree or disagree with the view that "United Russia" is the party of swindlers and thieves?

When surveyed Response option	April 2011 (%)	June 2011 (%)	November 2011 (%)	January 2012 (%)	April 2012 (%)	August 2013 (%)
Either definitely agree or inclined to agree	31	33	36	41	38	44
Either definitely disagree or inclined to disagree	45	47	45	43	48	35
Hard to say	23	19	20	15	15	11

Source: levada.ru/print/16–09–2013/schitayut-li-rossiyane-edinuyu-rossiyu-partiei-zhulikov-i-vorov.

Note: N = 1,601.

it resonated with the experience of a sizeable fraction of the Russian public. To cite Latynina again, "There are things you can make people buy, and there are things you can't make people buy. . . . People will never buy it if you tell them that new roads are being built in Russia, that high ranking officials don't run over people with their limousines and that police are busy catching criminals."[53] Both survey data and anecdotal evidence testify to how pervasive the label became and why Putin has quietly distanced himself from United Russia. Lev Gubkov and his Levada-Center group reported that in their April and June 2011 national surveys 31 and 33 percent, respectively, had answered affirmatively to the question "Do you agree or not with the view that United Russia is the Party of Swindlers and Thieves?" The number agreeing climbed to 36 percent in November 2011. In January 2012 it had reached 41 percent but decreased to 38 percent in April of that year. The proportion disposed to a negative answer gradually decreased from 45 percent disagreeing in April 2011 to 43 percent in January 2012 and then went up to 48 percent in April 2012. By August 2012, the proportion agreeing had achieved a slight plurality, 45 percent to 42 percent. A year later in August 2013 the number agreeing and disagreeing had reached 44 and 35 percent, respectively (Table 9.3).

Anecdotal evidence strengthens the sense that nationwide Navalny's characterization had effectively undermined United Russia as a brand name. Hale points out that in one of the debates on state-owned Rossiya

---

[53] Latynina, "Every Man for Himself," p. 9.

1 prior to the Duma election, Vladimir Zhirinovsky successfully baited a spokesman for United Russia, Aleksandr Khinshtein, into retorting that it was "better to be a party of swindlers and thieves than a party of murderers, robbers, and rapists."[54] This was then distorted by United Russia opponents to claims that "United Russia had itself *admitted* it was a party of swindlers and thieves."[55] And in fact in one remarkable advertisement prior to the Duma election an individual on the United Russia ballot actually did so. One Robert Shlegel declared, "Russians should vote for the party of thieves and swindlers. . . . Whatever they call us, we love our country and work together for its good. . . . Vote for United Russia."[56] Similarly, in Novosibirsk the local Fair Russia party was charged with defaming United Russia by posting a bus advertisement urging citizens to vote for a Russia Without Swindlers and Thieves. No explicit mention was made of United Russia in the ad — evidently the police assumed that virtually everybody in Novosibirsk made the connection between United Russia and the Party of Swindlers and Thieves.[57]

Navalny's impact was not limited to a strategy for maximizing the total votes cast against United Russia or to a slogan that became common parlance across the Russian Federation. By and large, initially the central theme of the rallies that followed the Duma election was that presidential selection should be based on a free and fair election. (The establishment parties were ambivalent about the rallies. Zyuganov, for instance, bought into the argument that the leaders of the rallies were following the example of Viktor Yushchenko, the former Ukrainian president, and Mikhail Saakashvili, the then president of Georgia.[58]) By this, those participating in the rallies largely had in mind an essentially Schumpeterian conception (above, p. 245) involving a near universal selectorate who would choose from among a list that included candidates from across the board. Putin, of course, had announced a process whereby he and Medvedev selected themselves, a selection process that was made closer to a sure thing by manipulating the pool of candidates so that potentially viable candidates (e.g.,

---

[54] Hale, "Putin Machine Sputters," p. 4.

[55] Ibid, p. 4, italics in original.

[56] "Government Deputy Tells Russians to Vote for Party of Thieves and Swindlers," www .rferl.org/content/ruling_party_deputy_calls_on_russians_to_vote_for_the_party_of _thieves_and_swindlers/24409518.html.

[57] "Novosibirsk Equates United Russia with Swindlers and Thieves," *The Other Russia*, November 13, 2011.

[58] "Parliamentary Opposition Distances Itself from Street Protestors," *CDRP*, Vol. 63, No. 51 (December 19, 2011), p. 7, dlib.eastview.com/browse.doc/26509861. He changed his tune somewhat as the presidential elections drew nigh.

Grigory Yavlinsky, Boris Nemtsov, Mikhail Kasyanov) were found in-eligible on spurious grounds.

Navalny's public utterances at rallies and in interviews after the December 4 Duma election were straightforward. For him, the goal was "the transformation of Russia into a normal democratic state, where power is always achieved by honest democratic elections," he told a BBC interviewer. It is a goal that requires "an indeterminate process and a long time." "Vladimir Putin," Navalny observed, "will naturally put off that date as long as possible."[59] He did not "think the regime will change as a result of an election."[60] Nor did his conception of the change process envisage emulating the "colored" revolutions epitomized by the events in Ukraine after the 2004 elections. Rather, he saw the change of regime as taking place in a way analogous to the 1989 "velvet" revolutions in Eastern Europe.

This, in his mind, would at some stage culminate in something akin to roundtable negotiations. To achieve that goal would entail the efforts of an ejectorate using a plurality of tactics "of varying intensity: from negotiations to thousands-strong street protests and throngs of people who toss officials out of office and string them up."[61] "We are peaceful people and we won't do that yet. But if these crooks and thieves keep cheating us, we will take what is ours," he declared at the December 24, 2011, rally.[62]

From Rallies to Reelection

The demonstrations tapered off (but did not cease) after the February 4 rally, scheduled intentionally to occur a month before the presidential election. The Kremlin acted as though it realized that it had treated the Duma elections too casually, a mistake not repeated in the run-up to the presidential election. In the immediate aftermath of the rallies it also behaved as if it were really alarmed by the rallies. By way of concession to the protesters, Medvedev proposed a return to the election of governors and the reduction of barriers to party formation. (There

---

[59] "Navalny: Sistema Putina ne prozhivet dol'she polutora let," p. 1, www.bbc.co.uk /russian/russia/2012/02/120214_navalniy_interview.shtml.

[60] "I Believe Good Will Triumph over Evil," Aleksei Navalny interview, *New Times*, Nos. 44–45 (December 26, 2011).

[61] Ibid.

[62] Lynn Berry and Vladimir Isachenkov, "Putin Protests: Tens of Thousands Demand Free Elections," *Huffington Post*, December 24, 2011. For subsequent events, see below, pp. 304–05.

were the usual denials in such circumstances that the policy innovations were in any way a response to the protests. Of course not.) As in several other instances during the Putin period, the proposed changes had a democratic cast to them, but the devil was in the details. In this instance, the devil's work was accomplished in the texts adopted after Putin's reelection had been secured.

Both the bill reintroducing the election of governors and that altering the rules on party formation were adopted in greatly modified form, that is, with hedges that cynics could readily interpret as rendering them easily subject to manipulation by the establishment. In proposing the restoration of the election of governors, Medvedev's foresight was better than it had been in September 2009 when he asserted he could not envisage "conditions in which we would renounce the decision [to eliminate the election of governors] not now nor in a hundred years"[63] The bill that finally passed the Duma provided that the president would be consulted and in addition there would be a "municipal filter" requiring the signatures of somewhere between five and ten percent of members of the region's municipal councils."[64] As was the intention of the majority members of the Duma, this will make it harder for someone not a member of United Russia to become governor. (A communist member of the Duma, Anatoly Lokot, invoked a pseudo-biblical "It will be easier for a camel to go through the eye of a needle than for an opposition candidate to become governor" in emphasizing how difficult it will be.[65])

The other major change pertained to party formation. Grigory Golosov points out that reducing the barriers to entry—most obviously the number required to form a party decreased from forty thousand to five hundred—was readily open to manipulation by the ruling party, the biggest danger being the ease with which proregime parties could be formed, their main purpose being to take away votes from other more serious challengers to the powers that be. Having entered caveats of which this is the most important, Golosov still concludes that the

[63] "Medvedev: Rossiya ne vernetsiya k prezhnei sisteme vyborov gubernatorov," *Gazeta.ru*, September 9, 2009, www.gazeta.ru/news/lenta/2009/09/15/n_1403803.shtml.

[64] Descriptions of the requirements may be found in Atle Staalesen, "Governor Elections Are Back," *Barents Observer*, June 1, 2012, barentsobserver.com/en/politics/governor-elections-are-back and Lilya Biryukov and Maxim Glikin, "Filter for Whoever Does Not Belong," *Vedomosti*, April 16, 2012. *JRL*, No. 70 (April 16, 2012). For the argument by Igor Kokin that the "municipal filter . . . will not benefit the municipal voters themselves," see *JRL*, No. 123 (July 9, 2012), No. 11.

[65] Cited by Maria Rybakova, "Kremlin Bill Passes Parliament, but Barely," *JRL*, No. 76 (April 25, 2012), No. 2.

"simplification of the registration process is . . . a significant victory for the democracy movement in Russia . . . [if it can] once more impose its own rules on the government [as it did winter 2011–12 and not just] . . . obediently toe the line."[66]

THE MARCH 2012 ELECTION

Despite the concessions in response to the rallies, the presidential election and its campaign were in many respects anticlimactic. The concessions were accompanied by a vigorous campaign supporting the status quo, stability and nationalism, fostering fear of an orange revolution,[67] accusations that the protesters were being paid and orchestrated by the United States, and bizarre suggestions by Putin himself that the opposition was "looking among well-known people for a sacrificial victim." "They could, I'm sorry, knock someone off and then blame the authorities."[68] These accusations were coupled with the application of administrative resources of the sort employed in previous elections throughout the decade, 2001–10, and the mobilization of large counterrallies to offset the impact of the rallies by his opponents. These efforts were extensive. They were, moreover, built on a foundation of prior actions—especially eliminating the "against all" option and denying several candidates a place on the ballot who might have influenced favorably the total vote for the opposition candidates.

Despite all these efforts, the presidential election was an election with a substantial selectorate—once it became clear that the public was not going to roll over passively as it had in 2008 and concede the decision by Putin to choose himself as president. Putin appealed to a broad coalition disproportionately drawn from pensioners, the military, and the working class. The 2012 presidential election was not an "election-type event," the regime's vigorous efforts to reduce the uncertainty characteristic of a genuinely contested election notwithstanding. Until quite late in the electoral process, Putin had cause to worry whether he would achieve a majority of the votes in the first round. Gordon

---

[66] "Medvedev's Party Reform: Concession or Convenience?," p. 5, www.opendemocracy .net/od-russia/grigorii-golosov/medevedev's-party-reform-concession-or-convenience.

[67] This resonated well at that juncture with the communist leadership. See note 58 above for Zyuganov's comments.

[68] Fred Weir, "For Vladimir Putin, Winning Russia's Presidency may be the Easy Part," *Christian Science Monitor*, March 1, 2012, and cited in *JRL*, No. 38 (March 2, 2012), No. 6.

Hahn[69] mustered the results of several polls (the Levada-Center, the Public Opinion Foundation, the All-Russian Center for the Study of Public Opinion [VTsIOM]) conducted in December and early January to argue Putin was likely to obtain less than 50 percent in the first round. A month before the March 4 election, Putin acknowledged that possibility. "'There is nothing horrible'[70] about a runoff," he declared, even though it might result in "'a certain destabilization, a continuation of the political battle.'"[71] The bravado notwithstanding, Putin was acknowledging the uncertainty that Levitsky and Way[72] associate with competitive authoritarianism and, implicitly, recognizing that the political system was on the cusp between full authoritarianism ("Officials in full authoritarian regimes can rest easy on the eve of elections"[73]) and competitive authoritarianism. Not only was the Kremlin determined to win the presidential election, it was determined to thwart a fundamental system shift to competitive authoritarianism. Every effort was made to achieve a majority in the first round rather than satisfice with a level of certainty that would make them confident about the outcome of a second round. This required that under no circumstances should someone other than the house-trained, within-system candidates be allowed to seek the presidency and the vast deployment of money, media dominance, and mobilizational capability.

It worked. By mid-February, the tide had shifted sufficiently for VTsIOM to predict Putin would win comfortably by obtaining 59 percent of the vote.[74] Striking a chord that resonates with Levitsky and Way, Putin's former chief of staff, Aleksandr Voloshin, wrote on Twitter in late February that "the news [that Putin would win 59 percent of the vote] . . . would make many 'sleep more soundly.'"[75] VTsIOM nailed the result pretty well. According to the CEC, Putin received 63.6 percent (45.6 million valid votes cast in his favor) of the vote—considerably more than he had received in 2000 but much less than in 2004.

---

[69] "Problems of Putinism," February 5, 2012, cited in *JRL*, No. 21 (February 6, 2012), No. 19.

[70] Aleksandra Odynova, "Putin Says He's Prepared for Runoff," *Moscow Times*, February 2, 2012, cited in *JRL*, No. 19 (February 2, 2012), No. 2. See also Vladimir Isachenkov, "Putin Admits He May Face Runoff in Russia's Presidential election," *AP*, February 1, 2012, and cited in *JRL*, No. 18 (February 1, 2012), No. 1.

[71] Ilya Arkipov, "Putin Aims to Dodge Kremlin Runoff as Stability Loses Appeal," *Bloomberg*, February 2, 2012, as cited in *JRL*, No. 19 (February 2, 2012), No. 6.

[72] Levitsky and Way, *Competitive Authoritarianism*, p. 12.

[73] Ibid., p. 12.

[74] Guy Faulconbridge, "Putin to win Russian First Round: Poll," www.reuters.com /article/2012/02/20/us-russia-election-putin-idUSTRE81G1J920120220.

[75] Ibid., p. 2.

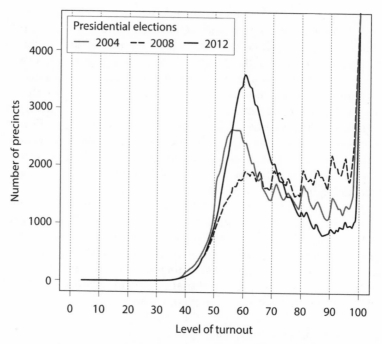

Figure 9.1 Turnout for the 2004, 2008, and 2012 presidential elections. The figure was generated by my research assistant, Kirill Kalinin.

Ironically, the 2012 presidential election was less open to charges of fraud than the December 2011 Duma election had been. Figure 9.1 shows the difference in the turnout by precinct for the 2004, 2008, and 2012 presidential elections. The fact that several republics reported Soviet-style turnout largely explains the turnout concentration at 100. That aside, the difference in the reported turnout for the 2012 presidential election as opposed to that reported for 2004 and 2008 is striking. The 2012 presidential election was more fair and involved less padding of the results. The reduction in electoral manipulation was to a considerable extent the Kremlin's reaction to the rallies that occurred after the December election. An overwhelming majority (reportedly 90,000 of a total of 94,000) of the precinct polling locations had web cameras installed so that the voting could be monitored. Putin agreed to allow the League of Voters to send volunteers to precinct stations to observe the election. Thousands from the within-system parties (including Yabloko) served as election observers. The election in Moscow (but not, evidently, in St. Petersburg) was notably less falsified than it had been in December 2011 (when it had been considerable). Combining the analytical modeling of many methodologists and the best of the exit polls, Anatoly Karlin places the overreport for Putin nationally as being on the order of 3 to 4 percent, a figure roughly half again less than the distortion favoring United Russia on the occasion of the December 2011 Duma election and, obviously, less than the gap between 50 percent and the 63 percent reported by the CEC.[76]

That said, Russia still fell well short of deserving to be characterized as democratic in Schumpeterian terms. Its biggest shortcomings in this regard were the regime's overwhelming but not exclusive presence on the major media, and the exclusion of potentially serious candidates, whose presence on the ballot might well have prevented Putin from winning in the first round. His opponents were retreads (Zyuganov, Zhirinovsky) or persons whose independence from Putin (Sergei Mironov, Mikhail Prokhorov) was suspect, at least at the outset of the presidential competition. The opposition was not much better than it had been when Medvedev won in 2008 against a troika (Zyuganov, Zhirinovsky, and Andrei Bogdanov) who were easily dismissed as insubstantial.[77]

The beginning of Putin's third term is an appropriate time to end the narrative dimension to this volume. A conclusion written in the summer 2011 would have likely been fraught with unqualified pessimism about the prospects for democracy in Russia at least within the policy-relevant future. It would have been easy to conclude that, in light of nearly a century of Russian politics, 1917–2012, there were only two real options for future Russian politics in the first quarter of the twenty-first century. Either Medvedev would have been reelected in 2012—an option foreclosed in September 2011—with Putin the man behind the throne or Putin might be president until 2024. (Logically, there was a third alternative. Medvedev might have been reelected. Putin could then have served for the twelve years, 2018–30.)

The remarkable events that took place in the winter and spring December 2011 to June 2012, require us to think more about the possible options for Russia over the long haul in comparative perspective. These comparisons need to be cross-temporal—and thus require in part a reprise of the evolution of Russian politics 1917–2012. Several of

---

[76] www.darussophile.com/2012/03/provincialization-russian-fraud.

[77] For an even more dismissive characterization see above p. 224, where I report a quote from *Times Online*, February 29, 2008, as cited in Levitsky and Way, *Competitive Authoritarianism*, p. 200.

Russia's leaders have taken public positions valuing Russia's becoming a normal (by which they mean Western) country. All have in turn often considered themselves or their personal choice indispensible and deferred that goal until some future time. Such comparisons also call for taking into account the secular changes in Russia in that time period. Most important in this regard has been the emergence of an articulate and strategically oriented urban populace, most specifically in Moscow but in other large Russian cities as well. They, in classic postmodernist fashion,[78] having achieved a level of material satisfaction roughly similar to that of comparable West Europeans and North Americans, demonstrated their attachment to characteristically postmaterialist values. These included demanding that they play the kind of substantial role in the fair selection of leaders as do their counterparts in Western Europe and North America. In the next chapter, I stick my neck out and assess the probable outcome circa 2020 for the nature of the Russian political system of the interaction of secular change and society, on the one hand, and the political leadership, on the other.

[78] See the many publications of Ronald F. Inglehart, e.g., *Modernization and Post-modernization* (Princeton, NJ: Princeton University Press, 1997).

CHAPTER 10

The Past and Future of Russian Authoritarianism

I BEGAN THIS BOOK with something of an apology, it having turned out that I devoted only modest attention throughout to ascertaining the extent to which, in cross-national comparative terms, Russia had become a normal democratic polity, focusing instead on the evolving nature of the various Russian political systems, 1917 to Putin's reelection and its immediate aftermath following the March 2012 election. It turns out, though, that the reference points Russian leaders and students of Russian politics have in mind when they determine that Russia is or intentionally is not normal provide a useful hook on which to hang some of the story of the evolution of Russian political systems across time.

As we saw (above, pp. 14–39), in the early days of Soviet rule, Lenin's thinking was governed in large part by considerations of what would render Soviet ideology distinctive and less fraught by the possibility of converging with Western social democratic ideas. To accomplish this, he set out, long before the October Revolution, to formulate a strategy for power seizure the guts of which proved to be an argument for a small, closed, and tightly knit party of a new type. When, in the context of World War I, the Bolsheviks with Lenin at the head overthrew the tsarist autocracy they moved quickly, though not without controversy, to extricate themselves from that war and to develop the institutions that would permit them to maintain themselves in power. This initially involved a small oligarchy of decision makers. Within that oligarchy, the Bolsheviks observed procedural niceties as they went about extricating themselves from the war. They succeeded. In a matter of a few years they quickly produced a European-style army, a civilian work force that emulated the hierarchical structures one typically associates with military institutions, and governing institutions that mimicked Lenin's strategy for power seizure, the latter a conscious rejection of the organizational structures of European socialist parties. In the process, the numbers of persons who might be considered the selectorate dropped, especially if one (inappropriately) takes as one's initial frame of reference the election of the Constituent Assembly. That election did occur after the Bolsheviks had seized power. But they did not initiate it; indeed they closed down the Constituent Assembly almost immediately. But even against the standards of the early days of Soviet power, the size of the selectorate shrank precipitously. Those whom they defined as clear-cut exemplars of the old regime were disenfranchised by the 1918 Constitution. The same document gerrymandered the peasantry as well.

Within a short time span, moreover, even the workers became "residents."[1] The trade unions lost their independence and the workers lost the right to strike. They were mobilized in much the way the army had been and effectively excluded from the Congress of Soviets the membership of which, as was noted on page 17, by the end of 1919 was 97 percent Bolshevik in composition. By 1922, Party membership, no longer status as a worker or a toiler, defined membership in the selectorate. Moreover, the resolutions adopted at the Ninth Party Congress (March–April 1920) committing the regime to implementing one man rule in the enterprises to considerable extent eliminated ordinary workers from constituting the selectorate, even within the enterprise, much less at a national level. This became even clearer in the winter 1920–21 when a major debate among the communist leadership broke out over the relation of trade unions to the state and Party (discussed above, pp. 29–35). What was not at issue among the members of the Central Committee (including the Democratic Centralist leadership) was whether the communists in the trade unions should be elected by their members or appointed by the central organs of the Party— whether in a proletarian state, the governing principle would be the dictatorship of the proletariat or the Party dictatorship over the proletariat. The Central Committee members opted for the second choice.

The outcome of the trade union debate was that the Bolsheviks effectively asserted their claim to appoint trade union leaders, thus basically disenfranchising the workers, communist and noncommunists alike. The centralization of decision making proceeded apace in the 1920s. The Party apparatus grew rapidly. With the growth of "the organs" and their use of the appointment and transfer weapon, the selectorate narrowed substantially. What Roeder termed reciprocal accountability and Daniels described as the circular flow of power (described above, p. 12) became standard practice, thus making it increasingly possible for the Secretariat and the Politburo to control those in the institutions (initially the Congress, then the Central Committee) who were notionally charged with the task of appointing the central organs.

At the same time, the regime sought a (temporary) accommodation with the peasantry. The New Economic Policy (NEP) was such an arrangement. It differed radically from the War Communism that

---

[1] Bueno de Mesquita et al., *The Logic of Political Survival*, p. 39.

preceded it, not to mention the collectivization and Five-Year Plans that came after. War Communism represented an effort to harness the populace in a manner consonant with our notions of a totalitarian regime (Introduction, pp. 4–6) while NEP with respect to regime-society relations more corresponded to a traditional ("full" for Levitsky and Way) authoritarian regime. In lieu of forced requisitions, the market was allowed to operate, thus creating incentives for the more successful peasants to maximize the growth of grain. In addition, NEP involved the denationalizing of all but the commanding heights of the economy (which increased the peasants' propensity to consume because there were things to buy) and the stabilization of the currency. Stabilization gave meaning to the currency and resulted in it serving as a means of exchange, as it had not been during the hyperinflation of War Communism.

Collectivization contrasted sharply with NEP. Coupled with a Cultural Revolution and the Great Breakthrough in the cities, it involved a blend of repression and mobilization (Chapter 2), the goals of which were a radical transformation of both the village and in the cities. The publication of many documents from the archives in recent years has made it clear that the result was civil war. The peasants not only engaged in widespread passive resistance but active resistance as well. According to a secret police report,[2] roughly 2.5 million persons participated in mass disturbances in 1930 and almost 1,200 officials and other supporters of collectivization were murdered in that same year. That said, the number harnessed to the regime's transformative goals was huge. They were incarcerated in camps, used in constructing such things as the Belomor (White Sea) Canal, and exiled to the far reaches of the northeast.

The transformative impulse had seized the cities as well. In many domains, calls went out for the replacement of bourgeois (normal) science by socialist, proletarian science. In some areas the emphases of the scientists and scholars harmonized with Stalin's transformative impulses. A particularly notable example was Trofim Lysenko's fraudulent proposals for the transformation of agriculture, a con that matched with Stalin's and later Khrushchev's transformative goals. In other areas, the Cultural Revolution prompted radical proposals for the transformation of major institutions in law and education, for example, that ran afoul of Stalin's modernizing impulses. The latter entailed underlining the importance of the state, institutions such as the conventional school, and historical narratives in which state builders such as Peter the Great played important and positive roles.

[2] Cited above, p. 58 and reproduced in English in Viola et al., *The War Against the Peasantry*, pp. 341–43.

Concomitant with these developments, the boundaries between the regime and society eroded during the 1930s. In the setting of the terror, the worst years being 1937–38, all manner of persons came under suspicion. Prediction of the consequences of one's actions became virtually impossible. There were some categories of people who were systematically purged—Old Bolsheviks, priests, persons the ethnicity of whom was that of ethnic groups bordering on the Soviet Union, persons who had traveled abroad or otherwise had contacts with foreigners. But in general the purge was stochastic: while obviously one could be purged for underfulfilling or merely fulfilling the plan, one could just as easily be targeted for overfulfilling it. As Stalin put it, "saboteurs disguise themselves by over fulfilling the plan," or in Ilya Ehrenburg's words, "the fate of a man was not like a game of chess but like a lottery."[3]

This applied both to mass publics and to the leadership. The arena of politics narrowed throughout the 1930s. At the outset of that decade, members of the Politburo could conspire (unsuccessfully) to inveigle Stalin to assume the role of head of the government (as Lenin had been). The intention, Khlevniuk argues, was to tie up the general secretary with prosaic matters and thus to strengthen the Politburo as an institution. By the end of the decade, the Politburo was no longer the selectorate even though by that time it was composed entirely of Stalin's appointees. By the mid-1930s Stalin was systematically undermining the norms that had set off the Politburo from moves directed at some segment of the masses or even at senior Party officials. Instead, smaller "commissions"—"quintets," "sextets"—of the Politburo became the relevant decisional group when Stalin did not act alone—as he did increasingly. Members of the Central Committee and even the Politburo could be arrested and shot without even the pretext of a Party hearing. All but Stalin and his closest associates had become disenfranchised residents. Not even the Politburo could be considered a selectorate.

The Great Terror went on at full force during 1937 and 1938. In early 1938, Stalin began to rein in what he had unleashed. The NKVD was blamed for "excesses" and the position of its head, Nikolai Yezhov, undermined. Within a year he was arrested. In 1940 he was executed and the mass arrests, but not the threat thereof, ended. (As Solomon points out, the legal basis for resuming the purges was not eliminated.) In theory, moreover, the distinction between Party member and others was restored in that the arrest of the former required clearance by the Party organization at the relevant level. These events were paralleled chronologically with gestures intended to persuade the man in the street that

---

[3] Both quotes introduce chapter 5 of Alexander Dallin and George Breslauer, *Political Terror in Communist Systems* (Stanford, CA: Stanford University Press, 1970), p. 57.

goods were becoming more available and that the state would serve as the provider of such collective goods as inexpensive education, housing, and entertainment. Whether in the absence of terror the provision of such goods would be adequate to ensure the effective mass mobilization that distinguished the Soviet system from more conventional authoritarian systems raised an enormously important question. In his last months, Stalin seems to have concluded the answer was in the negative. He was in the process of preparing to launch another mass purge when he died in March 1953, thus very likely extending the life span of several senior Politburo members along with many other lesser lights as well.

Stalin's death had some immediate consequences but the changes were largely fitful and over an extended time period of time. What did happen immediately was the abrupt termination of the Doctors' Plot and the arrest and demise of the secret police chief, Lavrenti Beria, and several of his subordinates. That accomplished, the executions of key government and Party officials ended. Over time, the fitful trends away from totalitarianism in the direction of a more normal authoritarian system—already apparent in Stalin's last years—continued. At the elite level norms about the consequences of losing a factional fight slowly evolved. The failed effort in 1957 to remove Nikita Khrushchev from his position as CPSU first secretary was quashed by members of the Politburo/Presidium, the military who sided with Khrushchev, and an appeal to the Central Committee, the latter assuming the role of the selectorate, given the division in the Politburo/Presidium. The leading coconspirators were not shot but exiled, Molotov to a hardship post as ambassador to Ulan Bator, Malenkov to manage a power station in northern Kazakhstan. Under Leonid Brezhnev, losing in such a fight typically resulted in an attractive ambassadorial appointment far removed from Moscow, forced retirement, or appointment to a minor government position but in Moscow. Central Committee members in the Brezhnev era exemplified the principle of "stability of cadres." Brezhnev, doubtless mindful of Khrushchev's ouster in 1964, basically made much the same deal with Central Committee members as the regime had made with the citizenry: to routinize mobilization and to grant them what amounted to job security in return for acquiescence.

Elite turnover was rapid in the Khrushchev era, as Khrushchev attempted to bring into line his aspirations to transform Soviet society with the political composition of the Politburo. The effort to mobilize the Soviet system to the accomplishment of grandiose schemes in the absence of terror as an instrument of control was not marked with success. Instead, throughout the Khrushchev era we discern a slow but monotonic decrease in the ability of the regime to mobilize its citizenry (above, pp. 161–63). This decrease, coupled with an increased proliferation of elite and subelite articulations of preferences, had the consequence of rendering increasingly inappropriate the proclivity to employ a simple dichotomy between intraselectorate politics and regime-society relations. This trend continued throughout the Brezhnev era. The players increasingly involved a small selectorate, an attentive public somewhat attuned to plural messages emanating from different sources, some subelites embedded in institutions in such a way that they could articulate claims on resources, and a vast conformist but unmobilized mass. The latter, by the time of Brezhnev's death, had largely bought into a kind of social contract. It was the best and the brightest who were least so disposed.

That notwithstanding, elite turnover was almost negligible in the Brezhnev era and, as several have observed, rather akin to a lifetime peerage in the British House of Lords. A driving factor in the turnover that did occur was natural attrition. While Brezhnev lived (he died in 1982) and in the immediate aftermath of his death, many of those who had been major figures in the Soviet regime also expired: for example, Kosygin (1980), Suslov (1982), and Ustinov (1984). Brezhnev was replaced by Yury Andropov, who, as was the case of his successor, Konstantin Chernenko, played nontrivial, albeit brief, roles in creating a milieu in which Mikhail Gorbachev was the overwhelming choice as general secretary by the Central Committee (pp. 167–70 above). The Politburo's right to select its own chair was honored in principle; as long as the Politburo got it right—read, picked Gorbachev—it remained the group that selected the general secretary. Members of the Central Committee and regional Party secretaries made it quite clear, though, that honoring the principle presupposed the Politburo getting right the answer to the question, "Who should be the next general secretary?" It did. The Politburo members chose Gorbachev.

Gorbachev hit the ground running. By Soviet standards, his transformation of the Secretariat, the Politburo, and the Central Committee in the first year of his tenure as general secretary was nothing short of astonishing: more than two-fifths (43 percent) of the voting members of the Central Committee were newly elected in Gorbachev's first year. (For more figures of the transformation of these three key institutions, see pp. 169–73 above.)

Initial readings of Gorbachev's behavior were often based on conventional notions of Soviet high politics. But Gorbachev was determined, especially in the three-year stretch from 1988 to 1990, to go beyond what Philip Roeder termed "normal politics"[4] and to change the rules of the game. As I noted above (p. 174), Gorbachev sought *both* to

[4]Roeder, *Red Sunset*, p. 212.

enhance his power position and to change the system. Had these efforts succeeded, he would have launched measures that would have fundamentally changed the composition of the Soviet selectorate: in choosing the president to be elected in 1995 (Gorbachev would have served a term at that juncture), the selectorate would have entailed the country's nonincarcerated adults. Even before that, the selectorate had been expanded substantially—though well short of what was implied by having a powerful president elected by the adult population—by virtue of a change in the rules for selecting the general secretary. Under the new rules, the general secretary would be chosen by the Party Congress. But to elect a president of the Soviet Union implied the migration of power from the Party institutions to governmental institutions including two national legislatures, the Congress of People's Deputies and the Supreme Soviet, and the continued existence of the Soviet Union.

Two-thirds of the first members of the Congress of People's Deputies were elected by popular vote, the remaining third being selected by "public organizations" ranging from the CPSU to the All-Union Society for the Struggle for Sobriety. The voting for the first two-thirds produced some extraordinary results (described at pp. 180–82). It was the first genuine national election since that of the Constituent Assembly in 1917. Communists, especially from the northern regions and in the capital cities, suffered huge defeats. For Gorbachev (who was safely ensconced among those selected by a public organization, the CPSU), the many defeats were real evidence of change and a part of "a normal process, a democratic one, that we must not regard as some kind of tragedy."[5] Rather, the elections were part of a larger process of system change. It was, he declared, "why we started everything in the first place—so a human being can feel normal, can feel good, in a socialist state."[6]

We will never know whether a human being felt good for any period of time in the last years of Soviet Union. The elections to which Gorbachev referred had taken place against the backdrop of enormous changes within and on the periphery of the Soviet Union, including, inter alia, the rapidly burgeoning demands for independence from multiple republics in the European parts of the Soviet Union, including Russia itself.[7]

These plans came to naught because the agreement that was scheduled to be signed on August 20, 1991, was thwarted by a coup—led by the self-described State Committee for the State of Emergency in the

---

[5] Above, p. 181 and drawing heavily on Urban, *More Power to the Soviets*, p. 112ff.
[6] Kaiser, *Why Gorbachev Happened*, p. 276 and above, p. 181.
[7] Beissinger, *Nationalist Mobilization*, especially pp. 422–25.

USSR (GKChP)—executed on August 19 by key Soviet figures who were determined to remove Gorbachev from his leadership position and to preserve the Soviet Union. The coup leaders had fantasized themselves an ejectorate that would remove Gorbachev and restore authoritarian Brezhnevism, a political system that far more resembled Levitsky and Way's full authoritarianism than the totalitarianism of the Stalin era. For them, as for Vladimir Putin twenty years later, the abnormal was the lack of stability. In the words of Vice President Gennady Yanayev, what they were addressing was an "uncontrollable situation in which there are no clearly defined spheres of authority . . . [in which] normal life is impossible."[8] The coup failed ignominiously.

Rather, it contributed mightily to clinching the demise of the Soviet Union the coup leaders had aspired to perpetuate. Gorbachev was notionally restored to power, but his restoration was a hollow one. The Ukraine declared its independence on August 24, less than a week after the coup had failed. It was, Mark R. Beissinger notes, "the final death-blow to the USSR."[9] In a matter of months Gorbachev was a president without a country. The coup leaders had lost, but so had Gorbachev. The relevant country was now Russia and the relevant president was Boris Yeltsin, who, unlike Gorbachev, had been elected by a selectorate composed of the adult population of his country, Russia.

Yeltsin and Gorbachev shared some things in common. Each declared that they sought to create a normal country, and both were self-described social democrats. For present purposes, it bears emphasizing that, their public stances notwithstanding, each had problems with the uncertainty of contested elections and the conflict partly engendered by their respective visions of their country's domestic transformation. Yeltsin's transformative vision led to a conflict with the Duma. That conflict led to the storming of the White House, this time with Yeltsin outside and members of the Duma inside and declaring its legitimacy; the approval of a new Constitution that, somewhat surprisingly, has persisted to this day (2013) and, less surprisingly, was heavily weighted in favor of the executive branch. With the new Constitution as backdrop, Yeltsin proceeded to renege on the early presidential election he had promised and defer it to 1996. Yeltsin was adverse to experiencing the uncertainty that accompanies democratic or competitive authoritarian elections, though somewhat less so than his predecessor or successor. In December 1995, he announced (above, p. 204), that "[w]e need to win the elections in order to quickly begin to live freely and with dignity, as do all normal people in normal

---

[8] For the source of this statement, see chapter 6, note 100.
[9] Beissinger, *Nationalist Mobilization*, p. 429.

countries."[10] He then came within a hair of deferring the election again in 1996. But he didn't and after the fact expressed chagrin that he had almost done so. The combination of lobbying by domestic and foreign influentials and shaming by his daughter and Anatoly Chubais resulted in the election taking place as scheduled.

What many Russian and Western scholars described as democratization seemed well launched in the mid-1990s but the implicit trend did not continue. The 1996 election was far more competitive than the 2000, 2004, or 2008 presidential elections. When compared with the elections that came after it, "the early and mid-1990s" in Russia seem truly admirable. Those were years characterized by "elections [that] were highly competitive"—Yeltsin successfully framed the election as a choice between communism and democracy; a "legislature [that] wielded considerable power, and private mass media . . . [that] regularly criticized Yeltsin and provided a platform for opposition."[11] There was another side of the coin as well. Both Zyuganov and Yeltsin's teams were open to charges of fraudulent behavior, with Yeltsin's forces being most open to suspicious behavior in Tatarstan and Dagestan in the second round. The same kind of broad coalition that had urged Yeltsin to resist the temptation to postpone the election rendered enormous financial support—by common recognition far in excess of spending limits. They also made abundantly clear their support for Yeltsin via symbolic gestures. All three major television networks supported Yeltsin. The president of NTV joined the group running Yeltsin's election campaign, thus obfuscating the line between state and commercial television, television being the overwhelming source for news at that juncture.

The expectation shared by many that subsequent elections would be increasingly democratic was not to be. Instead, the decade that followed was characterized by repressive measures that undermined claims concerning favorable trends in Russia. Selective enforcement of the tax code led to key oligarchs either fleeing the country or their incarceration. Elections of governors were eliminated. Barriers to introducing new parties were raised. The mass media, notably television, became even more biased. Potential candidates found themselves thwarted in their efforts to run for office. Ballot box stuffing became routine, especially in some of the republics.

For 2000, specifically, Yeltsin cleverly structured his resignation so that Vladimir Putin would be elected, something that, given his popularity, would have happened without the voter fraud and intimidation in several republics that was employed to ensure his victory, though

[10]Baturin et al., *Epokha Yeltsina*, p. 554.
[11]Levitsky and Way, *Competitive Authoritarianism*, p. 191.

conceivably it might have required a second round. Myagkov et al. report that in 2000 the gain from increases in turnout was four to one for Putin over Zyuganov, whereas in 1996 Zyuganov had actually gained more from turnout than did Yeltsin.[12]

The presidential elections of 2004 and 2008 were even less democratic. For all intents and purposes the 2004 election was essentially uncontested. The 2008 election constituted an event reminiscent of Daniels's circular flow of power (above, p. 12). Putin chose Medvedev to run for president. Medvedev in turn announced that Putin would be the prime minister. To make it even more clear that the selectorate had been reduced to a single person, the one possible alternative, Mikhail Kasyanov, who had held a major governmental post, was denied a place on the ballot ostensibly because a large fraction of the signatures were inauthentic. The 2008 election was easy to code. In Levitsky and Way's terms, the 2008 presidential election amounted to "full" authoritarianism and strong evidence of the absence of democracy in Schumpeterian terms. Just how rigged the election was is best illustrated by Figure 8.2 on page 266 where the reported turnout in oblasts just happens to cluster at points divisible by ten (and to a lesser extent five) for turnout figures greater than fifty.

A reminder that events in Russia sometimes surprise came in the 2011–12 parliamentary-presidential cycle. In late September 2011 the then prime minister, Vladimir Putin, announced that he was going to run for the presidency in March 2012 and that the then president, Dmitry Medvedev, would succeed him as prime minister. This "castling" did not sit well with a sizeable fraction of the Russian populace. Initially they were stalled by a variant of the first mover problem and did little by way of public demonstration until November when Putin was whistled (booed) at a boxing event in Moscow. But the castling, when combined with the cumulative hostility to United Russia, the focal point of which was its being labeled "the party of swindlers and thieves," had profound implications for the December 2011 Duma elections. United Russia, the dominant party, failed to obtain a majority in the Duma, even using the dubious calculations of the Central Electoral Committee. Set against a background of changes in the economy, a diminishing assessment of Putin's performance, media tolerance, and widespread corruption, Aleksei Navalny and others successfully tarred United Russia with the brush of being the party of swindlers and thieves. Even though many people had not heard of Navalny, his charges struck close to home for many. The labeling stuck. Navalny became highly visible; he told a BBC

---

[12] Myagkov et al., "Fraud or Fairytales," p. 105.

interviewer his goal was for Russia to become a "normal democratic state where power is always achieved by honest democratic elections."[13]

Subsequent to the December 2011 election a raft of mass demonstrations occurred. The protests evidently alarmed the leadership. Part of Putin's response was to accuse the United States of aiding the protesters and to assert that those protesting were endangering the nation's security. In addition, concessions were made, most notably providing for the return to the election of governors and altering the rules on party formation. Both came with qualifications that could invalidate the goals of the protestors.[14] There was the danger that the drastic reduction in the barriers to entry for parties (to form a party now required five hundred rather than forty thousand signatures) and to nominate a candidate for governor (requiring "filters" — consultation with the president and approval by a fraction of the members of the region's municipal councils), but Grigory Golosov was right to assert that on balance the reduced barriers to entry for parties potentially constituted "a victory for the democracy movement."[15]

But the real question was, "Could the regime obtain the requisite votes in the first round such that Putin would regain the presidency in the March 4 election?" Nothing brought home more clearly that in 2012 Russia had become once again a competitive authoritarian regime rather than a full authoritarian system. About halfway through the interim between the December 2011 Duma election and the March 2012 presidential election it became manifestly evident that Putin was confronting a nationwide selectorate and that the public passivity that had enabled him effectively to appoint Medvedev president in 2008 was no longer operative, even though his electoral opponents were quite weak. As late as a month before the election, Putin was publicly broaching the possibility of a runoff. Meanwhile, the regime launched an all-out effort to ensure that no serious candidates would enter the race. It deployed vast amounts of money, exploited its media dominance, and demonstrated that two could play the game of mobilizing the street. These efforts worked. Two weeks before the election, VTsIOM declared Putin would win comfortably, which he did, garnering, by the CEC's account, 63.6 percent of the vote against weak opposition.

* * *

A year and a half after the May 2012 presidential inauguration, it is difficult to project with great confidence the future evolution of Russian politics.

[13] "Navalny: Sistema Putina," p. 1.
[14] Further discussed above at p. 285.
[15] "Medvedev's Party Reform," p. 5.

At one level, this is a cause for modest optimism. Had I been writing these pages in the fall of 2011 when Putin and Medvedev announced they were going to switch positions, my message would have been almost entirely a pessimistic one for the near-term future evolution of Russian national politics. It would have been difficult to contemplate a leadership circa 2018–2020 who strongly endorsed the West and Western values and for whom the centrality of their claims were something other than stability and Russian distinctiveness. This would imply a political system with national elections much the shape of the 2008 presidential election with a selectorate amounting at most to a handful of people and more likely limited to Putin alone. In such a system, the passivity of mass publics would be ensured by their mobilization, the regime's control over the military and other armed forces, its dominance of the media, and threats to groups dependent on the regime for salaries or pensions. Potential rivals would be dealt with by selective intimidation, as would those political parties or organizations disposed to use the street to influence policy or leadership issues. This intimidation would typically involve cherry-picking those who seem most threatening to the regime or whose intimidation would seem least likely to engender protest.

Events in the fall of 2011 and the winter of 2011–12 suggested a different future narrative might be possible. Putin and Medvedev announced in September 2011 that they were going to exchange roles, with Putin becoming president and Medvedev becoming prime minister. Putin in particular emphasized that they had worked this out long before the announcement. The announcement initiated a series of events that led to mass demonstrations subsequent to the December 2011 Duma election. Even though the CEC announced that United Russia had received slightly less than a majority of the votes cast, the 2011 Duma elections were still widely perceived to have involved gross discrepancies between the real vote and the results announced by the CEC. Corrupt behavior by elites often came at the expense of ordinary citizenry. Illegal acts by elites went unpunished. The assessment of Putin by mass publics, as evidenced by survey data, remained high but on many dimensions declined steadily. In early February it seemed possible to many, including Putin himself, that he might not get a majority in the first round of voting in early March.

He did. What has followed has been discouraging for those who envisage a more democratic outcome for Russia. Against a backdrop of appeals to security and patriotism, the Duma has made opposition a higher risk exercise. In 2012, it withdrew immunity to a Communist and a Just Russia deputy. It has passed several laws that could be used to thwart criticism of domestic behavior as constituting treason. Of special importance, the Duma passed a bill that provides legal cover for efforts to constrain the exchange of views on the Internet. It also severely restricted unauthorized demonstrations and required NGOs that receive funds from abroad who are active in policy matters to declare themselves as "foreign agents."

The latter proved to be highly contentious, with contradictory results thus far. The NGOs refused to accept the status of foreign agent and resorted to various artifices to avoid being so labeled. In a few instances they received severe fines.[16] Others were harassed by the authorities. In response to what seemed initially almost infinitely elastic interpretations of the laws and in some instances draconic fines, the NGOs have resorted to multiple strategies with varying degrees of success, and so evidently has the Russian government. Even Golos, a particular target of some of the authorities—it received a heavy fine and was suspended for six months—has managed to keep its head above water by constituting itself as a movement. In this, leaders of Golos claimed to be drawing an analogy from Putin's All Russia People's Front. In mid-July 2013 the scope of the law was narrowed somewhat both by Putin and by regional courts.[17] In late August. the press agency ITAR-TASS announced that Golos would be among those receiving funds from a presidential grant. Almost simultaneously, an Alliance of Independent [Election] Observers, "set up earlier in August by the Golos movement," "was evicted from its office in Moscow."[18]

Readers who will recall the typology laid out in the Introduction will not be surprised by this blend of rent sharing and repression. Unlike totalitarian systems, authoritarian regimes adjust their policies to complicated large-scale societies (in this instance the reality of the articulate population of the two capitals), but the Kremlin has been determined to deny NGOs the potential leverage that comes from receiving funds from external sources. To accomplish this goal, they are even in some instances willing to provide the funding that some NGOs have heretofore received from external sources. At the same time the regime tolerates and may even encourage other efforts to minimize the NGOs' effectiveness. This blend of funding—adjusting policies to the reality of

---

[16] For a list of those NGOs that have been either threatened or sanctioned, see rferl.org /section/crackdown-on-ngos-in-Russia/3272.html.

[17] "Perm NGO Cleared over Refusal to Register as 'Foreign Agent,'" *Moscow Times* (July 18, 2013). Also Aleksei Anishchuk, "Russia's Putin Urges Moderate Changes in NGO 'Foreign Agent' Law," *Reuters*, July 4, 2013, *JRL*, No. 122 (July 5, 2013), No. 4.

[18] "Kremlin Gives Money to 'Foreign Agents,'" *Russian Press Review*, August 22, 2013, *JRL*, No. 154 (August 22, 2013), No. 19; BBC Monitoring, "Russian Election Watchdog Reports Being Ejected from Office," *Ekho Moskvy*, August 22, 2013, *JRL*, No. 155 (August 23, 2013), No. 12.

twenty-first-century Russian capital cities—and repression—resisting external influence—is not surprising based on what one might infer about authoritarian regimes from the typology articulated in the Introduction to this volume (p. 5 above).

A similar message has been conveyed to the Levada-Center. In May 2013 prosecutors had informed the Levada-Center that its influencing public opinion amounted to political activity and therefore it needed to register as a foreign agent. (This was not the first time it had been pressured by the authorities.) In August 2013 RIA Novosti announced that the center would receive R2,800,000 (approximately $90,000) from Russian government sources.[19]

Likewise, since President Putin's May 2012 inauguration, the regime has sapped the propensity to protest publicly, at least thus far. If one thought that taking to the street was the most consequential act one could envisage as a response to the postinauguration acts of intimidation, one would despair in late 2013 for the forces of change. Defined in these terms, the response since Putin's inauguration has been underwhelming. Protests have been minor when compared with the largest in the winter of 2011–12. Leaders of the opposition (Sergei Udaltsov, Aleksei Navalny, Ilya Yashin, and others) have been arrested on various charges, with possible jail terms ranging from fifteen days to ten years, with only a modest response in the streets.

Navalny's trial in Kirov began in April 2013, a week after he had announced his intention to run for president in 2018.[20] With Hegel, my Minerva's owl flies at dusk, but I would be remiss if I did not report on what has transpired in the interim between then and late 2013. As expected, in mid-July Navalny was found guilty and sentenced to five years in a corrective labor colony. A day after his sentencing (after protests had broken out in Moscow) in an almost unprecedented action, he was released pending the outcome of an appeal. He resumed campaigning for mayor of Moscow. These elections took place on September 8, 2013. He finished second, with a reported 27 percent of the vote. The current mayor, Sergei Sobyanin, was credited officially with 51 percent of the vote. In the meantime, President Putin in early August 2013 declared that he "found it strange" that "a defendant, whom you mentioned" (until the beginning of September Putin had never mentioned Navalny's name publicly) had been "hit with a real term of five years" considering the treatment of someone else who had confessed and cooperated with the authorities.[21]

---

[19] "Kremlin to Finance 'Foreign Agent' NGOs Report," *RIA Novosti*, August 26, 2013, as reported in *JRL*, No. 157 (August 27, 2013), No. 14.

[20] "Navalny Announces Presidential Ambitions," *Moscow Times*, No. 5104 (April 8, 2013).

[21] "Putin Questions Jail Term for Opposition Leader Navalny," *RIA Novosti*, August 2, 2013, and cited in *JRL*, No. 140 (August 2, 2013), No. 4.

That statement should be read in combination with the amnesty anticipated for December 2013 (it occurred) and the Constitutional Court's ruling of October 9 that with the exception of those receiving a life sentence, in the words of its chairman, Valery Zorkin, "*permanently depriving citizens of their right to be elected turns into the cancelation of the electoral right, which is impermissible.*"[22] They provide a backdrop to the Kirov appeals' court decision October 16 to give Navalny a suspended sentence. Despite the suspended sentence, Navalny may yet serve a prison term even if the December amnesty is applied to him. He faces other criminal charges and he could easily be charged for a misdemeanor for participating in some unauthorized political protest.

How in these circumstances his role will change is difficult to assess. At some level, (almost certainly above that of the three appellate judges in Kirov and probably considerably higher than that) it was decided that he would be less of a force as a person freighted with the burden of a suspended sentence with the monitoring that accompanies that status—along with defending himself in additional trials—than as a martyr in a corrective labor colony. He will still be the person who ran rather well in the Moscow election and for whom many went into the street to challenge a politically inspired trial and conviction. But he will also be the "suspended leader of the opposition."[23]

Operating with that burden will be a difficult task even if he manages not to be incarcerated. And the problems that have faced the opposition will remain regardless. He and others will have to come to grips with their internal quarrels and demonstrate that they can mobilize the citizenry. Even in the immediate aftermath of the suspension of his sentence, Navalny was being accused of being a collaborator with the regime by Eduard Limonov who charged that he had accepted the Kremlin's "nice offer . . . instead of prison to pretend that you're one of the opposition. There is no doubt about his collusion with the authorities."[24] At the same time, Navalny the nationalist disturbs many of those who went into the streets in the winter 2011–2012.[25] One can nevertheless imagine scenarios—more likely if Navalny is jailed—

[22] "Russia's Constitutional Court Allows Former Convicts to run in Elections," *RT*, October 10, 2013. Italics in article.

[23] BBC News, "Russia's Alexei Navalny's Sentence Suspended on Appeal," October 16, 2013 citing a "mocking hash tag."

[24] Interfax, "Russian Politicians Welcome Navalny News but Zhirinovskiy Wants him Banged up," (October 16, 2013). *JRL*, No. 186 (October 17, 2013), No.13.

[25] Navalny has been quite explicit in insisting on his willingness to embrace a large segment of the populace as his statement on p. 281 above illustrates. For a shrewd statement about what a successful posture might involve, see the observation by Matt Taylor that the greatest threat to the government is "a savvy pol who knows how to play to nativist sentiment . . . while simultaneously tapping into growing concern about the legitimacy of the legal system." "Why is Russia's legal system taking it easy on Alexei

where for once the opposition will act in a coordinated manner and mass protest will occur in numbers comparable to those that populated the streets in the winter 2011–2012.

Those in opposition will also have to build ties with some sizeable fraction of the elite as well. This may be easier than mobilizing the street. It is conceivable that under some circumstances such as Navalny's jailing, a fraction of the elites might react sharply. We have already seen powerful and influential persons distance themselves from Putin to some degree. These include Mikhail Prokhorov, Aleksandr Lebedev, and, most importantly, Aleksei Kudrin.

Kudrin has emerged as a potential mediator between the regime and the opposition. He has been the moving force behind the organization of a Civil Initiatives Committee (not [yet] a party) that will "openly oppose" the government.[26] His views about the trial of Navalny and the law on NGOs have been quite explicit: In April 2013 he stated on his blog that the case against Novalny in Kirov "cast [doubt] on the basics of the market economy in Russia" and likened the case to "time travel back to Soviet times."[27] Likewise, he has characterized the law on NGOs as "an obvious restriction of civil society."[28] Prior to Putin's 2012 election he appeared to be one of the people about whom there was the greatest buzz as a potential member of Putin's government whether as finance minister (again) or as a replacement for Medvedev. Kudrin's utterances in 2013, however, were not the words of someone who expected to be appointed to a major position by the Putin whose policies overall since his inauguration have emphasized restrictions on mass demonstrations and preventing NGO support from abroad. Indeed, in July 2013 Kudrin announced that the Civil Initiatives Committee would be "prepared to perform" the election monitoring function that Golos had done until it was sanctioned for refusing to register as a "foreign agent." Notwithstanding Putin's narrowing of the interpretation of the NGO law and the funding of some NGOs heretofore tarred with the label "foreign agent," I doubt whether either Putin or Kudrin will alter his basic orientation in the very near term, even if the latter takes on a major role in the Putin government. This means our crystal ball concerning the evolution of the Russian political system involves a time frame that incorporates the 2016–18 electoral cycle.

Navalny? *Blouin News* (blogs.blouinnews.com), (October 16, 2013), *JRL,* No.186 (October 17, 2013), No. 14.

[26] themoscownews.com/politics/20120405/18956145.html

[27] Cited in many places including RFE/RL, "Russian Opposition Leader's Trial Adjourned in Kirov," April 18, 2013.

[28] Brian Whitmore, "Putin's Game and Kudrin's Choice," *The Power Vertical,* May 20, 2013, p. 2.

What are the prospects for major transformations taking place in the Russian political system by roughly 2018 when Putin, health permitting, will presumably run again for president? If we return to the schema laid out in the beginning of this book, all four systems that most fit the columnar cells—democracy, competitive authoritarianism, full authoritarianism, and totalitarianism—are possibilities. Least likely of them is a return to totalitarianism. It is not an option that can be entirely excluded. There might be a war with China or with independence movements simultaneously in both the Northern Caucasus[29] and Siberia. To cope with those developments, a Russian ruler, specifically but not only Putin, might impose a thoroughly repressive regime and use the exigencies of war or the threat of war to return to the pre–World War II level of mobilization in the Soviet Union. Generally, though, totalitarianism has proved to be what Richard Lowenthal termed a disease of the transition from a preindustrial society to an industrial one. It is also very expensive. Even the Stalinist regime apparently acted as though welfare authoritarianism was the preferred means for social control and mobilization, though as we saw in concluding chapter 4 above Stalin appeared to have concluded near the end of his life that a return to terror was imperative. Barring a war-induced mobilization, we can rule out a totalitarian outcome.

Sad to relate, the prospects for democracy are almost equally slim. There is some evidence that younger Moscow elites—here defined as elites born 1970 or later—are more inclined to support Western-style democracy than those born in the 1960s. The latter are in turn more favorable to it than those born before 1960. In a survey of Moscow elites conducted in 2012,[30] of those who responded, 40 percent of those born 1970 or later favored Western-style democracy ($n = 14$). Of those born in the 1960s, 34 percent ($n = 30$), and of those born before 1960, 25 percent ($n = 16$), considered it the most suitable political system for Russia (tau$_c$ = .16, $p < .01$). This suggests there is a weak secular trend supportive of Western democracy in Moscow—where the strongest opposition to the Kremlin and Putin resides. (Unfortunately, that support was not matched by endorsement of key values associated with effective Western-style democracy, where the trend generally seems to be in

---

[29] Lost in accounts of Putin's skillful use of the Second Chechen War as a stepping stone to the presidency in 2000 is the fact that the agreement ending the First Chechen War stipulated that disputes between Russia and Chechnya would be settled on the basis of international law, i.e., that Russia recognized Chechnya's independence.

[30] The principal investigators were Eduard Ponarin and myself; 240 were interviewed. It was the sixth (1993, 1995, 1999, 2004, 2008, 2012) such survey, all done by the same firm, now named Bashkirova and Partners.

the opposite direction.[31]) While, as we saw above, the demonstrations in the winter of 2011–12 did suggest some movement in the direction of favoring a more democratic political system, they did not provide support for believing that pressure for democracy will increase qualitatively by the time of the 2018 election. Moscow is now a democratic city. Whether the democratic disease will spread to multiple large cities, much less small towns and the countryside, remains to be seen.

It could happen. There were some signs of political life in several large cities other than Moscow in the run-up to the September 8, 2013, local elections.[32] But there remains a need for the formation of a serious opposition party or parties (if more than one, parties united in the conviction that, whatever else their views, Putin or his designated replacement has to go). This might occur by overturning the leadership of the KPRF and the Liberal Democratic Party or by generating rival parties that, along with attracting the democratically inclined nationally, also appeal on a nationwide basis to the left and moderate nationalists as well.

Absent such developments, this leaves us with two alternatives: full or normal authoritarianism and competitive authoritarianism. Neither can be excluded as a serious shot on the board. We have had ample opportunity to identify times when both the Soviet system and the post-Soviet Russian system mapped well with the stylized characterization of full authoritarianism laid out in the scheme presented in the Introduction to this book. Even Stalin eased off during World War II. Brezhnev offered the citizenry a deal that implied a kind of normal relation between regime and society in which the citizenry conformed and worked well. In return, they could expect "to breathe easily . . . and live tranquilly." In this he was in many respects emulating the NEP of the 1920s. Vice President Yanayev, in rationalizing the coup against Gorbachev, defended it by asserting that he and the other coup members were determined to re-create a normal situation—by which he meant domestic stability a la Brezhnev and the continuing cohesiveness of the Soviet Union—not a return to something akin to Stalinism. Especially in his early tenure as president, Putin sometimes spoke as though Western party systems were the norm, but before, during, and after the

[31] William Zimmerman, "2020 Vision: Russian Elites in 2020 Perspective—Political System Preference and National Interests" (draft prepared for a Valdai presentation via video conference, July 31, 2013).

[32] Running on Prokhorov's Civic Platform, Yevgeny Roizman placed first (with a third of the vote) in the September 2013 mayoral election in Yekaterinburg. Robert Coalson, "Controversial Opposition Wildcard Yevgeny Roizman Takes Over in Yekaterinburg," RFE/RL, September 9, 2013.

temporary Medvedev[33] hiatus he defended a stability in which he was paramount over other alternatives and employed selective repression and the dispersal of rents to ensure a political system that more corresponds to full authoritarianism than to competitive authoritarianism.

This suggests that the prospects for full authoritarianism may be better than those for competitive authoritarianism. There is too little by way of independent institutions—thoroughly independent courts, genuinely competitive parties other than United Russia or its possible successor, independent media—to envisage a democratic outcome by the end of Putin's current term. The Duma has been busy systematically promoting a bevy of restrictions to deter the recurrence of large demonstrations. So far they have prompted little that would send people into the streets in large numbers, especially in cities other than Moscow. This points to a dim view of the prospects for competitive authoritarianism, not to mention democracy, as not much different from what was the case prior to at the time of the castling announcement in September 2011.

That pessimism turned out to be ill-founded at least for the short run. I may have relied in my judgment too much on the regime's domination of the media, its control over the military, and its ability to mobilize the street. Some objective considerations may undermine my pessimism yet again. Putin might find himself with serious sleep problems extending even beyond the March 2018 first round. Fracking may render the United States a net exporter of gas and oil, a development that diminishes Russia's leverage on Europe, for which Putin might be blamed. Generational change is in process. That may have implications for the support he will receive in 2018. A clear-cut and highly visible alternative to Putin may emerge. The proliferation of electronic devices may make it difficult to prevent the rapid spread of information despite the Duma's efforts to stymie the countermobilizational capacities of social media. This may make it possible for an organization such as a restructured Golos or, directly or indirectly, the Civil Initiatives Committee to oversee the presidential or Duma elections without resorting to Western financial support. The opposition may have challenged the regime's efforts to deter protests and found that the sanctions possible under the new laws are in practice not fully implemented.

Each of these things seems unlikely at this writing (late 2013). The likelihood that all of them would occur seems remote. But I was surprised by both how contemptuously the falsifications of the December 2011 Duma elections were flaunted and how readily available for mobilization were the ordinary citizens of Moscow when they realized

---

[33]For a knowledgeable if optimistic assessment of the Medvedev presidency, see Hahn, "*Perestroyka* 2.0," pp. 472–515.

they had been had. Putin may attempt to appoint himself president again in 2018. Changes in the context—the diminished role of television relative to other means of communication, a continuation in the downward trend in the assessment of Putin in the polls, less by way of profits from the export of energy sources—when compared with the 2011–12 electoral cycle might make it possible for someone (Navalny? Kudrin? Someone else?) to rally some nontrivial fraction of the citizenry, which when coupled with elite defections might unify around the theme that it was time for Putin to go.

The more likely outcome, though, is that, unless there are far more by way of elite defections than we have thus far witnessed in the aftermath of the 2011–12 electoral cycle, the policy of selective repression of potential leaders of the opposition and an occasional demonstrator, when coupled with payoffs to those mass publics, organizations, and elites who have been or might be recruited into Putin's support base, will be adequate to prevent the mobilization of a serious opposition in 2018. If that is so, the 2016–18 electoral cycle (likely with a diminished role for United Russia) will be reminiscent of the 2008 "election-type event," with Putin once again heading the ticket perhaps of United Russia but more likely of the All-Russia People's Front with something approximating competitive authoritarianism a possible characterization of the 2024 presidential election.

Selected Bibliography

Allison, Graham T. *Essence of Decision: Explaining the Cuban Missile Crisis.* Boston: Little, Brown, 1971.

Anderson, Richard, et al. *Postcommunism and the Theory of Democracy.* Princeton, NJ: Princeton University Press, 2001.

Antonov-Ovseenko, Anton. *The Time of Stalin: Portrait of a Tyranny.* New York: Harper & Row, 1981.

Anweiler, Oskar. *The Soviets: The Russian Workers, Peasants, and Soldiers Councils, 1905–1921.* 1st American ed. New York: Pantheon Books, 1975.

Atwal, Maya. "Evaluating *Nashi*: Sustainability: Autonomy, Agency, and Activism." *Europe-Asia Studies* 61, no. 5 (2009): 743–58.

Barber, John. *Soviet Historians in Crisis, 1928–1932.* Studies in Soviet History and Society. London: Macmillan, 1981.

——. "Stalin's Letter to the Editors of *Proletarskaya Revolyutsiya*." *Europe-Asia Studies* 28, no. 1 (1976): 21–41.

Baturin, Iu. M., et al. *Epokha Yeltsina: Ocherki Politicheskoi Istorii.* Moscow: Vagrius, 2001.

Bauer, Raymond A. *The New Man in Soviet Psychology.* Russian Research Center Studies. Cambridge, MA: Harvard University Press, 1952.

Beissinger, Mark R. *Nationalist Mobilization and the Collapse of the Soviet State.* Cambridge: Cambridge University Press, 2002.

Blank, Stephen. "The 18th Brumaire of Vladimir Putin." In Iuri Ra'anan, ed., *Flawed Succession: Russia's Flawed Power Transfer Crises.* Lanham, MD: Lexington Books, 2006: 133–70.

Breslauer, George W. *Gorbachev and Yeltsin as Leaders.* Cambridge: Cambridge University Press, 2002.

Brovkin, Vladimir N. *Behind the Front Lines of the Civil War: Political Parties and Social Movements in Russia, 1918–1922.* Princeton, NJ: Princeton University Press, 1994.

——. "The Mensheviks' Political Comeback: The Elections to the Provincial City Soviets in Spring 1918." *Russian Review* 42, no. 1 (1983): 1–50.

——. "Workers' Unrest and the Bolsheviks' Response in 1919." *Slavic Review* 49, no. 3 (Fall 1990): 350–73.

Brown, Archie. *The Gorbachev Factor.* New York: Oxford University Press, 1996.

Bueno de Mesquita, Bruce, et al. *The Logic of Political Survival.* Cambridge, MA: MIT Press, 2003.

Chaisty, Paul. "Majority Control and Executive Dominance: Parliament-President Relations in Putin's Russia." In Alex Pravda, ed., *Leading Russia.* New York: Oxford University Press, 2005: 119–37.

Chamberlin, William Henry. *The Russian Revolution, 1917–1921.* 2 vols. New York: Macmillan, 1935.

Chernyaev, Anatoly S. *My Six Years with Gorbachev*. University Park: Pennsylvania State University Press, 2000.

Clark, Katerina, et al. *Soviet Culture and Power: A History in Documents, 1917–1953*. Annals of Communism. New Haven, CT: Yale University Press, 2007.

Cohen, Stephen F. *Bukharin and the Bolshevik Revolution: A Political Biography, 1888–1938*. New York: Vintage Books, 1975.

Colton, Timothy J. "Putin and the Attenuation of Russian Democracy." In Alex Pravda, ed., *Leading Russia: Putin in Perspective*. Oxford: Oxford University Press, 2005: 103–18.

——. *Transitional Citizens: Voters and What Influences Them in the New Russia*. Cambridge, MA: Harvard University Press, 2000.

——. *Yeltsin: A Life*. New York: Basic Books, 2008.

Colton, Timothy J. and Jerry F. Hough, eds., *Growing Pains: Russian Democracy and the Election of 1993*. Washington, DC: Brookings Institution, 1998.

Colton, Timothy J. and Michael McFaul. *Popular Choice and Managed Democracy: The Russian Elections of 1999 and 2000*. Washington, DC: Brookings Institution, 2003.

Conquest, Robert. *The Great Terror: A Reassessment*. New York: Oxford University Press, 1990.

Coulloudon, Virginie. "Putin's Anti-corruption Reforms." In Dale R. Herspring, ed., *Putin's Russia: Past Imperfect, Future Uncertain*. Lanham, MD: Rowman & Littlefield, 2003.

Crotty, Jo. "Making a Difference? NGOs and Civil Society Development in Russia." *Europe-Asia Studies* 61, no. 1 (2009): 85–108.

Crowley, Stephen. *Hot Coal, Cold Steel: Russian and Ukrainian Workers from the End of the Soviet Union to the Post-Communist Transformations*. Ann Arbor: University of Michigan Press, 1997.

Dallin, Alexander and George Breslauer. *Political Terror in Communist Systems*. Stanford, CA: Stanford University Press, 1970.

Daniels, Robert V. *The Conscience of the Revolution*. Cambridge, MA: Harvard University Press, 1960.

——. "Office Holding and Elite Status: The Central Committee of the CPSU." In Paul Cocks, Robert V. Daniels, and Nancy W. Heer, eds., *The Dynamics of Soviet Politics*. Cambridge, MA: Harvard University Press, 1976: 77–95.

——. *The Rise and Fall of Communism in Russia*. New Haven, CT: Yale University Press, 2007.

——. "Soviet Politics since Khrushchev." In John W. Strong, ed., *The Soviet Union under Brezhnev and Kosygin: The Transition Years*. New York: Van Nostrand Reinhold, 1971: 16–25.

Davies, R. W. "The Syrtsov-Lominadze Affair." *Soviet Studies* 33, no. 1 (1981): 29–50.

Deutscher, Isaac. *Stalin: A Political Biography*. 2nd ed. New York: Oxford University Press, 1967.

Duncan, Peter. "Russia, the West and the 2007–2008 Electoral Cycle: Did the Kremlin Really Fear a Coloured Revolution." *Europe-Asia Studies* 65, no. 1 (January 2013): 1–25.

Easter, Gerald M. "The Russian State in the Time of Putin." *Post-Soviet Affairs* 24, no. 3 (July–September 2008): 199–230.

Emmons, Terence. *The Formation of Political Parties and the First National Elections in Russia.* Cambridge, MA: Harvard University Press, 1983.

Enteen, George. "Marxist Historians during the Cultural Revolution: A Case Study of Professional In-Fighting." In Sheila Fitzpatrick, ed., *Cultural Revolution in Russia.* Bloomington: Indiana University Press, 1984: 154–68.

——. "More about Stalin and the Historians: A Review Article." *Europe-Asia Studies* 34, no. 3 (July 1982): 448–54.

Erickson, John. "The Origins of the Red Army." In Richard Pipes, ed., *Revolutionary Russia.* Cambridge, MA: Harvard University Press, 1968: 224–58.

Fainsod, Merle. *How Russia Is Ruled.* Cambridge, MA: Harvard University Press, 1953.

Firsov, B. M. *Istoriia Sovetskoi Sotsiologii 1950–1980–kh godov: Kurs Lektsii.* St. Petersburg: European University in St. Petersburg, 2001.

Fischer, Louis. *The Soviets in World Affairs: A History of the Relations between the Soviet Union and the Rest of the World.* 2 vols. London: J. Cape, 1930.

Fish, Steven. *Democracy Derailed in Russia: The Failure of Open Politics.* Princeton, NJ: Princeton University Press, 2005.

——. *Democracy from Scratch.* Princeton, NJ: Princeton University Press, 1995.

Fitzpatrick, Sheila, ed. *Cultural Revolution in Russia, 1928–1931.* Studies of the Russian Institute, Columbia University. Bloomington: Indiana University Press, 1984.

——. *Everyday Stalinism: Ordinary Life in Extraordinary Times. Soviet Russia in the 1930s.* New York: Oxford University Press, 1999.

——. *Stalin's Peasants: Resistance and Survival in the Russian Village after Collectivization.* New York: Oxford University Press, 1994.

Gelman, Vladimir. "Treshchiny v stene." *Pro et Contra,* January–April 2012, 94–115.

——, ed. *Tretii elektoralnyi tsikl v Rossii, 2003–2004 gody.* St. Petersburg: European University Press, 2007.

——. *Iz ogniya da v polymya: Rossiiskaya politika posle SSSR.* St. Petersburg: BKhV-Peterburg, 2013.

Gessen, Masha. *The Man without a Face: The Unlikely Rise of Vladimir Putin.* New York: Penguin, 2012.

Getty, J. Arch. *Origins of the Great Purges: The Soviet Communist Party Reconsidered, 1933–1938.* Soviet and East European Studies. Cambridge: Cambridge University Press, 1985.

Gill, Graeme J. *The Origins of the Stalinist Political System.* Soviet and East European Studies. Cambridge: Cambridge University Press, 1990.

Ginzburg, Yevgeniya Semenovna. *Journey into the Whirlwind.* New York: Harcourt, Brace, 1967.

Gorbachev, Mikhail. *Memoirs: Mikhail Gorbachev.* New York: Doubleday, 1995.

Graham, Loren R. *The Ghost of the Executed Engineer: Technology and the Fall of the Soviet Union.* Russian Research Center Studies. Cambridge, MA: Harvard University Press, 1993.

———. "Quantum Mechanics and Dialectical Materialism." *Slavic Review* 25, no. 3 (1966): 381–410.

———. *Science in Russia and the Soviet Union: A Short History.* Cambridge History of Science. Cambridge: Cambridge University Press, 1993.

Gregory, Paul R. *Before Command: An Economic History of Russia from Emancipation to the First Five-Year Plan.* Princeton, NJ: Princeton University Press, 1994.

———. *The Political Economy of Stalinism: Evidence from the Soviet Secret Archives.* Cambridge: Cambridge University Press, 2004.

Gregory, Paul R. and Norman M. Naimark, eds. *The Lost Politburo Transcripts: From Collective Rule to Stalin's Dictatorship.* The Yale-Hoover Series on Stalin, Stalinism, and the Cold War. New Haven, CT: Yale University Press, 2008.

Gudkov, Lev. *Prezidentskiye vybory v Rossii 2012 goda: post-elektoralnyi analiz.* Moscow: Levada-Center, 2012.

———. *Rossiiskiye parlamentskiye vybory: elektoralnyi protsess pri avtoritarnom rezhime.* Moscow: Levada-Center, 2012.

Hahn, Gordon M. "Perestroyka 2.0: Toward Non-Revolutionary Regime Transformation in Russia?" *Post-Soviet Affairs* 28, no. 4 (September–December 2012): 472–515.

Hale, Henry E. "Putin Machine Sputters: First Impressions of the 2011 Duma Election." *Russian Analytical Digest*, No. 106 (December 2011).

———. *Why Not Parties in Russia? Democracy, Federalism, and the State.* New York: Cambridge University Press, 2006.

Hale, Henry E., et al. "Putin and the 'Delegative Democracy' Trap: Evidence from Russia's 2003–04 Elections." *Post-Soviet Affairs* 20, no. 4 (October–December 2004): 285–319.

Hanson, Stephen E. *Time and Revolution: Marxism and the Design of Soviet Institutions.* Chapel Hill: University of North Carolina Press, 1997.

Hazard, John N. *Settling Disputes in Soviet Society: The Formative Years of Legal Institutions.* Studies of the Russian Institute, Columbia University. New York: Columbia University Press, 1960.

Hirschman, Albert O. *Exit, Voice, and Loyalty.* Cambridge, MA: Harvard University Press, 1970.

Hoffmann, David L. *Stalinist Values: The Cultural Norms of Soviet Modernity, 1917–1941.* Ithaca, NY: Cornell University Press, 2003.

Horvath, Robert. "Putin's 'Preventive Counter-Revolution': Post-Soviet Authoritarianism and the Spectre of Velvet Revolution." *Europe-Asia Studies* 63, no. 1 (January 2011): 1–25.

Hunter, Holland and Janusz Szyrmer. *Faulty Foundations: Soviet Economic Policies, 1928–1940.* Princeton, NJ: Princeton University Press, 1992.

Huntington, Samuel P. *The Third Wave: Democratization in the Late Twentieth Century.* Norman: University of Oklahoma Press, 1991.

Huskey, Eugene. *Presidential Power in Russia.* Armonk, NY: M.E. Sharpe, 1999.

Hutcheson, Derek S. "Disengaged or Disenchanted? The Vote 'Against All' in Post-communist Russia." *Journal of Communist Studies and Transition Politics* 20, no. 1 (2004): 98–121.

Inglehart, Ronald F. *Modernization and Post-modernization.* Princeton, NJ: Princeton University Press, 1997.

Joravsky, David. *Soviet Marxism and Natural Science, 1917–1932*. Studies of the Russian Institute, Columbia University. New York: Columbia University Press, 1961.

Jowitt, Kenneth. *New World Disorder: The Leninist Extinction*. Berkeley: University of California Press, 1992.

———. "Soviet Neotraditionalism—The Political Corruption of a Leninist Regime." *Soviet Studies* 35, no. 3 (1983): 275–97.

Kaiser, Robert G. *Why Gorbachev Happened*. New York: Simon & Schuster, 1991.

Karatnycky, Adrian. "Ukraine's Orange Revolution." *Foreign Affairs* 84, no. 2 (March–April 2005): 35–52.

Karlin, Anatoly. "Measuring Churov's Beard: The Mathematics of Russian Election Fraud." www.sublimeoblivion.com/2011/12/26/measuring-churovs-beard.

Kecskemeti, Paul. *The Unexpected Revolution: Social Forces in the Hungarian Uprising*. Stanford, CA: Stanford University Press, 1961.

Kharkhordin, Oleg. *The Collective and the Individual in Russia: A Study of Practices*. Studies on the History of Society and Culture. Berkeley: University of California Press, 1999.

Khlevniuk, O. V. *Politbiuro: Mekhanizmy Politicheskoi Vlasti v 1930–e gody*. Moscow: Rosspen, 1996.

———. *1937–i: Stalin, NKVD i Sovetskoe Obshchestvo*. Moscow: Izdatel'stvo "Respublika," 1992.

———, compiler. *Stalinskoe Politbiuro v 30–e gody: Sbornik Dokumentov*. Moscow: AIRO-XX, 1995.

Khlevniuk, O. V., Donald J. Raleigh, and Kate Transchel. *In Stalin's Shadow: The Career of "Sergo" Ordzhonikidze*. The New Russian History. Armonk, NY: M.E. Sharpe, 1995.

Khrushchev, Nikita Sergeevich. *The Anti-Stalin Campaign and International Communism: A Selection of Documents*. New York: Columbia University Press, 1956.

———. *K Pobede v Mirnom Sorevnovanii s Kapitalizmom*. Moscow: Gosizdat, 1959.

Kinder, Donald R. and D. Roderick Kiewit. "Sociotropic Politics: The American Case." *British Journal of Political Science* 11 (1981): 129–61.

Kleimola, Ann M. "The Duty to Denounce in Muscovite Russia." *Slavic Review* 31, no. 4 (1972): 759–79.

Kotkin, Stephen. *Magnetic Mountain: Stalinism as a Civilization*. Berkeley: University of California Press, 1995.

Kowalski, Ronald I. *The Bolshevik Party in Conflict: The Left Communist Opposition of 1918*. Pitt Series in Russian and East European Studies. Pittsburgh: University of Pittsburgh Press, 1991.

Kryshtanovskaya, Olga. "Has Beens: Trends of Downward Mobility of the Russian Elite." *Russian Social Science Review* 46, no. 2 (March–April 2005): 4–51.

Kryshtanovskaya, Olga and Stephen White. "Putin's Militocracy." *Post-Soviet Affairs* 19, no. 4 (October–December 2006): 289–306.

———. "The Sovietization of Russian Politics." *Post-Soviet Affairs* 25, no. 4 (2009): 283–309.

Konitzer, Andrew. *Voting for Russia's Governors*. Washington, DC: Woodrow Wilson Press, 2005.

Kuran, Timur. "Now Out of Never: The Element of Surprise in the East European Revolution of 1989." *World Politics* 44, no. 1 (October 1991): 7–48.

———. *Private Truths, Public Lies: The Social Consequences of Preference Falsification*. Cambridge, MA: Harvard University Press, 1995.

Lapidus, Gail Warshofsky. "Educational Strategies and Cultural Revolution: The Politics of Soviet Development." In Sheila Fitzpatrick, ed., *Cultural Revolution in Russia*. Bloomington: Indiana University Press, 1978: 78–104.

Leeson, Peter T. and William N. Trumbull. "Comparing Apples: Normalcy, Russia, and the Remaining Post-Socialist World." *Post-Soviet Affairs* 22, no. 3 (July–September 2006): 225–48.

Lenin, Vladimir Ilyich, Richard Pipes, David Brandenberger, and Catherine A. Fitzpatrick. *The Unknown Lenin: From the Secret Archive*. Annals of Communism. New Haven, CT: Yale University Press, 1996.

Levitsky, Steven and Lucan Way. *Competitive Authoritarianism: Hybrid Regimes after the Cold War*. Problems of International Politics. New York: Cambridge University Press, 2010.

Lewin, Moshe. *Russian Peasants and Soviet Power: A Study of Collectivization*. The Norton Library. New York: Norton, 1975.

Lih, Lars T. *Bread and Authority in Russia, 1914–1921*. Studies on the History of Society and Culture. Berkeley: University of California Press, 1990.

Lih, Lars T., Oleg V. Naumov, L. Kosheleva, and O. V. Khlevniuk. *Stalin's Letters to Molotov 1925–1936*. New Haven, CT: Yale University Press, 1995.

Lipman, Masha and Michael McFaul. "Putin and the Media." In Dale Herspring, ed., *Putin's Russia: Past Perfect, Future Uncertain*. Lanham, MD: Rowman & Littlefield, 2003: 63–84.

Lohmann, Susanne. "The Dynamics of Informational Cascades: The Monday Demonstrations in Leipzig, East Germany." *World Politics* 47, no. 1 (October 1994): 42–101.

Loory, Stuart and Ann Imse, *Seven Days That Shook the World*. Atlanta, GA: Turner, 1991.

Löwenhardt, John. *The Reincarnation of Russia: Struggling with the Legacy of Communism, 1990–1994*. Durham NC: Duke University Press, 1995.

Lowenthal, Richard. "Development vs. Utopia in Communist Policy." In Chalmers Johnson, ed., *Change in Communist Systems*. Stanford, CA: Stanford University Press, 1970: 33–116.

Lukinova, Evgeniya, et al. "Metastasized Fraud in Russia's Presidential Election." *Europe-Asia Studies* 63, no. 4 (June 2011): 603–21.

Malia, Martin E. *The Soviet Tragedy: A History of Socialism in Russia, 1917–1991*. New York: Free Press, 1994.

Mathewson, Rufus W. *The Positive Hero in Russian Literature*. New York: Columbia University Press, 1958.

Matlock, Jack F. *Autopsy on an Empire: The American Ambassador's Account of the Collapse of the Soviet Union*. New York: Random House, 1995.

McFaul, Michael. "The Fourth Wave of Democracy and Dictatorship: Noncooperative Transitions in the Post Communist World." *World Politics* 54, no. 2 (January 2002): 212–44.

———. *Post-Communist Political Reform*. Washington, DC: Carnegie Endowment for International Peace, 2004.

———. *Russia's 1996 Presidential Election: The End of Polarized Politics*. Stanford, CA: Hoover Institution Press, 1997.

———. *Russia's Unfinished Revolution: Political Change from Gorbachev to Putin*. Ithaca, NY: Cornell University Press, 2001.

McFaul, Michael, et al. *Between Dictatorship and Democracy*. Washington, DC: Brookings Institution, 2004.

McFaul, Michael and Kathryn Stoner-Weiss. "The Myth of the Authoritarian Model." *Foreign Affairs* 87, no. 1 (January–February 2008): 68–84.

Meisel, James H. and Edward S. Kozera, eds. *Materials for the Study of the Soviet System: State and Party Constitutions, Laws, Decrees, Decisions, and Official Statements of the Leaders*. 2nd ed. Ann Arbor, MI: Wahr, 1953.

Melvin, Neil. "Putin's Reform of the Russian Federation." In Alex Pravda, ed., *Leading Russia: Putin in Perspective*. New York: Oxford University Press, 2005: 203–27.

Meyer, Alfred G. *Marxism: The Unity of Theory and Practice; a Critical Essay*. Russian Research Center Studies. Cambridge, MA: Harvard University Press, 1970.

Myagkov, Mikhail, et al. "Fraud or Fairytales: Russia and Ukraine's Electoral Experience," *Post-Soviet Affairs* 21, no. 2 (April–June 2005): 91–132.

Myagkov, Mikhail, Peter Ordeshook, and Alexander Sobyanin. "The Russian Electorate, 1991–1996." *Post-Soviet Affairs* 13, no. 2 (April–June 1997): 134–66.

Myagkov, Mikhail, Peter Ordeshook, and Dimitri Shakin. *The Forensics of Election Fraud: Russia and Ukraine*. Cambridge: Cambridge University Press, 2009.

Nation, R. Craig. *Black Earth, Red Star: A History of Soviet Security Policy, 1917–1991*. Ithaca, NY: Cornell University Press, 1992.

Nichol, Jim. "Russia's March 2008 Presidential Election: Outcome and Implications." CRS Report for Congress, March 13, 2008.

Oates, Sarah and Laura Roselle. "Russian Elections and TV News: Comparison of Campaign News on State-Controlled and Commercial Television Channels." *Harvard International Journal of Press/Politics* 5, No. 2 (2000): 30–51.

Odom, William E. *The Collapse of the Soviet Military*. New Haven, CT: Yale University Press, 1998.

O'Donnell, Guillermo and Philippe C. Schmitter. *Transitions from Authoritarian Rule: Tentative Conclusions about Uncertain Democracies*. Baltimore: Johns Hopkins University Press, 1986.

Orttung, Robert and Christopher Walker. "Putin and Russia's Crippled Media." *Russian Analytical Digest*, no. 123 (February 21, 2013).

Osokina, E. A. *Our Daily Bread: Socialist Distribution and the Art of Survival in Stalin's Russia, 1927–1941*. The New Russian History. Armonk, NY: M.E. Sharpe, 2001.

Petrov, Nikolai and Darrell Slider. "Putin and the Regions." In Dale R. Herspring, ed., *Putin's Russia: Past Imperfect, Future Uncertain*. Lanham, MD: Rowman & Littlefield, 2003: 203–24.

Pipes, Richard. *Russia under the Old Regime*. History of Civilisation. New York: Scribner, 1974.

———. *The Russian Revolution*. 1st Vintage Books ed. New York: Vintage Books, 1991.

Pollock, Ethan. *Stalin and the Soviet Science Wars*. Princeton, NJ: Princeton University Press, 2006.

Przeworski, Adam. *Latin Democracy and the Market: Political and Economic Reforms in Eastern Europe and America*. Cambridge: Cambridge University Press, 1991.

Putin, Vladimir. *First Person: An Astonishingly Frank Self-Portrait*. London: Random House, 2000.

Rabinowitch, Alexander. *The Bolsheviks Come to Power: The Revolution of 1917 in Petrograd*. 1st ed. New York: Norton, 1976.

———. *The Bolsheviks in Power: The First Year of Soviet Rule in Petrograd*. Bloomington: Indiana University Press, 2007.

Radkey, Oliver H. *Russia Goes to the Polls: The Election to the All-Russian Constituent Assembly, 1917*. Studies in Soviet History and Society. Ithaca, NY: Cornell University Press, 1989.

———. *The Unknown Civil War in Soviet Russia: A Study of the Green Movement in the Tambov Region, 1920–1921*. Stanford, CA: Hoover Institution Press, Stanford University, 1976.

Reddaway, Peter and Dmitri Glinski. *The Tragedy of Russia's Reforms: Market Bolshevism against Democracy*. Washington, DC: U.S. Institute of Peace, 2001.

Reiman, Michal. *The Birth of Stalinism: The USSR on the Eve of the "Second Revolution."* Indiana-Michigan Series in Russian and East European Studies. Bloomington: Indiana University Press, 1987.

Remington, Thomas F. "Ménage à Trois: The End of Soviet Parliamentarism." In Jeffrey W. Hahn, ed., *Democratization in Russia: The Development of Legislative Institutions*. Armonk, NY: M.E. Sharpe, 1996: 106–40.

———. "Patronage and the Party of Power: President-Parliament Relations under Vladimir Putin." *Europe-Asia Studies* 60, no. 6 (2008): 959–87.

———. "Putin, the Duma, and Political Parties." In Dale R. Herspring, ed., *Putin's Russia: Past Imperfect, Future Uncertain*. Lanham, MD: Rowman & Littlefield, 2003.

———. *The Russian Parliament: Institutional Evolution in a Transitional Regime, 1989–1999*. New Haven, CT: Yale University Press, 2001.

Remnick, David. *Lenin's Tomb: The Last Days of the Soviet Empire*. New York: Random House, 1993.

Rivera, Sharon Werning and David W. Rivera. "The Russian Elite under Putin: Militocratic or Bourgeois." *Post-Soviet Affairs* 22, no. 2 (April–June 2006): 125–44.

Robertson, Graeme B. "Managing Society: Protest, Civil Society, and Regime in Putin's Russia." *Slavic Review* 68, no. 3 (Fall 2009): 528–47.

Roeder, Philip G. *Red Sunset: The Failure of Soviet Politics*. Princeton, NJ: Princeton University Press, 1993.

Rose, Richard and William Mishler. "How Do Electors Respond to an 'Unfair' Election? The Experience of Russians." *Post-Soviet Affairs* 25, no. 2 (April–June 2009): 118–36.

Rosefielde, Steven and Stefan Headlund. *Russia since 1980: Wrestling with Westernization*. Cambridge: Cambridge University Press, 2009.

Ruble, Blair A. *Soviet Trade Unions: Their Development in the 1970s*. Soviet and East European Studies. Cambridge: Cambridge University Press, 1981.

Sakwa, Richard. *The Crisis of Russian Democracy: The Dual State, Factionalism, and the Medvedev Succession.* Cambridge: Cambridge University Press, 2011.
——. "The Dual State in Russia," *Post-Soviet Affairs* 26, no. 3 (July–September 2010): 185–206.
——. *Putin: Russia's Choice.* London: Routledge, 2004.
——. *Putin: Russia's Choice.* 2nd ed. London: Routledge, 2008.
Schapiro, Leonard Bertram. *The Origin of the Communist Autocracy: Political Opposition in the Soviet State, First Phase, 1917–1922.* London: London School of Economics and Political Science, 1955.
Schumpeter, Joseph A. *Capitalism, Socialism, and Democracy.* 2nd ed. New York: Harper, 1947.
Scott, John. *Behind the Urals: An American Worker in Russia's City of Steel.* Boston: Houghton Mifflin, 1942.
Seton-Watson, Hugh. *From Lenin to Khrushchev: The History of World Communism.* Books That Matter. New York: Praeger, 1960.
Sheinis, Victor. "The Constitution." In Michael McFaul et al., *Between Dictatorship and Democracy: Russian Post-communist Political Reform.* Washington, DC: Carnegie Endowment for International Peace, 2004: 56–82.
Shirk, Susan L. *The Political Logic of Economic Reform in China.* California Series on Social Choice and Political Economy. Berkeley: University of California Press, 1993.
Shlapentokh, Vladimir. *A Normal Totalitarian Society: How the Soviet Union Functioned and How It Collapsed.* Armonk, NY: M.E. Sharpe, 2001.
Shleifer, Andrei. *A Normal Country: Russia after Communism.* Cambridge, MA: Harvard University Press, 2005.
Shleifer, Andrei and Daniel Treisman. "A Normal Country: Russia after Communism." *Journal of Economic Perspectives* 19, no. 1 (Winter 2005): 151–74.
Shvetsova, Olga. "Resolving the Problem: The 1999 Parliamentary Election as a Presidential 'Primary.'" In Vicki L. Hesli and William M. Reisinger, eds., *The 1999–2000 Elections in Russia: Their Impact and Legacy.* Cambridge: Cambridge University Press, 2003: 213–31.
Solnick, Steven Lee. *Stealing the State: Control and Collapse in Soviet Institutions.* Russian Research Center Studies. Cambridge, MA: Harvard University Press, 1998.
Solomon, Peter H. *Soviet Criminal Justice under Stalin.* Cambridge Russian, Soviet and Post-Soviet Studies. Cambridge, UK: Cambridge University Press, 1996.
Solzhenitsyn, Aleksandr Isayevich. *Stories and Prose Poems.* London: Bodley Head, 1971.
Stepankov, V. G. and E. K. Lisov. *Kremlevskii zagovor.* Moscow: Izdatel'stvo 'Ogonek,' 1992.
Strong, John W. *The Soviet Union under Brezhnev and Kosygin: The Transition Years.* New York: Van Nostrand Reinhold, 1971.
Taubman, William and Jane Taubman. *Moscow Spring.* New York: Summit Books, 1989.
Timasheff, Nicholas S. *The Great Retreat: The Growth and Decline of Communism in Russia.* New York: E.P. Dutton, 1946.

Tkacheva, Olesya. "Federalism and Democratic Consolidation and Beyond." University of Michigan dissertation, 2009.

Tkacheva, Olesya, et al., eds. *Internet Freedom & Political Space.* Santa Monica, CA: RAND, 2013.

Tompson, William. "Putin and the Oligarchs." In Alex Pravda, ed., *Leading Russia.* New York: Oxford University Press, 2005: 185–94.

Treisman, Daniel. "Deciphering Russia's Federal Finance: Fiscal Appeasement in 1995 and 1996." *Europe-Asia Studies* 50, no. 5 (July 1998): 893–906.

———. *The Return: Russia's Journey from Gorbachev to Medvedev.* New York: Free Press, 2011.

Tucker, Robert C., ed. *The Lenin Anthology.* New York: Norton, 1975.

———. *The Soviet Political Mind: Stalinism and Post-Stalin Change.* Rev. ed. New York: Norton, 1971.

———. *Stalin in Power: The Revolution from Above, 1928–1941.* New York: Norton, 1990.

———, ed. *Stalinism: Essays in Historical Interpretation.* New York: Norton, 1977.

Urban, Michael. "December 1993 as a Replication of Late-Soviet Electoral Practices." *Post-Soviet Affairs* 10, no. 2 (April–June 1994): 127–58.

Viola, Lynne. *The Best Sons of the Fatherland: Workers in the Vanguard of Soviet Collectivization.* New York: Oxford University Press, 1987.

———, ed. *Contending with Stalinism: Soviet Power and Popular Resistance in the 1930s.* Ithaca, NY: Cornell University Press, 2002.

———. "The Other Archipelago: Kulak Deportations to the North in 1930 (Dekulakized Peasant Families in the Soviet Union)." *Slavic Review* 60, no. 4 (Winter 2001): 730–55.

———. *The Role of the OGPU in Dekulakization, Mass Deportations, and Special Resettlement in 1930.* The Carl Beck Papers in Russian & East European Studies. Pittsburgh: Center for Russian & East European Studies, University of Pittsburgh, 2000.

Viola, Lynne, et al., eds. *The War Against the Peasantry, 1927–1930: The Tragedy of the Soviet Countryside.* New Haven, CT: Yale University Press, 2005.

Wheeler-Bennett, John. *Brest-Litovsk: The Forgotten Peace, March 1918.* New York: Norton, 1971.

White, Stephen. *Understanding Russian Politics.* New York: Cambridge University Press, 2001.

White, Stephen and Olga Kryshtanovskaya. "Changing the Russian Electoral System: Inside the Black Box." *Europe-Asia Studies* 63, no. 4 (June 2011): 557–78.

Wilson, Kenneth. "Party-System Development under Putin." *Post-Soviet Affairs* 22, no. 4 (October–December 2006), 314–48.

Yeltsin, Boris Nikolayevich and Catherine A. Fitzpatrick. *Midnight Diaries.* New York: Public Affairs, 2000.

———. *The Struggle for Russia.* 1st American ed. New York: Belka, 1994.

Zimmerman, William. "Mobilized Participation and the Nature of the Soviet Dictatorship." In James R. Millar, ed., *Politics, Work, and Daily Life in the USSR: A Survey of Former Soviet Citizens.* Cambridge, UK: Cambridge University Press, 1987: 332–53.

———. "'Normal Democracies' and Improving How They Are Measured: The Case of Russia." *Post-Soviet Affairs* 23, no. 1 (January–March 2007): 1–17.

———. *The Russian People and Foreign Policy: Russian Elite and Mass Perspectives, 1993–2000*. Princeton, NJ: Princeton University Press, 2002.

———. "Slavophiles and Westernizers Redux: Contemporary Russian Elite Perspectives." *Post-Soviet Affairs* 21, no. 3 (July–September 2005): 183–209.

———. *Soviet Perspectives on International Relations*. Studies of the Russian Institute, Columbia University. Princeton, NJ: Princeton University Press, 1969.

Index

Page numbers in italics refer to figures and tables.

membership diluted, 133; role and evolution of, 9, 36–37, 75, 84–101; role in selecting Gorbachev as general secretary, 167–170; unilateral actions of Stalin including arrests of Politburo members, 86–87, 95–96. *See also* dictator's curse; Lominadze-Syrtsov affair; permanent commissions

Political systems: Brzezinski on, 6; Levitsky and Way on, 4, 8; typology used in text, 5

Poskrebyshev, Aleksandr , 10

Presidential Council, 176

Primakov,Yegeny: as prime minister, 225; withdraws from presidential race, 232, 234

Prokhorov, Mikhail, 269, 289, 306

Pshenichnikov, Maxim, 275

Psychology, 70–71; New Soviet Man and, 70

Public Opinion Foundation, 287

Purge, the Great (also the Great Terror), 102–129

Putin, Vladimir, 1, 267; acts presidential, 229; blames US for rallies, 286; booed (whistled), 278; changing evaluation of, 271– 277; differences between Putin and Medvedev, 270–274; election results of 2000 questioned, 233, 289; and law on parties, 247; reduces asymmetrical regionalism, 248–249; runs for president, 3, 229–231; and Second Chechen War, 229–230

Radek, Karl, 23

Radkey, Oliver H., 15, 44

Rallies, 280, 283

Ranks and orders, 111–112

Reciprocal accountability, 38, 42; institutional changes by Gorbachev that would eliminate, 175; Roeder on, 38

Red Army of Workers and Peasants (RKKA), 29, 43, 46–51; desertion from, 53; failure in Poland, 50; impact of Great Purge on, 123; increasingly like normal army, 48; multiple tasks of, 49–50; role in thwarting coup, 191; Trotsky's role in building, 46, 52

Red Terror, 44–45

Reds. *See* Greens

Referendum of 1993, 199–200

Regime–society relations, changing patterns of, 10

Residents, Bueno de Mesquita et al. on, 10, 19, 205, 292

Roeder, Philip: conception of selectorate, 3, 17; on reciprocal accountability, 38, 42, 137, 175

Roizman, Yevgeny, 308n32

RNII (rocket research institute), 113–114; and links to purge of Tukhachevsky, 113

Russian Association of Proletarian Writers (RAPP). 69–70. *See also* Union of Writers

Russia, viewed as normal country, 1–3; and coup of 1991, 182–194; as viewed by Gorbachev, 193, 196; as viewed by Muskovites, 196; as viewed by Putin, 247; as viewed by Yanayev, 188; as viewed by Yeltsin, 1, 197

Russia's Choice, 202

Rutskoi, Aleksandr, 200–201, 203

Sakrai, Sergei, 209

Sakwa, Richard, 246–247

Schumpeter, Joseph: conceptions of democracy, 3, 12, 220–221, 245, 262, 283, 289

Secretariat, Party: growth of, 37–38; gutted, 175

Selectorate, 10, 75, 197, 267, 286; defined, 3; changing sizes in Soviet and Russian political systems, 14, 20, 28–42, 222; contrasted with ejectorate, 5

Shakty trial, 61–62

Shlapentokh, Vladimir, 6, 133, 156

Shleifer, Andrei, 1

Shulgin, V. N., 68, 74

Sobchak, Kseniya, 279–280

Social welfare, monetization of, 258. *See also* ejectorate

Socialist realism and the New Soviet Man, 70–71

Socialist Revolutionaries (SRs), 15, 35. *See also* Left SRs

Sokolov, Sergei, 13

Sokolovsky, V.D., 151–152

Soskovets, Oleg, 208, 210

Soviet systems, differences between, 4